Bosom Friends

Bosom Friends

*The Intimate World of
James Buchanan and
William Rufus King*

———◆———

THOMAS J. BALCERSKI

OXFORD
UNIVERSITY PRESS

OXFORD
UNIVERSITY PRESS

Oxford University Press is a department of the University of Oxford. It furthers
the University's objective of excellence in research, scholarship, and education
by publishing worldwide. Oxford is a registered trade mark of Oxford University
Press in the UK and certain other countries.

Published in the United States of America by Oxford University Press
198 Madison Avenue, New York, NY 10016, United States of America.

Library of Congress Cataloging-in-Publication Data
Names: Balcerski, Thomas J., author.
Title: Bosom friends : the intimate world of James Buchanan and
William Rufus King / Thomas J. Balcerski.
Description: New York, NY : Oxford University Press, [2019] |
Includes bibliographical references and index.
Identifiers: LCCN 2018054956 (print) | LCCN 2019001017 (ebook) |
ISBN 9780190914608 (updf) | ISBN 9780190914615 (epub) |
ISBN 9780190914592 (hardcover : alk. paper)
Subjects: LCSH: Buchanan, James, 1791–1868. | King, William R. (William Rufus), 1786–1853. |
Male friendship—United States—History—19th century. |
Presidents—United States—Biography. | Legislators—United States—Biography. |
United States—Politics and government—1815–1861.
Classification: LCC E437 (ebook) | LCC E437 .B36 2019 (print) |
DDC 973.6/80922 [B]—dc23
LC record available at https://lccn.loc.gov/2018054956

3 5 7 9 8 6 4 2

Printed by Sheridan Books, Inc., United States of America

Contents

Acknowledgments

I HAVE MADE many friends and incurred even more debts in the research and writing of this book. This book grew out of my doctoral work at Cornell University. I thank my graduate committee members—Edward Baptist, Mary Beth Norton, Aaron Sachs, and Shirley Samuels—for their intellectual guidance and support at that early stage, as well as professors Derek Chang, Jefferson Cowie, and Suman Seth for their fine instruction. At Cornell, I workshopped early versions of this project with members of a reading group sponsored by the Society for the Humanities and at the History Americas Colloquium, the Graduate History Colloquium, and the Global Nineteenth Century Graduate Conference. I also must acknowledge the support of the dedicated staff at Olin Library and praise the 2CUL sharing program that permitted me access to Butler Library at Columbia University.

This book benefited from critical funding from numerous institutions. From Cornell, I received support in the form of the Henry W. Sage Fellowship, the Joel and Rosemary Silbey Fellowship, the Graduate School Research Travel Grant, the Walter and Sandra LaFeber Research Travel Grant, the Ihlder Research Fellowship, the Paul W. Gates Research Fellowship, the American Studies Program Graduate Research Grant, the Mary Donlon Alger Fellowship, and the Graduate Student Public Humanities Fellowship from the Society for the Humanities. From Eastern Connecticut State University, I received both the Faculty Research Grant from the Connecticut State University American Association of University Professors and the John Fox Slater Research Fund. These funds permitted research travel to archives and the purchase of microfilm collections that proved valuable to the project. From Eastern Connecticut State University, I also obtained reassigned time for research, travel funds to attend multiple conferences, and professional development support. A special thank you to Dr. Stacey Close, Vice President for Equity and Diversity, whose assistance supported the inclusion of several illustrations in this book.In addition, I thank the institutions that have provided me with research travel funds: the Library Company of Philadelphia and the Historical Society of Pennsylvania for providing housing during my research in Philadelphia, the Virginia Historical Society for awarding me its Mellon Research Fellowship, the Newberry Library for granting me status as a Scholar-in-Residence, and LancasterHistory.org for offering me a research fellowship through the National Endowment for the Humanities.

My project benefited from the assistance of librarians and staffers at a great number of federal and state institutions, historical societies, and libraries. I thank especially the devoted staffers at the Manuscript Division, Library of Congress; the careful stewards of the Buchanan Papers at the Historical Society of Pennsylvania; Connie King at the Library Company of Philadelphia; Heather Tennies, Patrick Clarke, and the knowledgeable staff at LancasterHistory.org; Jim Gerencser at the Archives and Special Collections, Dickinson College; Nancy Dupree, Norwood Kerr, and the unfailingly polite staff of the Alabama Department of Archives and History; the helpful research staffers at the David M. Rubenstein Rare Book & Manuscript Library, Duke University; the always cheerful staff at the Southern Historical Collection, University of North Carolina; Jenna Sabre and Alexandra Bainbridge at the Eberly Family Special Collections Library, Pennsylvania State University; Cheryl Custer at the Fendrick Library, Mercersburg, Pennsylvania; Mike Lear at the Archives and Special Collections, Franklin & Marshall College; and Mazie Bowen at the Hargrett Rare Book & Manuscript Library, University of Georgia. Special thanks also are due to the hard-working and dedicated staff at the J. Eugene Smith Library, Eastern Connecticut State University.

Historians of James Buchanan and William Rufus King are few in number, but they lack nothing in the way of enthusiasm for their research subjects. I particularly thank Michael Connolly for his interest in this project at an early stage; John Quist, Michael Birkner, Randall Miller, Thomas Horrocks, Michael Landis, and Joshua Lynn for engaging conversations about Old Buck; Pastor Ron Martin-Minnich, Upper West Conococheague Presbyterian Church, Mercersburg, for hunting down elusive church records; and Daniel Fate Brooks for sharing his passion for William Rufus King. Other historians and stewards of all things Buchanan and King deserve attention, too. Thanks to Doug Smith of Mercersburg Academy for sharing Harriet Lane Johnston materials, Nick Yakas of Phoenix Lodge No. 8, Fayetteville, North Carolina, for confirming King's Masonic information, and Bland Simpson at the

University of North Carolina for arranging access to the portrait of William Rufus King that graces the cover of this book.

I also thank the professional organizations and societies that have provided venues for my work. These include the American Historical Association, the New York Metro American Studies Association, the Society for Historians of the Early American Republic, the Organization of American Historians, the Association of British American Nineteenth Century Historians, LancasterHistory.org, the Early American Republic Working Group at the City University of New York, the Faculty Scholars Forum at Eastern Connecticut State University, the New England Historical Association, and the Pennsylvania Historical Association. For their valuable advice and camaraderie at various stages of this project, I thank Kelly Brennan Arehart, Diane Barnes, John Belohlavek, Mark Boonshoft, Robyn Davis, David Doyle, Douglas Egerton, Thomas Foster, Joanne Freeman, Craig Friend, Richard Godbeer, Amy Greenberg, Jessica Linker, Jake Lundberg, Stacey Robertson, Rachel Shelden, Manisha Sinha, Frank Towers, Elissa Wade, and Timothy Williams. To my colleagues in the History Department at Eastern Connecticut State University—Caitlin Carenen, Bradley Davis, David Frye, Stefan Kamola, Anna Kirchmann, Joan Meznar, Scott Moore, Jamel Ostwald, and especially Barbara Tucker—thank you.

Several people provided careful readings of individual chapters of this book. I thank the wonderfully generous Barbara Tucker for her first read of early chapter drafts. I also acknowledge the outstanding work of undergraduate research assistants who helped with the preparation of this book: Sara Dean, Joshua Turner, Katerina Mazzacane, Jordan Butler, Uriya Simeon, and Allen Horn. At Oxford University Press, I have benefited from the guidance of my editor, Susan Ferber. Three excellent readers' reports from Mark Summers, Michael Birkner, and Nicholas Syrett substantially improved this book. Thank you also to the Oxford University Press production team, especially Jeremy Toynbee, for its dedication in bringing this book into print. Finally, a portion of chapter 3, which appeared as "The Bachelor's Mess: James Buchanan and the Domestic Politics of Doughfacery in Jacksonian America" in *The Worlds of James Buchanan and Thaddeus Stevens: Place, Personality, and Politics in the Civil War Era*, edited by Michael J. Birkner, John W. Quist, and Randall M. Miller (Baton Rouge: Louisiana State University Press, 2019), is reproduced here with permission.

I have shared my journey into the friendship of James Buchanan and William Rufus King with many friends of my own. In addition to the colleagues noted above, I want to thank my academic friends, especially Alex

Black, Jillian Spivey Caddell, Mark Deets, Brigitte Fielder, Shyla Foster, Rae Grabowski, Amy Kohout, Henry Maar, Daegan Miller, Jacqueline Reynoso, Mark Rice, Stephen Sanfilippo, Jonathan Senchyne, Kathleen Volk, and Xine Yao. Other friends listened patiently to me talk about my project and played host to me during research visits—thanks to Samuel Aronson and George Cooper, William Cammuso, John Carpenter, Jeffrey and Kristin Kayer, Hanny Martinovici, Thomas Ricketts, David Rimshnick, Peter Rimshnick, Zachary Samuels, Preston Shimer, and John Vaughan. Thanks also to mentors and friends John Cebak, Warren Dressler, and David Stuhr.

Finally, my greatest debt is owed to my family. Without the support of my parents, William and Christine Balcerski, I would not have been given the freedom to explore my interests in college and beyond. To siblings Bill, Stephen, and Tracy Balcerski, you now know more about James Buchanan and William Rufus King than nearly anyone else on the planet. I owe also to Dorothy Halperin similar sentiments of gratitude; like my family, she never stopped believing in me and this project. Lastly, to Marc Halperin, I bestow upon you an honorary master's degree in American history and offer to you the dedication of this book; come what may, I love you.

Bosom Friends

Introduction

REMEMBERING

IN THE AFTERMATH of the Civil War, few wished to remember the politics of the prior generation. Perhaps fewer still wanted to reminisce about the vibrant social landscape of the nation's capital before the war. To many, such recollections must have recalled a tragic scene from a disastrous era in American history. Fittingly, a historian, Elizabeth Fries Lummis Ellet, took up the challenge of placing the calamities of the war years into a broader story about social elites from days gone by. In her final works Ellet turned to the more recent past, using the papers of prominent women to enliven the people, places, and events of high society. In reviewing the administration of President John Tyler (1841–1845), she ascribed a peculiarly communal aspect. "Members from the various sections of the Union, intending to domesticate with their families for a session, arranged what was styled a 'mess,'" Ellet noted, "generally formed of persons professing the same politics, having an identity of interest, associations, feelings, &c." Ellet then cited the two most famous messmates from that period, the Democratic senators and lifelong bachelors James Buchanan of Pennsylvania and William Rufus King of Alabama. "Buchanan and King were called 'the Siamese twins,'" she asserted. "They ate, drank, voted and visited together."[1]

This intriguing characterization of James Buchanan and William Rufus King as "the Siamese twins" drew upon a phrase that had been evolving for forty years in the American lexicon. It first appeared in 1829, when Scottish promoter Robert Hunter brought the conjoined twins Chang and Eng Bunker—the "Twins from Siam"—to the attention of the American public. During the 1830s, these original Siamese twins became a media sensation, as they toured the United States and England. Soon thereafter, the phrase took on new, more literary qualities. English writer Edward Bulwer titled an 1833 satirical poem "The Siamese Twins," while a cartoonist lampooned the "unnatural alliance" of Great Britain and the newly formed nation of Belgium as a conjoined pair. American journalists and cartoonists seized upon the designation in ways that were both more political and gendered. In 1837, for example, a reporter compared the governors of the neighboring states of Mississippi and Arkansas to the "Siamese twins, as they both act and think alike."[2]

Of all the new meanings attributed to "the Siamese twins," the political one spread widest and lasted longest. By the 1840s, politicians closely aligned in the public eye were likened, usually in a satirical or pejorative way, to Siamese twins. In the presidential election year of 1840, for example, a Whig cartoonist attacked the partisan and allegedly corrupt connection between Democratic newspaper editors Francis Preston Blair and Amos Kendall by depicting the men conjoined by an oversized ligature at their torsos. In response, a Democratic newspaper editorialized that the Whig presidential candidate William Henry Harrison was a political Siamese twin to his vice presidential running-mate John Tyler. Again in 1844, the duo of John Quincy Adams and Henry Clay warranted the same description. In the heat of the 1856 presidential election, when James Buchanan was a candidate, a pro-Democratic newspaper espoused the connection between the opposition Republican Party and northern abolitionists to be "like Eng and Chang . . . the death of one would kill the other." Eight years later, Republicans caricatured the Democratic presidential ticket of Civil War general George McClellan of New Jersey and George Pendleton of Ohio as a conjoined pair, bound by a farcical ligature on which read the words "the party tie."[3]

Like these other metaphorical couplings, Ellet's pairing of Buchanan and King certainly warranted the nickname. Even so, this curious label prompts many questions. Who were these two men from the nineteenth-century past? How and why did they enter politics? Why did neither one ever marry, and how unusual were they for not doing so? From there, questions about their "mess" relationship follow. What exactly was the nature of their domestic arrangement in Washington? Did it include a sexual element, or was it merely a platonic friendship? Did eating, drinking, and socializing together really translate to voting together on political issues? Since the phrase "Siamese twins" typically stemmed from a partisan critique, questions about their public personae ensue. What did their political opponents think of them, and what did they write about them in turn? And how did they manage to achieve their political successes in spite of it all? Finally, how did the historian

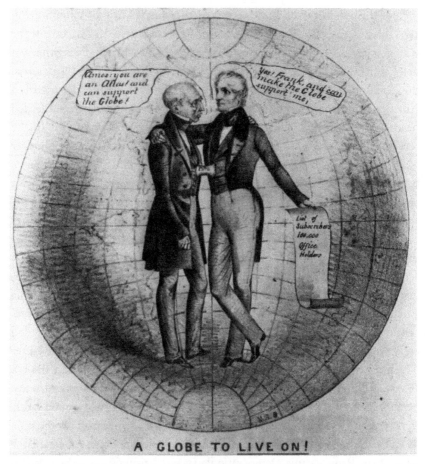

FIGURE I.I "A Globe to Live On!" Francis Preston Blair (pictured on the left) says: "Amos: you are an Atlas! and can support the Globe," to which Amos Kendall, holding a list that reads "List of Subscribers 100,000 Office Holders," replies, "Yes! Frank, and *can* make the Globe support me." Lithograph. Washington, DC: Printed and published by Henry R. Robinson, 1840. Prints and Photographs Division, Library of Congress, LC-USZ62-21235.

Elizabeth Ellet come to remember them as the Siamese twins, and, more to the point, how have they been remembered since?

* * *

The older of the pair by five years, William Rufus DeVane King (1786–1853) was born on the eve of the US Constitutional convention and died as the nation's sitting vice president. After attending the University of North Carolina, he rapidly thrived in public life. Elected to the state House of Commons in 1808, he was chosen for the US House of Representatives in 1811, one of the youngest men ever to serve in that body. A fierce War Hawk during the War of 1812, he subsequently served abroad as secretary to the foreign legation in the Kingdom of Naples and then at St. Petersburg, Russia. Upon his return to America, King headed southwest as part of the great cotton boom and settled near the new town of Selma, Alabama. Elected to the US Senate in 1819, he served continuously until President Tyler appointed him American minister to France in 1844. By the time of his first mess arrangement with Buchanan, begun a decade earlier, he was firmly established as both a confirmed bachelor and a southern spokesman for national unity in the Democratic Party.[4]

By comparison, James Buchanan (1791–1868) was born during the administration of President George Washington and died publicly discredited during his own postpresidential retreat to Wheatland, his country estate near Lancaster. In his education at Dickinson College, legal training, and early political engagements, he shared a trajectory similar to King's. As a Pennsylvania Federalist and state legislator, however, he opposed the War of 1812 and received the warm support of his Lancaster townsmen for the stance. His failed engagement to Ann Coleman ended tragically with her death in 1819, after which time he recommitted himself to a life in politics. Elected to the US House of Representatives soon thereafter, he served five terms in that body. Next exiled to Russia by President Andrew Jackson, he returned triumphantly in 1833, with a successfully negotiated commercial treaty in hand. At the time of his election to the US Senate in 1834, he was the leader of the Amalgamator wing of the Pennsylvania Democratic Party and a rising star on the national scene. Like King, he was a bachelor, though a far more reluctant one, and a northern voice for compromise and conciliation within the Democratic Party.[5]

The period of their active friendship, from their initial mess arrangement in December 1834 to King's death in April 1853, spanned more than eighteen years. Within this timeline, their relationship contained two discrete phases: first, the period from December 1834 to May 1844, when they overlapped in the US Senate and often lived together while in Washington; and second, the period from May 1844 to April 1853, when, with a few notable exceptions, the two men lived apart and operated independently. In its initial phase, their friendship centered around the institution of the Washington boardinghouse, or mess, where they ate and drank together in relative domestic harmony. They also attended social functions together, which often centered around still more eating and drinking. By thus intertwining their domestic fortunes while in Washington, they slowly but steadily forged an intimate personal friendship. In time, Buchanan and King intermingled members of their own families, notably their two nieces Harriet Rebecca Lane and Catherine Margaret Ellis, into an extended network of affective kinship. During this first, more intimate phase of their friendship, they became one of the best-known and most successful examples of a domestic political partnership in American history.[6]

In many ways, the structure of congressional service in the early American republic dictated the first phase of their friendship (1834–1844). Even after Congress relocated from Philadelphia to the unfinished city of Washington, DC, at the close of 1800, the average congressman spent surprisingly little time in the capital. Congressional sessions, divided into two-year spans to match the length of terms for members of the House of Representatives, followed an unusually long cycle from election to service. Many representatives were selected fully a year or more before the start of their terms of office, a situation that did not change officially until 1875. In the case of William Rufus King, for example, he was elected to his seat in the fall of 1810, but did not arrive in Washington as a member of the 12th US Congress until November 1811. From there, the first session of the new Congress most typically lasted until the late spring or early summer months, after which the body recessed until fall (this pattern persisted well into the 1930s). Only then did most congressmen return home, where, as it turns out, the majority had consciously chosen to live apart from their wives and families while in Washington.[7]

Several factors compounded the decision of most congressmen to separate from loved ones. For one, the great difficulty and slow rate of travel in the era before widespread railroad connections made a trip to Washington an uncertain proposition. At the start of his congressional career, for example, King endured a four- to five-day journey from North Carolina to Washington, while Buchanan's trip from Lancaster took the better part of two days, with stops in Philadelphia and Baltimore. For another, most lawmakers were not compensated sufficiently to cover the expenses of maintaining both a residence in Washington and another back home. Until 1816, representatives were paid a per diem rate of $6 (unchanged since the first Congress in 1789), after which a salary of $1,500 was set. However, this new allotment proved wildly controversial, and the subsequent Congress was forced to return to the per diem rate system, with a twist—representatives and senators were granted an $8 per diem and another $8 per twenty miles traveled to Washington. The convoluted pay scheme lasted until 1855, with one result being that even congressional sessions without much business lasted the full time allotted. If the

paltry salary were not enough to turn away elected officials from serving multiple terms, many congressional districts practiced a strict system of rotation
in office, called a "yearling policy" by one historian, such that turnover in office was comparatively much higher in the early nineteenth century than it is
today. On top of that, many congressmen withdrew early from their terms in
office, often motivated by entirely personal factors. Washington could be a
lonely place.[8]

The living conditions of early Washington also drove the parameters of
social life in the capital and thus the early years of the friendship of Buchanan
and King. Far from the modern city that it later became, the capital in these
years was very much a work in progress. The roads were muddy and the surrounding landscape dotted with swamps. Even if a congressman could afford
to bring his family to Washington, accommodations were often communal
and cramped. Few politicians, save members of the cabinet, ever owned their
own homes. To solve the problem of housing, congressmen lived together
in boardinghouses, which were called by the name "mess." From the earliest
Congresses of the 1790s until after the Civil War, these boardinghouses most
commonly accommodated congressmen while in Washington. For the rea-
sonable rate of around ten dollars a week, individuals could obtain single
rooms within a shared house that might contain as many as a dozen other
bedrooms, each often furnished with little more than a bed, dresser, and night-
stand. In the era before indoor plumbing, the boarders relied on domestic
servants, often enslaved African Americans, to meet the everyday needs of ab-
lution. Although boardinghouses existed in every American city during these
years, the Washington boardinghouse differed in that its inhabitants were the
country's leading elected officials.[9]

There was an essential communal element to boardinghouse life in the
capital. Dinner, the most important of the meals, was served between three
and six o'clock, with a menu that featured an assortment of meats, fish,
berries, and pies. Alcoholic beverages such as wine, brandy, and madeira
often accompanied meals, though congressmen provided these items at their
own expense. The messmates regularly congregated in the shared parlors,
especially around the fireplaces in the colder months, where they smoked
cigars and discussed politics and the social doings of the capital. Since many
boardinghouses featured the mixed company of men and women, such
gatherings could be quite formal. From these parlors, calls were made and
returned around the Capitol Hill neighborhood, such that congressional
messes functioned as social centers in the early republic. Congressmen frequently entertained their fellow politicians with food and drink, just as they

might have hosted guests back home. And without access to formal offices—congressmen worked primarily from their desks in the chambers of the Capitol—boardinghouses functioned as auxiliary office space as well. From these "parlor politics," much important legislation germinated.[10]

On the one hand, the basis for the relationship of James Buchanan and William Rufus King was not particularly uncommon. Whether as cause or effect of their boardinghouse connection, Buchanan and King followed a remarkably similar political course as congressional messmates. As Elizabeth Ellet noted, they almost always voted in common with one another. Stalwart Jacksonians, they offered unwavering support for the Democratic agenda, including the independent subtreasury system, a compromise tariff, and the expansion of federal land-holdings. But each man counseled careful moderation on sectional issues. For his part, King consistently balanced the interests of the slaveholding South with those of the national Democratic Party; however, his political partnership with the patriotic Buchanan required that he prioritize the permanent continuation of the Union. In turn, Buchanan joined King in combating abolitionism; he even devised a key aspect of the Senate's infamous gag rule that forbade the reception of anti-slavery petitions. Along with their Democratic messmates, Buchanan and King constituted a powerful voting bloc in the Jacksonian era. By the end of their shared mess, they agreed implicitly that the principles of their increasingly conservative creed offered the best way to preserve the national Union.[11]

On the other hand, their nearly ten-year boardinghouse relationship appears quite unusual in retrospect. After all, the two men originally hailed from very different parts of the country (King from the South, Buchanan from the mid-Atlantic), from varying socioeconomic statuses (King, a scion of wealthy slaveholding planters; Buchanan, the son of a yeoman shopkeeper on the western frontier), and opposite political parties (King an adherent to the Democratic-Republican Party, Buchanan a devoted Federalist). They nevertheless shared a few essential personal factors in common. Being descendants of Scots-Irish immigrants, both men shared similar ethno-cultural origins. They also attended college in an age when higher education was a luxury. Most critically, neither man married. In their capacities as lifelong bachelors, they forged an enduring political partnership that withstood the many challenges of their public lives.

In the second phase of their relationship (1844–1853), separated by distance, their friendship lost something of its earlier personal intimacy and devolved into a more overtly political alliance. While King served as American minister to France, Buchanan transitioned from the senate to the cabinet as secretary of state under President James Knox Polk. Thus separated, the inherent weaknesses of their friendship forged by domestic propinquity—witnessed in the scattered nature of their correspondence and the widening gulf between their romantic pursuits—became painfully evident. Even as King's counsel proved personally beneficial to Buchanan at critical moments, they drifted apart politically, especially over foreign policy questions. Under the expansionist Polk, Buchanan promoted territorial conquest, from Mexico to Cuba, for the benefit of southern slaveholders; ironically, King advised against the acquisition of these same lands. In their final years, they approached political questions at cross-purposes. During the congressional debates of 1850, Buchanan attempted to remain above the political fray, while King actively worked for a lasting compromise. Even so, glimpses of their old domestic intimacy resurfaced, as Buchanan occasionally visited with King in Washington. But these later-life efforts proved fleeting. In the end, the alienating effects of distance and time, compounded by a subtle divergence in their political views, had reduced the former intimacy of their friendship.

Nevertheless, the symbolic meaning of their political union soared to new heights in its final years. During the second phase of their friendship, each man reached, and nearly obtained together, the nomination of the Democratic Party for the vice presidency (King) and presidency (Buchanan). In the presidential cycles of 1844, 1848, and finally 1852, they worked tirelessly for a combined Buchanan-King ticket, but each time the political tides turned against a "bachelor ticket" in favor of other combinations. All the same, their brand of political conservativism appealed to their fellow partisans, as a safe choice in the face of ever-mounting sectionalism. In 1852, the Democratic Party selected King as its vice presidential nominee to run alongside Franklin Pierce of New Hampshire, while it chose Buchanan as its presidential candidate in 1856. Like the other pairs of political Siamese twins of the era, each man had proven integral to the success of the other. Yet conjoined as they were, their individual identities had been merged before the councils of the national Democratic Party. In consequence, only one of the two men seemed capable of political advancement at a time.

The active lifespan of these Siamese twins thus spanned from the partisan years of the Jacksonian era to the more sectional ones of the late antebellum period. During those same eighteen years, the United States expanded from a nation circumscribed by rivers for its western border to one bounded by oceans; grew its population, both free and enslaved, at unprecedented rates; and finally deadlocked its politics over the divisive issue of slavery. Indeed, at the heart of the friendship of Buchanan and King lay a solemn pact, developed in the boardinghouses of Jacksonian Washington, that the Union must not split over the question of slavery. As a politically conservative northerner, Buchanan acquiesced to protect southern interests at almost any price, while as a politically moderate southerner, King stemmed the tide of radical sectionalism in favor of compromise. As such, they comprised a cross-sectional, conservative force in American politics for nearly a generation. Theirs was an interwoven, intertwined, and finally interdependent union that worked primarily to better one another, the Democratic Party, and, by extension, the nation as they conceived it. This book tells their story.

* * *

The duo of Buchanan and King received much criticism, often rendered in the form of gossip, from their opponents. This gossip can be understood as gendered language in the "grammar of political combat." For some adversaries, character attacks allowed for the easy dismissal of political rivals, such as when Andrew Jackson supposedly called King by the name "Miss Nancy" in the 1830s or when John Quincy Adams recorded in his diary that King was "a gentle slave-monger" in 1844. For others, colorful insults levied against opponents endeared them to their correspondents, such as when Aaron Brown of Tennessee variously ridiculed King as "Aunt Nancy," "Miss Fancy," and Buchanan's "wife" in an 1844 letter to Sarah Childress Polk, wife of the future president. In turn, King and Buchanan gossiped among themselves, and with various female family members and friends, in the refined diction of highly educated men. In so doing, they established their own "grammar of manhood," in which the exigencies of a political agenda intersected with the private realm of thought and feeling. Gossip thus circulated across the private correspondence of multiple circles of male and female political actors.[12]

While their political adversaries could only speculate about the relationship of Buchanan and King, the scholarship of subsequent generations has uncovered far more evidence about the pair. In the 1880s George Ticknor Curtis published the first major biography of James Buchanan, which included a now infamous letter from Buchanan to Mrs. Cornelia Roosevelt, dated May 13, 1844. "I am now 'solitary and alone,' having no companion in the house with me," he complained following King's departure from Washington. "I have gone a wooing to several gentlemen, but have not succeeded with any one of them," he reported, before adding: "I feel that it is not good for man to be alone; and should not be astonished to find myself married to some old maid who can nurse me when I am sick, provide good dinners for me when I am well, & not expect from me any very ardent or romantic affection." In the early 1900s John Bassett Moore, editor of the largest collection of Buchanan letters and papers, reprinted this letter and several others from the Buchanan-King correspondence, though he offered little context for them. This new evidence notwithstanding, neither Curtis nor Moore replicated the characterization of Buchanan and King as Siamese twins.[13]

Matters began to change with the next generation of Buchanan biographers. In an article from 1938, biographer Philip Auchampaugh, likely drawing on the reference provided by Elizabeth Ellet, included a footnote that described King as "Buchanan's 'Siamese Twin,' United States Senator for Alabama." In 1962, Philip Klein published the definitive biography of Buchanan. About Buchanan's relationship with King, however, Klein largely repeated the chatter of previous generations: "Washington had begun to refer to [King] and Buchanan as 'the Siamese twins.'" While Buchanan's major biographers quietly elided this gossip, the Polk biographer Charles Sellers expanded upon it. King's "conspicuous intimacy with the bachelor Buchanan," he wrote in 1966, "gave rise to some cruel jibes around Washington." Sellers then repeated the salient gossip of Andrew Jackson, John Quincy Adams, and Aaron Brown, and, in a footnote, excerpted King's reply to Buchanan's May 1844 letter. "I am selfish enough to hope you will not be able to procure an associate, who will cause you to feel no regret at our separation. For myself, I shall feel lonely in the midst of Paris, for there I shall have no Friends with whom I can commune as with my own thoughts." The pieces of a new interpretation were gradually falling into place.[14]

Nevertheless, the intimate nature of male friendships little concerned the narratives constructed by older forms of political history. Indeed, the relationship of Buchanan and King may well have remained a footnote to American history, had it not been for a new interest in the study of historical gender and sexuality, especially same-sex sexuality, in the past several decades. In turn, the popular view of Buchanan's various intimate attachments, and especially his relationship with King, began to change radically beginning in the 1980s. Tabloid journalism played a critical role in the transformation. On the front cover of its November 1987 issue, for example, *Penthouse Magazine* pronounced: "Our First Gay President, Out of the Closet, Finally." In the linked article, New York gossip columnist Sharon Churcher pointed to a forthcoming book by historian Carl Anthony as evidence for the assertion. But even before the publication of Anthony's *First Ladies* (1990), Churcher's sensational article attracted the notice of journalist Shelley Ross, who opined

in her own book about presidential sex scandals: "Perhaps Buchanan's dark se-
cret was that he was a homosexual, a notion that has crept through historical
literature for decades." For his part, Anthony, who drew heavily upon both
Klein and Sellers, concluded: "Whatever manifestations it might have taken,
Buchanan maintained a longtime relationship with King."[15]

Once the question of the nature of Buchanan's relationship with King had
been raised, more imaginative answers became inevitable. Although he had
pledged in his play *Buchanan Dying* (1974) that he would not publish any
more about Buchanan, writer John Updike returned to his fellow Lancastrian
in his novel *Memories of the Ford Administration* (1992). He detailed the
mess life shared by Buchanan and King, surmising at one point that the pair
enjoyed "the leathery, cluttered, cozy, tobacco-scented bachelor quarters
where, emerging from separate bedrooms and returning from divided duties,
they often shared morning bacon and evening claret." Updike variously labeled King a "beau ideal" and "a love object" of Buchanan's, but he ultimately
found "little" in the way of "traces of homosexual passion." Buchanan, he
concluded, looked to King as an "older brother." Many academic historians
embraced the Updike reading, with one critic calling it the "best thing that
has happened to James Buchanan since 1856."[16]

Regardless, Updike's relatively circumspect characterization of their relationship has not stopped a veritable torrent of speculation about the pair. For
the most part, these surmises have addressed the question of each man's sexual
orientation. Typical of these new interpretations are the views of one historian who equivocated that Buchanan and King "were likely gay," or that of
another who asserted more forcefully, "I'm sure that Buchanan was gay." Still,
even these scholars have based their arguments, however flawed, in the historical record. By contrast, the Internet has enabled an explosion in gossip, mis-
information, and erotic imagination about Buchanan and King, with only the
slightest basis in evidence. At the start of the twenty-first century, it has become practically *de rigueur* in many popular circles to call King and Buchanan
America's first gay vice president and president, respectively.[17]

At the heart of this new understanding lay a growing interest in discovering
and assessing the sexual orientation of figures from the American past. The
search for a usable queer past, begun in earnest during the 1970s, has widened
in scope and scale and evolved into the academic study of LGBT history. The
difficulty of locating, with certainty, examples of same-sex behavior—to say
nothing of identities and orientations—in the early American past has defined
a major methodological problem of the field of LGBT history. Accordingly,
how one conceives and describes same-sex attractions and relationships has

provoked a debate between those taking an "essentialist" view, who believe that same-sex attractions, behaviors, and identities as lived today similarly existed in past eras, versus those who take a "social constructionist" view that the same require attention to the societal definitions and practices during the period in question. Nevertheless, this ongoing dialogue has generated more careful attention to the nature of historical sources and the possibility of new interpretations.[18]

In the case of Buchanan and King, an essentialist view of the two men as gay has certainly predominated the popular and scholarly imagination. However, this book finds that the surviving evidence neither supports a definitive assessment of either man's sexuality, nor the occurrence of a sexual liaison between them. Instead, this book argues that their relationship conformed to an observable pattern of intimate male friendships prevalent in the first half of the nineteenth century. Like many words, the present understanding of "intimacy," which today primarily connotes a physical closeness, has evolved from its earlier meaning, when it usually conveyed a shared trust on a personal level. For their part, politicians understood their associations with other public men to include two distinct, if overlapping, categories: the first of these, *personal* or *affective* friendships, involved a significant level of intimacy, while the second, *political* or *public* friendships, functioned more instrumentally to advance common interests. Of course, politicians commonly built relationships with one another that contained elements of both kinds of friendships; as Buchanan himself later wrote, his friendship with King was an "intimate personal & political association" unmatched by any other.[19]

This conception of intimate male friendship places the relationship of Buchanan and King at the heart of a vital part of the political process and, in so doing, clarifies the possibilities for political partnerships in early America. Borrowing another term from this period, Buchanan and King may be understood as sharing a "bosom friendship," one suggestive of a particular kind of domestic intimacy common in the eighteenth and nineteenth centuries. In the 1750s, Dr. Samuel Johnson noted in his dictionary that bosom friendship included a "communication of secrets." Later lexicographers also stressed the connection to sharing private thoughts and feelings. For the most part, such "romantic friendships" were the special domain of women. Yet by the middle of the nineteenth century, the American novelist Herman Melville could use the term to describe the symbolic marriage of Queequeg and Ishmael in his chapter titled "A Bosom Friend" from *Moby Dick* (1851). The special bond of Melville's sailors, built as it was on the close quarters of the whaling ship, paralleled the similarly confined setting of the Washington boardinghouse.

But unlike the close companionship of Melville's sailors, politicians often viewed their bosom friendships in more instrumental ways.[20]

Indeed, friendships among politicians had long been an important way to knit together the disparate strands of democratic societies. Following the American Revolution, historian Richard Godbeer has argued, "Americans turned to friendship as an emotional anchor for the new nation itself as it struggled to establish social and political stability." In this way, these friendships enabled critical connections otherwise unavailable on the national level, which in turn promoted greater partisan development. Similarly, Ivy Schweitzer noted in her study of friendship that such relationships represented the "privileged and dominant affiliative modes" available to political men, often at the expense of women and enslaved people. As educated elites, politicians modeled the intellectually restrained manhood common among the genteel classes. In their dress, appearance, and manly comportment, they paid careful attention to the cultural norms expected of gentlemen, whether on the dueling grounds or in the halls of Congress. The political culture of the party system, constructed upon the idealized notion of friendship among elites from different cultural, social, and economic backgrounds, thus operated to bind men together.[21]

By the nineteenth century, the concept of "bosom friends" was already part and parcel of American politics. Less pejorative than "Siamese twins," the term most often appeared in a positive light—whether as an elegiac for statesmen who had passed away or as a suggestion of personal intimacy among politicians. Upon the death of the old Jeffersonian Nathaniel Macon of North Carolina in 1837, for example, he was noted as the bosom friend of Thomas Jefferson, James Madison, and Andrew Jackson. In the 1840s, Martin Van Buren of New York was tagged as a bosom friend to fellow New Yorker Silas Wright. The same went for the duo of James Polk and Andrew Jackson, both from Tennessee, whose bosom friendship was applauded at the 1844 Democratic nominating convention. Similarly, Franklin Pierce of New Hampshire was called the bosom friend of Alfred Nicholson of Tennessee during the Democratic nominating convention in 1852. As with all political terms, however, the phrase could also be used in less charitable ways. Democratic rivals dismissed the pairing of Buchanan and King as mere bosom friends. As late as 1856, Buchanan and Van Buren were still lumped together as bosom friends, even though they had long since parted political ways.[22]

The bosom friendship of Buchanan and King represented something new in the political process. As the era of the founders gave way to the leadership of the second generation, the resulting partisanship eventually hardened into an entrenched two-party system. During the bitter partisan wars of the late 1820s and 1830s, political advancement operated on the tenets of loyalty, primarily to Andrew Jackson and by extension the Democratic Party. The opposition Whig Party soon followed suit, making the succeeding decade of the 1840s rife with political cronyism and corruption. In the transformation of the earlier vision of cross-sectional friendship by baser partisanship, the intimate friendships of the Jacksonian period yielded a bitter stew of political resentments. Although ostensibly the kind of cross-sectional bonding envisioned by the founders, these later friendships required a specific version of partisan politics. For Buchanan and King, the imperatives of partisan loyalty subsumed the older view of friendship as essential to patriotic politics.[23]

The relationship of Buchanan and King thus highlights the changing nature of friendship, manhood, and partisan politics during a critical period of American history. They united in a reciprocal relationship that sustained their respective ascension to the highest of executive offices. Most significantly, they tested the limits of cross-sectional cooperation in an increasingly divided Democratic Party and nation. They formed a bosom friendship, one conceived out of domestic convenience, which solidified through a shared conservativism into a symbolically powerful partnership between North and South. In this way, they embodied both the political benefit and the moral difficulties of cross-sectional collaboration in the three decades before the Civil War.

* * *

Biographers of early American politics typically consider the origins, highlight important events, and assess the major accomplishments of an individual subject. However, to appreciate the bosom friendship of James Buchanan and William Rufus King requires a modification of the traditional approach. This book instead offers a dual biography of the men which intermixes the events of their lives from beginning to end. Of course, their relationship also included other people in their political and personal circles. As such, this book interconnects the traditional emphases on the major events that drove the rise of party politics and the coming of the Civil War with the smaller biographical details of their friendship. The result is a surprisingly intimate glimpse into the nineteenth-century past.

The early lives of Buchanan and King coincided with the rise to prominence of the second generation of Americans. Accordingly, chapter 1 ("Leavening") begins with their respective family backgrounds, educations, friendships, and early legal and political careers. While their formative political experiences differed considerably, bachelorhood shaped their personal lives in similar ways. As such, this chapter scrutinizes both men's efforts at romantic courtship—King's dubious foray during his time as secretary to the Russian legation and Buchanan's failed engagement to Ann Coleman of Lancaster. These romantic pursuits not only legitimated their later bachelorhood, but also solidified their embrace of intimate male friendship, especially with other bachelors, as a constitutive part of their rise to political power. Moreover, their early experiences began a process of leavening that shaped their later political forms: Buchanan as a northern man who supported the southern agenda for political gain, and King as a southern man who placed national concerns over purely sectional interests.

Chapter 2 ("Hardening") turns to how they established themselves within the Democratic Party of Andrew Jackson. In both cases, intimate male friendships and the Washington boardinghouse played critical roles in developing a cross-sectional, though partisan, approach to their politics. At the same time, each man remained deeply embedded within the political climate at home: King quarreled with Democratic factions in his adopted state of Alabama, while Buchanan struggled against the various elements of the Democratic Party in Pennsylvania. Both men also gained valuable experience in diplomatic service. Unwittingly, Buchanan's foreign exile as the American minister to Russia connected him to King, who had served in that country fifteen years earlier. These formative years corresponded to a hardening of their political principles—on the questions of tariffs, banking, land sales, and, most critically, slavery—and their personal convictions, especially about marriage.

In that vein, chapter 3 ("Messing") explores the "bachelor's mess" and its many intersections with the overlapping identities of partisan politics. Besides King and Buchanan, the boardinghouse included a variety of Democratic politicians, among them Edward Lucas of Virginia, Robert Carter Nicholas of Louisiana, John Pendleton King of Georgia, Bedford Brown of North Carolina, William Sterrett Ramsey of Pennsylvania, and William Henry Roane of Virginia. As their voting records demonstrated, their congregation into a single boardinghouse produced a politically potent unit that influenced key aspects of the legislative process. For example, the members of the bachelor's mess supported an independent subtreasury system and quelled public discussion of slavery by instituting a gag rule. For Buchanan and King, the mess provided an effective site for their continued quest for power within the national Democratic Party. In turn, the pair grew ever more

personally intimate and established bonds strong enough to survive the political turmoil of the decades ahead.

Toward that end, chapter 4 ("Wooing") examines the period from the triumph of the Whig Party in 1840 to the dissolution of the bachelor's mess
in 1844. In these years, the mess diminished in size, paralleling the waning
political fortunes of the Democratic Party. The 1840s also seriously fueled
Buchanan and King's collective presidential fires. First in 1840 and again in
1844, each man aspired for either the presidential or vice presidential nomination. The struggle occasioned a great deal of personal gossip from their
political enemies. In April 1844, President John Tyler's appointment of King
as the American minister to France dissolved the old mess. Nevertheless, the
separation precipitated a regular, if one-sided correspondence, including
the now controversial letter in which Buchanan complained of his failure
to "woo" new gentlemen to join him, and the equally provocative reply in
which King hoped that his messmate would not easily find a new associate
with which to "commune." All the same, Buchanan remained alone in their
Washington boardinghouse. His inability to attract new members paralleled
the bachelor messmates' failed efforts to woo the Democratic presidential and
vice presidential nominations, first in 1840 and again in 1844.

Next, chapter 5 ("Ministering") traces a period of extended separation
between Buchanan and King, from the years 1844 to 1848. During the administration of President James K. Polk, each man turned his attention to
foreign policy concerns, with Buchanan serving as secretary of state and King
as American minister to France. As such, their relationship transformed from
an intimate boardinghouse friendship into one of superior to political subordinate. But their continued collaboration proved critical, as the nation
navigated first the territorial crisis in Oregon and then the War with Mexico.
For King, his removal from the domestic political scene caused consterna-
tion, but his growing estrangement from Buchanan's affections proved even
more bothersome. For Buchanan, personal disagreements with President
Polk plagued his time in office, though it did not prevent him from engaging,
however perfunctorily, in new courtships with women half his age. Ironically,
even as the forces of manifest destiny and the Young America movement
clamored for attention, these two old bachelors gradually became venerable
statesmen worthy of the nation's respect. They once more stood to obtain the
nomination of the Democratic Party in 1848.

Consequently, chapter 6 ("Running") considers the years between the
presidential election of 1848, when neither man obtained the nomination,
and the election of 1852, when the Democratic Party nominated King for

vice president. During the great debates in Congress known to history as the Compromise of 1850, the friendship of Buchanan and King cooled. Each man followed a separate political path: King remained committed to a combination of the Union and Democratic principles, while Buchanan attempted to place himself above the political fray in semiretirement at Wheatland. Above all, King valued the political success of Buchanan (more so than Buchanan felt for King in turn). In 1852, however, the Democrats passed over Buchanan for the dark horse Franklin Pierce. In turn, to pacify Buchanan and his supporters, they selected King as Pierce's running mate. King's death in April 1853 ended a decades-long political and personal friendship with Buchanan. But in truth, it had long before diminished into a mere shell of its former intimacy. As if on cue, Buchanan accepted an appointment as the American minister to England.

A final chapter ("Presiding") follows the sudden rise and even more precipitous fall of the Buchanan presidency. Upon his return to the United States in 1856, Buchanan was selected as the Democrats' standard-bearer. In the presidential campaign of 1856, the party touted Buchanan's friendship with southerners, including King, to suggest his pro-southern principles. During his four years in office, he sustained the pro-southern Lecompton Constitution in Kansas, promoted the acquisition of Cuba, and watched mounting sectional tensions culminate in the secession winter of 1860–1861. He also presided over an active social calendar, administered by his niece and First Lady Harriet Lane and often joined by King's niece Catherine Ellis. At times he invoked the memory of King to promote national unity, such as when he delivered a commencement address at the University of North Carolina (King's alma mater). Yet Buchanan's continued reliance on intimate friendships, a tendency that had served him well in earlier years, eventually left him bereft of political support during the secession crisis. More than a mere failure of personal character, the Buchanan presidency revealed the limitations of cross-sectional intimate male friendship in American politics. In retirement Buchanan took special care to reconnect with Ellis, who in turn bonded once more with the newly married Harriet Lane Johnston.

As detailed in the epilogue ("Preserving"), both nieces diligently saved the correspondence of their respective uncles and worked to memorialize them for later generations. Due to their careful efforts, the record of their extraordinary friendship yet survives. Indeed, the legacy of these Siamese twins has reverberated through the decades and centuries ahead in other notable same-sex friendships of subsequent generations. In fact, echoes from the bosom

friendship of Buchanan and King may still be heard in the political parlance
of modern times.

* * *

Since the inception of presidential rankings, historians have consistently
placed James Buchanan at the bottom of the list. Likewise, William Rufus
King is often dismissed to the lower echelons of vice presidential rankings.
This book does not explicitly seek to rehabilitate the reputation of either
Buchanan or King, though it implicitly argues that both men deserve better
scholarly treatment than they have typically received. Instead, by taking
the long view of their lives, this book provides a view of American history
through the lens of a significant friendship and offers a unique glimpse into
how growing sectional tensions divided even the most intimate of friends and
their families.[24]

As such, this book reconceives Elizabeth Ellet's evocation of Buchanan
and King as the Siamese twins. It posits a world at once more personally intimate and more politically important than previously imagined. By studying
just how they ate, drank, voted, and visited together, the many bright
possibilities, as well as the numerous treacherous pitfalls, of intimate friendship among politicians comes into sharper view. To riff on the familiar pro-
verb, politics makes not only for strange bedfellows, but for intimate ones as
well. In remembering these bosom friends from the early American past, this
book contends that friendship was, and continues to be, a fundamental part
of American politics.

I

Leavening, 1786–1819

THE SECOND GENERATION of Americans, born between the years 1776 and 1800, inherited the promises and pitfalls of the founding mothers and fathers of the Revolutionary era. Raised in small villages, frontier outposts, and remote plantations, they joined others who took advantage of new lands farther west, as well as economic opportunities closer to the established cities on the eastern seaboard. As the presidential administrations of George Washington and John Adams gave way to those of Thomas Jefferson, James Madison, and James Monroe, they formed a bloc of younger politicos who pushed their elders in riskier directions: as war hawks, they promoted conflict with Great Britain in 1812; as western expansionists, they championed American extension into new territorial possessions. By the start of the nineteenth century, they were already itching to seize the exciting promises of new lands, new inventions, and new ideas about society. In effect, those who inherited the American Revolution demanded and ultimately obtained an American polity far more expansive than the one envisioned by their forefathers. From their ever-reaching grasp, both economic and political, grew the seeds of future conflict.[1]

The era also witnessed a disruption of the traditional social and family values inherited from earlier generations. The forces of economic dislocation strained the traditional relationships of parents and children, as the second generation struggled to thrive in the usual familial settings. Although such changes were slower in reaching the south, urbanization and the beginnings of industrialization presaged further dislocation in the northeast. Even the institution of marriage came under pressure. A growing number of young men followed new professional paths available through college education. As such, they married much later in life, or perhaps not at all. For those young professionals who did marry, the number of children produced from their unions dwindled in what has been termed a "fertility transition."[2]

Both William Rufus King and James Buchanan came of age in this changing political, social, and marital climate. Indeed, their family backgrounds and early personal and professional experiences paralleled many of these same changes taking place across American society. Both men were born into prosperous and large families: King in the booming agricultural economy of Piedmont North Carolina and Buchanan on the bustling frontier of south-western Pennsylvania. Their parents prepared them for future success: the two young men attended school from an early age, where they each gained a lifelong love of all things literary. As they grew older, they were each sent to one of the newly founded American universities. From there, both men left the small towns of their youth to rising new cities—King to Fayetteville, North Carolina, and Buchanan to Lancaster, Pennsylvania—to study law and become practicing attorneys at the bar.

As each man came into his own, King and Buchanan derived advantages from their relationships with their respective families. King's father, a prominent legislator, enabled an easy entry into politics, while Buchanan's father aided his son in attending and then graduating from college. Somewhat estranged from their respective patriarchs, they were much closer to their mothers and female siblings. After their fathers passed away, both men became the de facto heads of their respective clans at relatively young ages. And in a world where marriage was still expected and common, both men counted multiple family members who never married. Although questions about their marital status never disappeared entirely, these early claims to patriarchal status tempered the expectations surrounding marriage among their family members. As sons and as brothers, the basic outlines of lifelong bachelorhood fell into place.

In time, politics, not marriage, became the single most important calling in their lives. Following the success of their legal practices, each man traveled a well-trodden path into politics through election to local office. Ironically, they started on opposite sides of the political divide, King as a Democratic-Republican and Buchanan as a Federalist. However, the intense partisan-ship of the 1790s and 1800s did not embitter them; instead, it left each man with an enduring sense of the conjoined necessities of party unity and cross-sectional cooperation. As their political careers flourished, their involvement extended beyond the borders of their home states. Taken together, the nec-essary ingredients fell into place for their leavening into two of the foremost bachelors of the second generation of American statesmen.

Carolina's Second Son

The life of William Rufus DeVane King followed a trajectory similar to many of the leading southern politicians of his day. Born on April 7, 1786, in Sampson County, North Carolina, he was the second son of William King Sr., whose father Michael King had descended from a family of Scotch-Irish immigrants that first immigrated to Virginia in the latter part of the 1600s, and Margaret DeVane, whose father Thomas DeVane had descended from French Huguenot ancestry by way of Scotland. His birth family eventually consisted of eight children who survived to adulthood, including two brothers (Thomas DeVane and John DeVane) and five sisters (Elizabeth Ann, Margaret, Tabitha, Helen Louisa, and Catherine). His numerous King and DeVane relations provided the young King—who was sometimes called William King Jr., or more commonly William Rufus King to distinguish him from his father—with an extended kinship network.[3]

King appears to have enjoyed a carefree and happy childhood. The best surviving account of his earliest years derives from his grandniece Bessie Hogan Williams, who in 1917 recorded many anecdotes about him. In one story, the young William Rufus demonstrated the gentlemanly manners that defined his character as an adult. "When he was 10 years old the boys in the neighborhood formed a Cavelry Company," wrote Williams in her idiosyncratic spelling. "All road stick horses. William had a very fine stick horse named Roebuck—which would out run all the other horses—for sometimes he would let one of his cousins . . . ride his horse. And Robuck would always win the race. I aske my mother how could that be—Oh Uncle was the swiftest rider runner and he would just hold the horse he was riding back and let the other boys come in a head." Even as a child, such were the inclinations of the young William Rufus toward conciliation and compromise that he sacrificed his own pride to permit others to claim victory. These traits would prove critical in later life.[4]

The Piedmont region of King's youth comprised a primarily agricultural society. Once home to the Tuscarora Indians, yeoman farmers, largely of Scots-Irish stock, had claimed the land by the mid-eighteenth century. Looking back on early Sampson County, William Dickson, a Pennsylvania transplant, recalled these early white settlers: "The first Inhabitants of this place were generally Rude and uncultivated in their Manners, but Sociallity and Civilization has progressed considerably in all Classes of our Citizen since the Revolution." Given its upland climate, the region did not promote large-scale, slave-based agriculture. For the most part, these "rude" farmers grew subsistence crops, such as corn, cowpeas, wheat, and small grains, though the

FIGURE I.I North Carolina. King was born and raised in Sampson County, part of the Piedmont region of the state. Map by Samuel Lewis and Henry Schenck Tanner, ca. 1802. Courtesy Geography and Map Division, Library of Congress.

cash crops of tobacco, rice, and cotton also fared well in the loamy soil. Great stands of pine provided raw building materials, and in time, sawmills sprung up to meet the demand for finished wood. In short, the upcountry Piedmont proved prime territory for its independent-minded inhabitants.[5]

In many ways, the Kings exemplified the patterns of settlement in the late eighteenth-century Piedmont. Yet unlike most of their neighbors, they enjoyed considerable material wealth as measured by land and enslaved people. The 1790 census recorded that William King Sr. owned thirty-one enslaved African Americans, a number that grew with time. He deployed his workforce to improve his land with profitable crops, raise cattle, and operate a sawmill. From this successful economic position, he naturally became a leading member of the community: he represented Sampson County at the state's constitutional ratification convention in 1788, served as a justice of the peace, and attended the state legislature as his county's representative. William Rufus King would follow this formula of planter, slaveowner, and politician pioneered by his father and many other leading men of his state.[6]

From the start, William Rufus King had been groomed for life among the planter elite. He first attended the Grove Academy in Kenansville, followed by a stint at the Donaldson Military Academy in Fayetteville. In 1799, he joined his older brother Thomas DeVane King at the nearby Preparatory School in Chapel Hill, and subsequently followed him into the University of North Carolina. At age fifteen, King and seven other classmates joined the Philanthropic Society, one of two literary societies that dominated student life on campus. Among King's society classmates was John H. Eaton, who later became secretary of war under Andrew Jackson. In his time, King held nearly every office of the Philanthropic Society, including corrector, councillor, supervisor, and president. During this period, collegians commonly formed bonds of intimate attachment with one another, especially through memberships in literary societies. King appears to have been particularly close to John A. Thornton of Virginia, as both young men were routinely fined for such offenses as "irregularity" in their attendance at society meetings and "laughing." Indeed, a mischievous streak ran deep in King. One tale has him running through town in the middle of the night to steal beehives.[7]

Despite having enjoyed many happy student days, King did not officially graduate from the university. At age eighteen, he apparently concluded that he was already prepared to study the law. He may also have been motivated by guilt. In May 1804 he had been called to serve on a jury in Sampson County, but he failed to heed the summons, which cost him twenty shillings and public rebuke. Notwithstanding, he quickly busied himself with the full-time study of law under Judge William Duffy in Clinton and was admitted to the bar in 1806. He began a legal practice in Fayetteville, and by February 1807, Sampson County had appointed him as its solicitor. Although a practicing attorney, King could also be counted as a planter, thanks to a generous transfer from his father of 600 acres of land and numerous enslaved people. Just a few years after leaving college King had established himself as a wealthy and promising young lawyer and planter.[8]

Like so many ambitious young men, he quickly became absorbed in the affairs of his community. In 1807 King became a Freemason by joining Phoenix Lodge No. 8 in Fayetteville, and three years later, he advanced to the level of Master Mason. He maintained a lifelong connection to the fraternal society, in large part because many of his closest political and personal friends were members. In addition, King was called in 1808 to local militia service under the command of Captain Joseph Westbrook. From these early military experiences, he earned the lifelong sobriquet of "Colonel King." These early years in North Carolina were, by his own retrospective account, the "happiest portion of my life," where "were all those tender associations" of youth. Whether as freemason or militia officer, King found the company of other men to be critical to his social, professional, and political advancement.[9]

Part of King's happiness stemmed from his growing interest in politics. As a Jeffersonian Democratic-Republican, King was first elected to serve a term in the North Carolina House of Commons in 1808. The following year he became solicitor in the fifth circuit of the state superior court, a position that required constant travel around the Piedmont. When Thomas Kenan declined to seek a fourth term as Sampson County's representative to the US House of Representatives, King, though not quite twenty-five, decided to run for the vacant congressional seat in 1810. After a nominal campaign that included stump speeches at local picnics, he was elected that fall. King maintained an element of dignity in his campaign style. Robert Strange, a fellow North Carolinian, later remembered that King "was not a man to stoop to the arts of the demagogue."[10]

Upon arrival in the capital in December 1811, King was immediately concerned with his choice of a boardinghouse. "While affiliation with a particular party did not preclude associations with persons of another party," a historian of the subject has observed, "members of Congress tended to socialize with their political compatriots." King typified this trend in his decision to form a mess with several incoming young Democratic-Republicans, including fellow North Carolinian Israel Pickens, at Mr. Claxton's boardinghouse. In the charged atmosphere prevailing across Washington, the boardinghouse fraternities tended to unify the political views of its members, as evidenced by King's mostly southern mess. Of the thirteen other representatives at Mr. Claxton's boardinghouse, for example, eight joined King in voting for war with Britain in June 1812, marking them as a solidly "War Hawk" mess. In subsequent congressional sessions, King continued the earlier arrangement and grew especially close to Pickens.[11]

The handsome and youthful King quickly became a favorite of Washington society. Sarah Weston Gales Seaton, the wife of journalist William Winston Seaton, remembered one dinner party at the Dolley Madison White House. "Mr. King came to our side *sans cérémonie*, and gayly chatted with us until dinner was announced," she recalled. Nevertheless, King could also be quite awkward and even standoffish around women. At another White House dinner hosted by Dolley Madison, King appeared frozen in the company of a woman of polite society. "I was crossed by Wm R. King, who pass'd a lady neither of us knew," Jonathan Roberts of Pennsylvania noted. "I motioned to him to bring her on, but like a hauberk he said he did not know her." King, it seems, did not always care much for the niceties of social life in Washington, nor for the partisan politics of the early American republic.[12]

As King began his second term in the House, the ominous rumbles of war were converging around the capital. On the evening of August 24, 1814, the British marched unopposed into Washington and torched the White House, the Capitol, and several other public buildings. When the congressional representatives returned in September, they found a charred remnant of the former city and available lodgings scarce. King scrambled to form a mess with three other southerners and the sitting vice president, the elderly Elbridge Gerry of Massachusetts, a connection that proved significant. King later recalled how he had "enjoyed a long intimacy with [Gerry], and had derived much knowledge from his long experience in public affairs." From Gerry, King reinforced his already strict republican tendencies and, just perhaps, his adherence to wearing powdered wigs. But the old habits of an earlier era could not forever lay claim to the second generation of statesmen. The congressional session that followed the devastation wrought by war proved a turning point for the second son of Carolina.[13]

The Young Buck

The life of James Buchanan epitomized the democratic possibilities of those who came of age in the early Keystone State. James Buchanan Jr. was born on April 23, 1791, the second child of Scotch-Irish immigrants: his father was James Buchanan Sr., a Scotch-Irish immigrant who had been born in County Donegal, Ireland, and who had immigrated to the United States in 1783; his mother was Elizabeth Speer, whose own parents had also recently arrived in America from Ireland by way of Scotland. Following their marriage in 1788, the family of James and Elizabeth Speer Buchanan eventually numbered seven children to reach adulthood (in order of age, James, Jane, Maria, Sarah, Harriet, William Speer, and Edward Young). The young James, whom his family called "Jimmie," seems to have had experienced something of a tense relationship with his father and namesake—he never included the epithet of junior in his signature or on official papers, for example. Nevertheless, the son recalled his father as "a sincere friend, and an honest and religious man." By comparison, Buchanan cared deeply for his mother, with whom he remembered spending "hours pleasantly and instructively in conversing with her." From his mother, especially, Buchanan gained a passion for reading, books, and poetry.[14]

The young James Buchanan was a product of the borderlands of the Middle Atlantic, a thriving agricultural region that straddled the Mason-Dixon Line separating the North from the South. At a crossroads called Stony Batter, the Buchanan family prospered, trading necessary supplies for animal skins with the Native Americans and white settlers who lived in the nearby mountains. William Findlay, a future governor of Pennsylvania and an early resident of Mercersburg, later observed that James Buchanan was "cradled amid these wild scenes of nature and the rude din of frontier life." As a precaution, Elizabeth Speer Buchanan tied a cowbell around the young Jimmie's neck so that she could keep the boy within earshot at all times. In addition to their trading post at Cove Gap, James Buchanan Sr. had purchased the Dunwoodie farm and grew a profitable wheat crop; he later owned several hundred acres of land in the region. In 1796 James Buchanan Sr. physically relocated his log cabin and his family from Cove Gap to the crossroads town of Mercersburg, where they operated a general store. This bustling town would be Jimmie Buchanan's home for the remainder of his childhood years.[15]

In addition to learning the routines of frontier life and his rudimentary letters, he was introduced first-hand through his nurse to the lingering effects

FIGURE 1.2 The Buchanan boyhood home today. The cabin stands on the grounds of Mercersburg Academy in Mercersburg, Pennsylvania. Collection of the author.

of slavery in the state. About Hannah, a Mercersburg historian recalled, Buchanan "always remembered an old colored nurse that he had when he was a small boy and would buy for her things that he thought she could use." Although Pennsylvania had abolished slavery in 1780, it had done so gradually and thus permitted the continuation of the institution for decades to come—its peculiar presence in Buchanan's early life was a foreshadowing both of future political disagreement and of his intimate connection to the maintenance of the slave system.[16]

Buchanan followed a typical path to his formal education. He was first schooled at the Old Stone Academy in Mercersburg—under the tutelage of James R. Sharon—then by a Mr. McConnell, and finally by Jesse Magaw. By the suggestion of the family's neighbor and pastor Dr. John King of the Presbyterian Church at Mercersburg, he headed east to Dickinson College in Carlisle. Although smaller than its peers, Dickinson was notable among American colleges for its mix of northerners and southerners; for example, Roger Taney of Maryland, the future Supreme Court Chief Justice, graduated in 1795. When Buchanan enrolled in the fall of 1807 at age sixteen, he found the college in a "wretched condition" with "no efficient discipline." Nevertheless, Buchanan diligently prepared for his examinations. He wrote out hundreds of questions and answers on such topics as logic, grammar, rhetoric, chronology, history, metaphysics (or pneumatology), and moral philosophy, which included sections on the morality of slavery and the duties of friendship. Although he passed his qualifying exams, Buchanan was expelled in the fall of 1808 "on account of disorderly conduct," possibly for violations of the school's prohibition on the consumption of alcohol. In turn, he promised both his father, who had delivered the news by silently passing him the letter of expulsion and then leaving the room, and Dr. John King, who was also a trustee of the college, to remain on good behavior thenceforth.[17]

Duly readmitted, controversy followed him in other ways. He had joined the Union Philosophical Society, which, along with the competing Belles Lettres Society, was a major force in the intellectual and social life of the college. As treasurer of the society, he collected membership dues and fines from members for "not debating." Ever the devotee of poetry, he purchased such tracts as the collected works of Alexander Pope and Mark Akenside's derivative poem "Pleasures of the Imagination." Upon graduation, his fellow society members unanimously chose him as their commencement speaker. Yet the faculty denied Buchanan the top honor, mostly because he seemed unrepentantly proud. Outraged by the arbitrary decision, the society petitioned college President Robert Davidson on his behalf, but to no effect. Finally, the faculty intervened and permitted him his first public oration.[18]

The petty squabble altered Buchanan's previously rosy view of the nature of mankind. His father consoled him with a truism that shaped the outlook of the future politician: "The more you know of mankind the more you will distrust them." In his recollection of these events, though, the young Buchanan remembered especially that "friendship [had never] been manifested towards me in a more striking manner than by all the members of the society to which I belonged . . . I left college feeling little attachment to the Alma Mater." The sting of resentment for Dickinson persisted in the years ahead, as he instead devoted time to the growing Marshall College (later Franklin & Marshall College). But he had equally learned the value of intimate companionship during the most difficult of times.[19]

As a young man starting out in the world, Buchanan proceeded along a strikingly similar path to his future messmate King. After graduating from Dickinson in 1809 he determined to move to Lancaster, a city which was fast assuming its place as the most important link between Philadelphia and the state capital at Harrisburg. His father had encouraged the move, even paying for his son's legal education. Buchanan Sr. thought the new city held good opportunities for a young lawyer. All the same, he warned his son to "guard against the temptations that may offer themselves." The younger Buchanan seems to have complied with those wishes, as he studied law under the tutelage of the Federalist judge James Hopkins. Many years later, Buchanan remarked of his legal training that he had "never known a harder student than I was at that period of my life."[20]

Three years of intense study passed in this way, but before long, Buchanan considered going west. In 1812, with the nation drifting toward war with England, he was setting his sights on Kentucky, where his father had previously purchased acreage on his children's behalf. Yet only James ever left Pennsylvania, albeit briefly, and largely with the intention of settling his father's land claims and obtaining a fair price in the sale. As an ancillary benefit, his father believed, Buchanan would gain "the restoration of your health." His frontier itch satisfied, Buchanan returned to Lancaster. He was promptly admitted to the Pennsylvania bar, and he established a legal practice in the fall of 1812. He earned a handsome living as a practicing attorney in the bustling town. Over the next three years alone, he appeared in more than one hundred fifty cases.[21]

Buchanan busied himself with social organizations that naturally linked him to public affairs in Lancaster. In 1813 he began an association with the

Union Fire Company. His great strength, one remembered, made him a natural favorite for carrying "the large ladder to the fire, and returning it to its
proper place." He was also awarded his first public office in 1813 as the pros-
ecutor for the newly established Lebanon County. The news gave his father
"pleasure to find you have so many good friends as to procure you the appointment." As they had for King, friendships with other men had proven
essential to Buchanan's initial foray into public life.[22]

The later stages of the War of 1812 provided the backdrop for Buchanan's
first entry to elected office. In the summer of 1814, the British army threatened
to invade Baltimore and possibly march on to Pennsylvania. At a meeting in
Lancaster to raise volunteers for a militia, he "addressed the people, and was
among the first to register my name as a volunteer." The impromptu militia
organized by Judge Henry Shippen became a mounted dragoon company and
began its march to Baltimore under the command of Major Charles Sterrett
Ridgely on August 27. These "Shippen Guards" joined an encampment of
regulars from the army and militia contingents from across the region. Never
formally listed on the official rolls of the War Department, the company
was honorably discharged in early September. Unlike his future messmate,
Buchanan earned no honorary rank from his military service.[23]

Though the militia was short-lived, Buchanan attracted the widespread
admiration of his fellow citizens. Within days of his discharge he was
nominated as a representative to the Pennsylvania State Assembly, and the
people of Lancaster duly elected him to the office in October 1814. Buchanan
took a natural liking to politics. His brother Edward later wrote of these early
years that "his mode of expressing his views, was then, as afterwards clear
and convincing." Buchanan's father, who had earlier cautioned him about
diverting attention from his legal practice, was glad to hear that his son was
so well "pleased at being a member of the Legislature." By June 1815, however,
Buchanan was questioning whether to return for a second session. Perhaps he
was concerned about the consequences of a planned oration scheduled for
the upcoming July 4 celebration, in which he would declare himself an ardent Federalist and an opponent of the late war with Britain. In that speech,
he pilloried President Madison, whom he claimed should have "shed his last
drop of blood in . . . [the] defence" of Washington rather than abandon the
city to its fate. Only a return to "Washingtonian policy," he believed, could
bring the country back to the right spirit of the Revolution. Despite having
"many political enemies to criticize your oration," as the elder Buchanan
averred, the citizens of Lancaster re-elected their young Federalist representative for another year.[24]

By 1816, Buchanan had determined to conclude his public service and focus on his prosperous legal career. All the same, the signs of his later leavening into a full-time politician were already present. He had aligned himself with the reactionary Federalist Party, which in one historian's view was "essentially passive, depending upon the force of tradition, the stimulus of good example, and the mistakes of the opposition to hold the party together." He had delivered a patriotic oration that so often brought attention to a politician from beyond the local stage. Yet an important aspect of Buchanan's personal life remained unsettled: his marital status. As the eldest son, the traditional responsibilities of carrying on his family's name fell on his shoulders. Whether he could translate his professional success and political popularity into a marital union remained unclear.[25]

Youthful Folly

The conclusion of the War of 1812 brought the termination of William Rufus King's service in the US House of Representatives. During the congressional recess in the spring of 1816, he decided to resign his seat in the House. Quite likely, he did so to avoid the embarrassment of being turned out of office for his support of the unpopular Compensation Act of 1816 that granted higher pay to congressmen. Instead, he sought an appointment as secretary of the legation to Naples in the Kingdom of the Two Sicilies (not yet unified into the modern nation of Italy), under the auspices of the new American minister William Pinkney, a Maryland Federalist. Once secured, King prepared for his journey and began to keep a private journal, a common practice among Americans traveling abroad. To start his diary, King began somewhat disingenuously: "Actuated by a desire to visit the Continent of Europe which I had fostered from a very early period of my life . . . I determined to resign my situation in Congress." But whatever his true motivations, this period abroad would prove life-changing.[26]

In June, William Rufus King departed for Europe from Annapolis, sailing initially at his own expense. King proved a capable secretary and, given his aptitude for learning French, the official diplomatic language, he became an essential part of the operation of the Pinkney mission. Pinkney soon accomplished his assigned task of settling indemnity claims with the Kingdom of the Two Sicilies, after which Secretary of State James Monroe ordered him to continue on to St. Petersburg to negotiate a commercial treaty. As secretary of the legation, King arrived in the Russian capital in advance of the minister to make the necessary arrangements for their mission. He also carried Pinkney's implicit trust; to the outgoing chargé d'affaires in Russia, Pinkney concluded his views on a legal matter with the note: "Colonel King, who knows perfectly my views, will supply verbally what be deficient in this letter." In January 1817, Pinkney reported to president-elect Monroe that King had been "very graciously received" by the Russian court circle. The American delegation to St. Petersburg appeared to be off to an auspicious start.[27]

Then matters took an unexpected turn. During the summer of 1817, the high society of St. Petersburg prepared for the royal marriage of Grand Duke Nicholas (later Emperor Nicholas I) to Princess Charlotte of Prussia (the future Empress Alexandra Feodorovna). By the protocols of the Russian court, the members of the American diplomatic corps were regularly invited to attend the many "fêtes, balls, [and] felicitations," as William Pinkney put it in a letter to new secretary of state John Quincy Adams. Accordingly, the members of the legation attended "*the fiancailles & marriage*" of the royal couple at the Grand Church of the Winter Palace on July 1. The royal wedding brought an especially "great pomp" and, with it, an unexpected existential crisis in the life of William Rufus King.[28]

From later accounts, the sight of the nineteen-year-old Princess Charlotte moved King, then thirty-one, to a theretofore unrealized affection for the young woman. Grandniece Bessie Hogan Williams recounted the sequence of events in this way: "When Colonel King was presented to the Bride he kissed her hand and squeeze it more than he ought to have don. He said to his Friend Mr. Pinkney—When I am presented to the Charming Bride—I am going to give her pretty hand a little squeeze just to see what she will doo—Which he did—She flushed and with drew her hand putting it behind her back—in anger." The purported move was certainly risky on the young American's part. An onlooker, perhaps Pinkney, warned King: "You will land in Siberia if you aren't careful." But, as the story goes, King need not have worried. "Before he arose next morning," another historian recounted, "there was a knock on his door and an officer of the Czar's household greeted him. When he opened the door, he thought his time had come; but very much to his delight there was a note in English from the Czar's daughter to the effect that it was a pleasure to meet him the night before and that he would be welcome to call again at the Czar's Palace." Williams conceded that the "story may be all fiction," but she concluded cheerily, "it's a pretty good story."[29]

In the years ahead, the story of King's unrequited love for the Russian czarina circulated with some regularity. In fact, King himself often hinted at it in his correspondence with trusted political and personal friends, usually as a way to explain his lifelong bachelorhood. In response to the death of the wife of his friend Israel Pickens, he alluded to his own comparative personal misery. "I am almost induced to envy you," he wrote, "when I contrast your

FIGURE 1.3 Czarina Alexandra Feodorovna, formerly Princess Charlotte of Prussia. The love story of King and the czarina persisted during his lifetime and beyond. Portrait by Pyotr Sokolov, early 1820s. Photograph by Natalia Antonova and Inna Regentova and copyright the State Hermitage Museum, St. Petersburg, Russia.

situation with mine." In a revealing passage from the letter—a small square of which was ripped out by later readers—King hinted at the reason for his inability to marry:

> What are my prospects; a cheerless winter of life; no "smiling babes to lisp their sire's return, and climb his knees the envied kiss to share." You ask why should it be. I can only say such is the decree of fate; mine is a wayward heart, that loves but once and loves forever. Of [St.]

Petersburg or of those residing in its vicinity, I know but little between me and them there never was a community of sentiment, vanity, and youthful folly may have misled me for a moment, but returning reason convinced me that "perfect esteem, enlivened by desire ineffable, and sympathy of soul; thought meeting thought, and will preventing will, with boundless confidence" was entirely wanting.

King's poetical quotations evoked classic images of marriage and the joys of family and thus underscored the unhappiness of his own unmarried state. In the first quote, he alluded to Thomas Gray's "Elegy Written in a Country Churchyard," while in the second, he drew on the "Spring" section of James Thompson's lengthy poem "The Seasons." The choice of Gray's poem was especially ironic, since as one scholar has argued, the "Elegy" can be read as containing "the indirect and subtle effects of . . . sexual frustration and internalized homophobia" following the death of the poet's young friend Richard West. Whether or not King understood the poem in this way, his use of poetical allusion effectively foreclosed his prospects for marriage by conflating the images of family with death. In so doing, the application of sentimental poetry permitted him to gloss over the details of his bachelorhood.[30]

Although he kept detailed notes of his Italian sojourn, King recorded nothing of his time in Russia. Since accounts from family tradition and references in his correspondence offer only traces of the affair, a comparison to other contemporary southerners provides an insight into King's later management of this far-fetched story of an unattainable love. For example, historian Craig Friend described the vexed case of one Cyrus Stewart of South Carolina, a son of a blacksmith, who discovered that a successful wooing required "family, wealth, and social and courtship skills." While at home King counted himself among the planter elite, at the Russian court, his status as secretary to the American legation marked him as a social inferior. If credible, King's kissing and squeezing of the hand of the princess at her wedding was poor form. All the same, John Mayfield noted in his study of southern manhood that for many men, "Life became a series of public displays in which the male literally performed . . . for the approval of his peers." The presence of his fellow legation staff, Pinkney among them, may well have goaded him into enacting the romantic mischief.[31]

As his letter to Israel Pickens attested, King's story of his love for the future Russian czarina revealed an inner conflict in his private thoughts and feelings. His declaration to Pickens that he had loved once and thus could not love again fit neatly within a pattern of dramatic alienation not

uncommon among southern intellectuals. But while not unusual for widows
and widowers not to remarry, King had not taken the marriage vow. He was
certainly still young enough to love once more and, accordingly, to marry.
Moreover, the literary quality of his prose in this and other letters related to
the topic of marriage suggested that he invented, or at least embellished, the
story of his love for Princess Charlotte. Such a reading easily lends itself to the
conclusion that King was romantically uninterested in, or perhaps sexually
repelled by, women. In point of fact, he carried an aversion to romantic marriage throughout his adult life.[32]

Indeed, King's romantic estrangement toward women may have
corresponded with a sexual attraction toward men. Same-sex desire, literary
scholar David Greven has observed, "was subjected to an especially rigorous
cultural silencing," which has caused considerable methodological difficulties
in establishing its presence. A recent study of the intimate friendship of
Abraham Lincoln and Joshua Speed makes a similar point. "The key issue is
shame," psychobiographer Charles Strozier concludes. "Sex among men, because it was so strongly condemned, inevitably . . . would generate a pervasive
shame among those who crossed that line, with implications for attitudes and
behavior." At the start of the nineteenth century, the repression of same-sex
desires included a severe legal component as well; sodomy remained a crime
punishable by death in many places until the American Revolution, and
subsequently, it carried a prison sentence. The hostile environment toward
same-sex intimacies and attractions in early America, when combined with
King's unceasing ambition for public office, almost certainly led to a form of
sexual repression. As such, he can hardly be described as actively, or perhaps
even consciously, same-sex oriented. Given the incredible human capacity for
sexual repression—a fact borne out especially in historical same-sex desire—
King's sexuality seems to have been intensely and consistently suppressed
throughout his lifetime.[33]

Over time, the story of King's "youthful folly" underscored a critical fea-
ture of political bachelorhood—the constant need to explain one's unmarried
state. By ascribing his bachelorhood to "a decree of fate," he safely attributed
his failure to marry to a "wayward heart, that loves but once and loves forever," rather than any innate sexual inability to love women. That King revealed these deep-seated feelings to another man (and the sitting governor
of his home state) may seem unusual, but discussions of sexuality were a hall-
mark of bosom friendship in the early American republic, both in the north
and the south. Even so, he could not avoid questions about why he had never
married, especially from his most intimate political associates. The story of a

long-lost love for the Russian czarina, King may have grasped, provided just such an explanation. By the conventions of the day, a story of an unrequited love protected him from further scrutiny of his failure to marry. That it had taken place thousands of miles from American soil only served to heighten its romantic appeal.[34]

One month after his charged encounter with Princess Charlotte, the American minister William Pinkney reported to secretary of state John Quincy Adams that King had "quitted me on his return to the U.S." What accounts for his departure? Perhaps King had overstepped his boundaries in his ardent affections for the czarina and decided that he ought to remove himself from the scene of his unrequited love. Possibly he had perceived the futility of Pinkney's mission to Russia—in the course of events, the American minister failed to accomplish his chief diplomatic objective of a commercial treaty with the emerging power. Certainly, King wished to pursue the lucrative economic opportunities emerging for cotton planters in the southwestern territories; he had previously recommended his friend Israel Pickens for the position of receiver of public lands in the new Alabama territory. Finally, he may have desired to return to his family. Not long after his departure, the health of William King Sr. began to decline, and he died in late 1816, with his second son thousands of miles away. The news of his father's death would have taken months to reach him, but when it did, the dutiful second son probably felt compelled to go home. Whatever the reasons, it would not be the last time that King traveled overseas, or for that matter flirted with society women abroad, in the service of his country.[35]

Lancaster Lamentations

Life in the new city that Buchanan called home was, in the words of an early historian of Lancaster, "neither busy, nor were [its] concerns vast." Yet the lawyer was busier than ever, thanks in large part to his successful defenses of the Federalist judge Walter Franklin from impeachment charges by his Democratic opponents in the Pennsylvania state legislature. In 1818, Buchanan's name appeared in more cases than any other attorney in the state of Pennsylvania. His practice flourished: in 1818, for example, he earned $7,915 for legal services—a princely sum in those days. Professionally, he came into frequent contact with many of the leading men of Lancaster. One such figure was John Passmore, memorably described as a "man of great weight, at one time weighing 480 pounds," who was a lawyer, alderman, and then the first mayor of Lancaster. The two men became especially close when, in partnership with Passmore, Buchanan bought a building in which the two men both lived and worked.[36]

Through intimate friendships such as these, Buchanan further intertwined his professional and personal affairs. He befriended Moulton C. Rogers, the son of former Delaware governor Daniel Rogers. The two young men, born a few years apart, bonded over the finer things in life and regularly dined together; as a Buchanan biographer memorably put it, "both were bon vivants and members of the exclusive fraternity which relishes steamed terrapin and brandy." By 1816, their friendship had been transformed into a legal partnership that lasted for several years. Other social accolades followed, including an invitation to serve as a manager for the town's annual ball. At the sponsorship of Rogers and John Reynolds (another lifelong friend), Buchanan became a member of the Free and Accepted Masons, when in December 1816, he was initiated into the prominent Masonic Lodge No. 43. In his capacity as a freemason Buchanan eventually became Junior Warden in 1820, Worshipful Master in 1822, and the First District Deputy Grand Master for southeastern Pennsylvania in 1823. Through his Masonic affiliation, Buchanan shared a connection with numerous other politicians of the period, including King. When an anti-masonic political movement gathered steam in Pennsylvania in later years, Buchanan decried it as "acting under a delusion." His commitment to the masonic fraternity was whole cloth.[37]

During these years in Lancaster, Buchanan might have been the town's most eligible young bachelor. All that changed in early 1818, when he became aware of Ann Coleman, the daughter of the wealthy iron magnate Robert Coleman. Although Moulton Rogers introduced him to Ann Coleman, he already knew her father Robert Coleman in other capacities; the two men shared a connection as volunteers of Union Fire Company No. 1, and members of Buchanan's immediate family were also communicants of the St. James Episcopal Church, to which Coleman was attached as a prominent vestryman. Buchanan subsequently called upon Ann Coleman, who at twenty-three was nearly beyond the socially acceptable age of marriage. Over the course of the winter, the pair evidently fell in love, Buchanan even penning romantic verse to his betrothed, declaring, "I pledge my all to you!" in one poignant line. The couple became engaged in the late summer of 1819.[38]

In the months ahead, the press of business and political affairs—made worse by the Panic of 1819 afflicting the nation—engrossed Buchanan and caused him to neglect his new fiancée. In particular, a suit against the Columbia Bridge Company, which was represented by Buchanan, required his constant travel back and forth between Lancaster and Philadelphia. In

FIGURE I.4 Ann Coleman. Buchanan, his family members, and his political supporters protected the purity of his romantic attachment to Coleman during his lifetime and beyond. Oil portrait on canvas by Hannah Mee Horner, 1939, copied from the original by Thomas Sully, 1820. Courtesy James Buchanan Foundation Photograph Collection, LancasterHistory.org, Lancaster, Pennsylvania.

November 1819, after one such trip, Buchanan returned to Lancaster and thoughtlessly paid his first call at the home of his friend William Jenkins, who had also studied law under Judge Hopkins, and his wife Mary Field Hubley Jenkins. Besides Jenkins, his wife, and their young children, Grace P. Hubley, an unmarried sister of Mrs. Jenkins, was present with the family. Buchanan apparently enjoyed the call and stayed for a full hour in an engaging conversation with Miss Hubley. When Ann Coleman heard of this visit—likely by way of an unsolicited and possibly malicious note from Hubley—she decided to break off the engagement. Coleman penned a furious note, which, one account has it, "she sent by messenger in hot haste, the note being handed to Buchanan while he was in the court house." After receiving the note, his face turned noticeably pale. Buchanan later described the reason for their break as "trivial," but one Lancaster observer thought the split resulted as "a consequence of his coolness" following months of neglect of his betrothed.[39]

Early the next month, Ann Coleman's parents urged her to visit with relatives in Philadelphia to lift her lingering depression following the break with Buchanan. However, events unexpectedly spiraled in a tragic direction. On her way to Philadelphia Coleman had apparently caught cold, and, quite possibly, she took laudanum, an opiate commonly prescribed to cure illness but which could be lethal in higher dosages. On the evening of December 8, Ann Coleman was examined by a physician and found to be suffering from "hysterical convulsions," according to a diary entry of Philadelphia judge and Buchanan friend Thomas Kittera. She died just after midnight. Rumors quickly circulated that Coleman had committed suicide, though the surviving evidence suggests otherwise.[40]

Whatever the actual cause of her death, the news electrified Lancaster and stirred sorrow, gossip, and bitter resentment toward Buchanan. "I believe that [Coleman's] friends now look upon him as her Murderer," Lancaster townswoman Hannah Cochran wrote to her husband Samuel in the days following the tragedy. Buchanan himself was genuinely afflicted by grief and wrote an appropriately sorrowful letter to Robert Coleman, dated December 10. The note was likely never sent or perhaps returned unopened, for it survives among Buchanan's personal papers. "I feel that happiness has fled from me forever," he wrote and asked to be able to "follow her remains to the grave as a mourner." The request did not come to pass. He spent the next several days secluded with friends, though he may have roused himself sufficiently to write a touching obituary notice.[41]

What can be made of this failed romance with Ann Coleman? Unlike King's love for the Russian czarina, Buchanan's relationship with Coleman is thoroughly substantiated by the historical record. Nevertheless, the affair produced the only known instance in which Buchanan destroyed a portion of his personal papers that he otherwise carefully preserved for posterity. Whatever the true nature of his feelings for Coleman, the relationship carried significant consequences in the ensuing years. Perhaps most importantly, the story of his love for Ann Coleman permitted Buchanan to claim quite credibly that he could not again consider a serious romantic relationship with another woman—he had loved once and could not do so again. Yet he also became an object of sympathy and even gained "a sort of romantic appeal" to other women, which he quite often reciprocated from the relative security of middle age. Bachelorhood, although inherently undesirable to the convivial Buchanan, begrudgingly grew on him.[42]

The tragic tale of Ann Coleman's death did not detract from Buchanan's future political prospects. On the contrary, this story of long-lost love became an essential part of his public persona. Indeed, Ann Coleman's death provided a powerful justification for his bachelorhood to the wider world. Once established as such, Buchanan, his family members, and his political supporters were equally beholden to maintain the purity of this early romance. In 1856, when *Harper's Magazine* published a story claiming that Buchanan had left Coleman for another woman, his defenders loudly detracted the piece. Even long after his death, Buchanan's heirs and the executors of his estate remained on the lookout for any libelous claims related to the affair. In 1883, when the Boston *Herald* printed a lurid account by Emma Jacobs Thompson that she had been the cause of the break with Ann Coleman, Buchanan's executor Hiram Swarr immediately threatened a law suit, and the paper issued a retraction. These later examples reveal the multi-generational investment required to protect the purity of Buchanan's bachelorhood from potential aspersion.[43]

After the Coleman tragedy, the years ahead witnessed an explosion of political activity that brought Buchanan's name into the national spotlight. But the catalyst for his entry into politics, as he later recounted to his intimate friend Samuel M. L. Barlow, directly followed from this personal sorrow. "I never intended to engage in politics," Barlow remembered Buchanan saying in 1856, "but meant to follow my profession strictly . . . but I saw I must leave my home or fight my way—as a distraction from my great grief and because I saw that through a political following I could secure the friends I then needed." Buchanan returned to his beloved Federalist Party, which in Pennsylvania had combined forces with a splinter group of the Democratic Party to form a loose coalition called the Independent Republicans. In turn, the Lancaster Federalists chose Buchanan as their candidate in the district's congressional election in the fall of 1820.[44]

During the campaign, Buchanan's relationship with Ann Coleman and even members of his own family became targets of political attack. The dispute centered on the legal status of Buchanan's old nurse Hannah, who in 1801 had been sold by James Buchanan Sr. to Archibald Irwin of Mercersburg, the father-in-law of the Democratic Governor William Findlay. Following Irwin's death Hannah sued for her freedom, thus involving Findlay as executor of the estate. Federalist newspapers charged Findlay with being a slaveholder, which resulted in a reply from an anonymous "Investigator" who accused Buchanan of being behind the attacks. The charge infuriated James Buchanan Sr., who wrote to his son that the piece was "well calculated to irritate & hurt your feelings." In another public letter signed by "Colebrook"—a not too subtle jibe at the name of Buchanan's recently deceased fiancée—he was further taken to task for his alleged involvement. "Your attack on Governor Findlay for being the owner of a slave was rash in the commencement and exceedingly unfavorable in the end to the cause it was designed to support," the letter claimed. Buchanan denied his involvement in the affair, but the ill-will generated against him in some parts of Pennsylvania continued for many years to come.[45]

In the congressional contest that October, the popular Federalist Buchanan won handily over his Democratic opponent. Due to the timing of the election, more than a year passed before he took his seat in the Capitol. In the interim, his private affairs became more tragic still. On June 11, 1821, James Buchanan Sr. was thrown from his horse and died after hitting his head against the iron wheel of his carriage. Buchanan dutifully returned to Mercersburg for the funeral and to arrange his family's affairs. Soon thereafter, his sister Sarah Buchanan Huston died at a young age from disease and his younger brother William Speer Buchanan, a promising young attorney who had attended Princeton, met a similar fate. At age thirty, Buchanan looked to leave these weighty family responsibilities behind him. Unlike King, he did not travel overseas for a change of scenery, but instead searched for a greater purpose to his life in Washington.[46]

* * *

At first glance, the early lives of King and Buchanan seem to have shared little in common. Born six years and hundreds of miles apart, they came of age and entered public life in two very different regions of the country. From the Piedmont, the young King had taken to politics based on the strength of his family name; exceptionally eloquent and of patrician demeanor, his tall and slim figure appealed to the state's rural voters. After leaving Mercersburg, the young Buchanan relied upon hard work and natural intelligence to make his way in the world; his oversized frame and dignified manner likewise made him a natural favorite among the people of Lancaster. One was attracted to the principles of the Democratic-Republicans, the other to those of the Federalist Party; one urged war with England to prove American independence, the other served begrudgingly in a war unpopular at home. At the start of the 1820s, they stood at opposite ends of the political spectrum.

Nonetheless, their lives had been shaped by similar forces. Educational opportunities and civic duties defined their early years: both men attended college, trained for the law, participated in militia activities, joined fraternal societies and community organizations, and attended social functions.

Equally, intimate friendships with other men had proven critical to their early successes in their educations, professions, and political activities. So, too, had events taken them farther afield from the scenes of their childhoods: King went first to Naples and then on to Russia; Buchanan left tiny Mercersburg for Carlisle, followed by Kentucky, before settling in Lancaster. Like others of the second generation of Americans, they refused to be limited by their provincial upbringings.

Of all their similarities, lifelong bachelorhood eventually became their most salient commonality. Each man had unsuccessfully flirted with romance—King never took serious steps toward the altar, while Buchanan tried, but failed, to follow the traditional route to marriage. Throughout their political careers, both men relied upon stories of loves long-lost. These tales provided a necessary explanation to satisfy the demands of the inquisitive public and those of their intimate friends and family members. Of course, these stories could also help to disguise same-sex attractions and erotic desires condemned by American society, as seems likely to have been the case with King. Bachelorhood became for both men a defining part of their personal and political identities. The political developments of the decades ahead only hardened the early convictions of these young bachelor politicians.

2

Hardening, 1820–1834

THE EARLY POLITICAL careers of William Rufus King and James Buchanan straddled the transition from the First Party System, of Federalists and Democratic-Republicans, to the Second Party System, of Democrats and Whigs. Similarly, their lives echoed the evolving political culture of the early republic. When each man entered Congress, the republican comportment of the prior era was fast receding—the powdered wigs, knee-length breeches, and silk stockings gave way to flowing manes of hair, waistcoats, and trousers. Not surprisingly, King and Buchanan each maintained a signature sartorial style during their respective lifetimes. They also witnessed a changing social milieu in the capital, reflected especially in the increasingly partisan arrangement of boardinghouses. Prior to the election of Andrew Jackson, the court culture of the early republic favored the elite establishment; following Jackson, the boisterous capital society matched the nation's mood. Both men cut their political teeth in this democratizing social world.[1]

The decade of the 1820s witnessed the high watermark of the "Era of Good Feelings." Under the presidential administration of James Monroe, the partisan bickering of the prior decades receded from public view. In its place, previously buried sectional differences over slavery—witnessed most visibly in the crisis over the admission of Missouri—threatened the national union. This momentary peril notwithstanding, the greatest political problem of the era was not slavery, but the question of President Monroe's successor. The failure of the congressional caucus system to produce an acceptable nomination yielded five "favorite sons" vying for the top office: Andrew Jackson, John C. Calhoun, John Quincy Adams, Henry Clay, and William H. Crawford. In the election of 1824 Jackson received the most votes, both in the popular and electoral columns, but he had failed to win a clear majority in either category; accordingly, the election was thrown to the House of Representatives, which selected Adams as the winner. This astonishing result harbingered the end of a unified rule by the Democratic-Republican Party.[2]

Amidst these political changes, King remained decidedly fixed in his bachelorhood. King's "youthful folly" in St. Petersburg permitted him to focus instead on the new possibilities for material wealth in cotton planting and electoral success in state and national politics. Upon his return from Russia, he relocated with members of his family to the new territory of Alabama, where he established a plantation at King's Bend, near the town of Selma. He also quickly rose to prominence in the public affairs of his adopted home state. Elected as its first United States senator, he argued on behalf of Alabamians for easier access both to credit and the lands of Native Americans. Re-elected to the Senate, he found that he remained vulnerable to other kinds of challengers, as demonstrated by a near duel in 1831. A supporter of Andrew Jackson, he nevertheless found himself at odds with the old general over issues of states' rights during the nullification crisis of 1833. The 1820s and early 1830s, in short, found King struggling to achieve distinction both within and beyond the South.

By comparison, Buchanan spent considerable effort during these years in new romantic pursuits, almost always with much younger women. Although none advanced beyond the stage of flirtation, the political career of the Young Buck flourished. His Lancaster townsmen elected him five times to the House of Representatives, where he happily became an "instruction man" first for his beloved Federalist Party and then for the new Jacksonian Democracy. His incautious involvement in the election of 1824 revealed the costs of these shifting political alignments, as did the factional infighting between the Amalgamation Party and the Family Party in Pennsylvania. Like King, partisan politics exhausted Buchanan, yet he too could not quench his ambition for higher office. Though conflicted, he accepted President Jackson's appointment as American minister to Russia in 1831. His triumphant return to Pennsylvania two years later brought him a just political reward; in 1834, the Pennsylvania state legislature selected him for the US Senate. Once again, Buchanan headed to Washington a bachelor.

This seemingly banal connection to bachelorhood proved, in time, to be a vital political asset in King and Buchanan's conjoined rise to power. They had forged their earliest and strongest partisan associations with fellow bachelors from their respective political parties. As they faced factional conflicts at home, the realities of bachelorhood reinforced the need for intimate political and personal friendships. In Washington, their unmarried status cast them as objects of curiosity, recipients of sympathy, and targets for the matchmakers of high society. They also both took the initial steps toward becoming the bachelor patriarchs of their extended families. Like their married counterparts, their romantic choices defined a crucial aspect of their public personae.

Alabama Planter Politician

By the fall of 1817, King had returned from Russia to his native North Carolina. In February, he traveled to Washington to meet with political friends, his former congressional messmate Israel Pickens among them. There he discussed his plans to relocate to Alabama, where he hoped to seek his fortunes in the cotton boom taking place across the southwestern territories. In October 1818, he purchased 750 choice acres from the federal land office based out of the Georgia state capital in Milledgeville. By March of the following year, he helped to found the Selma Land Company at a meeting in the first territorial capital of Cahawba. He became an enthusiastic booster of the new town of Selma and may even have provided its name; from his college days, he likely remembered the place-name from the poetry of "Ossian." Regardless, King remained forever proud of his part in founding the town.[3]

Soon the three King brothers, William Rufus, Thomas DeVane, and John DeVane, established a plantation along a prominent curve in the Selma River, which they called King's Bend, and purchased more land in the town of Selma proper. Their family's initial dwelling consisted of a large log cabin at "Chestnut Hill" or "Pine Hill," variously so named for the native hardwoods and conifers prevalent in that region. In 1820, William Rufus King began work on a larger oak-planked structure that became his home for the remainder of his adult life. Although he shared the house with other family members, he determined to live as freely as possible, as evidenced by a separate entrance to his ground-floor bedroom. From Chestnut Hill, King thus established himself in the public affairs of Selma and the new territory.[4]

In time, the King clan branched out across Alabama. Older brother Thomas DeVane King moved with his family to the new state capital at Tuscaloosa, while King's mother Margaret, several of his sisters, and younger brother John DeVane all remained behind at King's Bend. Brother John, who was also unmarried, managed the various plantations and often stood in for the family's business interests in Selma. William Rufus grew quite close to Thomas DeVane's two children, William Thomas King—who eventually inherited the entirety of the King's Bend plantation—and Margaret William King. Similarly, he became intimately attached to Margaret Eliza Beck, the daughter of his sister Margaret King Beck (who died in 1822) and her husband

FIGURE 2.1 Chestnut Hill, the plantation of William Rufus King at King's Bend, Dallas County, Alabama. The door on the left side of the house served as a separate entrance to King's bedroom. Charcoal on paper. Courtesy Alabama Photographs and Pictures Collection, Alabama Department of Archives and History.

John Beck (who died in 1824). Following these deaths, King grew particularly close to Eliza, as evidenced by one letter where he wrote: "I have the greatest confidence, and my affection for you is unbounded." In 1828, King became custodian to the children of his sister Tabitha King Kornegay, whose husband had abandoned them back in North Carolina. Though yet a bachelor, he was fast becoming a surrogate father to the extended King family.[5]

Of all his nieces and nephews, the one to whom King eventually grew fondest was Catherine Margaret Parish. Her mother, Catherine King Parish, had died during childbirth in 1816, leaving the infant to the care of relatives. William Rufus considered the orphaned Catherine, whom he affectionately called "Cate," as an adopted daughter. In 1832, sixteen-year-old Catherine married Harvey Ellis, who had served in the state legislature and as mayor of Tuscaloosa. Although Harvey Ellis was more than a dozen years older than Catherine, King evidently did not object to the marriage on the basis of age; as he once wrote to a colleague whose own daughter had recently turned sixteen: "Youth is the season for enjoyment." At just past forty, King must have taken comfort in his role as the prominent uncle of the extended family. In this way, too, King shared another commonality with Buchanan—both men presided as guardians to several children of their younger sisters.[6]

The King family relocated to Alabama for the economic opportunities afforded by the nearly limitless demand for cotton from textile manufacturers worldwide. William Rufus King legally owned and managed various estates, including the King's Bend plantation in Dallas County and others in nearby Lowndes County. By 1860, the Dallas County lands alone totaled 2,436 acres, while the King family collectively owned as many as 500 enslaved people. At the time of his death, William Rufus King claimed 180 enslaved African Americans, up from 80 enslaved people in 1820. Contemporaries considered him a "humane master," a veritable contradiction in terms, but one very much in keeping with the racial hierarchies of that time. Regardless, King prospered economically thanks to the high prices and great demand for short-staple cotton. The investment of his personal fortunes in the region's cotton market further connected him to his Alabama constituents and served the planter politician well in the years ahead.[7]

Despite moving to Alabama for cotton, King focused most of his attention on politics. During the summer of 1819 he attended the territory's constitutional convention in Huntsville, where he made so strong an impression on the delegates that they chose him as their chair. Albert Pickett, the early Alabama historian and King's contemporary, captured his appeal. "In all the relations of his life, Colonel King has maintained a spotless reputation," he wrote, "his frank and confiding disposition, his uniform courtesy and kindness, has endeared him to numerous friends, and commanded for him the respect and confidence of all who have had the pleasure of his acquaintance." The proceedings of the constitutional convention dragged on through the hot summer months, but King presided with an unshakable equanimity. For his efforts, the new Alabama state legislature chose him as one of its first two US senators.[8]

From the start, King stood out among the power players of the new state. Convention delegate John Campbell remembered King as being a "very gay elegant looking fellow." A fellow bachelor, Campbell also shared an essential personal commonality with King, and unsurprisingly the two became "very intimate." As Campbell told his brother, King "has some very fine qualities and I cannot but feel gratified in seeing him occupy any situation he wishes. He would do any thing in his power for me and I feel a correspondent disposition towards him." In Campbell's view, King compared far more favorably than rival John W. Walker, the state's other US senator, whom he found "amazingly *spoilt*." Through bosom friendships such as these, King advanced his rising political fortunes.[9]

Nevertheless, fierce rivalries soon developed within Alabama that challenged the strength of his political network. On the one side were the members of the "North Carolina Faction," which included King and Israel Pickens. On the other side were the supporters of the "Georgia Faction," variously called the "Broad River Group" or the "Royal Party," which counted Judge William Crawford, Charles Tait, and Senator John W. Walker among them. For the most part, the factions split along geographical lines, with the northern and southern halves of the state receiving equal representation in the distribution of federal offices. The elections for state level offices were particularly contested in this environment; for example, the 1821 gubernatorial election featured one candidate from each faction, Israel Pickens from the North Carolina group running against Henry Chambers of the Georgia clique. The primary issue dividing the two candidates concerned banking, with the North Carolina Faction supporting the creation of a state bank and the Georgia Faction promoting private banks instead. King's ally and intimate friend Israel Pickens, who proclaimed himself a representative of the "People's Party," handily won the election.[10]

In 1822, factional politics once more surfaced when the legislature considered the fate of King's nearly expired term in the US Senate. In 1818, Senator William H. Crawford of Georgia had offered King a profitable land receivership in Huntsville in the hopes that it would remove him from consideration for one of Alabama's two US senate seats. But King rejected the deal and eventually accepted a partial term in the Senate. Prior to the selection in 1822, Crawford again enticed King with a plum prize: a diplomatic assignment to South America. Once more, King spurned the offer, deciding to take his chances against three other candidates. In the contest, the legislature voted to give King a full six-year term in the Senate. King clung to a lingering resentment against Crawford. As Crawford noted to a friend: "The proceedings in relation to them, have produced, or given full development to, feelings of great acerbity towards me, in the bosom of Wm. R. King." A reflection of the unsettled era of one-party politics, Crawford felt compelled to reconcile publicly with King, thus resolving the conflict between the two southern Democratic-Republicans.[11]

On the national level, the decade of the 1820s had begun in a relatively quiet mode. As senator, King worked to ensure the easy sale of public lands in Alabama, which included supporting all efforts to purchase the large tracts owned by the Creek Nation in the northwestern part of the state. As such, he argued for the ratification of the Treaty of Indian Springs, which had been signed in 1825 and ceded approximately two million acres of land to the state of Alabama. The US Senate ultimately disagreed and passed a substitute treaty in 1827 that King deemed a "villainous fraud." Nevertheless, he succeeded in extending greater credit for land purchases, which he hoped would "save Alabama from the ruin which was impending over it." He opposed any increase in import duties, a battle he lost. Equally, he resented the intrusion of the Bank of the United States into Alabama, since its branch competed with the state-level bank that he had worked diligently to fund based on the "valuable staple of Alabama," namely its cotton crop. Overall, King's political philosophy during these years can be characterized as a southern Democratic-Republican who had not yet realized the full partisan potential of his later Jacksonian Democratic views.[12]

Similarly, Democratic-Republican politics on the national level had just begun to divide over the presidential contest of 1824. From the outset, King voiced his strong support for Andrew Jackson. He naturally rejected Jackson's political challenger William H. Crawford as following the mode of "King Caucus" that had traditionally selected presidential candidates since 1800. In a move coordinated with messmate Nathaniel Macon of North Carolina, King returned to his old home state to stump for Jackson. The experience moved him to report to Israel Pickens: "I have great hopes the old Chief will defeat the Caucus Gentry there." King had good reason to be hopeful, as North Carolina went for Jackson in the fall. Jackson's subsequent loss to John Quincy Adams in the House of Representatives stunned King, but Old Hickory's allies in Alabama did not easily lose faith. A new campaign to support Jackson's election in 1828 began almost immediately. By early 1827, King once more reported to Israel Pickens that Jackson's "stock is rising in the market, nothing but destiny can prevent his success at the next election."[13]

In Washington, the court culture of the early republican era insulated itself from the political changes afoot. The late 1820s was the highwater mark for members of the elite society whose presence dated to the turn of the century. Washington itself was prospering once more in the decade following the devastation of the War of 1812. Dozens of new buildings arose, especially residential structures, and the number of wives of congressmen and cabinet officers residing in local boardinghouses substantially increased. The amplified presence of women became "both cause and consequence," as one historian put it, of an expanding social life. With the old political divisions lessened, boardinghouses increasingly became centers for social contact among congressional members, irrespective of party affiliation or section. In the capital's social life, good feelings were widely and truly felt.[14]

For his part, King continued to find personal and political commonality with mostly unmarried southern congressmen. During the years of the

Quincy Adams presidency, King quite often united with old Republicans such as Nathaniel Macon (a long-time widower) and Samuel Smith of Maryland (a widower and long-time president pro tempore of the Senate) in a boardinghouse arrangement. At times, King shifted toward smaller mess groups with fellow southern senators, such as his Alabama ally John McKinley, his erstwhile opponent William Walker, Philip Pendleton Barbour of Virginia, John Bell of Tennessee, and Willie P. Mangum and Bedford Brown of North Carolina. On multiple occasions, King and his messmates returned to an establishment operated by Alfred R. Dawson (also spelled Dowson), whose boardinghouses famously promoted music and refined conversation with younger, unmarried women. Thus King had found a home, both in the domestic and political sense, as an administration critic among a group of pro-Jackson partisans. These connections helped to solidify his standing in the emerging Democratic Party.[15]

An Instruction Man

The Lancaster lawyer who entered the nation's capital in late 1821 was, by all accounts, impressive to behold. The Young Buck cut an attractive figure, especially to female admirers. Few descriptions survive of him from these early years, but well into his thirties, journalist Anne Royall thought him "quite a young man (and a batchelor, ladies) with a stout handsome person; his face is large and fair, his eye, a soft blue, one of which he often shuts, and has a habit of turning his head to one side; his countenance is open and manly, and to crown the whole, a Chesterfield in his manners, and a great politician." At just about six feet in height, he was "almost a giant in size, as well as mind." Most every social commentator noticed Buchanan's squint in one eye, his large head and frame, and his polite manners. And, of course, they all noted his bachelor status.[16]

Buchanan's entry to the House of Representatives was ill-timed. He was a freshman member of the Federalist Party, by then a scattered contingent of rump delegates. Yet he insulated himself somewhat from his Federalist affiliation by becoming "an instruction man," whereby he committed to following the specific instructions of his state legislatures on critical issues. For Pennsylvania, this most notably meant urging a strong protective tariff to promote domestic manufacturing in the state. But before he could tackle the important issues of the day, the first order of business was to settle his domestic arrangements in Washington, preferably in conjunction with other men of the same party. As a Federalist, Buchanan struggled to find fellow partisans with whom he might form a mess. During one session, he settled upon a mess

FIGURE 2.2 James Buchanan of Pennsylvania. This is the earliest surviving likeness of
Buchanan. Mezzotint engraving by John Sartain from painting by Jacob Eichholtz, 1834.
Prints and Photographs Division, Library of Congress, LC-USZ62-17650.

with two Massachusetts Federalists, as well as with Andrew R. Govan and
George McDuffie from South Carolina, who had recently switched party allegiance from the Federalists to the Democratic-Republicans.[17]

Considering his later domestic arrangement with King, the early
connections to these South Carolina politicos were noteworthy. While
Buchanan's primary association with Govan and McDuffie stemmed from
their former affiliations as Federalists, personal factors also played a part.
Roughly the same age as Buchanan, they were like him bachelors. At the same

time, Govan and McDuffie held radically different views of proper manhood, stemming from their upbringing in the honor culture prevalent across the South. Since entering Congress, for example, George McDuffie had become infamous for a series of duels with William Cumming of Georgia. Similarly, the southern representatives brought Buchanan into closer contact with the enslaved people who attended them in the boardinghouse (an institution that also relied upon the labor of free African Americans). In turn, he aligned himself with southern colleagues whenever possible on the slavery question. During a congressional speech in 1826, for example, Buchanan proudly joined his former messmate McDuffie, when he proclaimed that he would "without hesitation, bundle on my knapsack, and march . . . in defense of their cause." From an early period, congressman Buchanan became intimately familiar not only with the chivalric culture of southern politicians, but with a pleasant domestic lifestyle in Washington predicated on the labor of perceived racial inferiors.[18]

Beyond the confines of the boardinghouse, William Lowndes of South Carolina exerted an especially strong political influence on Buchanan. As with his prior political friends, Buchanan was drawn to the grace of Lowndes's character: "His eloquence partook of his own gentle and unpretending nature." In his "social intercourse," Buchanan remembered, "he was ever ready and willing to impart his stores of information on any subject." From Lowndes, Buchanan gained his first opportunity to speak before Congress on the question of the War Department's expenditures. He even adopted many of the rhetorical strategies—what one historian has called the "Lowndes formula"—including the appearance of impartiality and nonpartisanship, extensive knowledge of the subject under debate, and unassailable logic in the presentation of argument. These traits became hallmarks of Buchanan's oratorical style in Congress.[19]

By 1823, Buchanan had begun to shift his political allegiance in the direction of the Democratic-Republicans (he now described himself with the half-way appellation of "Federal-Republican"). Not long before then, a messmate had written to Henry Clay, the charismatic speaker of the House, that Buchanan was "a gentleman from Lancaster—a Lawyer of Considerable Eminence & whom I have made Very much your Friend." Yet Buchanan's views on presidential politics in the election of 1824 hinted at a different direction. After the untimely death of Lowndes in 1822, he followed the advice of his messmate McDuffie that the "safest course" was to support John C. Calhoun for the presidency and not to back Clay. When Calhoun himself realized that he could not obtain the highest office, he instead positioned himself in the second spot under whomever was selected in 1824. Still Buchanan remained uncertain about his allegiance. By the end of the year, he had privately come to support both Andrew Jackson and to a lesser extent Henry Clay for the presidency.[20]

In its peculiar course, the election of 1824 proved nearly fatal to Buchanan's political career. When the electoral college failed to produce a clear result, Buchanan was urged by fellow Pennsylvania representative Philip Markley and others to find common ground between Jackson and Clay, who represented the state's first and second choices, respectively. On December 30, Buchanan paid a call on Jackson at his boardinghouse, and the two men went for a walk. He repeated a widespread rumor that if the general were elected to the presidency, Jackson would continue with Adams as secretary of state, which would preclude Clay from the office. Jackson rejected the rumor outright, but he left the conversation under the impression that an offer was being made by Clay's supporters in return for Pennsylvania's votes. However, on January 24, Clay threw his support behind John Quincy Adams, who defeated Jackson in the vote taken by the House of Representatives. Soon thereafter, Adams named Clay as his secretary of state. Outraged, Jackson claimed a "corrupt bargain" had taken place between Adams and Clay. Worse still, anyone associated with the outcome became an object of suspicion to the general. Not only had Buchanan's strategy of playing kingmaker failed miserably, but he had also earned Jackson's lasting resentment.[21]

The rift between Buchanan and Jackson only worsened in the ensuing years. Since Jackson had already made clear his intentions to challenge Adams for the presidency in 1828, Buchanan was bound to be implicated at some point for his prior involvement in the negotiations among the competing camps. In the summer of 1827, a controversy erupted when a letter from Jackson to a Democratic associate became public. By way of reply, Clay used the occasion to issue an "Address to the Public" that pilloried Jackson for his "corrupt bargain" claims. Buchanan labored to defend his actions; he lamented that Jackson considered him "an emissary from Mr. Clay," but he also felt unfairly abused by the process. He complained to a Pennsylvania colleague at having been "dragged before the Public" and "being the emissary of Mr. Clay in making a corrupt proposition to him." Yet he equally determined to stay the course and hoped that neither Jackson, nor his Tennessee ally John Eaton, would "force me to reply," and thus "use the weapons in my possession for my defence." The controversy eventually died down and Buchanan and Eaton reconciled, but the old accusations stubbornly persisted as late as the presidential election of 1856. For better or for worse, Buchanan had hitched his political wagon to the powerful star that was Andrew Jackson and the Democratic Party that supported him.[22]

Back in Pennsylvania, Buchanan faced internal challenges to his status as a leading son in the state. Over the course of the 1820s and early 1830s, two factions, the Family Party, so named for the clubby nature of their leadership, and the Amalgamation Party, so called for their absorption of the former Federalists, battled for supremacy in Pennsylvania politics. For the most part, their differences stemmed from the usual disagreements over spending, such as the appropriate level of funding for internal improvement projects. In time, Buchanan became one of the leaders of the Amalgamators, while George Mifflin Dallas of Philadelphia became the figurehead of the Family Party. Even as they stood in political opposition to one another, Buchanan and Dallas shared much in common: both possessed legal training, both were active in Masonic affairs, and both claimed to be staunch Jacksonian Democrats. The two factions stayed divided, until the emergence of the Whig Party once more changed the political dynamics of the Keystone State. Even after the rifts healed within the state's Democratic party, Buchanan and Dallas remained lifelong rivals.[23]

In Washington, Buchanan retrenched and quickly aligned himself with representatives from his region and his new party. After the election of 1824, he had also shifted the composition of his mess, boarding near exclusively with other Pennsylvania congressmen. As before, the intimate confines of mess life fostered bosom friendship. While he had once found Isaac D. Barnard, one of the state's US senators, to be "backward and reserved," Buchanan gained a new appreciation for the man after becoming his messmate: "At the commencement of the present Session, I felt for Gen: Barnard that sort of regard which gratitude will I trust never fail to excite in my bosom. Since I have become his messmate, that feeling is changed into friendship & respect. He is frank, manly, & high minded & will never be improperly under the influence of any family or any individuals." Besides their newfound propinquity, personal considerations once more shaped the friendship. Barnard and Buchanan were the same age and of similar political temperament, as they shared a desire to integrate the factions within Pennsylvania politics.[24]

As the 1820s turned to the 1830s, Buchanan neared his tenth year in the US House of Representatives. He was by this time a proud supporter of Andrew Jackson in Pennsylvania and in Washington. Yet by March 1831, he had determined to resign his position in Congress. He was growing bored of congressional politics, which he now complained as being "very dull." Moreover, he found himself embattled in endless conflict with the opposition party back

home, as the Amalgamators had failed to obtain the nomination of their gubernatorial candidate. While he did not formally retire from public service,
he had decided to return full-time to his lucrative law practice in Lancaster.
That did not stop his name from being bandied about as a potential member
of Jackson's cabinet, especially following the political fallout from the mass
resignation of the president's first cabinet, or as a vice presidential candidate
to replace the estranged John C. Calhoun in the upcoming election of 1832.
Even as a private citizen, Buchanan remained ever attuned to shifts in the political winds.[25]

Andrew Jackson was not about to help Buchanan in his quest for higher
office. After Jackson's election in 1828 the two men came into greater direct
contact and conflict, as the rough-and-tumble frontier president clashed
with the more buttoned-up Lancaster lawyer. In one memorable anecdote,
Buchanan happened upon Jackson in his private quarters at the White House
while the latter was dressed only in shirtsleeves. Young Buck reminded Old
Hickory that he was scheduled to receive a visit from a lady and encouraged
the president to change into more suitable clothes. After a second such re-
minder, Jackson supposedly replied, "Mr. Buchanan, I once knew a man in
Tennessee who made a large fortune—by minding his own business." The personal friction between the men did not fail to attract notice from the opposition. John Quincy Adams, a keen observer of all things Jackson, recorded in
his diary in January 1831 that "Jackson's aversion to Buchanan is more immediately personal and vindictive.... [Jackson will] never forgive him nor miss
any opportunity of inflicting punishment upon him." The general would yet
have an even greater opportunity for revenge.[26]

Factional Fighting

As the age of Jackson dawned in Alabama, the conflict between the two political factions temporarily subsided. In April 1825, the American visit of the
Marquis de Lafayette to Alabama signaled a hope for political unity. Governor
Israel Pickens directed William Rufus King to work with a committee of the
state's leading men to receive the general during his time in Alabama. But
the goodwill produced by the French visitor could not stop the usual business of politics. In the following year, the Alabama state legislature appointed
Pickens to fill the vacant seat in the US Senate left by the death of Henry
Chambers, but he served for only a few months before resigning for health
reasons. Pickens traveled to the seaside town of Matanzas, Cuba, in search of
healthier climates to cure his worsening tuberculosis. His efforts were to no

avail, however, and he died there in April 1827. Bereft of one of his earliest and closest allies, King faced an uncertain re-election in 1828. However, the uneasy coalition between the northern and southern factions of the state held, and King was elected for another six-year term.[27]

Although safely returned to the Senate, King knew that the rough and tumble politics of the Alabama frontier always carried the potential for violent conflict. Starting in the spring of 1831, he endured a months-long affair of honor with Michael Johnston Kenan, a member of a powerful North Carolina

FIGURE 2.3 William Rufus King of Alabama. Although undated, King's youthful appearance dates this print to the 1820s. Courtesy Albert Newsam Print Collection, Historical Society of Pennsylvania.

family who had also relocated to Alabama. In the ensuing months, the affair expanded to include Kenan's second from the initial challenge, former state treasurer John C. Perry, and finally culminated in multiple challenges to duels. Although some have supposed that the affair resulted from gossip circulating about King's sexuality, the surviving evidence places its origin squarely within the internecine struggle for power among the members of the North Carolina Faction. In this way, the affair mirrors others among politicians of opposing factions within Alabama and across the Old South more generally.[28]

According to later published correspondence, the precipitating event of the affair between King and Kenan took place on the evening of May 21, 1831. The two men met on the streets of the old capital of Cahawba, where a political argument ensued. Kenan accused King of campaigning for John Murphy—a member of the North Carolina Faction, former two-term governor of Alabama, and candidate for representative from the state's fifth congressional district—and blamed him for blocking his own appointment as the register of the land office at Cahawba. The verbal disagreement quickly escalated and became physically violent, after Kenan, who was drunk, pushed King aside. In turn, King drew his sword cane and slashed the flat of the blade across Kenan's face. The affair escalated from there, with Kenan challenging King by letter the next morning. In the exchange of formal notes that followed, King denounced Kenan as unworthy of his honor as a gentleman and thus of accepting any challenge to duel. Without any other recourse, Kenan publicly posted King as a coward. By striking Kenan with a sword cane and ignoring the subsequent written challenges as ungentlemanly, King followed the dictates of the southern *code duello* and honorably sidestepped a duel for now.[29]

Then, in June 1831, the affair became more complicated. In the process of receiving the challenge, King had become entangled with Kenan's letter-bearer, John C. Perry. King apparently did not expect a formal challenge to materialize, for he thought Perry a gentleman. But Perry was insistent that King accept Kenan's challenge. Following protocol, Perry agreed to take Kenan's place in the proposed duel, wherein an official challenge issued forth once more. King wrote to his friend John Coffee of Tennessee, who, working through future Supreme Court justice John McKinley, had given his "assent to attend [King] to the field." In that letter, King characterized the nature of his struggle with Kenan in no uncertain terms: "The quarrel is entirely political, and I was very desirous to have for my Friend one whose political integrity, and personal firmness could not be questioned." Still the affair persisted.[30]

Over the ensuing months, the affair expanded to include additional players. While John Coffee had agreed to serve as King's second, King's unmarried brother John DeVane King acted as intermediary in the negotiations that followed. Likewise, William S. Taylor, a member of the Georgia Faction and a future commander of the Alabama state militia, came to the aid of John Perry as his second. But King cleverly set odd terms for this new duel—he chose swords for the weapons, he picked the distant Chickasaw Agency for the site, and he set the nearby date of August 8 for the meeting. These details proved predictably unsatisfactory, and in turn, both sets of seconds then became entangled with one another. As before, they published their correspondence for public view (John DeVane King went so far as to write out a will). Yet as was so often the case, the affair of honor never fully blossomed into a duel, largely due to King's handling of the terms of the meeting. In the end, he had outmaneuvered Perry, whose involvement in the affair was peripheral from the start.[31]

The short-term effects of the abortive duels were minimal, largely due to the ingrained nature of affairs of honor among southern elites. Although King had lamented the "unprincipled denunciations of that base fellow Kenan," he seems to have stabilized relations with the Kenan clan in the long term. Both before and after the affair, King remained close to Thomas S. Kenan, the uncle of King's recent antagonist and the man whose congressional seat he had first occupied as a young representative from North Carolina back in 1809. Given his polite manners and likeable character, King must have lamented that such disagreements were a regular part of politics in the Alabama cotton kingdom. Nevertheless, the incident demonstrates his readiness and ability to defend his honor as a man against political enemies.[32]

By the 1830s, King was entering high middle age. Nevertheless, contemporary observers noted his genteel comportment and handsome appearance. Journalist Anne Royall thought that King possessed "a young look with a good figure and every quality of person and mind to render him no ordinary member of society, his manners being of the first order." From appearances in numerous portraits, he cut a dashing figure. Colleagues also took special note of his polished and polite manners describing him variously as "the Chesterfield of the Senate" and the "Alabama Chesterfield." The description was especially apt, as the English Lord Chesterfield was famous for his guide to polite manners. Careful attention to Chesterfield's provisions constituted, in the words of one historian, an "obsession" among southern elites. Not surprisingly, James Buchanan was also considered a Chesterfield of the US Senate.[33]

Neither King's bachelorhood nor appearance detracted from his commitment to the Democratic political agenda. He was in many ways a typical senator of the cotton South: he promoted the sale of public lands, and he pushed
Congress to purchase additional tracts from native tribes in the new southwestern states. In view of these interests, he became chairman of the Senate
Public Lands Committee. However, King did not always place his section's
narrow interests above national considerations. For example, he supported the
proposed increase in duties related to manufactured goods in the Tariff of 1832,
which was generally thought to hurt the southern states that relied heavily on
foreign imports. The stance damaged his political standing in Alabama, but
King, being "personal as well as political friends of the President," stuck by
the position. To start 1832, he declared his political independence from the
Calhoun faction and fell in line with the loyal Jacksonians.[34]

That May, King was selected to the Alabama state delegation to the first
ever Democratic National Convention. With Jackson already presumed to
be the candidate, the delegates primarily worked to determine an appropriate
vice president to replace John C. Calhoun, who had by then broken with the
Jackson administration. King was appointed chair of the rules committee to
determine the process by which a nomination could be made. The committee
proposed a rule that would prove enormously consequential in the years
ahead. When "a difference of opinion prevailed" on the best candidate for the
vice presidency, the committee proposed a compromise. To reduce objections
among the delegates, King favored nominations "made by two thirds of the
whole body of the representatives of the people," which he thought "would
show a more general concurrence of sentiment in favor of a particular individual, would carry with it greater moral weight, and be more favorably received." An effort to block the two-thirds rule failed, which meant that King
and his committee, perhaps unwittingly, had set a standard for presidential
nomination that persisted well into the twentieth century. In time, the two-
third rule came to benefit disproportionately slaveholders' control of the
presidential selection process; yet it had originated in King's quest for party
unity on the lower half of the ticket.[35]

Following the convention, events tested King's moderate unionism. For
years, he had warned against "the monster nullification," but events had moved
the thorny issue into the national spotlight. In November 1832, the state of
South Carolina convened a nullification convention and publicly declared the
Tariff of 1832 to be null and void in the Palmetto State. When the Congress
convened in December, President Jackson declared the action unconstitu-
tional. During the ensuing debate in the Senate, King made the unusual choice

to work with Henry Clay to craft a compromise tariff. He later regretted the pact; to Martin Van Buren, he admitted: "When the danger of a disruption of the government becomes imminent, Clay will step forward as the mediator, the great pacificator, the work will be done, and the Presidency will be his reward." If such an outcome took place, King expressed his hopes to new Alabama governor John Gayle that at least the "absurd and mischievous doctrines of the nullification will now die a natural death; and fraternal feelings return, and render our Union perpetual." But the crisis only worsened.[36]

At the same time, King questioned Jackson's response to nullification. He did not condone Jackson's proposed Force Bill to punish South Carolina for its opposition to the tariff. He feared the "tremendous power" such a bill would give the president. In turn, Jackson lumped King "with the nullifiers." Nevertheless, King remained enough in Jackson's good graces to call socially at the White House, such as when he accompanied the old Alabama brigadier general Sam Dale during a visit to Washington. Likewise, when Louis McLane, Jackson's former secretary of state, publicly feuded with Martin Van Buren, then the vice president, the old chief asked King to intervene. King's standing in Alabama and among southern moderates could not so easily be dismissed, even by Jackson. The two men eventually reconciled.[37]

Since his appointment to the US Senate in 1819, King had plotted a course for moderate unionism in the southern wing of the Democratic Party. His views could ensnare him into unexpected conflicts; his balanced approach had proved successful at a time when many in the South were developing more extreme views. The emergence of the Whig Party, the first viable opposition to the Democrats in more than a decade, was fast changing the dynamics of partisanship, however. If King hoped to be successful in his moderate program, he would need the help of others in the party, particularly northern allies. And if the past examples of his personal and political relationships were any indication of his future path, he would be most likely to find such help from fellow bachelors.

Russian Exile

In the spring of 1831, Andrew Jackson settled on a new strategy regarding the fate of James Buchanan. When John Randolph of Roanoke notified the president of his resignation as the American minister to Russia, Jackson instructed secretary of war John Eaton to offer the position to Buchanan. As Jackson supposedly explained years later, he sent Buchanan to Russia because "it was as far as I could send him out of my sight . . . I would have sent him to the North Pole if we had kept a minister there!" Such politically motivated ministerial appointments were not uncommon. Jackson himself had nearly been the target of a similar attempt by President Monroe, who contemplated sending him to Russia in 1818 until Thomas Jefferson dissuaded the president from doing so. He was similarly offered (and declined) the mission to Mexico in 1823. Jackson's standing as a national hero had permitted him to turn down these appointments, but what excuse did ex-representative Buchanan have? To spurn Jackson risked the president's further wrath, which he could little afford if he ever hoped to advance within the Democratic Party. Buchanan was trapped.[38]

A trip to Russia was not without its charms, political and personal. After ten years in the House of Representatives, Buchanan's political career had plateaued; his legal practice in Lancaster, as before, continued to provide insufficient professional satisfaction. The appointment to Russia carried a full ministerial rank, equivalent to those of the ministers at other European courts. At age forty, Buchanan had never before left the United States. Still unmarried and without dependents, his domestic situation afforded him the necessary flexibility to leave the country. But his elderly mother strongly objected. "Your political career has been of that description which ought to gratify your *ambition*," she wrote to her son in October 1831, and exhorted him: "If you can consistently with the character of a gentleman & a man of honor, decline, how great a gratification it will be to me." But decline he could not and did not. In August, he informed Jackson of his acceptance of the mission. As she had morbidly predicted, Elizabeth Speer Buchanan passed away while her son served abroad.[39]

Before his departure, Buchanan took the time to travel across the country. He visited New England, where he made the acquaintance of Jared Sparks, a Harvard history professor. Once more, Buchanan was keenly aware of his bachelorhood. "My excursion could not have been more agreeable than it was unless I had got a wife," he later wrote to Sparks. Evidently the two men had bonded quite closely together over the trip. From New York in April 1832, on the evening prior to his departure across the Atlantic, he penned Sparks a touching note. "If you knew how much pleasure it would afford me to see you, you would meet me there for a few minutes," he pleaded, but to no effect. As he boarded his packet ship the next day, Buchanan steeled his nerves for the journey. By his own account he suffered terribly on the overseas voyage, which included an initial stop in Liverpool, before continuing overland to London and then by ship to Hamburg, arriving in St. Petersburg on June 3, 1832.[40]

Buchanan's time abroad was made more pleasurable through shared domestic intimacy with other Americans abroad. Much as he had done with friends in Lancaster and in Washington, he bonded closely with his new colleagues. He grew intimate with his personal secretary, John Waller Barry (son of Jackson's postmaster general William Barry), with whom he had made the overseas voyage, and with John Randolph Clay, the previous chargé d'affaires to Russia. Both Barry (born in 1809) and Clay (born in 1808) were much younger than Buchanan and as yet unmarried. For his part, Barry acknowledged his appreciation for Buchanan, as he wrote to his sister: "I am more pleased with Mr. Buchanan the more I know of him." In turn, Buchanan reciprocated his appreciation for his young staffers, writing to his younger brother Edward: "Mr. Clay and Mr. Barry are very agreeable young gentlemen." Their mutual feelings of admiration only intensified in the days ahead. As Buchanan reported to his sister Harriet Buchanan Henry, "My domestic arrangements are comfortable . . . Mr. Clay the Secretary of the Legation, and Mr. Barry are members of my family." Of the two, Buchanan was especially protective toward Barry. This domestic arrangement of inter-generational bachelors continued for Buchanan's two years as minister.[41]

Buchanan's reaction to the Empress Alexandra Feodorovna is particularly noteworthy given King's youthful passion for her. Like King, Buchanan found the former princess, now fifteen years older and into her early middle age, to be "a fine looking woman," and like King, he especially looked forward to kissing her hand as part of the customary diplomatic receiving line. Describing the experience in a letter to his friend Stephen Pleasonton, he wrote: "It is the custom here for a minister upon his presentation to kiss the hand of the Empress . . . a task which I performed with much pleasure." Outside of the royal court, however, Buchanan did not find himself at all attracted to the native Russian women. Russia lacked "what would be termed a good looking woman in the United States," he complained to a friend back home. Nevertheless, he forged a lifelong bond with Princess Lieven, the Russian minister to England, when the pair traveled on the same boat to the continent. More importantly, Buchanan gained a deeper appreciation for the wider world.[42]

One additional episode from his time in Russia bears closer inspection. Buchanan was ever a keen observer of the social obligations required of him by the court at St. Petersburg and of the customs of the Russian people more generally. Like King before him, he kept a travel journal. In one passage, he described an encounter with a Russian Orthodox monk, Father Antoine. "Upon taking leave of Antoine," he recorded, "I submitted to be kissed by him according to the Russian fashion, first on the right cheek, then on the left, and then on the mouth. This was my first regular experiment of the kind." Although some historians have interpreted the encounter as evidence of same-sex attraction, Buchanan himself thought the incident to be so much "bagatelle," a favorite word of his that implied play-acting.[43]

The Russian mission presented many challenges for an aspiring American diplomat. A commercial treaty to regulate the trade of the two powers, which had remained unresolved for nearly two decades, was the greatest of them. The Russians hoped for increased export duties on iron, sail duck, and hemp sent to the United States, while the Americans insisted on higher import duties to protect domestic production (though these had been made lower by the measures set in the Tariff of 1832). Buchanan spent the first several months acclimating himself to the customs of the Russian court before beginning his negotiations in earnest by the fall. In December 1832, Buchanan accomplished that which had eluded his predecessors for decades, when Emperor Nicholas I signed a commercial treaty with the United States. The purpose of his mission largely completed, he remained in Russia through August 1833.[44]

Before returning to the United States, Buchanan traveled across the European continent and to England. Once back in Pennsylvania in late November 1833, he attended a public dinner in his honor at Saint's Hotel in Philadelphia and reacquainted himself with the domestic political situation. In December, the Pennsylvania state legislature gathered to choose a new US Senator, but they passed over Buchanan in favor of Samuel McKean. The following December, the legislature met again to fill the vacancy left by the resignation of William Wilkins, a fellow Amalgamator who ironically had been nominated by Jackson to replace Buchanan as minister to Russia. Fittingly enough, the legislature selected Buchanan to fill the Senate vacancy. Despite his professed desire to continue as a private citizen, the opportunities for higher political visibility afforded by the US Senate must have appealed. Besides, as he wrote to fellow bachelor Mahlon Dickerson of New Jersey, he felt "too young to be without employment." Whether or not he cared to admit it, politics had become his most earnest, lifelong avocation.[45]

Buchanan prepared to go to Washington still a bachelor. Indeed, the high society of the capital had done little to advance his marital prospects; as he wrote one Lancaster intimate in 1826: "I have not yet made the least progress in falling in love though there is nothing which I so earnestly desire." He seemed equally unable to move beyond the failings of his long-ago courtship. In 1829, he had purchased from his Lancaster townsman Simon Gratz a grand brick townhouse at the corner of East King Street and Duke Street, a mere block from the residence of his former fiancée Ann Coleman. Then in 1833, he purchased for the price of eight thousand dollars the Coleman house itself, from sons William C. Coleman and Edward Coleman and the widow Anne C. Coleman (whose husband Robert Coleman had died in 1825). From this same house Buchanan's life took another strange turn, when he pursued a business interest in the same industry that Robert Coleman had once mastered: iron production. Along with his Lancaster neighbor John Reynolds, Buchanan became the co-owner of the Lucinda Furnace in Clarion County, Pennsylvania. The specter of the Coleman family seemed ever to shadow him.[46]

Like King, Buchanan also faced marital pressures from his many surviving siblings. Of the nine children of James and Elizabeth Speer Buchanan to reach adulthood, six married—the five sisters Jane, Maria, Sarah, Elizabeth, and Harriet, and the youngest brother, Edward Young Buchanan—while two younger brothers, William Speer and George Washington, died before being able to do so. Nevertheless, as the eldest brother, James often advised his younger siblings about the ways of the world. To Harriet, who was then unmarried, he admonished: "When you have determined (as I trust you will not) never to marry I shall cheerfully provide you a comfortable home." He then condescended with the smugness of an older brother: "It would afford me great pleasure & promote my own comfort & happiness to have you for a

FIGURE 2.4 View of East King Street, first block, south side, 1858. From 1834 to 1849, Buchanan lived in the former Coleman townhome, located on the northeastern corner of what is today East King Street and North Christian Street. Courtesy General Collection, LancasterHistory.org, Lancaster, Pennsylvania.

house keeper. Still I think you ought to marry, should a favorable opportunity offer. There is nothing very desirable in the situation of an old maid; still it is less comfortless than that of an unhappy wife." Harriet eventually married despite this advice. Would her older brother follow suit?[47]

Perhaps. From his new home on East King Street, which he glumly called his "solitary Bachelor's abode," the forty-three-year-old Buchanan engaged in half-hearted efforts at courtship. Starting in 1834, Buchanan expressed romantic interest in at least one of the unmarried women living in the household of his Philadelphia associate Judge Thomas Kittera, the same man who had observed the rapid deterioration of Ann Coleman more than a decade earlier. He concluded a letter to Kittera with the cryptic note, "Please to remember me to your mother & sister & be particular in giving my love to my intended." Whether the "intended" was niece Mary Kittera, who was only thirteen years old, or sister Ann Kittera, who was closer to Buchanan's age, or someone else altogether is unclear. Perhaps it was just another example of his lifelong penchant for "bagatelle."[48]

But Buchanan's romantic pursuits persisted. Three years later, he concluded a draft of a letter to Eliza Violet Gist Blair, daughter of the influential Democratic editor Francis Preston Blair, with a telling comment: "I expect to be married & have the cares of a family resting upon my shoulders." Whether he ever sent this letter is unclear, but months later, he again wrote to Thomas Kittera and once more closed that his reader not forget "that portion of [his family] in which I feel a peculiar interest." He vacillated in his flirtations. By 1839, the topic had dropped from his correspondence with Kittera; then three years later, the old charm was back. Remember "me most kindly to Ann & my portion of this world's goods," the second half of which line may have referred to Mary (now closer to twenty-two). Whatever his true intentions, Buchanan eventually ceased his pursuit of the Kittera women. To confidante Eliza Blair, he opined: "I believe a bachelor becomes more & more undecisive as he grows older." His later course during the 1830s and 1840s affirmed the accuracy of this view. For the time being, he clung to the life of a bachelor. In Washington, he would find many other like-minded men of marital uncertitude.[49]

* * *

To start the age of Jackson, King and Buchanan had found a political party that would define their remaining years. Both men were naturally conservative in their politics, a tendency that hardened their loyalty to the Democratic

Party. They both supported the party's promotion of commerce, even as they harbored reservations about the speculation of too-easy credit that had precipitated the financial panic of 1819. Each man believed in the inherent dangers of bringing attention to the slavery question on the national level. For them, the issue had been settled years earlier by the Missouri Compromise. Finally, each man attached himself to the larger than life politics of Andrew Jackson, while being personally disliked by the general. To end 1834, each could rightly be said to have earned his respective stripes among the ranks of the Jacksonian Democrats.

In this new era of partisan rancor, each man adjusted his political course to ride the rising tide of American democracy. They had achieved great success at home: King was elected on multiple occasions to the US Senate from Alabama, while Buchanan abandoned his Federalist affiliations for the presiding Democratic banner. Both men had served abroad in the royal court of St. Petersburg, a place that very few Americans could claim to have seen. So too did each man attempt to gain national prominence in the party of Jackson. King tried to chart a moderate unionism, while firmly representing his section's interests on the crucial questions of land and labor. By necessity he aligned himself with southern members, even as he kept an eye out for political allies from the other side of the Mason-Dixon Line. By contrast, Buchanan vainly tried to please the twin masters of his divided constituency in Pennsylvania and the often-willful dictates of his new party's chieftain. His struggle to maintain the support of his home state would be lifelong.

During the 1820s and 1830s, King and Buchanan had risen to prominence through intimate personal and political friendships forged in Washington boardinghouses with other members of their party. More often than not those men were, like them, hardened bachelors. If they could not follow the marital example of most politicians, they at least appreciated the need for a similar kind of bond, that of bosom friendship, to unite their personal and political lives for the duration of the congressional term. From this shared commonality of bachelorhood, the groundwork had been laid for a combination of political power rarely equaled in Washington.

3

Messing, 1834–1840

DURING THE DECADE of the 1830s, the Democratic Party of Andrew Jackson and his successor Martin Van Buren dominated Washington politics. In both the House of Representatives and the Senate, Jacksonian Democrats held a numerical majority and directed the legislative agenda. Yet the era was rife with political controversies, among them the veto of the rechartering of the Second Bank of the United States, the nullification crisis and the Force Bill, the controversy over the reception of abolitionist petitions and the resulting "gag rule," the issuance of the "Specie Circular," and the subsequent Panic of 1837. The many arguments over policy and politics precipitated the rise of a permanent opposition party—the Whigs. The Second Party System, born of this bitter stew of political and personal differences, defined the course of electoral politics over the next two decades.[1]

The divisions produced by the legislative contest of the 1830s also shaped the contours of domestic politics in the capital. In this charged atmosphere, boardinghouse groups drifted in a noticeably partisan and sectional direction. However, the basic patterns of life in the capital had changed little from the previous decades. These boardinghouse families still stood in as proxies for the domestic, as well as for the affective, needs of congressmen away from loved ones at home. To survive these unusual conditions, one historian has argued, most congressmen "essentially lived as bachelors" while in Washington. An unexpected corollary followed from this: since unmarried politicians knew how to navigate the idiosyncrasies of life in bachelor's quarters, lifelong bachelorhood could well prove a political advantage in the Washington boardinghouse. Bachelors, in essence, were ideally suited for domestic life in Washington.[2]

Democrats King and Buchanan demonstrated precisely this advantage during their years together in Congress. Without the burdens of immediate family members, they freely formed political and personal friendships with like-minded politicians, relationships that often intensified through the medium of the boardinghouse. They organized a boardinghouse group based on one salient personal commonality: bachelorhood. In this vein, Buchanan declared to a Pennsylvania friend, "I shall be delighted to welcome you to the Bachelor's mess." The invitation, though seemingly ordinary, revealed more than a passing pronunciation—the identification of the bachelor's mess supports the longstanding view that "mess group affiliation was recognized as a mark of identification among legislators," so much so that "some boardinghouse groups were given distinctive names." But in the charged climate of 1830s Washington, Buchanan's boardinghouse group practiced a noticeably partisan and sectional form of politics that promoted Jacksonian aims and protected the institution of slavery from abolitionist assaults. For the new Pennsylvania senator, participation in the bachelor's mess also meant implicitly embracing the role of a "doughface," or a northern man with southern principles.[3]

For seven years, from 1834 to 1841, the bachelor's mess housed an ever-shifting composite of mostly unmarried Democratic senators, including Edward Lucas of Virginia, Bedford Brown of North Carolina, Robert Carter Nicholas of Louisiana, John Pendleton King of Georgia, William Sterret Ramsey of Pennsylvania, and William Henry Roane of Virginia. The various messmates collectively controlled two major Senate committees: Buchanan chaired Foreign Relations, of which both William Rufus King and John Pendleton King had been members; William Rufus King chaired the Commerce Committee and served as president pro tempore of the Senate for over six years; and Nicholas and Buchanan both sat on the Senate's Finance Committee, while Buchanan also served on the Judiciary Committee. In an era when the US Senate numbered anywhere between forty-eight and fifty-two members, their group represented a critical voting bloc (see Appendix A).

The bachelor's mess also revealed the triumph of a more sectional, partisan, and gendered politics in the Jacksonian period. Dominated by southern Democrats, it cannot be understood outside of the political context of the Second Party System; certainly, the members' commitment to Jacksonian principles was a prerequisite to inclusion in this partisan mess. More than politics motivated the arrangement, though. The bachelor messmates also developed intimate friendships that outlasted their congressional service. Taken together, these relationships illustrate the operation of domestic politics among a key boardinghouse group, the nature of bosom friendships among congressmen, and the possibilities of political bachelorhood in Jacksonian

America. For Buchanan and King, their union in the bachelor's mess marked the beginning of their rise to new heights of national prominence.

The Bachelors of the Mess

Among congressional officeholders in early America, marriage held a widely acknowledged political value. In Washington during the 1830s, the marital partnership of Congressman James K. Polk of Tennessee and his wife, Sarah Childress Polk, presented one such power couple, while the continued presence of the indomitable Dolley Madison reminded the unmarried politician of the immense practical advantages of a socially adept and politically active partner. Toward that end, the newly arrived unmarried congressman seemed to gravitate toward the altar. In some cases, these men became prime targets to assume social obligations, and given that the work of politicians required their attendance at receptions, balls, and parties of all kinds during a congressional session, the occasions for such escorts were numerous. Through the fulfillment of these responsibilities, an entering congressional bachelor might well conclude his years of service as a married man.[4]

Yet unmarried politicians were more common than might be expected. Compared to the estimated national average of fewer than 3 percent, more congressmen were bachelors, widowers, or otherwise unmarried during their terms of service than has previously been recognized (they numbered perhaps as much as 7 percent). Although the late nineteenth century has been declared the "age of the bachelor," the roots of its normalization and mainstream acceptance may be traced to earlier decades. In a study of bachelorhood in the early American republic, one scholar found that by mid-century, new developments in American society had "created the bachelor as a legal identity, a cultural ideal, and a lived experience" and made him "a permanent fixture of American society." By the 1830s such men were publishing newspapers, forming their own social clubs, and participating in an emergent literary sensibility. Henry David Thoreau embraced his moniker as "America's bachelor uncle." Political bachelors, King and Buchanan among them, were everywhere.[5]

During the campaign preceding the election of 1828, marriage itself had proven a highly divisive issue in the partisan wars of the era. Nothing had enraged Andrew Jackson more than aspersions against the legitimacy of his marriage to Rachel Donelson Robards. Her untimely death in late 1828 embittered Jackson and likely reinforced his inherent tendency to defend women subjected to political attacks. The marriage of his secretary of war, John Eaton, to the much younger widow Margaret "Peggy" O'Neale—under circumstances similar to Jackson's own marriage—caused the new president to defend the virtue of the younger woman. The ensuing Petticoat Affair, in which the wives of his cabinet officers refused to accept the new Mrs. Eaton into polite society, led the president to dismiss nearly the entire group (excepting the widower Van Buren) and caused one of the greatest internal controversies of his administration. The Washington society of 1834 was thus still scarred from the gender-related wounds of the past.[6]

As a consequence, a new kind of partisanship, one that centered on views about Andrew Jackson, was rapidly taking shape. Like the House of Representatives, the Senate was split among Jacksonian stalwarts and their anti-Jacksonian opponents, this latter group well on its way to coalescing into the new Whig Party. As noted by observers, the leading Jackson Democratic senators included William Rufus King, Bedford Brown, John Pendleton King, and president pro tempore Hugh Lawson White of Tennessee, while the anti-Jacksonians counted Henry Clay, Daniel Webster, Willie P. Mangum of North Carolina, John Bell of Tennessee, and John Tyler of Virginia among their ranks. Nevertheless, these were fluid times for partisan identity: Hugh Lawson became a Whig, while John Tyler, a nominal Whig, never truly abandoned the principles of the Democracy. The age of Jackson was accordingly a time of choosing and switching sides alike.[7]

As might be expected, partisanship filtered into the domestic world of the boardinghouse families. When King's messmates Mangum and Bell adopted an anti-Jacksonian persuasion, he replaced them with two more solid Democrats, Bedford Brown of North Carolina and then Edward Lucas of Virginia. In the ensuing sessions, the group of King, Brown, and Lucas sought to identify an additional messmate whose Jacksonian principles were unwavering and, just as importantly, whose personal qualities made him a congenial social companion. In 1834 they turned to Buchanan, who well knew the practical necessity, political potential, and personal benefits of belonging to a partisan congressional mess. The new group relocated to Saunder's boardinghouse on E Street, near the post office. Significantly, all four messmates were staunch Jacksonians, and three of the four were bachelors (Brown was married).[8]

In many respects, the Washington world of the bachelor's mess was a primitive one. Since Buchanan first arrived in Washington more than a decade earlier, the city had grown in the size of its population, from just over twenty-four thousand people, enslaved African Americans included, in 1810, to over forty thousand by 1830. In terms of buildings, the capital expanded from the "Seven Buildings" of the 1790s to many dozens of structures by the 1830s. Even so, one resident reminisced that "the streets were deep with mud in wet weather and thick with dust at other times." Few fashionable neighborhoods existed, though Dolley Madison's drawing room stood out as a center of social life in the young city. That situation began to change in 1837, when larger, more stately residences appeared on C Street (alongside the Patent Office, a grand edifice in the neoclassical mold, and the Treasury Building, also of Palladian design). Soon thereafter new homes were erected on F Street—only recently made into a proper road—near the Executive Mansion, including several permanent dwellings for prominent political figures. Ex-president John Quincy Adams resided there, as did members of the cabinet. Washington during these years, one historian of the capital observed, "bore the air of a city without driving ambition."[9]

Like the city in which they resided, the Democrats who gathered together at Saunder's boardinghouse mixed partisan views with fixed personal habits. Of the group, King exuded social polish and congeniality. "Colonel King is about six feet high, remarkably erect in figure, and is well proportioned," wrote one contemporary. "Brave and chivalrous in his character, his whole bearing impresses even strangers with the conviction that they are in the presence of a finished gentleman." A later publication described him as an "old

FIGURE 3.1 Washington, DC. The capital was still an assemblage of unfinished streets and wide-open spaces during the 1830s. Drawn by J. R. Smith, engraved by J. B. Neagle. Boston: S. Walker, 1834. Prints and Photographs Division, Library of Congress, LC-USZ62-17823.

gentleman, a bachelor, who wears a prim wig, and is precise in his manners, as well as his notions of legislation." King's fellow Democrats often derided him for these punctilious qualities. Ironically, unmarried men often leveled the harshest critique against him. Caleb Cushing, himself a bachelor upon his entry into the Congress in 1835, found King to be a "frivolous Jesuit," while Martin Van Buren, a long-time widower, thought him a "gentleman of colder temperament." Even as King had found personal security in his bachelorhood, he remained politically vulnerable for the same aspects of his intellectually refined, even effeminate, manhood.[10]

By contrast, Bedford Brown presented a roughhewn appearance and embodied the frontier in his personality. Yet the two southerners had much in common: they both originally hailed from North Carolina, both attended the University of North Carolina, and both found success in politics at a young age. However, in 1816 Brown married and began his career

FIGURE 3.2 William R. King of Alabama. The print captured a youthful looking King in a romantic pose (he was over 50 at the time of the creation of the lithograph). Print by P. S. Duval from drawing by Charles Fenderich, 1840. Courtesy Prints and Photographs Division, Library of Congress, LC-DIG-pga-06427.

as a planter-politician and father of seven. Although primarily interested in local issues, a vacancy occasioned his selection for the US Senate in 1829. Reflecting on the turbulent decade of the 1830s, Martin Van Buren noted that Brown was "an old and constant friend of Genl. Jackson and my own, one on whom as much as any other man, we relied for support of our respective administrations in the Senate." A contemporary described the North Carolinian as possessing a "dignity ... so studied that it was a little pompous." In addition to his unwavering commitment to Jacksonian principles, Brown manifested a fierce loyalty for his political and personal friends.[11]

If King and Brown represented one pair entering the new arrangement at Saunder's boardinghouse, Lucas and Buchanan formed the other. Born in 1790 in Shepherdstown, Virginia (today West Virginia), Edward Lucas attended Dickinson College and graduated in the same class as Buchanan. Along with his college friend, Lucas had likewise "got into drinking bouts sufficiently rowdy to come to the attention of the faculty." After graduation, he returned home and served in the Virginia militia during the War of 1812. Like

FIGURE 3.3 Bedford Brown of North Carolina. The only married member of the mess, he continued to correspond with his former messmates after leaving Congress. Courtesy US Senate Historical Office.

Buchanan, he established a prosperous legal practice and pursued a mercantile career. He served several terms in the Virginia House of Delegates, followed by election to the US House of Representatives in 1833, which made him the only such member of that body in the new mess. Like his new messmates, Lucas was an ardent Jacksonian. At forty-three he was unmarried upon his entry into Washington society.[12]

Of the foursome lodging at Saunder's boardinghouse, Buchanan seems to have been the most personally agreeable. Washington contemporaries found the forty-two-year-old Pennsylvanian immensely likeable. Typical was a description by Democratic congressman John Fairfield of Maine, who called Buchanan "a great favorite of mine." As Fairfield wrote to his wife, "I liked him the first time I put my eye upon him." He was witty and possessed a voice suitable for public speaking. Yet he was also beginning the transition into middle age. A Philadelphia newspaper reported that he was "a bachelor, probably on the wrong side of forty"; in fact, he was only thirty-nine when that article was printed. Nearly fifteen years after the death of Ann Coleman, he still considered himself something of a charity case. To one friend, he bemoaned that "it is but charity for the friend of an old bachelor occasionally to pass a day with him to assist him to drive away the blue devils." In the years ahead, the signs of this transformation became more apparent: his blonde hair began to turn white, his waistline increased, and his old-fashioned style of dress looked increasingly out of date. "He is a bachelor, and always wears a white cravat," a reporter noted dryly.[13]

The bachelor's mess thus brought together different strands, one southern and one northern, one longstanding friendship and one connection made during the previous congressional session. But the question remains as to whether Buchanan and King had already come to know one another before then. Quite likely, the answer is yes, since they had served in opposite chambers in the Capitol from 1822 to 1831. They almost certainly met in passing; the two might also have encountered each other socially during their overlapping years in Washington, perhaps at one of the many formal receptions hosted by First Lady Elizabeth Kortright Monroe or at a ball arranged by Louisa Catherine Adams, wife of secretary of state John Quincy Adams. However, neither man mentioned the other in his correspondence prior to the formation of this mess, nor do the contemporary records conclusively put them together in the same place during these years. If they had known one another before 1834, the connection was most likely a superficial one. Now the communal atmosphere of the boardinghouse provided an inimitable setting for them to forge new friendships with men of similar political views and personal temperament.[14]

A Residence for Us

The messmates at Saunder's boardinghouse returned to their respective states following the short session of the lame-duck Congress that ended in March 1835. When Congress resumed in December 1835, the messmates went their separate ways: Brown and Buchanan attempted to join a mess with Democratic Senator Garret Wall of New Jersey at Mr. Birth's boardinghouse on Third Street, while King and Lucas wanted to return to Saunder's boardinghouse. Personal considerations dictated the dissolution of the original group. As Buchanan recounted years later to Wall's son: "With the exception of Col. King, I never was in terms of more intimate personal & political association with any friend than with your excellent father." But a problem emerged: Wall wanted to bring his wife and children with him, and they could not find an appropriate establishment to house the enlarged group.[15]

Buchanan scrambled to rearrange his lodgings in the months leading up to the new congressional session. He noted that he had received a letter from John Pendleton King of Georgia "urging me to unite with King of Alabama, Brown of N. Carolina, & himself in forming a mess." Yet such was not his desire, as he admitted to Wall: "The truth is I had wished to form such a mess & to include yourself; but I could not bring them to act specifically on the subject." In the same letter, he further outlined his reasons for preferring a smaller mess group, referring to his early years in the House: "I cannot live in a large mess & would reluctantly go into one where there were members of the House." His indecision continued for weeks, ultimately forcing him to secure a private residence for the next session.[16]

With the Congress in recess beginning July 1836, political attention turned toward the upcoming presidential election. Andrew Jackson had reached the now customary two-term limit. In turn, the Democrats had nominated a ticket of Martin Van Buren of New York and Richard Mentor Johnson of Kentucky to succeed the old general. In opposition, the Whig Party ran a series of regional favorite sons, including William Henry Harrison of Ohio, Hugh L. White of Tennessee, Willie Mangum of North Carolina, and Daniel Webster of Massachusetts. As in the 1824 contest, the Whigs hoped to garner enough electoral votes among their several candidates to throw the election to the House of Representatives, and, once there, to replicate its results in their favor. A general anti-Masonic sentiment had sprung up by this time, further diluting the electoral pool. All in all, victory for Van Buren and the Democrats was by no means assured.[17]

The nomination of Van Buren produced little enthusiasm with King. In October, he wrote to Buchanan about the Democratic Party's prospects in the South. "Van Buren will get the vote of this State," he correctly predicted of his native Alabama, though he further worried, "Money commands every whore & tremendous influence." King was also adamantly committed to Buchanan's reelection to the US Senate, going so far as to tie his own political fortunes to that of his former messmate. "One thing is most certain should you be left out of the Senate & Harrison made President, I shall take my leave of public life forever," he wrote. King need not have worried, for in the actual event, the Pennsylvania legislature granted Buchanan a full six-year term in the Senate, while Van Buren and Johnson carried both the popular vote and the Electoral College, though barely. The pair faced an uncertain re-election four years hence.[18]

With another session of Congress approaching in December 1836, Buchanan again attempted to arrange lodgings with his former bachelor messmates. Affairs remained unsettled through the fall. Subsequently, William Rufus King asked Buchanan to "oblige me by securing a residence for *us*, I cannot say what are [John Pendleton] King's arrangements. I have requested him to write you, and say whether he will live with gentlemen or [bring] himself as usual." Buchanan acceded to the request, for he wrote a Lancaster confidant that "I have engaged to take lodgings for Mr. King the President pro tempore of the Senate & myself." The October 1836 letter from King to Buchanan—the earliest to survive between the two men—suggests that their friendship had grown more personally intimate over the prior year. In an earlier letter (now missing), Buchanan had written King about an "annual pilgrimage" to the mountain resort at Bedford Springs, where Pennsylvania politicians gathered en masse to discuss politics and enjoy a "gay & agreeable time." In response, King teased his messmate about a flirtation with one unnamed young woman: "Miss L—, the romping rosy girl you saw at the springs, who would probably have been fortunate had some kind friend whispered in her ear, 'that old Bachelors are mighty uncertain.'" That Buchanan mentioned this flirtation was unusual, for he typically confined his discussion of romantic matters to his letters with women. But with King, he had become comfortable enough to share stories of his romantic pursuits.[19]

To start the second congressional session in December 1836, the trio of Buchanan, King, and Lucas reunited at Mrs. Galvin's boardinghouse on C Street. In addition, Robert Carter "Cary" Nicholas, a sugar planter from Terrebone Parish, Louisiana, joined the mess. Like Lucas, Nicholas originally hailed from a wealthy Virginia family. An 1803 graduate of the College of

William and Mary, the slaveholding Nicholas attempted to make his fortune in Virginia but eventually decided to move farther south in 1820. Like the other men in the mess, he traveled abroad but remained close to political friends at home. For example, as the chargé d'affaires of the American legation in Livorno, Italy—a position previously held by William Rufus King—Nicholas wrote to his friend James Preston, the governor of Virginia, using a phrase common to bosom friendship of that time: "When I shall have the pleasure of taking you and my other friends in Virginia by the hand is very doubtful." More significantly, Cary Nicholas was, at age forty-three, still a bachelor.[20]

During the congressional session, the bachelor congressmen faced a heavy workload, which tended to bond them closer together. "The truth is I have no time to enjoy the company of any of my friends," Buchanan complained to one Lancaster associate, "except those who live in the house with me." But the new mess of the unmarried did not last long—Lucas had not stood for

FIGURE 3.4 Robert Carter Nicholas of Louisiana. A bachelor and sugar planter, "Cary" Nicholas was a favorite of both Buchanan and King. Lithograph by Charles Fenderich, 1840. Prints and Photographs Division, Library of Congress, LC-USZ62-58500.

re-election in 1836 and returned to his native Virginia in March 1837. Next, President Van Buren offered the Austrian mission to King. Although an attractive assignment, King felt obligated to decline the post. As the *Washington Daily Globe* reported, he considered "his present position more important at this crisis than any other, and has sacrificed his predilections to the interests of his constituents, and the duty he owes them." John Catron, the recently nominated Supreme Court justice, reported with disbelief to James Polk that "King refused *openly*, the Austrian mission & said he'd been up to the Presdt's to refuse." Two years later, after the resignation of Felix Grundy as attorney general, Van Buren offered the cabinet post to Buchanan, who also promptly refused the position. King and Buchanan were determined to stay together in the Senate.[21]

The remaining three bachelors—Buchanan, King, and Nicholas—were equally dedicated to keeping their mess at the same size for the special session of the Congress scheduled to meet in September 1837. Accordingly, they turned to Democratic senator John Pendleton King of Georgia, who was also unmarried, to fill the fourth spot in the house. Born in 1799, John Pendleton King was in many ways the opposite of William Rufus King. A Kentuckian by birth, he was an ambitious lawyer and a fervently pro-development businessman. For his part, Buchanan apparently got along well with King of Georgia. He received a warm invitation from John Pendleton King to travel south, though Buchanan never made the trip and their correspondence lapsed soon thereafter.[22]

Despite their common last name, the two Kings often disagreed on matters related to their living arrangement. In one letter to Buchanan, King of Alabama referred to King of Georgia as "that strange fellow." Unlike his other bachelor messmates, John Pendleton King did not intend to remain in the US Senate, nor for that matter to stay unmarried. When the short first session of Congress ended in October, he resigned his Senate seat to pursue his interests in the emerging railroad industry. Not long afterward, he married Mary Louise Woodward, who at age twenty-three was fully twenty years his junior. In the years ahead, John Pendleton King drifted apart from his former congressional messmates, focused on his growing family and business concerns.[23]

As the residents of the bachelor's mess changed, the pair of Buchanan and King grew increasingly intimate. A notably playful and at times jealous tone entered their letters. In June 1837, King asked Buchanan—who was then in the midst of a potential courtship with one or the other of his Kittera neighbors—about the lapse in their correspondence: "Are you so engrossed

FIGURE 3.5 John Pendleton King of Georgia. Called "that strange fellow" by William Rufus King, he was a bachelor during his years in the US Senate. Courtesy US Senate Historical Office.

by the aspirations of ambition, or the hopes, and anxieties of love, that friendship can find no abiding place in your heart? Or have you been standing on your dignity; and waiting to receive the first card?" King had good reason to be upset with Buchanan's epistolary silence—back in Alabama, he had suffered a near-fatal carriage accident. What excuse did Buchanan have for the delay in writing? Accordingly, he closed his letter with a terse salutation: "I hope to see you in September, till then farewell." Buchanan certainly warranted the admonition, for while he was a dedicated correspondent with other political colleagues, he habitually disregarded the necessity of writing to King. He had not yet realized the full value of this friendship with his southern messmate.[24]

In October 1837, Buchanan returned to Lancaster following the end of the special congressional session. In late November, he invited King to visit him. This initial "flying visit" lasted less than a full day and left members of the local Democratic Party feeling ignored. "As soon as our Democratic citizens learned that [King] was amongst us, they immediately made arrangements for offering him a public dinner," editor John Forney of the pro-Buchanan *Lancaster Intelligencer* reported, "but, much to their disappointment, they were prevented from tendering him this honor by his unexpected departure." In contrast, the anti-Buchanan *Lancaster Examiner and Democratic Herald* criticized King's visit as evidence of an underlying conspiracy between the two men. "During Mr. King's visit to this place, a year or two ago," editor Robert Middleton later claimed, "Mr. Buchanan paid the greatest attention to him, and has ever since been using his influence in his behalf." Even a short visit divided public feeling in the intensely partisan climate of the day.[25]

Back in Washington for the new session, Buchanan, King, and Nicholas resumed the old mess. The social dynamic of the group shifted, as Cary Nicholas quickly became a favorite of both Buchanan and King. The two southerners, King and Nicholas, who served together on the Committee on the District of Columbia, often dined together with other Senate colleagues, sometimes without the knowledge of Buchanan. In May 1838, for example, Buchanan learned from his regular drinking companion, Daniel Webster, that the Massachusetts senator had "asked [Mr. Nicholas] & Mr. King to dine with me on *Thursday*" and that he hoped "for the pleasure of your company at the same time." Buchanan accepted the belated invitation.[26]

On other occasions, Buchanan and Nicholas operated without King. In June 1838 the pair traveled to Charlottesville, Virginia, where they visited with Thomas Jefferson Randolph, grandson of the former president, for nearly a week. Then, too, the messmates operated independently of one another. Two months after his trip to Charlottesville, Nicholas could be found vacationing alongside President Van Buren, members of the cabinet, and numerous other congressmen at the White Sulphur Springs resort in the Virginia Springs region of the state. The following summer King joined Nicholas at the springs, where the pair mingled with other members of elite society and took the mineral waters. In retrospect, these halcyon days of the bachelor's mess were numbered.[27]

The Conservative Body of the Republic

During the second half of the 1830s, the members of the bachelor's mess faced many political and economic issues, chief among them the financial health of the nation. As the bachelor messmates vacationed in the summer of 1837, the nation entered a severe depression. Known as the Panic of 1837, the crisis was precipitated when Andrew Jackson's administration withdrew federal funds from the Second Bank of the United States (BUS) and deposited them into various regional banks, known as "pet banks." Jackson's proclamation of the "Specie Circular," which mandated the payment of gold in the sale of public land, only worsened the monetary crisis. In response, President Van Buren proposed a subtreasury, or independent treasury, which placed the task of funding the federal government in the hands of state-level banks. He also took the unprecedented step to call the Congress into an emergency session to commence in early September.[28]

Thorough-going administration Democrats, Buchanan and King declared themselves publicly for the president's plan. Yet when both men returned home that summer, they found local conditions deteriorating. The withdrawal of the federal deposits from the BUS "has done us much mischief," King lamented to Buchanan. To his old North Carolina friend Asbury Dickens, he likewise reported that the removal of the federal deposits, "once considered a master stroke of policy . . . is now openly denounced." While King had supported Jackson's decision, he now blamed Van Buren for following "a mistaken delicacy towards his predecessor" and thus failing to modify the government's policy. For his part, Buchanan faced an angry electorate, one far more connected to financial interests than King's more agrarian constituency. While he privately blamed Van Buren for acquiescing to the "bidding of the New York Merchants," he nevertheless joined King in supporting the president. In so doing, Buchanan carefully modified his views on the economic questions of the day to align with the emerging Jacksonian orthodoxy.[29]

Buchanan determined to deliver a speech in favor of the subtreasury plan, which he did before the full Senate on September 29, 1837. In this oration, considered "one of the best speeches of his life," he warned of a "stimulus of excessive banking" and feared that the "banks are all-powerful." As the presiding officer, King avoided making a public address on the question, but he moved along the debate when possible and privately urged the passage of the subtreasury plan. After weeks of charged debate, the Senate passed the Independent Treasury Bill in 1837, but the House did not ultimately agree to its provisions for another three years. For their continued support of the subtreasury plan, the *Boston Courier* declared Buchanan and King to be "at the head . . . of the more moderate friends of the Administration."[30]

During these years the members of the bachelor's mess, especially Buchanan and King, built their reputations as respected and influential national figures of their party. They positioned themselves as among the only true conservative members of the Senate capable of uniting the Democratic Party in the decades ahead. In 1837 King declared the Senate to be "the great conservative body of this republic," where the "demon of faction should find no abiding place." Buchanan concurred: "This body is truly the conservative body of the country, and we are not to be deterred, through fear of giving offence, from marching forward in the course of our duty." Through invocations to conservatism in the dignified setting of the Senate, the politically ambitious Buchanan and King enhanced their standing across the country. Looking ahead to the 1840s, they hoped this formula of conservative partisanship would yield electoral success.[31]

In that same vein, the bachelor messmates found common cause to oppose the growing tide of abolitionist petitions. In January 1836, for example, Whig senator Thomas Morris of Ohio introduced two anti-slavery petitions to the Senate. In the House, James Henry Hammond of South Carolina proposed a strict "gag rule" on accepting any such petitions. Then, Senator John C. Calhoun similarly moved to suppress the petitions presented by Morris. Buchanan quickly enjoined the debate, using the occasion to decry abolitionists as "fanatics, [who] instead of benefiting the slaves who are the objects of their regard, have inflicted serious injuries upon them." After a brief but heated series of exchanges, the subject was postponed on Buchanan's motion. Nevertheless, the issue periodically resurfaced, with Buchanan opposing the reception of anti-slavery petitions each time. At first, he simply moved to table the motions. Later, he proposed that the Senate "receive and reject," a measure that he believed "the only mode of avoiding everlasting debate." This clever procedural move, which prevented the reading of anti-slavery petitions, held in the upper chamber until 1850.[32]

As president pro tempore of the Senate, King was pleased with his messmate's course of action. He temporarily left his presiding seat to urge his fellow senators to moderate their petitions and, by extension, to concur with Buchanan. "The course proposed by the Senator from Pennsylvania ... would, if adopted, be the most decisive that could be pursued," he said in a rare prepared speech on March 3, 1836. A reporter added that King was almost too embarrassed to add anything more to the "able argument . . . so strongly and clearly enforced by his friend from Pennsylvania." The Alabama senator agreed with Buchanan on every point, adding in the paternalistic language of the slaveholder that the enslaved were "well-fed, well-clothed, happy, and contented." Slavery, he insisted, must be forever protected. A few days later, he joined Buchanan in celebrating their gag rule victory over dinner, with South Carolina senators Calhoun and William Preston, at the home of Mahlon Dickerson, secretary of the navy (and yet another bachelor resident of the capital city).[33]

In the winter months of early 1837, new petitions to abolish slavery in the District of Columbia continued to inflame Congress. Although he had previously favored receiving anti-slavery petitions from his own constituents in Pennsylvania, Buchanan opposed receiving those pertaining to abolition in the District. In fact, Buchanan declared himself "never better satisfied with his own course" on the slavery question, because he "deprecated a renewed discussion of the question, which would only tend to keep up the excitement in the South and in the North, without any countervailing advantage." Nevertheless, Buchanan and King tried to block a resolution promoted by John Calhoun against further "intermeddling with slavery" in the District. He hoped that his earlier resolutions would serve as a "platform for the friends of the South in the Northern States, on which they might stand and defend themselves against the assaults of the Abolitionists; and that we of the North would have gone further than we had done . . . had it not been from a dread of public opinion at home." He had come to believe that the highly sensitive question of slavery had become too important to leave to the course of politics as usual.[34]

In Buchanan's support of the gag rule, the bosom friendships enjoyed with his southern messmates proved critical. More so than in his previous domestic arrangements, his intimate associations with southerners brought him into direct contact with men whose political and personal convictions about the issue superseded his own ambivalent views on the peculiar institution. The topic constantly surfaced among the messmates. At one point, King warned Buchanan that if northern abolitionists continued in their course to end slavery, "then we will separate from them." Buchanan's Pennsylvania associate Thomas Elder thundered in reply to "let them withdraw and wade in blood before six months"; as always, Buchanan took a more cautious approach. If he ever hoped to become a national candidate for his party's presidential nomination, he needed to cultivate southern friends. Much as Martin Van Buren had done before him, Buchanan hoped to present himself as a safe northern man, in a party largely dominated by southern interests and larger-than-life southern politicians. His public support for the protection of slavery was essential.[35]

Buchanan's views of slavery were shaped in more intimate ways within the bachelor's mess, as African Americans, both enslaved and free, enabled the cozy domestic arrangement. Moreover, Buchanan watched as King purchased a trio of enslaved African Americans, including a new personal valet or man-servant named John Bell. From these exposures to African Americans in the boardinghouse, the institution of slavery carried a softer, more personal face. When one of his family members inherited legal ownership of two enslaved people (Daphne Cook, age twenty-two, and her daughter Ann Cook, age five), he purchased their freedom and indentured them, as provided by the manumission laws of Pennsylvania. As an added advantage to Buchanan, the Cooks performed household work at his Lancaster home. Whether in his Washington or Lancaster household, he benefited from the domestic labor of African Americans.[36]

Buchanan's commitment to the Jacksonian legislative agenda reflected a wider partisanship embraced by politicians of the age. "America had known parties before," historian Harry Watson has observed, "but the earlier competition between Federalists and Democratic-Republicans had been amateurish compared to the rivalry between well-established and increasingly sophisticated organizations that came to dominate virtually all aspects of American politics in the 1830s and 1840s." The "shrine of party," as one historian put it, extended to voting behavior among congressmen. Senator Buchanan was not immune to the forces of partisan alignment. A multiyear roll-call analysis from 1834 to 1844 reveals that he accorded with his messmates on approximately four out of every five votes (excluding abstentions and missed votes). Likewise, the percentage of votes in common generally increased over the ten-year period, an apt reflection of the intensifying partisanship. With King, in particular, Buchanan voted in common nearly 88 percent of the time, with their votes aligning toward complete unity in their final year together in the Senate (see Appendix B).[37]

Beyond the general voting patterns, the voting congruities among messmates extended to nearly every piece of major legislation as well. From Buchanan's first Senate vote on a minor internal improvement matter in January 1835, he almost always found common cause with his messmates. In fact, Buchanan, King, and the various messmates voted the same way on all the landmark legislation of the period, including in favor of the Distribution Act of February 1836 that allocated surplus funds from tariff duties to the states, the gag rule on the reception of abolitionist petitions over 1836 and 1837, and the creation of a subtreasury system in 1837 to replace the BUS. In January 1835 King introduced a resolution to expunge the censure of President Jackson, passed by the Senate in March 1834 in response to his removal of federal deposits from the BUS. Although not immediately considered, King's expunging resolution was finally taken to a vote and passed in January 1837. Taken together, the messmates filled their roles as the loyal congressional supporters of the Jackson administration.[38]

The two men did occasionally disagree on issues reflective of their different sectional origins and constituencies. For example, King consistently voted in favor of distributing federal lands, while Buchanan voted against such measures. Likewise, Buchanan supported the pension applications of Revolutionary War widows and approved additional allocations to expand the collections of the Library of Congress, including the purchase of the public papers from the estate of James Madison. King typically voted against these additional expenditures. But these differences aside, the voting records underscored Buchanan's change from a pro-tariff, pro-bank Federalist to a pro-slavery, anti-bank Jacksonian populist. Similarly, King's alignment with Buchanan widened his purview from a sectional approach to encompass a more wholly national, albeit strictly partisan, view of politics.

Of course, the close-knit personal relationships among the various members did not alone determine the outcome of voting behaviors. But as their many concurring votes suggest, the messmates were remarkably consistent in their voting patterns. If the Jacksonian Democrats who joined the bachelor's mess held largely preformed political opinions, their experience living together hardened those views in the partisan climate of the 1830s. The setting provided an opportunity for members, as King put it, to "unite" together around those very issues and to plot their legislative agenda. For Buchanan, in particular, his voting record marked him as a "safe" northern man, whose principles included protection for the institution of slavery. In time, the bachelor's mess functioned as an incubator for partisan unity, a pro-slavery ideology, and, by extension, the entire Jacksonian legislative program on Capitol Hill.[39]

Peculiar Pleasure

At the beginning of 1838, the Democrats still firmly held power. Even as Congress preoccupied itself with the fallout from the economic panic of the previous summer, new issues presented themselves with unexpected partisanship. Chief among them was the future of the newly declared Republic of Texas, whether it ought to be immediately annexed to the United States or recognized as an independent nation. King and Buchanan joined Van Buren in standing against immediate annexation, but they used the occasion to debate their Whig opponents on the legalities of slavery in any new territory acquired by the United States. Besides the debates over the subtreasury and the Texas question, this session and the ensuing lame-duck session that ran through March 1839 were quiet times for the Democracy and for the members of the bachelor's mess. All eyes already seemed fixed on the presidential contest in 1840.[40]

At the bachelor's mess the trio of Buchanan, King, and Nicholas accepted an unusually young new colleague into its ranks. Born in 1810, William Sterrett Ramsey of Pennsylvania was, like Buchanan, a graduate of Dickinson College, and, like King, had served as an attaché to the legation of a foreign court. After a stint as a diplomatic courier for Washington Irving, Ramsey returned to America, continued his legal studies, and secured an appointment as commander of the Carlisle Light Infantry. At this point, Buchanan began to take a noticeable liking to the young man and promoted his case for various government appointments. Elected to the House of Representatives in 1838, Ramsey was at age twenty-eight the youngest member of Congress, a distinction King once held. Like his new messmates, Ramsey was also unmarried.[41]

Meanwhile, the aftershocks of the Panic of 1837 still hampered the nation to start 1840. In the Senate, the newly energized Whigs argued with Democrats, mostly over the proposed subtreasury bill and by extension, the low wages for laborers prevailing across the country. The exchange became particularly heated at times. In response to Henry Clay's dismissal of the subtreasury system, Buchanan systematically dismantled his opponent's position and argued for more a conservative economic approach. "I would, if I could, radically reform the present banking system, so as to confine it within such limits as to prevent future suspensions of specie payment," he declared. In reply, John Davis of Massachusetts came to Clay's defense and attacked Buchanan's proposal as designed to "bring to the cotton planters the extraordinary profits anticipated, at the expense of the other branches of industry." Davis then published his own speech, with detailed notes, as a pamphlet. Over the next few weeks, Davis and Buchanan published charges, and then countercharges, of misrepresentation. The issue was coming to a boil.[42]

On March 3, 1840, the rancorous debate exploded. Buchanan declared that Davis had made a "flagitious representation" in the characterization of his speech. Davis immediately struck back and called Buchanan's remarks "unparliamentary, ungentlemanly, and untrue." Buchanan refused further comment, but he called Davis "unworthy of the courtesy which one gentleman owes to another." By this point, their fellow senators and Buchanan's own messmates had witnessed enough. King expressed "unfeigned regret" at the direction of the debate, while Bedford Brown decried the "very extraordinary spectacle [that] had been presented to the Senate" and that the debate had been "highly irritating, and of a strictly personal character." Not to be deterred, both Davis and Buchanan published additional pamphlets of their printed speeches. Privately, Davis complained to his wife of Buchanan's "senility."[43]

At the bachelor's mess, the debate stirred William Ramsey to an anger that reflected his intimacy with Buchanan. In June, he issued a thunderous defense of the independent treasury bill that echoed Buchanan's views in both form and content. When Congress adjourned in July, the pleasant sociality of the previous session lingered in Ramsey's mind. To Buchanan, he expressed his hope for Van Buren's success in the upcoming election and added a touching personal note about the other messmates. "I am very glad that Col. King has come out of this war successful," he wrote of his messmate's re-election to the Senate. "I have his portrait and that of our good friend Col. Nicholas framed and hanging in my room. I intend to get yours also one of these days, to place along side of them."[44]

The intergenerational friendship between Buchanan and his new messmate was not altogether unique. Buchanan regularly cultivated intimate friendships with other aspiring young men from the Keystone State, notably with his Lancaster townsman Jonathan Messersmith Foltz. Also born in 1810, Foltz studied medicine and aspired to a military commission in the Navy; like Ramsey, he was still unmarried. Foltz even sought marital advice from the older bachelors of the mess; as he later remembered of one visit to Washington: "To the advice of the late lamented Col: King and yourself, I am indebted for getting married. Such was your combined advice at your fireside in W- years ago, you were my confidante then and still are." For bachelors, Foltz's recollection evinced, few settings were more intimate than the fireside hearth, in which they could think, in one scholar's estimation, "in the bachelor's dreamy, longing way, primarily of what it would be like *not* to be a bachelor." Buchanan and Dr. Foltz remained on "terms of intimate friendship" for decades to come.[45]

To Buchanan, the ambitious and politically active William Ramsey must have reminded him of his younger self. However, Ramsey also suffered from a severely troubled state of mind. On October 17, 1840, he checked into Barnum's Hotel in Baltimore, where he killed himself. Reports varied concerning the reason for his actions: some attributed the cause to alcoholism, others to depression. Whatever the cause, news of his death spread around the country and produced a sensation, since Ramsey was the first sitting congressman to commit suicide. Buchanan prepared a glowing obituary notice for the Lancaster *Intelligencer*. Philadelphia jurist John Meredith Read, knowing his friend's connection to the deceased, sent his condolences to Buchanan: "I was greatly shocked and grieved at poor Ramsey's death," as he well remembered the "gentleman's manner and deportment."[46]

Ramsey's death left King, Buchanan, and Nicholas once again looking for new members to join their mess. As before, they faced difficulty in finding a suitable replacement, since most of the remaining Democratic congressmen had already made their boarding arrangements for the lame-duck session scheduled for December 1840. But through a connection made by Nicholas, they added William Henry Roane of Virginia, a Democrat who had lost his seat to a Whig challenger in the last election, as a fourth. Born in 1787, Roane, a grandson of Patrick Henry, was predeceased years earlier by his much

FIGURE 3.6 William Henry Roane of Virginia. A widower, he urged a "frolick" with Buchanan and King. Courtesy US Senate Historical Office.

younger wife Sally Anne Lyons Roane, which left his eldest married daughter, Sarah Roane Harrison, as his closest confidante. To her, Roane admitted that he desired "to be alone" in his boardinghouse for the short session, though it was "not improbable that one or two vacant rooms may be taken." Despite his initial inclinations, Roane found himself happily situated with his new messmates and, in time, hoped to rekindle the intimate friendships formed there.[47]

For Cary Nicholas at least, the tragic news of Ramsey's death was offset by a felicitous development in his personal life. On October 15, 1840, he married Susan Adelaide Vinson, the daughter of an old military friend and a woman twenty-six years his junior. The news of Nicholas's marriage did not go unnoticed by political commentators. "Senators King, Buchanan, and Nicholas are at their old quarters, Mrs. Ironsides," the Washington correspondent for the *New York Herald* wrote in January 1841. "This was last year a bachelor mess, but Nicholas has become a Benedict of late," the reporter noted in reference to the bachelor character who eventually married in Shakespeare's *Much Ado about Nothing*, "and his two friends talked of having him tried by a Court martial for getting married without their consent." Jokes aside, the arrangement of the newly married and the still unmarried was necessarily impermanent, as Nicholas like Roane had lost his seat in the Senate.[48]

Despite their immediate separation, the messmates still hoped to continue their friendships. In June 1841, only a few months after his departure from the mess, Nicholas inquired about Buchanan's personal affairs. "I hope soon to hear from you or our friend the Col., not only something of your public doings but what I take no little interest in your domestic arrangements," he wrote in reference to King, adding, "Such as where you are located, who you have with you, & who in my absence does the scolding." The feeling of interest was mutual. Later that summer, Buchanan joined King and Nicholas at the fashionable White Sulphur Springs resort in Virginia. Prior to the trip, Buchanan wrote to Mrs. Nicholas; in reply, the new husband noted that his "wife received your kind message with great pleasure, & . . . desires me to say that forming your acquaintance is one of the highest gratifications she promises herself from her visit to the Springs." Likewise, former messmate Edward Lucas, who had married Mary Ellen Johnson in November 1838, had not forgotten his college friend and Washington companion; he even christened his second son James Buchanan Lucas in 1848. Despite their later life marriages, Nicholas and Lucas continued their feelings of attachment to their former messmates.[49]

In this same way, William Roane kept in touch with Buchanan in the months ahead. Much as he had done with other southern messmates, Buchanan expressed an interest in visiting Roane at his home. In the spring of 1842, Roane opened one letter: "If you knew how often I have thought of you and *anticipated* the pleasure of seeing you in *my House* this spring." The former messmate then revealed his plans for Buchanan's visit, writing with unusual candor:

> [Newspaper editor Thomas] Ritchie and other Democratic friends shall meet you at *Tree Hill*, and perhaps some pretty *girls*, so that you may have all sorts of a frolick . . . . I cannot say how much it would add to my pleasure if our esteemed friend Col. King would accompany you, please urge him in my name to do so, and I speak in all sincerity and truth when I say that it would rejoice me if you would wake up a *party* of my senatorial friends & give me a "*benefit*." [Ambrose] *Sevier* is generally fond of a frolick & there is no one I would be more pleased to see.

From Roane's reference to "pretty girls" and a "frolick," the letter suggested a playful, sexualized banter to be commonplace among the messmates. Equally so, Roane intimated much about their relative manhood: Buchanan stood somewhere in between the "swaggering style" of the Arkansas Democrat Ambrose Sevier and the more refined and reserved manhood of King. In other words, Buchanan could be counted on for an enjoyable time of drinking and flirting with "pretty girls."[50]

The frank tone of Roane's letter similarly comported with other correspondence with former messmate Bedford Brown. In a letter from July 1841, Buchanan beseeched his old messmate: "King orders me to command you to rouse yourself, to exert all your talents and energies in North Carolina and put down the d—d Whigs." He also poked fun at King's aging manhood, in a tone reminiscent of Roane's witty banter. "The beauties of a fine foot and anchle and a luxurious form no longer make the same impression upon him as formerly," he hinted. "He is sinking gracefully into the vale of years; but his will be a green old age." The references to King's diminished physical attraction to women were only thinly veiled: the innuendo of "a fine foot and anchle" was a common euphemism for female sexuality, even as his hope for a "green old age" suggested a continued sexual vitality. Although Brown never returned to the Senate, Buchanan could still be found recollecting fifteen years later with him about the "peculiar pleasure our intercourse in 'the auld lang syne.'" Their time together as messmates did not easily fade from view.[51]

Meanwhile, Buchanan faced mounting family obligations. As one tragedy after another struck the Buchanan siblings, the bachelor brother James found himself saddled with the management of their estates and eventually the legal guardianship of two young children. In 1839 he became responsible for the well-being of the nine-year-old Harriet Lane (daughter of his sister Elizabeth Jane Buchanan Lane), and, a year later, for the seven-year-old James Buchanan "Buck" Henry (son of his sister Harriet Buchanan Henry). In time, his commitment to supervising these two children grew as one and then the other relative joined their favorite uncle first in Lancaster and then in Washington. The job of raising the pair was made easier by the presence of Esther Parker, whom Buchanan hired as housekeeper and called "Miss Hetty." He had become a veritable bachelor father.[52]

Nevertheless, the responsibility for these orphaned wards seems to have pressured Buchanan to consider marriage once more. As he had with Ann Coleman years earlier, he took to poetic verse for self-expression. In March 1842, Buchanan copied out a sentimental poem written for an unidentified "Maid from Tennessee." The significant difference in age between Buchanan and the recipient became a central obsession. "Should I attempt to woo a youthful wife?" he asked. "A match of age with youth can only bring / The farce of 'winter dancing with spring,'" he answered glumly. "Blooming nineteen can never well agree / With the dull age of half century." Nothing came of this poetical wooing to the anonymous Tennessee maiden—given its inclusion among his papers and anonymous nature, he may not even have delivered it—but Buchanan did not stop the flirtations with younger women in the years ahead.[53]

Eventually, most members of the bachelor's mess married. For the most part, these later life nuptials followed a typical pattern of first marriages among elite older men: the grooms were nearly twice the age of their brides. Given that these former bachelors married soon after their arrival in Washington, a similar outcome might have been expected for Buchanan and King. However, they differed from their other messmates in one crucial respect. The marrying bachelors of the mess—Edward Lucas, Robert Carter Nicholas, and John Pendleton King—all married either after leaving Congress or as they were retiring from national politics. In contrast, Buchanan and King desired to remain in Washington and to achieve a greater political prize. For them, marriage was ultimately subservient to political advancement.

* * *

As the 1830s progressed, the bachelor's mess provided critical support to the Jacksonian agenda in the US Senate. Together, the messmates stood united on two of the most divisive issues before the Congress: the gagging of petitions calling for the abolition of slavery and the establishment of a subtreasury system to replace the defunct BUS. Their outspoken support of the Jacksonian agenda helped them to forge coalitions with politicians from different wings of the party. By decade's end, the local supporters of Buchanan and King began to advance them as possible presidential and vice presidential candidates of their party. That a personal union of two bachelors from Pennsylvania and Alabama might yet generate a fertile political bounty would have been impossible a generation earlier.

Of the messmates, Buchanan was by far the most ambitious and ultimately benefited the greatest from his fraternalization with the boardinghouse group. Already southern leaning in his Pennsylvania upbringing, his commitment to the party of Jackson necessarily led him down the road of becoming a northern champion of southern interests. Entering the Senate in 1834, his connections to southern messmates solidified these early inclinations into a characteristic lifelong form. Buchanan also grasped that his alliance with southern Democrats promoted his standing as a safe northern man who might one day be a potential candidate for the presidency. As such, he aligned his positions on the questions of slavery, the tariff, and the bank with these mostly southern moderates. Along the way, he found himself sharing intimate friendships with men, who likewise had ventured through life without getting to the altar. In this way Buchanan embodied the qualities of a northern doughface, as much for potential political advancement as for the personal satisfaction of his associations with his southern messmates. The conjoined identities of Jacksonian, bachelor, and doughface proved a potent combination in Buchanan's quest for higher office.

The bachelor's mess had been formed by the necessity of finding suitable lodging in the capital. In time, it had been transformed into something more: a boardinghouse group that combined the intensely political aspects of the Jacksonian Democracy with the equally personal aspects of middle-aged bachelors. Bachelorhood had become an unlikely political asset to these men. But such assets could quickly become liabilities. The bachelor's mess was formed during the high-water mark years of the Democratic ascendancy, when all could easily enjoy the fruits of partisan power regardless of marital status. Whether the bosom friendships cultivated there could last beyond the confines of Washington remained to be seen.

4

Wooing, 1840–1844

THE FLOWERING OF partisanship during the 1830s yielded an entrenched two-party system in the decade of the 1840s. Two important political legacies solidified in the years following Jackson's reign. The first and foremost of these developments concerned the Democratic Party itself, which by 1840 consisted of cross-sectional alliances among southerners, northerners, and westerners. The Jacksonian Democratic formula was simple enough: reward those loyal to the party banner and punish those who resisted its program. The Jacksonian administrative ethos of a small federal government did not preclude a commitment to patronage, as the "spoils system" pioneered in these years took hold with startling force in the ensuing decades. Equally so, the Jacksonian Democracy changed the nature of presidential politics. In the past, the Virginia Dynasty of Jefferson, Madison, and Monroe had relied upon deference to their elite class status and political standing as members of the founding generation. Jackson upended the traditional hierarchy. Now anyone could become a potential candidate for president of the United States.[1]

The evolution of the Jacksonian years corresponded with the second legacy of the era: the development of a permanent opposition party. In the contest between Whigs and Democrats, the basic outlines of the Second Party System fell into place. Real differences in politics—disagreements over tariff levels, internal improvements, the sovereignty of Native Americans, the fate of slavery, and territorial expansion, especially the question of the annexation of Texas—divided the two parties and their successors for another generation. Yet in other ways the greatest conflicts were personal, begotten among men of varying cultural backgrounds and divergent conceptions of the proper conduct of public men. From such disputes flowed gossip on both sides. Presidential elections became especially vitriolic, from the disgraceful accusations of 1828 to the boisterous singing and shouting of 1840. In this contest for the popular support of the American people, the Jacksonian era democratized the nation.[2]

The ongoing battle between Democrats and Whigs brought new challenges to James Buchanan, William Rufus King, and the other members of the bachelor's mess. If the 1830s had permitted them the freedom to develop intimate personal relationships, the 1840s tested them. Of the remaining bachelor messmates, all but Buchanan and King lost their bids for re-election to Whig challengers. The surviving pair struggled, and ultimately failed, to find new Democratic associates to reinvigorate their mess. In this period, Buchanan and King slowly evolved into "the Siamese twins" of Washington society. As events further politicized their relationship, they also lost something of the warm bonhomie that had characterized their previous domestic arrangements.

From their ongoing contest for power in the Senate, each man began to seek a path to greater prominence and higher office. In 1840 and again in 1844, Buchanan and King earnestly tested the presidential waters. As each man attempted to claim a share of the national leadership in the Democratic Party, they encountered resistance from the very quarters of Washington society that had provided their initial entry. In these whispered attacks, King became "Miss Nancy" or "Aunt Nancy," and Buchanan turned into "the Great Humbugger." Even their friendship, which in an earlier time would have been considered politically beneficial, became an object of scorn—to their critics, the marriage of "Mr. Buchanan and His Wife" represented an aberration both in function and form. Thus attacked, Buchanan and King consolidated their political position and in turn ridiculed their enemies in a more refined, though still highly critical, manner. Through such political gossip, each side bonded over shared dismissals of their opponents' presidential aspirations.

Aunt Nancy and the Great Humbugger

To start 1840, Democrats expected incumbent Martin Van Buren to seek another term of office, but some in the party sensed the vice presidency to be up for grabs. Since its inception the office had served a largely ceremonial function, and, except for John Adams, one that held dim prospects for presidential aspirants. Beginning with Thomas Jefferson, incumbent presidents commonly dropped their vice presidents from the first administration; whether for political reasons or because of death, they preferred new running mates in the second term. The presidency of Andrew Jackson further complicated the dynamic. After Jackson came into direct conflict with his first vice president John Calhoun, the party chose Martin Van Buren, his former secretary of state and minister designate to the Court of St. James, to fill the second spot on the 1832 ticket. Van Buren's nomination four years later meant that the vice presidency had suddenly become an electoral wedge by which presidential aspirants might make their way to the White House.[3]

For Van Buren's running mate in 1836, the Democrats selected war hero Richard Mentor Johnson of Kentucky, known popularly by his colorful nickname "Old Dick." The Democracy hoped that Johnson, who carried a heroic reputation as the killer of Tecumseh in the War of 1812, might balance the ticket; Andrew Jackson also favored him. Yet Old Dick proved a liability: his sexual relationship with his African American mistress Julia Chinn cost the Democratic Party in the South—the ticket failed even to carry Johnson's home state of Kentucky—and earned him a new reputation as a "great amalgamator," a pejorative term that suggested untoward racial mixing. The Democratic electors in Virginia, still smarting that their favorite son William Rives had been passed over for the vice presidential nomination, cast their twenty-three vice presidential votes for William Smith of South Carolina. Accordingly, while Van Buren won the election with 170 electoral ballots for president, the defection of the Virginia electors meant that Johnson had only received 143 electoral votes for vice president. Under the provisions of the Twelfth Amendment to the Constitution, the mismatch left Johnson one vote short of the necessary majority of ballots to secure victory. Accordingly, the decision fell to the Senate, which under the leadership of president pro tempore William Rufus King, dutifully voted to elect Richard Mentor Johnson as vice president.[4]

The earlier agitation over Johnson left the vice presidential field seemingly wide open for the 1840 contest. Predictably, Buchanan attempted to play executive matchmaker, this time on behalf of his messmate King. A shrewd political calculus animated his efforts. Of the two men, King possessed a better chance for the vice presidential nomination in 1840; his southern origins balanced the ticket with the New Yorker Van Buren. If King could be successfully placed in the position of vice president, the thinking went, he could be retained in the subsequent presidential election of 1844. At that point, Buchanan would be better positioned to succeed Van Buren as the leading northern Democrat and King would once again balance the ticket as the vice presidential nominee. The plan, though seemingly far-fetched, did have a political precedent; John Calhoun had served as vice president first under John Quincy Adams and then again under Andrew Jackson. By this logic, the successful election of King as vice president would clear the way for Buchanan in 1844.[5]

Before he could obtain the vice presidential nomination of the Democratic National Convention, King needed to secure the support of as many state-level nominating conventions as possible. Toward that end, Buchanan distributed a campaign biography of King to the Pennsylvania state press and wrote to his wide network of political correspondents on his messmate's behalf. To his former secretary of the Russian legation, John Randolph Clay, he wrote of the vice presidential question: "For my own part, I prefer Col. King of Alabama & believe that he would add much more to the strength of Mr. Van Buren in the doubtful Southern & South Western States, especially in North Carolina of which he is a native." Likewise, to his erstwhile correspondent Eliza Violet Gist Blair, he wrote coyly: "As a lady, however, possessing, as I know, the Colonel's esteem in an eminent degree, I thought you might reciprocate it by speaking a kind word for him among your friends & particularly among the sex who rightfully govern mankind." Not wanting to leave the impression that he wished to replace Richard Mentor Johnson outright, Buchanan added: "We were disposed to let things take their natural course, not however forgetting Col. King." In the summer, Buchanan courted the support of the influential Missouri senator Thomas Hart Benton, by inviting him and his family to join him for a week's vacation in the Pennsylvania mountains (though Benton declined). Based on the intelligence gathered, Buchanan reported to his brother-in-law in the late summer of 1839 that it was "now pretty certain" that King would obtain the vice presidential nomination at the Pennsylvania state convention in December.[6]

During the long congressional recess, King expressed his gratitude to Buchanan for the efforts made on his behalf. "I can but feel grateful at the lively interest you manifest," he declared. Yet King was quick to "assure you my Friend it is a matter in which I do not take the interest you imagine and I shall without one feeling of regret give my cordial support to any Republican who may be designated by a Convention or in any other way presented as the candidate of the party." In turn, King noted that the "Republicans of Virginia"—a holdover expression from his early affiliation with the Democratic-Republican Party—had begun to appreciate Buchanan and that "Alabama . . . is as safe for you as Pennsylvania." By winter, Alabama's state convention had formally nominated King for vice president on the Van Buren ticket; Buchanan's efforts also paid off in securing the same nomination for King in Pennsylvania. By the fall of 1839, King's chances for nomination had moved from merely theoretical to nearly imminent.[7]

Yet he was not alone in the race. John Forsyth of Georgia, Robert Walker of Mississippi, and James Polk of Tennessee also evinced interest. Of this

group, Polk possessed the strongest chance; he carried the endorsement of
Andrew Jackson, who had privately abandoned Richard Mentor Johnson
by late 1839. Just as King benefited from Buchanan's assiduous efforts, Polk
received aid from the equally diligent work of his own political ally, Aaron
Venable Brown. Given Brown's later part in creating the modern-day view of
Buchanan and King as a same-sex couple, it is interesting to note how much
Brown shared in common with King. Brown too attended the University of
North Carolina and became a member of the Philosophic Society, graduating
as valedictorian of the class of 1814. After college Brown moved not south to
Alabama, but west to Tennessee, where he began to practice law with Polk,
himself another ambitious migrant and graduate of the university. Like King,
Brown proved a staunch supporter of Andrew Jackson and all those favored
by the old general; for his loyalty, Tennessee elected him three times to the
House of Representatives. By the 1830s, Brown had become Polk's political
watchdog and protector of his reputation in Washington.[8]

As the end of 1839 approached, the battle for the vice presidency was
in full swing. While all sides pledged publicly to support whoever was
nominated, tensions were privately rising. In consultation with Buchanan,
King decided to withdraw his name from active consideration; as a result,
the Pennsylvania and Alabama state delegations switched their support to
Johnson. King was displeased by how events had unfolded and complained to
niece Catherine Margaret Ellis that Polk had "thrust himself forward and the
result has been precisely what I anticipated, the fixing of Col. Johnson upon
us." King complained that Polk had been "activated by . . . the most selfish
views." Resigned to the outcome, he declared somewhat incredibly that his
seat in the US Senate was "fully equal to my highest ambition for station, or
place." King was naturally conciliatory, even to a fault, but he had also gained
a new enemy in the form of James Polk and his Tennessee loyalists.[9]

Even though King had publicly bowed out of the race, Polk's supporters
still privately chastised him. Aaron Brown bashed King as "'Aunt Nancy,'
(K of Ala)" and called another rival, the physically miniscule Robert Walker
of Mississippi, by the epithet "Little Senator Walker" (a diminutive that he
also used for Van Buren). But unlike the slanders against Walker and Van
Buren, the characterization of King as "Aunt Nancy" carried more than a
hint of sexual deviancy, as the related phrase "Miss Nancy" had acquired a
euphemistic meaning to describe effeminate, possibly same-sex oriented men.
Brown was not the first to apply the term "Aunt Nancy" to King. Newspaper
correspondents, almost all of whom worked for anti-Jackson publications, had
referred to King as "Miss Nancy" since the early 1830s. In 1837, for example,

the *New York Herald* described King as "an old bachelor, very prim in his appearance, and old maidish in his habits; and has, on that account, I presume, been called Miss Nancy—a cognomen which he still bears." By 1844 King had acquired three nicknames: "Miss Nancy"; "the Father of the House," a reflection of King's standing in as the senior representative in Congress; and "old Love-gold," a reference to his supposed miserliness. According to John Quincy Adams, Andrew Jackson called King "Miss Nancy," as did the Washington fixture Benjamin Perley Poore. Whether as "Aunt Nancy" or "Miss Nancy," King's political enemies disparaged his character in an effort to weaken his public standing. In this, they largely failed.[10]

Buchanan also became a target of private scorn. "[Buchanan] carries his head more *one sided* than usual," Brown sneered; in the same letter to Polk, he added "The Great *Humbugger, affects* great impartiality—but 'all in my eye' depend upon it." Brown rejected Buchanan's claim to impartiality in the contest, calling him a "humbugger," or imposter, while also ridiculing Buchanan's

FIGURE 4.1 Aaron Venable Brown of Tennessee, ca. 1845. A Polk loyalist, Brown's private attacks against Buchanan and King were especially virulent. Oil portrait. Courtesy Tennessee State Library and Archives.

habit of squinting and cocking his head to one side. Brown was not alone in this scornful portrait of Buchanan. Harvey Watterson, a Polk stalwart from Tennessee, declared: "Buchannon [*sic*] is so anxious for the nomination that he has *almost* turned *crossed-eyed*." He also intimated the possibility of sexual deviancy in Buchanan's relationship with King: "I regard his prospects as peculiarly gloomy, but not more so than those of his friend Col King of Alabama who would like the best of all things in the world to be run upon *his* ticket for Vice President." The Tennesseans were out for blood.[11]

As the date grew closer to the convention, Buchanan and King came under further attack from opponents at home. "It has been apparent, for some time," the Lancaster *Examiner* editorialized in March 1840, "that an intrigue was going on between Mr. Buchanan and William R. King, of Alabama, in which Buchanan was to secure the nomination of King to the Vice Presidency; and King, in return, was at a proper time, to secure the vote of Alabama to Buchanan for the Presidency." As King's chances faltered, the messmates determined to prevent Polk's vice presidential nomination, as a way of depriving him of a national platform for a presidential run four years hence. The move infuriated Tennessee Democrats, who believed that King and Buchanan were "disposed to have Johnson nominated, right or wrong," adding that Buchanan "from hostility to Gov. Polk's future prospects had allied himself to King." Buchanan was already playing for the 1844 nomination, claimed his critics. In truth, they were right.[12]

The Democratic Party nominating convention met in Baltimore over May 5 and 6, 1840. As expected, the delegates nominated Martin Van Buren for a second term as president, but an unexpected problem ensued concerning the vice presidential nominee. The convention could not agree upon either the current vice president, Richard Mentor Johnson, or the leading challenger, James Polk, as no man could achieve the necessary two-thirds vote required by parliamentary rules. Instead, the delegates permitted the individual electors in each of the several states to select the vice presidential candidate of their choosing. Implicitly, the convention's nondecision meant that the Democracy continued with the ticket of Van Buren and Johnson. In the actual contest, Johnson received the majority of the vice presidential electoral votes cast for the Van Buren ticket, although both Polk and Littleton Tazewell of Virginia also received some electoral votes.[13]

The byzantine machinations of the Democracy proved for naught. Following the example of Andrew Jackson, the opposition Whig Party unified behind the war hero William Henry Harrison in a log cabin and hard cider campaign that appealed to the masses. In November, General Harrison, whom King had once derided to Buchanan as "that vain ridiculous fellow," was voted into office in a wave of popular enthusiasm. The Whig victory came as a major shock to many. Not since the election of Andrew Jackson twelve years earlier had the government faced a disruption of this political magnitude. In Washington, Henry Clay and the other congressional Whigs itched to seize the reins of power and begin the process of distributing lucrative patronage, while the Democrats prepared to oppose them at every turn.[14]

A Gentle Slave-Monger and Old Buck

After twelve years of Democratic rule, the Whig ascendancy proved formidable. In a special two-week session following the inauguration, President Harrison asked Congress to consider the appointment of new federal officers to expedite the transition of power from a Democratic-controlled government to a Whig one. The shortened special session proved acrimonious, however, and the feelings of ill will did not dissipate at its close or during the ensuing three sessions of Congress. Thenceforth, Democrats and their Whig counterparts engaged in a sustained battle for control of the legislative agenda. At times these debates spiraled into personal conflicts, many of which evolved into affairs of honor. Both Buchanan and King found themselves embroiled in numerous partisan disputes with others. These interpersonal conflicts tested not only their political willpower, but also the viability of the friendship they had forged over the previous six years.[15]

During this period King nearly resorted to violence twice with partisan opponents. The first incident involved William Seaton, the publisher of the Whig newspaper the *National Intelligencer* and an official printer of congressional business. In the weeks prior to the inauguration of William Henry Harrison, the editor issued a politically motivated welcome to the president-elect, to which King took particular offense. In his reply, King disparaged the character of both Seaton and his business partner Joseph Gales. Seaton demanded personal satisfaction with the predictable result of a challenge to a duel. The two men went so far as to arrange for seconds, with King's former messmate, Whig Willie Mangum of North Carolina, representing Seaton and William Preston of South Carolina standing in for King. But matters soon improved: "Finally, Mr. King's better feeling asserted itself," Seaton remembered, "he manfully and honorably avowed himself in the wrong; the result of the spirited correspondence was made public, and the friendship between Mr. Seaton and himself, begun in early manhood, was warmly renewed." Once again, King had averted a duel with a political antagonist.

But the newspaper editor Seaton did not forget the conflict, nor did he refrain from printing sexually suggestive characterizations of King's relationship with Buchanan in the years ahead.[16]

The second incident carried far more serious consequences. The origins of the affair began with the battle over procedural control of the Senate. The first test came when Buchanan moved to abolish the sergeant-at-arms position, a motion that Senate "bully" Henry Clay loudly resisted. Next, the debate turned to the printers of the *Congressional Globe*, the official journal of deliberations of the Senate. King asserted that the character of the Washington *Globe* editor Francis Blair, a Jacksonian stalwart, would "compare *gloriously*," or perhaps "compare *proudly*," to that of Clay's. As the Tennessee senator Alfred Nicholson reported to Polk, "Mr. Clay considered this remark as placing Blair on an equality with himself, and therefore pronounced it false and *cowardly*." King did not reply directly to Clay, but instead issued a written challenge by way of Missouri Democratic Senator Lewis Fields Linn. Next, the two men arranged for seconds: King chose Linn and also engaged Senator Ambrose Hundley Sevier, a Democrat from Arkansas, while Clay worked through William Archer, a Virginia Whig, as his second.[17]

To political observers on both sides of the debate, the affair appeared ominous. To outgoing President Van Buren, who had remained in Washington following Harrison's inauguration, the affair was "of such a nature, as, in the opinion of most persons, to make it impossible to adjust it." William Marcy of New York, who had served with King in the Senate, similarly fretted over the matter, observing: "King is a fighting man & I do not see how a duel can honorably be avoided unless Mr. C makes a retraction and an unequivocal apology." Matters might well have worsened had it not been for Senate sergeant-at-arms Edward Dyer, who arrested both King and Clay and turned them over to local authorities to prevent further violence. Clay immediately issued a bond for five thousand dollars, and he promised to keep the peace. The next week Clay apologized in full to King, who accordingly followed suit. There were apparently no hard feelings, since Clay, an inveterate consumer of snuff, approached King's desk and in a friendly manner said, "King, give us a pinch of your snuff." The peace offer made, King sprung to his feet and held out his hand, which Clay grasped in turn. The tobacco dutifully exchanged, the happy scene received applause from the gallery.[18]

The affair with Clay reinforced King's high standing in the masculine honor culture of the antebellum Congress. About this episode John Forney recalled King as "courtly a gentleman as ever breathed," but he "would have fought Mr. Clay without hesitation." Yet King's political opponents continued to degrade him as effeminate. A Whig periodical noted King's "ladylike" behavior and that he had "long been known as the sobriquet of Miss Nancy." John Quincy Adams privately described King as "a gentle slave-monger," as much an insult of King's widely perceived effeminacy as a dismissal of his ties to the world of slaveholding plantation owners. But like so many others, Adams failed to appreciate the effectiveness of King's "gentle" personality. For decades, King had utilized the culture of honor to his political benefit, and enhancing his standing as a "fighting man," Democrats once more applauded his handling of Clay. The affair also underscored the limitations of King's friendship with Buchanan, who was considered a "noncombatant" in the various violent conflicts that periodically erupted in Congress. Although one contemporary recalled that Buchanan was "a warm personal friend of Mr. King," the Southerner could not call upon his messmate, a Northerner and one not versed in the culture of honor, to serve as a second. Indeed, Buchanan may well have disapproved of his messmate's conduct, as he remained publicly silent during the incident. Certain cultural differences limited the fullness of their friendship.[19]

The first Whig administration lasted barely a month. William Henry Harrison caught pneumonia after delivering the longest inaugural address in presidential history and died soon thereafter. To Harrison's vice presidential running mate, John Tyler, fell the duties of the presidency. Many observers, Henry Clay among them, assumed that Tyler would follow the Whig platform. But Tyler was an aristocratic Virginia Democrat of the old school. His disdain for Andrew Jackson, latent from the start of the old general's rise, had emerged into public view during the nullification crisis. Although Tyler had aligned with the Whigs, he had never abandoned his Democratic—albeit anti-Jackson inflected—principles. His enemies started to call him by the epithet "His Accidency." The nickname stuck.[20]

Before his death, President Harrison had called for a special meeting of Congress to be held in the summer of 1841. For the members of the bachelor's mess, the timing of the session could not have been worse. Months earlier, William Rufus King had predicted to the Alabama Governor Arthur Bagby: "The time is coming when we shall require our ablest men to guard our rights, and protect our interests against federal incroachment." With their former messmates Cary Nicholas and William Roane rebuffed by their constituents, Buchanan and King struggled to locate fellow Democrats on whom they could rely to sustain their opposition to Henry Clay and the Whigs. Finally, they found such a man in the second senator from Alabama, Democrat Clement Comer Clay Sr. (of no relation to Henry Clay). Clay of

Alabama was not a bachelor, but such niceties must have seemed a relic of the distant political past in the face of the newfound Whig power. Although C. C. Clay did not actively participate in the debate, his staunchly Democratic views heightened political solidarity in the mess.[21]

Personal acrimony remained commonplace among the members of Congress. Now it was Buchanan's turn to clash publicly with Henry Clay, who "rarely missed an opportunity to mock Senator Buchanan." At one point, he facetiously apologized to Buchanan for his lack of "a more lady-like manner of expressing myself" and proceeded using more "mellifluous tones." Not to be outdone, Buchanan quipped that Clay's manner was "greatly improved," which ended the squabble for the time. On another memorable occasion, Clay ridiculed Buchanan's notorious squint—crossed eyes supposedly being a sign of stupidity. Similarly, Clay criticized Buchanan for never having taken "any fair lady" under his care, a jab which effectively silenced the debate once more. Buchanan's bachelorhood remained a touchy subject in a public forum.[22]

In the months ahead King, Buchanan, and the other Democrats in the Senate worked together to oppose the Whig Party's program of enhanced internal improvements, a higher protective tariff, and a new centralized bank. As such, the messmates voted together with even greater frequency. By July, Buchanan noted that the Democratic party in the Congress had never been "more firmly united than at the present moment." But their efforts proved insufficient, as the Whig majority jammed numerous bills through the Senate. President Tyler gave the Democrats unexpected aid, however, by regularly using his veto power to reject overtly Whig measures. In return, King and Buchanan publicly supported the president on numerous speeches in the Senate; privately, Buchanan thought Tyler "more egregiously humbugged than any man I have ever known." He was one to know.[23]

During these difficult partisan years, the members of the bachelor's mess retreated from social life in the capital. King acerbically described one congressional session to niece Catherine Margaret Ellis: "I have lived quite the life of a Hermit this winter and can give you no account of the fashion and gaiety of Washington. But as I understand it had differed not at all from the past, abounding in mustached gentleman without brains, and silly girls with whom they waltz." Nevertheless, the messmates could be generous entertainers when they so desired. As John Forney recollected, Buchanan was "a capital host," and King was "amusing in his dry way." Indeed, Buchanan still attracted numerous Washington admirers, especially among the young ladies of elite society. Julia Gardiner, then twenty-two years old and not yet married to the much older President John Tyler, remembered Buchanan well from his visits to the Gardiners' boardinghouse. She later described him, with only a little tongue-in-cheek given the stark difference in age between herself and Tyler, as "a young bachelor of *50* . . . a great beau among the young ladies; one of the first families and very wealthy." That Buchanan was also an active "candidate for the presidency" only enhanced his appeal.[24]

Even as he passed the mark of middle age, Buchanan's reputation as a northern champion of pro-southern interests expanded. He continued to defend the rights of southern slaveholders, building upon his earlier defense of slavery in the gag rule resolutions. In a speech on the question of the Webster-Ashburton Treaty, which defined the northern border with Canada, he added: "I might here repeat what I have said upon a former occasion— that all Christendom is leagued against the South upon this question of domestic slavery. They have no other allies to sustain their constitutional rights, except the Democracy of the North." He also more publicly identified as a bachelor. In one speech, he cheekily argued against a proposed tariff on tea and coffee that high taxes would "deprive the ladies—and especially the old ladies, who sipped their tea with so much zest—of this additional cup." In reply, a senator retorted: "Let the men give up their share. Let the old bachelors have none." Buchanan responded that "though he protested against being considered an *old bachelor*, yet he would willingly abandon his share to the ladies." By the middle 1840s, the combination of his doughface tendencies and bachelor identity had fully hardened into his new moniker as the "Old Buck."[25]

The next session brought little improvement to the Democrats' congressional prospects or the living arrangements at the bachelor's mess. C. C. Clay resigned his Senate seat in November 1841, which once more left Buchanan and King bereft of fellow messmates. From their former residence at Mrs. Beale's boardinghouse on Capitol Hill, the pair moved to Mrs. Dashiell's boardinghouse on C Street, between 4 ½ and 6th Streets. There King and Buchanan were joined for the term by John Catron, an associate justice on the Supreme Court, and by his wife Matilda Childress Catron. Also around this time, King came into possession of a "newfound dog." Although the messmates engaged in partisan battles on the Hill, the domestic pleasures of everyday life must have eased the burden of their labors.[26]

Buchanan and King determined to stick together for the lame-duck session of Congress that began in December 1842. They settled at Mrs. Miller's

FIGURE 4.2 South of F Street, Northwest, between 14th and 15th Streets, ca. 1861. Buchanan and King lived at various boardinghouses one block down on F Street, between 13th and 14th Streets. Courtesy Washingtoniana Collection, D.C. Public Library.

boardinghouse on F Street, between 13th and 14th Streets, and quite near to the Executive Mansion occupied by the widower John Tyler. The neighborhood was typical of many southern cities of the time, from its leisurely pace of life to its reliance on African American laborers. "There was an old-world atmosphere about the place in those days, and a smiling black boy, with a tall, thin glass, from a nearby bar, was always within easy hailing distance," an observer recalled fondly. Ironically, John Quincy Adams, the bachelor messmates' arch nemesis and antislavery stalwart, lived in the house next door. For the ensuing meeting of Congress in 1843, Buchanan and King stayed in the same boardinghouse and neighborhood, though now under the care of Mrs. King (of no relation to William Rufus King). With Adams and the Whigs surrounding them, the beleaguered pair settled in for yet another acrimonious session of Congress.[27]

Mr. Buchanan and His Wife

The sudden death of William Henry Harrison triggered an untimely start to the next presidential contest. Despite having lost to Harrison three years earlier, many in the Democratic Party still presumed Martin Van Buren to be its front-runner. In December 1843, however, the New Yorker badly hurt his chances for renomination by declaring himself against the annexation of Texas. In January 1844 the pro-slavery southern wing of the party began to search for a more solidly pro-annexation, pro-expansion candidate. New names surfaced for the presidency: Lewis Cass of Michigan, rear admiral Charles Stewart of New Jersey, former Vice President Richard Mentor Johnson, senator Levi Woodbury of New Hampshire, and, for the first time, James Buchanan. The vice presidency remained equally uncertain going into 1844. But as in 1840, James Polk and William Rufus King seemed likely candidates for the second honors. As such, a combined Buchanan-King ticket emerged as a viable option to Democrats.[28]

Of the two contests, the battle for the presidential nomination predominated the political conversation. As early as the winter of 1841 and continuing well into the summer of 1843, Buchanan's candidacy appeared to be strong. As before, King played a leading role in pressing his messmate's presidential claim. "Col. King assures me that the Legislature of Alabama were anxious to nominate me," Buchanan wrote a Pennsylvania colleague in 1841, "but he thought it indiscreet at the present moment." To his Lancaster intimate John Reynolds, he predicted: "The real contest would seem to be between Van Buren & myself," adding that "if the Democracy of Penna. would sustain me with an unbroken front I think my chances are fully equal if not superior to his." Nevertheless, Buchanan wanted to appear deferential to Van Buren, a man he believed could take back the White House in 1844. Over the course of 1843, Buchanan operated mostly on the local level, corresponding with his vast network of contacts and encouraging potential state party delegates to do the same.[29]

As Van Buren's chances grew brighter in late 1843, however, Buchanan determined to withdraw from active consideration. In December, he publicly expressed his "anxious desire to drive discord from the ranks of the party, and secure the ascendancy of democratic principles, both in the state and throughout the union." King noted to his niece Catherine Margaret Ellis that "our excellent Friend Buchanan, who has wisely & magnanimously determined to withdraw himself from the canvass, that, if possible, harmony may be restored, & concert of action be produced." Nevertheless, as late as the week before the Democratic nominating convention in May 1844, King still promoted Buchanan's candidacy; to a representative from the Alabama delegation, he described his messmate as "an able & safe" candidate. Buchanan thanked his many friends, especially King, for their support. Perhaps 1848 would afford a better opportunity. King agreed and further gushed to Ellis: "He is a most estimable man, and his liberal course will not I think fail to be appreciated by the country." If Van Buren could obtain the White House in 1844, the new thinking went, Buchanan stood a fair chance of becoming his successor in 1848.[30]

With Buchanan out of the running, King still held out hope of obtaining the vice presidential nomination and indirectly to pave the way for Buchanan's presidential nomination in 1848. Buchanan actively campaigned for King as the nominee of the Pennsylvania state nominating convention. Yet Buchanan curiously equivocated at times. When asked by a Democratic Party regular to prepare a campaign biography of his friend, he replied: "Intimate as I am with Colonel King, I do not possess the necessary information to write a sketch of his public life." Meanwhile, the powerful branch of the Tennessee Democracy closed ranks behind Polk for the vice presidential nod and quite possibly for the presidential nomination, too. As 1843 drew to a close, Jackson privately endorsed Polk, writing to Martin Van Buren that he believed "Young Hickory" to be "the strongest and truest man in the South." The fissures among southern Democrats foreshadowed even greater divisions in the coming months.[31]

The behind-the-scenes contest between King and Polk soon erupted into public view. In early 1844, Democratic editor Francis Blair published an anonymous letter signed only as "Amicus" in the Washington Daily Globe. In the lengthy letter, Amicus promoted King as the party's vice presidential nomination on the grounds of "seniority—length of service—more varied service—service in the war—Congress—service in a branch of government which requires more information and gives more experience—difference in the attitude of their respective friends towards Mr. Van Buren . . . and in the political condition of their respective states." Polk's confidant Cave Johnson thought the plodding style of Amicus smacked of Buchanan, but the letter likely was penned by King's ally and fellow Alabama congressman, William Winter Payne, who, unlike Buchanan, knew the particulars of his friend's biography.[32]

The Amicus letter elicited a swift rebuke from Polk's supporters. Once again, Aaron Brown came to Polk's aid, writing under the name "A Tennessee Democrat." Although conceived "without disparagement to the merits of Mr. Polk" or "without invidious comparison" of the same, Brown disproved of "such studied disparagement" on the part of Amicus. In reply, Amicus complained of the "deep malignity" shown by the "Tennessee Democrat" toward King and suggested that he "abandon that system of puffing, blowing, and swelling, by which a toad may be magnified into the dimensions of an ox." In turn, the Tennessee Democrat demurred that he "did not dream of instituting any comparisons" between Polk and King, but once engaged, he regretfully entered the fray. The debate continued in the pages of the *Globe* during the ensuing weeks, reaching an impasse in February with a final plea from Amicus to leave the decision "wholly to the people." As the Democratic Convention drew ever closer, no easy resolution seemed in sight.[33]

Even as the public debate raged, Brown continued his harangue against Buchanan and King in his private correspondence. The preceding four years had done nothing to soften his opinion of either man. On January 14, 1844, only days after the publication of the first Amicus letter, he wrote a four-page "confidential" letter to Sarah Childress Polk. Mrs. Polk held her own views about Buchanan and King; years earlier she had refused to be accompanied by them to a social occasion. In his letter, Brown was unusually vitriolic and even more salacious than he had been in 1840, writing that "Mr. Buchanon [*sic*] and *his wife*" yet remained a political unit, but he predicted that "*Mrs. B.*" might benefit from unhitching "her" political star from Buchanan. Then, drawing on the recent tit-for-tat published in the *Globe*, Brown submitted that Buchanan's withdrawal from the presidential race might actually have improved King's chances: "Mr. Buchanan looks gloomy & dissatisfied & so did *his better half* until a little private flattery & a certain newspaper puff which you doubtless noticed, excited hopes that by getting *a divorce* she might set up again in the world to some tolerable advantage." Continuing the metaphor, he further chirped: "*Aunt Nancy* may be now seen every day, triged [*sic*] out in her best clothes & smirking about in hopes of seeing better times than with her former companion." King got what "every prude deserves who sets herself up for more than she is worth," he concluded. Overall, these attacks once more aimed to emasculate King and, by extension, his vice presidential prospects.[34]

Although only Brown's words have survived, Sarah Childress Polk likely used those same colorful phrases in her correspondence about her husband's political opponents. For years she had proved critical to her husband's political success, and in 1844, she continued to aid his campaign for the vice presidency from behind the scenes. In Washington, she was especially well-liked by fellow Democrats; the gregarious Franklin Pierce of New Hampshire, for one, observed that he would rather talk politics with Mrs. Polk than with her husband. But Sarah Childress Polk was not above making, or at least consuming, personal attacks on her husband's many political enemies, often to the physical discomfort of her husband. Try as Polk might to temper his wife's immodest conversational style—often by flashing a knowing look her way—he could not control her private correspondence. Whether from the

FIGURE 4.3 Sarah Childress Polk, ca. 1845. The wife of James K. Polk, she provided unwavering support for her husband's political aspirations. Lithograph by Nathaniel Currier.
Prints and Photographs Division, Library of Congress, LC-USZC2-2849.

venomous pen of Aaron Brown or from women in the higher echelons of
Tennessee society, Sarah Childress Polk was especially well-suited to act as a
social mouthpiece on behalf of her notoriously dour husband.[35]

Few others of Polk's political rivals elicited so intensive a scorn, a sign of just
how serious King's chances were for the nomination. In turn, Buchanan and
King wielded their pens in making gentler, though wittier characterizations.
Of the pair, King could be quite cutting toward his enemies. Ever since the
election of 1824, he had detested John Quincy Adams, whom he color-
fully described to Buchanan and others as "that black hearted old witch"
(Buchanan more succinctly found Adams to be "mulish" in disposition). But
he was also critical of men of the "inferior" sort, in which group he included
Aaron Brown and Isaac Toucey of Connecticut. He found Polk especially
to be a "very inferior man." More cautious than King, Buchanan carefully
avoided personal attacks in his correspondence, though he did employ the
popular phrase "Little Van" for the diminutive president (by contrast, King

thought Van Buren an "intriguing selfish politician"). In comparison to the correspondence of their enemies, the attacks of Buchanan and King did not contain the same sexual undertones. As practitioners of an intellectually refined manhood, they aimed, but did not always succeed, at taking the moral high ground.[36]

Although King professed hope for the vice presidential nomination, he was resigned to being passed over again. By March 1844, however, two interrelated events had changed the course not only of King's vice presidential prospects but also of his future in the Senate. The first involved the accidental explosion of a heavy gun aboard the *U.S.S. Princeton* on February 28. The US naval warship was on a Potomac River cruise carrying President John Tyler, Secretary of State Abel Upshur, and Navy Secretary Thomas Gilmore, among other dignitaries, when one of its heavy guns exploded, killing six people, including Upshur and Gilmore. Following the accident, Tyler endeavored to pick up the pieces of his administration. As part of the administrative overhaul Tyler offered King, whom the president "highly esteemed," the post of American minister to France, a position left vacant since the resignation of Lewis Cass. In selecting the moderate King, Tyler hoped to avoid a repeat of the prior debacle in putting forward the divisive Henry Wise, who had failed to obtain Senate confirmation, while still assigning a proslavery southerner to the post. The Senate unanimously approved its former president pro tempore, and even opposing partisan newspapers, such as the *Baltimore Patriot*, described King as "a gentleman of the Old School, conciliatory, courteous and polished in his bearing." Support for the appointment was nearly universal.[37]

But would King accept the mission? On April 12, King received official word from John C. Calhoun, Tyler's new secretary of state, of the appointment. Two days later, King dutifully replied: "I accept the Situation thus conferred on me, and will be prepared to take my Departure, whenever required by the President." Nevertheless, he felt deeply conflicted about leaving the Senate. As he explained to Alabama Governor Benjamin Fitzpatrick, he had "yielded to the opinion and advice of friends on whom I rely, and not from any desire of office on my part," adding "I am free to say that it is was with this hope alone that I consented to abandon a more honorable situation—one every way congenial to my feelings—and for a season to place myself far distant from my home, my country and friends." In private, King equally lamented his fate; to Joseph White, a Baltimore lawyer and an intimate friend of Buchanan, he declared that "if I had acted in accordance with my own feelings, I should still be a Member of that honorable Body." Although King's decision was tempered, he could not ignore the "advice of his friends," foremost among them his messmate Buchanan.[38]

In retrospect, the decision to accept the French mission appeared intimately tied to the decline of Buchanan's and King's presidential and vice presidential prospects. John Catron, a confidant of both Polk and Buchanan, later blamed the "coarse brutality" of the Washington *Globe* toward Buchanan during the winter of 1843 to 1844. The newspaper "drove out Buchanan; as he believed no such folly, and that the party was too weak, to elect any one presdt," he wrote in a letter to Polk. Buchanan's presidential fate, Catron thought, influenced King's decision to leave the Senate. In language that echoed the view of the pair as Siamese twins, Catron concluded: "Hence he quit & hence King, (B's shadow) went to France." Newspaper reports likewise noted that the recent "diminishing" of King's chance "by the competition of Messrs. Polk, [Andrew] Stevenson [of Virginia], and Dick Johnson" for the vice presidential nomination also influenced the decision.[39]

In April 1844, neither messmate saw a viable path to higher office for either themselves or any Democratic presidential candidate, but especially Martin Van Buren. Worse still, they feared that the likely election of Henry Clay would bring four more years of bitter partisan conflict to the Senate. At the same time, King also grasped a potential upside to a Clay victory in the fall: he would most certainly be recalled from France, at which point he might regain his seat in the Senate. Equally so, a stint in the foreign service would strengthen King's resume for the vice presidential nomination in 1848, much as Van Buren's appointment as Minister to England had done in 1832. In short, the spring of 1844 marked both a dark hour for the Jacksonian Democracy and the end of the bachelor's mess. Ten years of a shared domestic association, much like the Jacksonian Democratic coalition itself, seemed to have run its course.

Gone A-Wooing

In the days and weeks following their separation, Buchanan and King collected their thoughts and recorded them in long, heartfelt letters to one another. The exchange of letters beginning in early May 1844 revealed much about the intertwined nature of their long-standing bosom friendship. A persistent theme of isolation ran throughout the correspondence. Equally, their letters produced two of the most often quoted lines about their relationship: "I have gone a wooing to several gentlemen, but have not succeeded with any one of them," Buchanan reported, to which King replied, "I am selfish enough to hope you will not be able to procure an associate, who will cause you to feel no regret at our separation." But what do these lines really mean?[40]

With his appointment made final, King prepared to transport himself and members of his household overseas. In early May, he left Washington for New York, a move that elicited the usual chatter from the gallery of partisan pundits. One Whig newspaper noted that his "departure will leave one of your Senators in quite a widowed state," a clear reference to Buchanan, and added, "I understand that they bade each other adieu today, as Senators, with great mutual signs of tenderness." Others were more respectful of King, including a reporter who ironically figured the elderly bachelor as "the Father of the Senate." Journalist Anne Royall praised King's kindness and generosity. "The poor man, the desolate widow, the friendless orphan, will lose their best friend in his departure!" she exclaimed; Royall probably went too far in concluding that King was "beloved by all who knew him" or that he "never had an enemy." But even his political enemies found little to complain about in King's appointment. With his prior experience in Europe, his knowledge of French, and his understanding of the state of affairs in Washington, he was better prepared than most politicians of his era for a ministerial post.[41]

While in New York, King stayed as the guest of former Democratic congressman James J. Roosevelt and his wife Cornelia Van Ness Roosevelt. Within days, King had made the necessary arrangements for his trip; he also found time to write Buchanan. "Could I have taken you by the hand to say God bless you, before leaving Washington," he intoned, suggesting that his had been an unexpected departure, "I should have left it without regret." Perhaps the impending separation was too painful: King avoided saying good-bye in person and later "regret[ted] now that I did not do so, but the truth is I wished to avoid the pain of saying farewell." The separation had been understandably difficult for the two men, both in the unexpected conclusion of their shared domestic arrangement and in the many political uncertainties that lay ahead. To close the letter, King added a telling interrogatory, "Did you not write to Mrs. Roosevelt?"[42]

In fact, Buchanan had written to Cornelia Van Ness Roosevelt. Given its proximity to their separation, Buchanan's letter dated May 13, 1844, provided one of the few written accounts of his feelings of bosom friendship with King. To begin, he described the typical routines of Washington society. But he soon turned his attention to the more attractive image of the gathering of his friends in New York, playfully remarking to Mrs. Roosevelt: "I envy Colonel King the pleasure of meeting you & would give any thing in reason

FIGURE 4.4 Cornelia Van Ness Roosevelt, ca. 1857. The wife of Congressman John J. Roosevelt of New York, she was an intimate friend of both Buchanan and King. Salted paper print from glass negative by Matthew Brady. Courtesy Gilman Collection, Metropolitan Museum of Art.

to be of the party for a single week." Then he fretted: "I am 'solitary & alone,' having no companion in the house with me. I have gone a wooing to several gentlemen, but have not succeeded with any one of them." As a result, he predicted that he "should not be astonished to find myself married to some old maid who can nurse me when I am sick, provide good dinners for me when I am well & not expect from me any very ardent or romantic affection." Loneliness thus consumed him.[43]

Understandably, though inaccurately, many have interpreted these sentimental expressions as clear evidence of a sexual relationship between the two men. However, many of these same expressions undergirded the language of intimate male friendship during this period. Moreover, such phrases commonly appeared in their correspondence with other public men. For example, Jonathan Messersmith Foltz, the Navy surgeon and erstwhile visitor to the bachelor's mess, used the same construction in a letter to Buchanan, as did Cary Nicholas and Bedford Brown in their letters with male friends. For his part, King quite frequently used the phrase "take by the hand." In another letter written shortly after his May message to Buchanan, he declared: "I shall be very happy to take by the hand my old & valuable Friend [Commodore Jacob] Jones before leaving the country." That King wished to "take by the hand" his friend Jones, who at the time was commander of the port of New York and by no means an intimate friend, suggests a more prosaic meaning. Rather than expressive of sexual intimacy, the phrase conveyed the desire of one public man to reinforce the sometimes-distant ties that bound them together.[44]

In the same way, the phrase " 'solitary and alone' " has been equally skewed by modern readers. Throughout his correspondence, Buchanan used these words, always within quotations marks, in a very particular way. He was alluding to a famous speech delivered by Thomas Hart Benton in January 1837 that had favored King's expunging resolution of President Jackson. In the speech, Benton railed against the congressional censure of Jackson and argued that the president ought to be "expunged" of any previous reprimand. "Solitary and alone, and amidst the jeers and taunts of my opponents," Benton concluded histrionically, "I put this ball in motion." His speech, and particularly the phrase "solitary and alone," caused an uproar in the popular press. One Whig cartoonist mocked the Missouri senator as a tumble bug dragging along the expunging resolution—with the names of messmates Buchanan, Brown, Nicholas, and King listed—in his oversized carapace, the text bubble above quoting Benton's speech. From there, other politicians adopted the phrase in their correspondence. As both Buchanan and King had voiced strong support for the expunging resolution, they had naturally internalized Benton's phrase and, like others from the period, sprinkled it throughout their correspondence.[45]

Similarly, few have recognized the intimate nature of the relationship between Buchanan and Cornelia Van Ness Roosevelt, the actual recipient of his letter. The daughter of Cornelius Van Ness, the former governor of Vermont and the American minister to Spain during the Jackson administration, Cornelia Van Ness (born 1810) enchanted Buchanan from the moment of

FIGURE 4.5 "N. Tom O'Logical Studies: The Great Tumble Bug of Missouri, Bent-on Rolling his Ball." The cartoon depicts an insect-like Senator Thomas Hart Benton of Missouri pushing a ball marked "Expunging Resolution," with the names of messmates Buchanan, Brown, Nicholas, and King included in the "List of the Black Knights." Benton speaks the line: "Solitary and alone and amidst the jeers and taunts of my opponents. I put this Ball in motion." Published by Henry R. Robinson, 1837. Prints and Photographs Division, Library of Congress, LC-USZ62-91422.

their meeting in the late 1820s or early 1830s. As Buchanan admitted to her many years later: "You captivated me at once & I have ever since remained faithful & true; & am now, in my old age, your devoted friend." Years later, Secretary of State William Marcy confirmed that Buchanan still "takes a wonderful interest in that family . . . and once courted . . . one of the daughters himself." Although Cornelia had apparently declined these advances—she married James J. Roosevelt in 1831—the pair still felt a deep affection for one another (Buchanan once traveled to see her in New York as the "principal object of my visit"). During James Roosevelt's single term in Congress from 1841 to 1843, the couple hosted numerous social gatherings, and in the process, the intimate circle of Buchanan and the Roosevelts expanded to include King. One year later, the new connection led King to stay with the Roosevelts during his time in New York.[46]

The letter of May 13, 1844, from Buchanan to Cornelia Van Ness Roosevelt also illustrated the practical difficulty of finding new messmates with whom to "unite." Whether or not he cared to admit it, Buchanan had thrown in his political and domestic lot with his bachelor messmates, of whom King had been the last surviving member. Most likely the unnamed "several gentlemen" whom Buchanan "wooed," or asked to join him at the mess on F Street, were quite content with their own living arrangements. They may also have been uninterested in joining the mess of an old bachelor and waning political operator. Thus rejected, Buchanan sought epistolary refuge in his bachelorhood, a recurring theme throughout his letters to female friends. His lament for "some old maid who can nurse me" was more theatrical performance than reality, for he had already hired Esther Parker to keep house back in Lancaster. Yet even at age fifty-three, a marriage to an "old maid"—a term to describe an unmarried woman beyond the socially accepted age of marriage—was not out of the question for an "uncertain" bachelor. Such a pairing would have relieved him of the "ardent or romantic affection" expected by a younger, more amorous female partner. This outcome must have appeared attractive to Buchanan. In fact, he would pursue exactly this sort of union in the years ahead.[47]

Cornelia Van Ness Roosevelt passed along Buchanan's letter to King, who wrote back immediately to his former messmate. "I am selfish enough to hope you will not be able to procure an associate, who will cause you to feel no regret at our separation," he responded with his usual sentimentality. He did not wish to feel replaceable by another congressman, after spending the better portion of the past ten years living with Buchanan. "For myself, I shall feel lonely in the midst of Paris, for there I shall have no Friends with whom I can commune as with my own thoughts." King's impending isolation in France would prevent further "communion"—a word that he used here and in other letters to mean sharing his thoughts—with his "Friends," a word he usually capitalized in reference to political friends, or allies. Although King brought relatives and younger staffers with him, the transatlantic separation cut him off from his network of political friends. Ultimately, his letter suggests, he wanted to believe that his friendship with Buchanan meant something more than a mere political expedient. But had it?[48]

This exchange of letters among Buchanan, King, and Cornelia Van Ness Roosevelt revealed the unequal terms of their relationship. King felt more respect and admiration for Buchanan than he received in return. To Buchanan, their separation proved personally painful only in the short-term. In an effort to woo as messmates Matilda Childress Catron and Supreme Court Justice John Catron, he hinted at how good it would be to lay his "old head on [the] young shoulders" of other men's wives, for "it is not good for a man to be alone." In reply, Judge Catron noted that he had arranged to form a mess with his wife and two other Supreme Court justices, James Wayne of Pennsylvania and Peter Daniel of Virginia, and that he would happily include Buchanan as well. Within a few weeks, the ever-ambitious Buchanan had moved on to new prospects. Simply put, King was more expendable to Buchanan than Buchanan was to King in turn.[49]

Washington society openly gossiped about the two men in the wake of King's departure. Observers often reached back to classical antiquity for a comparison. The Whig-controlled *National Intelligencer* thought them the "Orestes and Pylades of the Senate," a reference to the well-known pair of intimate male friends and lovers from Greek mythology. Concerning their separation, the still embittered Whig editor William Seaton wrote caustically: "The only regret I have heard expressed is that two such long-tried and faithful friends as Messrs. Buchanan and King should be separated after a social and political union of so many years. Talk of the cords of love, the *viniculum matrimonii* [Latin for "bond of marriage"], the loves of Jonathan and David, which passeth that of women—all is mere matter of moonshine compared to the regard which these two worthy bachelors entertain for each other." Although Whig editors rarely failed to disparage their Democratic rivals whenever possible, they accurately underscored the "social and political union" that Buchanan and King had forged over the previous decade.[50]

In political terms at least, King need not have feared that Buchanan would procure a new associate. By 1844, each man had become so publicly connected to the other that they had become the Siamese twins of the Tyler administration. The Whig-leaning Philadelphia *North American*, for example, dubbed King as Buchanan's "*alter ego*," while a reporter for the Charleston *Mercury* (another Whig rag) called them those "two princes of bachelors." Still, their intimate association had obtained for them a measure of political power, even a kind of political royalty, in the affairs of the national Democratic Party. Though the bonhomie of their domestic intimacy had ended, they would reach for greater heights together in the upcoming decade. For the time being, however, their efforts to woo the support of their political party, as well as the personal affections of their fellow congressmen, had proven a failure.[51]

* * *

To start 1841, the prospects for four years of Whig control cast a worrisome shadow on the future of the Democratic Party. But the Whig rise to power came with a catch. The accidental rise of President John Tyler reintroduced an irreconcilable partisan element between the Congress and the White House. As the Whigs dominated the legislative agenda, the president checked their program with his veto. For the Democrats, the unexpected turn of events preserved the status quo for nearly four years. The next presidential contest would thus prove crucial to both parties' futures, as each side actively sought to attract new voters to its ranks. By 1844, the contest for political supremacy had reached new levels of partisanship.

At the bachelor's mess, the events of the Tyler years proved equally pivotal. The friendships of the mess, inherently tenuous by nature, slowly weakened through the Whig ascendancy of the early 1840s. Buchanan and King watched as first Cary Nicholas, then William Roane, and finally C. C. Clay departed the mess and politics itself. By necessity Buchanan and King grew more interconnected. This happenstance fusion in the face of political events left them vulnerable to the changing political imperatives of the day and to the virulent gossip that circulated about them. Finally, in 1844, when the mess itself collapsed, Buchanan was left to fend for himself, without much success. He was on his own.

All along, the bosom friendship of Buchanan and King, forged by the political exigencies of the Second Party System and personal proclivities of unmarried men, had been defined by bachelorhood. At first a kind of political marriage, formed of convenience, the arrangement eventually turned into something more intimate. The two political bachelors shared a reciprocal relationship that placed the success of each man as its central aim. Yet like so many marriages, the terms of their attachment were unequal. In the long separation that followed, the uneven nature of their bond would become painfully evident.

5

Ministering, 1844–1848

BY 1844, THE country had collectively fixated its attention on a new issue: Texas. Ever since 1836, when Texas had won its independence from Mexico, the United States had been seeking a way to bring this vast southwestern country into the Union. Yet Jackson and then Van Buren hesitated to force the issue. Two major obstacles stood in the way of immediate annexation: first, the disputed western border between the independent Republic of Texas and Mexico, and second, the outstanding indemnity claims of many Americans against the Mexican government. Equally so, neither president wished to precipitate an unnecessary war when a peaceful resolution to these questions might be attained. In the minds of many politicians, Texas would naturally enter the Union in due time.[1]

The question of Texas annexation spurred a related concept of "manifest destiny." The popular doctrine held that the western lands of North America belonged to the United States by a preordained right. Ambitious politicians obsessed over the possible acquisition of the vast territories of Oregon, New Mexico, and California. Equally, they understood that the presidential election of 1844 would hinge on the issue of expansion. But who would guide the nation during this new era of American expansionism? On the eve of the 1844 presidential election, Whig candidate Henry Clay of Kentucky and his supporters believed him to be the most qualified man for the job. But Clay could not bring himself to support Texas annexation outright, and by a thin margin, the electorate rebuked him for a third and final time. Instead, they elevated a little-known Democratic challenger, James Polk, often called "Young Hickory" after his Tennessee forbearer Andrew Jackson, to the presidency. For the next four years, the Democrats controlled the levers of statecraft.[2]

The Polk victory set into motion a series of events that shifted the course of Democratic party politics and unexpectedly revived the political fortunes of Buchanan and King. For King, prolonged ministerial service brought mixed results. Diplomatically, he succeeded at his primary mission to assert America's right to annex Texas and thus to thwart Anglo-French efforts to entice the Lone Star Republic to remain independent. Likewise, he gracefully represented his country's position in France during the burgeoning American conflict with Mexico. While at times pleasant, his two years abroad separated him from his many friends back home. Nevertheless, he remained intimately attached to Buchanan. For more than two years, he ministered to the diplomatic needs of the nation and indirectly to those of his former messmate—he advised him about political and professional issues. By October 1846, he journeyed home with little prospect of returning to the scene of national power.

Buchanan appeared to fare better than his old messmate, at least initially. His selection to head the State Department placed him in a long line of political succession that had once carried several past secretaries of state—Jefferson, Madison, Monroe, Quincy Adams, and Van Buren among them—directly or indirectly to the presidency. Additionally, this position placed him at the center of a presidential administration absorbed with foreign policy issues. During the Polk years, he proved critical to enacting the president's twin foreign policy aims: to settle the occupation of the Oregon territory with Great Britain and to acquire land from Mexico. Yet war constantly threatened. On the Oregon question, his cautious and skillful diplomacy with the European powers prevented overt hostilities, even as it caused his first serious rupture with the president. In the lead-up to the American invasion of Mexico, he similarly managed the diplomatic effort, at least at first, to find a peaceful resolution to the fighting. As the events of the Polk administration progressed, he embraced a new expansionist philosophy; this represented a calculated maneuver to place himself as a leading presidential candidate in 1848.

Ironies abounded in the new roles assigned to King and Buchanan. Two inherently conservative politicians became spokesmen for the expansionist mood sweeping across the country. But the Polk presidency also transformed their bosom friendship from one of domestic intimacy to one of political superior (Buchanan) to subordinate (King). Although they still corresponded regularly, the personal intimacy of their friendship slowly receded, leaving a more purely political relationship in its wake. Simultaneously, their transatlantic separation occasioned renewed efforts at romantic courtship; Washington society expected both men to try once again to find wives. Though flirtations abounded, old age and their continued government service lessened the need for a companionate marriage. Instead, each man increasingly relied upon a favored niece to mitigate this ever-present societal expectation. By the end of the Polk administration, they had accepted their roles as bachelor uncles within their respective families and, in a larger sense, within their country as well. In this avuncular mode as bachelor statesmen, Buchanan and King ministered to the diplomatic needs of an expanding nation.

Godfathers to Their Young Countrymen

As a precursor to the eventual annexation of Texas, President John Tyler believed that the time had come to settle the ongoing boundary dispute and indemnity claims with Mexico. In the process the president, who lacked the support of either major party, hoped to attract a wider following for the upcoming presidential election. As such, Tyler arranged for a "Treaty of Annexation" between Texas and the United States and sent it along to the Senate. In the ensuing debate, Buchanan cautiously supported the agreement and issued a measured defense of annexation more generally. Without Whig support, however, the 1844 Treaty of Annexation failed.[3]

On the same day that the Senate received the Treaty of Annexation, King received the instructions for his French mission. Secretary of State Calhoun officially ordered him to "strengthen, if possible, the very friendly relations so happily subsisting between the United States and France." Yet Calhoun may have unofficially directed King to take a different approach to his mission. Just one day earlier, the secretary learned of renewed efforts of England and France to prevent the American annexation of Texas. Although the Monroe Doctrine compelled the United States to resist European intervention in the western hemisphere, France equally demanded settlement of its citizens' indemnity claims with Mexico; to enforce their claims, France sent warships to Mexico. Additionally, both England and France sent diplomatic envoys to Texas urging the government to remain independent. Such a course would materially benefit the Europeans by preventing the further expansion of the United States. Thus, King's true mission in 1844 was diplomatically weightier and more vital to foreign policy concerns than it might appear at first glance. He was charged with nothing less than to determine the intentions of England and France and to stake firmly the American claim to Texas annexation.[4]

From New York, King arranged to travel overseas. He informed Calhoun that he would "sail on the 16 direct to Havre—that being the first packet in which I could procure comfortable accomodations." The party that embarked upon the *Silvia de Grasse* included legation secretary Dr. Jacob L. Martin, niece Catherine Margaret Ellis (age twenty-eight), nephews Alfred J. Beck (age twenty-six) and William Thomas King (age nineteen), and his personal valet, the enslaved African American man John Bell, who was probably in his late teens. Once in France, King quickly established his official position and social standing in the city. Although he received an annual salary of nine thousand dollars, it barely enabled him to afford the rent on the grand home at 100 Rue St. Domingue. Not to be deterred, King's lavish entertaining style "left a classic fame in Paris" even years after his mission had ended.[5]

Of the group traveling with King to France, Catherine Margaret Ellis was the most intimate family relation. She had never been abroad and might never have done so had it not been for the sudden death of her husband two years earlier. From that point forward, Ellis became hostess and constant traveling companion to her uncle; in turn, King considered her like a daughter. Perhaps unsurprisingly, she had once tried to nudge her uncle toward marriage, but he evaded the effort with typical self-effacement, calling himself

FIGURE 5.1 William R. King. His mission to France separated him from Buchanan for four years. Engraving by W.H. Dougal from a daguerreotype by Whitehurst, 1854. The Miriam and Ira D. Wallach Division of Art, Prints, and Photographs, New York Public Library.

an "Old Bachelor" and adding in a telling note: "When I see you, we will
discuss the important subject of marriage to which you have called my attention; I will only say that I see but little prospect of giving you an aunt
very shortly." Whether or not King recounted the story of his long-lost love
for the Russian princess, Ellis dropped the subject of marriage in their future
correspondence.[6]

By 1844, Ellis had already come to know her uncle's most important friend
in Washington. Buchanan never failed to send his kind remembrances to Ellis,
and he may even have expressed a romantic interest in her. In a letter from
1842, King served as proxy for his messmate, writing to Ellis: "Your friend
Buchanan was highly flattered by your accession to the ranks of his friends,"
and added that he "counts most sanguinely on receiving the vote of Alabama
by means of your influence." To Buchanan, King remarked upon the "extrava-
gant terms of admiration" that his friend displayed for Ellis and in turn jested
to his niece that they "might excite the jealousy of a certain gentleman in
Tuscaloosa [namely, her husband Harvey Ellis] who professes to have claims
upon you, to the exclusion of all others." When possible, Buchanan warmly
recommended Ellis to his friends, such as when he told Cornelia Van Ness
Roosevelt in his May 13, 1844, letter: "I was acquainted with her some years
ago & liked her very much." In the years ahead Buchanan and Ellis remained
on cordial terms, their relationship always triangulated through King. In time
a fourth member joined their set: Buchanan's niece Harriet Lane.[7]

For King, other members of the travel party hoped that his second time
abroad would prove the marital charm. Nineteen-year-old nephew William
Thomas King wrote optimistically to his father: "The old man is looking exceedingly well and when he is dressed in his new wig and new hat I would
stake him against any old cad of his age, and perhaps you think his days of
conquest over, but I can tell you are very much mistaken, for I assure you
that there is a young lady here who never sees him without having hysterics
for an hour after he leaves her." But the nephew added glumly, "I fear he will
never add to the number of the family, as he seems now satisfied to give away
the young brides and stand Godfather to his young countrymen." Buchanan's
prior observation about King's waning sexual interest in women was confirmed once more.[8]

The remarks of the nineteen-year-old William Thomas King can be
dismissed as youthful naivete. Yet King's political friends at home also expected marriage from him. Francis Pickens of South Carolina, an intimate
friend of the bachelor's mess, wrote in this vein to Buchanan. "I hope if [King]
comes home he will bring a French lady it would suit him well," Pickens

observed of King's refined manners. "He was a little French before he went, and he must be very much so now. Tell him if he does intend to bring out a lady, for God's sake, let it be no French or Italian countess." Though tongue-in-cheek, Pickens did not jest entirely—the marriage of the famous English poet Lord Byron to the Italian noblewoman Teresa, Contessa Guiccioli, had filtered into the American popular imagination. Although often compared in his physical features to Byron, especially in his flowing curls, King's second European journey brought him no closer to wedding a woman than his first trip overseas thirty years earlier. His Frenchified ways apparently did not include marriage.[9]

On July 1, King presented his credentials to the French Court of St. Cloud. At a formal dinner held on July 4, French King Louis Phillipe discussed the US Senate's failed Texas annexation treaty with the new American envoy. King insisted that domestic political considerations had sunk the effort; in return, Louis Phillipe expressed his personal view that Texas should remain an independent state. King replied that such an outcome was short-sighted, as an expanded American nation presented more robust opportunities for trade with Europe. Following their conversation, Louis Phillipe assured him that "no steps would be taken by his government, in the slightest degree hostile" to the United States. Ashbel Smith, who joined King at the Court of St. Cloud as envoy from the Republic of Texas, seconded this view, arguing that "such a course would give umbrage to the American Government." However, Louis Phillipe's personal sentiments on Texas—to say nothing of his own genealogical connection to King's French Huguenot ancestors—did not encompass the full view of the French government. François Guizot, the French minister of foreign affairs, administered the nation's foreign policy. By the end of summer, King finally received assurances from Guizot that "France had acted for herself with no other power," as he reported to Calhoun. The question of European non-intervention in Texas appeared settled.[10]

To Buchanan, King presented a more revealing version of events. Confidentially, he questioned his own skill and talent as a foreign minister and wrote of how his "hands trembled like an alarmed school Boy before the dreaded Pedagogue." Although he had finished his prepared remarks, he lamented his perceived physical failings, likely due to the lingering effects of the overseas voyage. "My unfortunate delivery, convinces me that I am not fitted for diplomacy," he admitted, "& causes me to regret still more, that I ever consented to accept of a situation for which I am so illy qualified." But he added: "All this is for yourself alone, from whom I disguise nothing, but it had determined me absolutely to avail myself of the earliest occasion which offers, to get back to my own country & permit our high spirited & proud people, to be represented here by some one, who has more of the spirit of a man." These bodily failings aside, King keenly articulated the various dynamics at play in the Texas question. He ended his letter on a more amicable note, lamenting that Buchanan had not written to him. He further asked his former messmate to procure some "good Madeira Wine" for him in Paris. "In thus making you both Merchant & Banker," he wrote, "I can only say that it will afford me sincere pleasure to act in the double capacity, whenever you may require any articles the produce of France." Thus closed the first of many such letters exchanged between the two men.[11]

While King ministered to American interests abroad, Buchanan turned his attention to domestic politics. In May 1844 the Democrats gathered at the Egyptian Saloon of the Odd Fellows Hall in Baltimore. On the first ballot, former president Martin Van Buren received a simple majority of the votes. But he had not received the necessary two-thirds majority required by the convention's rules (King's old measure for party unity still held), likely because he had previously expressed opposition to the annexation of Texas. Then, in a surprising development, second-choice candidate Lewis Cass of Michigan surpassed Van Buren in the balloting, but he too failed to gain the needed two-thirds. After several further ballots neither Van Buren nor Cass obtained the nomination, largely because two separate handfuls of delegates remained steadfast in their respective support for Buchanan and Richard Mentor Johnson. A compromise candidate was clearly needed.[12]

Enter James Polk. His success in pushing King aside for the party's number two spot had simultaneously elevated his standing as a possible presidential candidate. At the convention, his Tennessee supporters persuaded George Bancroft of Massachusetts to propose Polk as a compromise candidate. The convention delegates quickly hurrahed their acclamation for Young Hickory, and one state after another switched its votes from Van Buren or Cass to Polk. To add personal insult to political injury, former bachelor messmate William Henry Roane solidified the convention's emerging consensus when he declared the Old Dominion's unanimous support for Polk. In an ironic twist, the convention chose George Dallas, a long-time supporter of Van Buren and Buchanan's great Pennsylvania rival, as Polk's running mate. "The Texas question," Buchanan later lamented, "was the Grecian horse that entered our camp."[13]

The news of Polk's nomination stunned the nation. He was quickly dubbed a "dark horse" candidate, as he had entered the national convention with little possibility for obtaining the nomination. With the selection of Polk and

Dallas, the national prospects of Buchanan and King fell to a new low. Yet neither man was easily discouraged by the setback. Publicly, Buchanan declared
his prior withdrawal from the presidential race to be an "act of deliberate duty
as well as of sound policy," while he called Polk "a faithful and true Democrat"
whose "character both personal & political is above reproach." Privately, he
was more candid. "When you & I served with Mr. Polk in Congress," he ac-
idly remarked to one old friend, "neither of us probably supposed that he
would ever be President." For his part, King thought that Polk and Dallas
were "bad selections." He now believed, incorrectly as it turned out, the election of Henry Clay to be a foregone conclusion. "Had you been the nominee which I had hoped," he complained to Buchanan, "Clay would never
have been President." Regardless, Buchanan campaigned across Pennsylvania
and parts of Ohio in support of the Democratic ticket and counseled Polk
on the tricky question of the protectionist Tariff of 1842. In the final count
Polk received 170 electoral votes, including those of both Pennsylvania and
Alabama, and soundly defeated Whig challenger Henry Clay.[14]

Our Antient Friendship

As his first task, President-elect Polk assembled a cabinet of subordinates
that balanced the Democratic Party's various regional and ideological wings.
These included William Marcy of New York as secretary of war, Robert
Walker of Mississippi as secretary of the treasury, John Y. Mason of Virginia
as attorney general, George Bancroft of Massachusetts at the navy department, and Cave Johnson as postmaster general. For secretary of state, Polk
chose Buchanan who had been strongly recommended by the Pennsylvania
delegates to the electoral college for the position. Nevertheless, Vice
President-elect Dallas privately complained about the choice. "I am resolved
that no one shall be taken from Pennsylvania who is notoriously hostile to
the Vice-President," Dallas warned cabinet nominee Robert Walker, adding
"if such a choice be made my relationship with the administration are at once
at an end." The old divisions engendered by Pennsylvania's factional politics
still ran deep.[15]

Dallas had good reason to fear a Buchanan nomination, since it would enhance an already powerful rival and further dilute his own ability to distribute
patronage. Dallas also did not particularly care for Buchanan. For years, they
had competed for high-level federal appointments in a game of political hop-
scotch. First, Jackson had appointed Buchanan minister to Russia, then Van
Buren appointed Dallas to the same post during his presidency. Next, Dallas

was elected to the US Senate, then Buchanan was elected following the end of his term. From there, Van Buren offered the vacant attorney general post to Buchanan, and after he had rejected the position, he turned to Dallas (who did likewise). And so it went. But in 1844, Vice President-elect Dallas could not stop the Buchanan nomination. To his wife, he confided that Polk had made "a most dangerous choice." Ultimately, Dallas stayed the course with Polk.[16]

If Polk's own vice president questioned Buchanan's selection, why did the president-elect choose him for the top cabinet post? Simply put, he needed Buchanan. Polk aimed to transform American relations with its continental and overseas neighbors. An industrious micro-manager, he also desired to control the foreign policy of his administration; the punctilious Buchanan made for the perfect henchman to execute the ambitious president's agenda. His pro-southern leanings equally appealed. Ironically, Polk's political operative Aaron Brown, who earlier slandered both King and Buchanan, also encouraged the appointment: "[Buchanan] is a man you know of calm temperament [in] foreighn [sic] affairs & he & his state can be more relied upon on by the South than the N.Y. Democrats." Even the usually embittered Andrew Jackson thought that Buchanan would "execute the duties [of office] with ability." Following these recommendations, Polk confirmed Buchanan's selection as secretary of state.[17]

From his mansion at Rue St. Domingue, King welcomed the belated news of Polk's victory. Though an ocean away, King grasped the complexities of the domestic political scene and advised his old messmate with clear-eyed realism. He greatly feared that the internal divisions within the Democracy threatened to overwhelm the seemingly pliable president-elect. "Were he a man of great firmness of character, which I fear he is not, and would take the helm of state into his own hands, regardless of cliques, or sectional influences, he probably would be able to steer clear of the breakers by which he will be surrounded," he wrote to Buchanan, "but if he wavers, he is lost and the party with him." King also welcomed the news that Buchanan might be appointed to head the State Department. Yet he correctly feared that Vice President Dallas would "look with an eye of jealousy on your being placed in the line of safe precedents" to the presidency.[18]

Although King counseled Buchanan from abroad, the former messmates no longer shared the same social customs and obligations. As such, Buchanan alone mingled with members of the Polk White House, now carefully managed by Sarah Childress Polk. Despite their earlier social friction, Buchanan and the new first lady were already well-acquainted from her husband's many congressional terms. "I shall both expect & desire to be a favourite" of Mrs. Polk, he wrote optimistically to Matilda Childress Catron, wife of the Supreme Court justice and a cousin to the first lady. In a reference to his bachelorhood, he declared, "I intend to make one more attempt to change my wretched condition, and should I fail under her auspices I shall then surrender in despair." Once again, marriage seemed a real possibility to Buchanan. Although nearing fifty-five, he took comfort from the knowledge that one after another of his former colleagues from the bachelor's mess had married much younger brides. With good reason, he had become convinced that his de facto position as a member of the president's inner circle offered a viable path to the altar.[19]

In spite of her earlier convictions, Sarah Childress Polk took a liking to the sole bachelor in her husband's cabinet, as did several of her unmarried relatives. While the Oregon territory boundary question raged during cabinet meetings in 1845, Buchanan engaged in a playful banter with Polk niece, Joanna Lucinda Rucker. To a relative, Rucker described Buchanan as "a bachelor of fifty; he is very grey but is decidedly the finest looking gentleman belonging to the Cabinet." Rucker also noted that he "says he is resolved upon marrying a Tennessean. I understand that he thought last night I looked young enough for him (he is but little older than Pa!)," she exclaimed. This comment notwithstanding, Buchanan and Rucker became intimate, though chaste, friends. "You are a girl after my own heart," he wrote Rucker as the Polk administration came to a close, "& I never can forget you." Thus slipped one more possibility for marriage into platonic friendship.[20]

However, Buchanan's most serious flirtation derived from his friendly association with another former first lady. Anna Coles Payne was the niece of the elderly Dolley Payne Todd Madison, by then a fixture of Washington society. In one letter, the "Lovely Miss Annie," as Buchanan called the twenty-five-year-old, requested that he "write poetry for her." Ever a self-conscious if maudlin poet, Buchanan demurred: "I have never been more successful in courting the Muses than in wooing the terrestreal fair." To Annie Payne—who one contemporary described as "not handsome, her features being irregular," but who Buchanan found to be "a cheerful, gay & fascinating girl"—he revealed that his friendships with women had been "more sincere & steady" than those with men. But "what am I now to Annie Payne?" he asked. He reminded her that he had once called her a "Harum-Scarum," a light-hearted reference to her famous merrymaking. Although he saved a silhouette cut-out of Payne's profile and also kept an album devoted to her (and perhaps others), he seemed unable to move beyond this avuncular interest in the young woman, instead praising her "devotion to her good & venerable Aunt." When he later learned of Payne's marriage to James Causten, a man much closer to her own age, he expressed sardonic surprise at the news, having been her "devoted admirer for so many years."[21]

Buchanan's flirtation with the mischievous Annie Payne typified his social course at middle age. On one level, he perceived a political advantage from a connection to Dolley Madison. She was an immense favorite of the Polk White House and a woman whose blessing still carried significant

FIGURE 5.2 Anna Payne and Dolley Madison. Buchanan called Payne the "Lovely Miss Annie," and he later served as an executor to the estate of Dolley Madison. Daguerreotype by Matthew Brady, 1848. Courtesy Greensboro Historical Museum, Greensboro, NC.

weight in Washington; accordingly, Buchanan could be found socializing with her around the capital. Likewise, as secretary of state, Buchanan was expected to host social events at his own residence. Without the help of the women of Washington, he was unlikely to turn his bachelor's quarters on F Street into a welcoming social environment. As the *New York Herald* noted, "Mr. Buchanan has not the materials with which to lead off in the Mazourka or La Polka." A proper hostess—and one who was the niece and adopted daughter of Dolley Madison—could enhance his standing in Washington.[22]

On another level, Buchanan likely never intended for his flirtation with Annie Payne to move beyond the playful "bagatelle" that he had so long practiced with younger women. The prospects of a May–December romance appeared even less likely when his adopted sixteen-year-old niece, Harriet Lane, arrived in Washington to attend the Georgetown Visitation Convent. With the Polks' blessing, Buchanan integrated his niece into the White House inner circle; soon she "presided at his hospitable board" at his F Street house, as one remembered. In time Harriet Lane became a favorite of both the Polks and Treasury Secretary Walker, with whose family she spent several summers. In a daguerreotype that perfectly captured the social circle of the Polk White House, Lane was pictured standing between her uncle and Joanna Lucinda Rucker, followed by Cave Johnson, Sarah Childress Polk, Robert Walker, James Polk, Dolley Madison, and former Buchanan messmates Matilda Childress Catron and John Catron. So close were Buchanan and Dolley Madison that she named him an executor of her estate. Anna Payne, curiously absent from the White House photograph, may have resented her former suitor's lack of romantic will. Still she cherished her friendship with the Old Buck in the years ahead.[23]

As Buchanan flirted his way through Washington society, King grew more distant in his affections for his former messmate. "I had sworn in my wrath that I would never again employ my almost disabled hand in writing to you, untill you condescended to give me an answer," he scolded Buchanan in one letter. After several months without a reply, he glumly concluded that Buchanan's letters must have failed to reach France. "My pride, to say nothing of friendship, brings me to this conclusion," he said. King continued to seethe with annoyance at having received "not a single line since I have been in France." Yet Buchanan had followed his former messmate's instructions in other ways; King reported that he received a box of Madeira wine on the last steamer. The gesture mollified King, and he hoped that Buchanan might yet visit Paris to "enjoy the gayeties of this city of pleasure." He once more offered the

FIGURE 5.3 The Polk White House social circle. The photo shows (from left to right) James Buchanan, Harriet Lane, Joanna Lucinda Rucker, Cave Johnson, Sarah Childress Polk, Robert Walker, James K. Polk, Dolley Madison, Matilda Catron, and an unidentified male (probably John Catron). Daguerreotype by an unknown artist, ca. 1848. Courtesy George Eastman Museum, Rochester, NY.

epistolary olive branch, admitting "in despight of all your neglect, I still cling with fondness to our antient friendship." Finally, after nine months abroad, King received his first private letter from Buchanan, and their friendly correspondence resumed.[24]

The reason for Buchanan's silence stemmed from both the torturously slow nature of transatlantic communication by packet ship and the intense pressures of governing. He faced a constant swarm of office seekers who beseeched him for political appointments (at this thought, King quipped that Buchanan "sent them away charmed with your affability"). Additionally, Buchanan confronted two immediate crises: Texas annexation and the Oregon boundary question. In March, Polk sent John Slidell as American envoy to Mexico; he was to negotiate a settlement to the boundary question, but ultimately the Mexican government rebuffed him for bureaucratic reasons. From Washington, Buchanan followed Calhoun's precedent and instructed American foreign ministers to thwart any European interference on Texas annexation. Consequently, he sent the first of his official letters of instruction to King, in which he expressed his surprise that France and Great Britain "were now acting in concert" to block Texas annexation. King replied that there was "scarcely any sacrifice which England would not make to prevent Texas from coming into our possession." Their official despatches and instructions followed in this vein over the coming months.[25]

In addition to the commotion raised by Texas annexation, Buchanan studied the disputed boundary between the United States and England in the Oregon territory. At his inauguration, President Polk announced the "clear and unquestionable" right of the United States to occupy the whole Oregon territory; this included a large portion of land extending to the 54° 40' latitude line in British Columbia. Polk sought clarification and instructed Buchanan to work with Richard Pakenham, the British minister to the United States. Accordingly, Buchanan noted the president's "determination ... that the British government will recognize his sincere and anxious desire to cultivate the most friendly relations between the two countries." He then attempted a compromise solution by fixing the border at the 49th parallel, a line that extended the existing boundary between Canada and the United States east of Oregon. But Pakenham rebuffed Buchanan's solution, largely over the division of Vancouver Island, leaving Polk to respond to the British obstinacy.[26]

As the events of 1845 unfolded, King received numerous official despatches from Buchanan. But once more, no personal communications accompanied this diplomatic correspondence. Again and again, King chafed and admonished Buchanan in his private letters: "You might have snatched a few moments to commune with an old Friend, who feels the liveliest in all that concerns you, personally and politically." When a personal letter finally arrived, King breathed a sigh of relief: "I had come to the conclusion that our friendly intercourse was destined to die a natural death." Following another period of silence, however, King return to his old complaint. "Now as my last four [letters] have commanded no attention," he wrote, "it seems to be time that I should take the hint, and annoy you no more." Still, he persisted in his unofficial correspondence, penning a private letter with every diplomatic despatch, and revealed his continued willingness to assist his former messmate. Eventually, he knew, Buchanan would write back.[27]

Though time did not often permit him to write, Buchanan carefully read each of King's private letters. From his friend, Buchanan received intelligence that both England and France might collectively contest, by force if necessary, the Oregon boundary issue. In April, King advised Buchanan in no uncertain terms: "If practicable avoid a war for the present if it can be done without sacrifice of our undoubted rights; and I trust I need not say that I know you too well to believe for a moment that you would make such sacrifices to avoid even greater evils than war." He also reminded Buchanan that "we should not hesitate to divide the Territory by fixing our northern boundary at latitude 49 to settle the question." Buchanan implicitly concurred, but President Polk demanded a stronger response to the Pakenham letter. Unlike the president, however, Buchanan's position as secretary of state afforded him a clearer picture of the ramifications of enflaming the Oregon question. The stage was set for a showdown between the president and the secretary of state.[28]

All Minor Annoyances

The first significant split between Buchanan and Polk took place at a cabinet meeting on August 26, 1845. In response to British minister Pakenham's rejection of the president's proposal to set the Oregon boundary at the 49th parallel, Polk wanted to withdraw the offer, to which Buchanan agreed. Yet the secretary of state counseled some kind of written reply, arguing that "the people of the U. S. would not be willing to sustain a war for the country North of 49°, and that if we were to have war he would like for it to be for some better cause, for some of our rights of person or property or of National honour violated." Polk ignored this plea and instructed Buchanan to withdraw the compromise offer. "Well," Buchanan said glumly at the next cabinet meeting, "the Deed is done." This first open rift with Buchanan so bothered Polk that he began to detail his thoughts in a private diary, starting with the events of that fateful August day. Over the next three and a half years, Polk's diary revealed a mixture of respect, exasperation, and bafflement for his secretary of state.[29]

Meanwhile, the Oregon question was far from settled. In October, after further negotiation had failed to produce a meaningful solution, Polk instructed Buchanan to deliver another letter that reiterated the American position. In this second meeting with Pakenham, Buchanan went beyond his strict instructions and noted that the British ambassador could not expect the United States to "abandon the ground" taken in the negotiations to date. When the interview abruptly ended, Polk blamed Buchanan for "laboring to prevent" the delivery of the more aggressive letter from the president. In Congress, factions within the Democratic Party variously pushed the president either to settle the boundary at the 49th parallel line or to fight for every inch of land to the 54° 40' latitude line. The Oregon dispute remained uncertain through the end of the year.[30]

As the struggle with the British became protracted, Buchanan attempted to align himself with the popular anti-British views of Lewis Cass, considered his chief Democratic competitor for the presidential nomination in 1848. Buchanan refused to allow Polk to publish his earlier, more conciliatory views or to help him draft a message to Congress about the proposed Oregon Treaty in June 1846. Unsettled by this intransigence, Polk confronted Buchanan. "The conversation became a very painful and unpleasant one," the president recorded, "but led to mutual explanations that seemed to be satisfactory." Soon enough, the two men found common ground in the language of friendship. "I told him I had never had any unkind feelings towards him personally or politically," Polk wrote, while Buchanan similarly "expressed his friendship for me and for Mrs. Polk." On June 18, the Senate approved the Oregon Treaty by a wide margin, and the friction between the two men subsided.[31]

Soon thereafter Buchanan became infuriated with Polk over an entirely different matter. In the previous year, Polk unilaterally decided to appoint George Woodward of Pennsylvania, a favorite of Vice President Dallas, to a vacancy on the US Supreme Court. The action so enraged Buchanan that he penned a letter of resignation, which he opted against submitting only "after a full and free conversation with Mr. P.," possibly in November 1845. For his part, King supported Buchanan's decision not to resign, admonishing him "to act with great deliberation and prudence" in any future decision relating to his tenure in the cabinet. By the end of the year, Buchanan was still complaining to Polk about Woodward's appointment, preferring instead judge John M. Read of Philadelphia; in addition, Buchanan may have actively worked against Woodward's nomination with his former Senate colleagues. In January the Senate rejected the nomination, with Democratic defections coming from Buchanan allies Simon Cameron of Pennsylvania, Thomas Hart Benton of Missouri, Ambrose Sevier of Arkansas, and others. Infuriated, Polk believed that Buchanan had influenced them. "Being responsible for my appointments," Polk recorded in his diary, "I cannot surrender the appointment power to anyone else, and if, because I will not do so, Mr. B. chooses to retire from my Cabinet, I shall not regret it." The conflict lingered for months.[32]

A related issue also seemed to irk Buchanan: his own sincere desire for a position on the Supreme Court. As the drama over Woodward's nomination unfolded, Buchanan wrote candidly to Louis McLane, the sitting American minister to England and a man widely presumed to be in line to succeed him at the State Department. "I should this day have been on the bench of the Supreme Court, had it not been for the critical state of our foreign relations," he wrote, adding "I very much desired this position, because it would have enabled me to spend the remainder of my life in peace." Indeed, from the outset of his legal career, Buchanan had long respected the arbiters of justice; he had famously defended Judge Walter Franklin against impeachment by the Pennsylvania legislature. Temperamentally, Buchanan was well suited for life on the bench. Already he was personally intimate with several members of the Taney Court, John Catron among them. Yet the rigors demanded of him as a member of Polk's administration also mattered, for Buchanan had once before rejected an offer to the same court vacancy by President Tyler. Indeed, a seat on the Taney Court offered a far more tranquil lifestyle than the hectic pace at the State Department.[33]

The failure of the Woodward nomination, the conclusion of the Oregon treaty, and the near passage of a lower tariff bill finally convinced Polk to offer the court vacancy to Buchanan in June 1846. The unexpected gesture, Polk noted, put the secretary of state into "an unusually pleasant humour." At a meeting soon thereafter, Buchanan expressed his "preference for the Bench." He desired an immediate nomination, as opposed to waiting until the end of the current congressional session as Polk proposed, but the president refused to commit to that course. Taken aback, Buchanan asked for more time to think the matter over. Still, he wrote to his brother Edward that "All things considered, I believe it to be best."[34]

In addition to the timing of the nomination, Buchanan delayed acceptance for two interrelated reasons, both connected in some way to King. First, Buchanan wanted to name his own replacement at State, where he hoped that King rather than Louis McLane would succeed him. At least at first, King had politely refused Buchanan's offer of the State Department, writing in February 1846: "I feel but too sensibly my inability, properly to discharge the duties of so important a station, to attribute the suggestion to any thing else than the personal regard of yourself." But the idea, once formulated, lingered with King, and he soon began to talk openly of his interest in the position. In the summer, rumors once more swirled that King might succeed Buchanan. In a letter to President Polk, McLane related how King and his niece Catherine Ellis had recently called on him in London. "I learned that [Buchanan] particularly desired Col. King should succeed him in the Department and sanguine expectations of that which had been raised with the latter gentleman," McLane informed Polk after the visit.[35]

In private, McLane was outraged. To his son, he found King to be "an imperious fellow" and alleged "a dirty intrigue between Buc. & King." The American minister to England thought King to be "filled . . . with disgusting vanity and self-conceit" and Ellis to be "a weak woman." Citing King's "monomania" for the presidency, McLane believed his interest in the State Department a mere "steppingstone to the higher object." In September, McLane returned to Washington and met privately with Polk. After the meeting, the president recorded in his diary that Buchanan had "determined to retain his place in the Cabinet" if King were not elevated in his stead. Although Polk contended that he never thought of "inviting [King] to take charge of the Department of State," he also noted that "as Mr. Buchanan is very intimate with Mr. King and in the habit of corresponding with him, I think it probable that without consulting me on the subject and without my knowledge he had written to Mr. King suggesting it." Nevertheless, King was not to be considered as a nominee.[36]

Second, and more importantly, Buchanan reassessed the Supreme Court offer in view of the advice given by King and other political advisers. Since first hearing of Buchanan's possible resignation over the Woodward nomination, King had strongly counseled him to reconsider. "In your present position and under existing circumstances, you can render important services to your Country, which cannot fail to command for you its highest rewards," subtly hinting at the possibility of the presidential nomination in 1848. In the spring of 1846, thanks to improved transatlantic shipping routes that made a better exchange of letters possible, the pair was once more writing "*long* and friendly letter[s]" to one another at regular intervals. As such, King's advice was not only valuable, but timely as well. "Retain your place, regardless of all minor annoyances," he urged. In July, King reported that "rumours reach me that you are still inclined to abandon your position and either go on the bench or as Minister to England." He advised Buchanan to let them "be the last if you are determined on a chance; as your political Friends can then call you back, for the great political race of 1848." King strongly encouraged him "to abandon all idea of the Judgeship, and to continue in your present position." Politically, King predicted that Buchanan would "find the field open for the presidency unless you place yourself on the shelf, by accepting of the Judgeship." To take that position would, King correctly believed, permanently sideline him.[37]

Although he advised against a court appointment, King did not discount another idea, namely that of Buchanan accepting an appointment as the American minister to England. As King knew from his own ministerial service, the post carried special significance in the charged diplomatic climate and could possibly be leveraged into higher public office. More immediately, though, King could not ignore the idea of being nearer to his old bosom friend. "If I were certain you would come to England," he admitted, "I should be almost reconciled to remain another year in France, as a few hours suffices for passing from Paris to London, and we could visit each other frequently without detriment to the public service." But Buchanan turned down both the Supreme Court opportunity and the ministerial assignment.[38]

On August 11, 1846, nearly one year after his initial break with Polk, Buchanan reconciled himself to his cabinet post. "Mr. Buchanan called about 6 O'Clock P.M. and informed me that he had decided to remain in the Cabinet," Polk recorded with astonishment, "and not to accept the offer which I had made him to appoint him Judge of the Supreme Court." Buchanan further informed the president that he "did this cheerfully, although he had long desired a seat on the bench, and now he would stick to me & go through my administration with me." Although many factors contributed to Buchanan's decision, the advice from King and other allies had carried the day. With another major conflict already underway, Buchanan may also have glimpsed the possibility of a prize greater than the Supreme Court bench in the upcoming election of 1848. Regardless, one thing was certain: Buchanan would stay the course with Polk.[39]

Bachelor Doughface Diplomacy

The year 1846 has been called a year of decision with good reason, for those months encompassed a war with Mexico that marked a turning point in American history. The conflict had long been brewing; after the refusal of the envoy John Slidell the year before, the Mexican government grew more militant in its attitudes toward the United States. In turn, Polk directed General Zachary Taylor to move the army to the newly annexed Texas territory to enforce American claims there. Finally, in April 1846, with the full support of his cabinet, Polk ordered Taylor to cross the Nueces River (then the undisputed border of Texas) to the highly-contested region bounded by the Rio Grande (or Del Norte) River to the south. Taylor encamped opposite the small town of Matamoros, where the Mexican army had positioned itself. Inevitably, as Polk must have known, skirmishes broke out between the two sides, with several American soldiers killed in the process. Known as the Thornton Affair, the clash started the ensuing Battle of Palo Alto and with it, the War with Mexico.[40]

Before they had heard news of the fighting, the president and his cabinet considered an appropriate course of action. Buchanan agreed that Mexico had given the United States "ample cause of war," but he alone in the cabinet counseled waiting for an overt act of hostility prior to asking for a declaration of war. When news arrived of the fighting at Matamoros, Polk and Buchanan once more clashed over the president's message to American ministers abroad. Based on his correspondence with King in France and McLane in England, Buchanan counseled caution. As Polk recorded in his diary, Buchanan "stated that our object was not to dismember Mexico or to make conquests . . . [and] that in going to war we did not do so with a view to acquire either California or New Mexico or any other portion of the Mexican territory." Polk firmly objected to this proviso, to which Buchanan replied "you will have war with England as well as Mexico, and probably with France also, for neither of these powers will ever stand bye and [see] California annexed to the U.S." Polk persisted, however, and ordered the more bellicose version despatched to King, McLane, and the other American foreign ministers. A daguerreotype taken of the Polk cabinet soon after the meeting—the oldest surviving photograph taken inside the White House—reveals the rupture: all cabinet officers were present except Buchanan.[41]

FIGURE 5.4 President Polk's Cabinet. The photo shows (left to right, standing): Cave Johnson, George Bancroft; (seated): John Y. Mason, William L. Marcy, James K. Polk, and Robert Walker. Buchanan is notably absent from the picture. Daguerreotype attributed to John Plumbe Jr., ca. 1846. Courtesy James K. Polk Memorial Association.

As the war with Mexico began, King's mission to France suddenly became far less urgent. Moreover, the damp Parisian climate aggravated King's already painful rheumatism. In his private letters to Buchanan, he complained repeatedly about his health, but he did not officially request his recall until the first of June 1846. At that time, he couched his request in personal terms, noting that "my private affairs renders it of the utmost importance for me to visit Alabama even were it on leave of absence." In his reply, Buchanan drew a fine distinction in their prior correspondence about the recall issue. "You have alluded to the subject only in private letters," he noted, "and we desire that your recall should appear on record to be your own act, & that the President, so far from desiring it, would have been most happy, had you consented to remain." To replace him, Buchanan settled upon Richard Rush, the American minister to England during the Monroe administration, secretary of the treasury under John Quincy Adams, and a prolific author on the history of American foreign policy. The switch made, Buchanan wished for the return of the "*auld lang syne*" of their former domestic harmony, while King lamented in turn: "Most sincerely do I wish that we had both remained in the Senate."[42]

Meanwhile, King's return trip to the United States nearly cost him his life. In late September, his official entourage boarded the *Great Britain*, a steamer bound from Liverpool for New York. Late in the evening, the ship foundered on rocks in Dundrum Bay to the north of Ireland, causing a "terrific" shock. But all the passengers and crew miraculously escaped unharmed. In November, aboard a slower and sounder packet ship, he safely transited back to America. King headed directly to Washington, where he called on the president for the customary formal interview. King also likely met with Buchanan to discuss his mission, but he did not stay long in the capital. He met with political friends along the journey back to Alabama, undoubtedly to assess the domestic political climate and especially his prospects for election to the Senate. His chances for an immediate return to public office, he ascertained, were not bright.[43]

In late 1846, the war with Mexico intensified. American victories at Monterrey, in Santa Fe, New Mexico, and across California transformed the scope of the conflict from a limited engagement along the Texas border to a full-scale invasion of Mexico. Buchanan dissented with this strategy, but he was overruled by Polk and other members of the cabinet. The president directed General Winfield Scott to prepare an expeditionary force against the port city of Vera Cruz. From there, Polk envisioned an overland march, supported by an additional ten regiments of soldiers, to capture the capital at Mexico City. As first the cabinet and then the Congress debated funding for the war, General Taylor scored a major victory at Buena Vista, followed in short order by General Scott's planned capture of Vera Cruz. From King, Buchanan received counsel that tempered his view of the conflict. "Close this Mexican war at the earliest practicable moment; and upon any terms which do not conflict with the honor of our country," he urged. "Abandon, if it is entertained, the idea of acquiring extensive Territory." Buchanan sidestepped this advice, however. As far as the administration was concerned, he wrote to King "the Mexicans can conclude a treaty at any moment; it is this cut and dry for them." The two former messmates were in open disagreement.[44]

Even as the military conquest of Mexico proceeded, the president prepared to negotiate a diplomatic settlement of the war. To avoid political infighting, Polk wanted Buchanan personally to negotiate with the Mexican government, but given the uncertain state of affairs, the president deemed such a course to be impractical. In turn, Buchanan suggested Nicholas Trist, a former consul to Cuba and recently appointed chief clerk of the State Department, as "an able man, perfectly familiar with the Spanish character and language." Buchanan had become an intimate friend of Trist and his wife Virginia, both of whom found the secretary of state to be "distinguished." As the chief clerk prepared for his Mexican mission, Buchanan reportedly jested, "If you succeed in this, we shall have to take you up as our candidate for the Presidency."[45]

Buchanan's diffidence toward the acquisition of additional territory alarmed King. The war must be ended, King believed, and the United States "shew our magnanimity; and thus free ourselves from the charge of being a grasping nation, readying to seize upon the Territory of our weaker neighbors regardless of right or justice." Yet King could not avoid intermingling his national views with his own concerns about Buchanan's conduct toward him. He took great personal umbrage at the long delay in reply from his former messmate and accordingly questioned the very foundations of their friendship. "I must confess your failure to answer my letters produced on me no such feeling [of mortification]," he averred, "as I never doubted your friendship; and in fact prized it too highly to consent to surrender it for any such cause. Perhaps I am too proud to believe that I can be an object of neglect." But, he warned, "Try me not too far however," adding coolly: "For as love it is said cannot long exist unless it is mutual; so with friendship. Coldness or neglect on one side will in the end produce a correspondent coldness on the other; and the warmly attached friends of years will part with indifference if not with unkindness. Such I trust will never be the case with you and myself." Once more, Buchanan had been warned.[46]

Leaving aside these complaints, King objected strenuously to Buchanan's handling of the peace process and the resulting political fallout. He noted that while in New Orleans, their former messmate Cary Nicholas had taken the "extraordinary move" of promoting the nominal Whig Zachary Taylor as a Democratic presidential candidate. King especially lamented the sectional tension created by the war, in particular the proposed Wilmot Proviso that would prohibit slavery from any territorial lands acquired as a result of the conflict. "For myself I wish to acquire no Territory which will cause the South to be insulted by the adoption of a Wilmot Proviso, and such I believe is the feeling of the Southern people generally," he wrote. "But," he insisted, "we cannot and will not consent to be excluded from a fair participation by the joint efforts of the confederacy." The former messmates were once again at fundamental odds over a crucial foreign policy issue and especially its effect on the political realities of sectional difference. The limitations of their friendship appeared to be expanding as rapidly as the nation's own boundaries.[47]

As the summer months of 1847 ticked away, the military situation in Mexico turned in the Americans' favor. Polk and his cabinet officers now began to consider claiming additional Mexican territory as part of the proposed settlement. In October, Polk ordered Buchanan to recall Trist, since the envoy's earlier instructions proposed to treat Mexico on much more limited terms. Buchanan gladly complied, sensing a political windfall by pushing for additional territorial concessions. "Had you not asked my opinion," King wrote with annoyance at the news, "I would not . . . have presumed to express an opinion," but he believed that "future action must be made to depend on a very great degree on the information you receive from Genl. Scott, and your agents in Mexico." Weeks later, Buchanan must have been pleased to hear of Trist's resignation by way of his wife. "Say so to Mr. Buchanan, with my kindest regards," Trist instructed his wife, "and my most poignant regret that I cannot again take my post and relieve him from parts of his labours." But, just a week later, Trist opted to ignore his recall, writing a rambling, sixty-page letter to Buchanan explaining his actions, and continued with the peace negotiations. The resulting treaty with Mexican officials at Guadalupe Hidalgo was unexpectedly delivered to Buchanan on the evening of February 19, 1848.[48]

Polk and Buchanan had little choice but to consider the treaty. At a full meeting of the cabinet, Buchanan objected to it on the grounds that the United States had "spent much money and lost much blood" in the war and that the president should push for a boundary line further south to the Sierra Madre Mountains. Polk was flabbergasted at the turnabout and recorded as much in his diary: "I cannot help laboring under the conviction that the true reason of Mr. Buchanan's present course is that he is now a candidate for the Presidency, and he does not wish to incur the displeasure of those who are in favour of the conquest of all Mexico." As the president prepared to send the treaty to the Senate, Buchanan attempted to engineer its defeat, a move that the president found "seriously embarrassing" to his administration. On March 10, 1848, despite Buchanan's efforts, the Senate passed the Treaty of Guadalupe Hidalgo by a vote of 38 to 14.[49]

Once more, Buchanan enjoined into controversy through a war of words in print. In February 1848, John Nugent, a correspondent of the *New York Herald* who wrote under the pseudonym "Galviensis," attacked Polk, Cass, and other leading Democrats, while promoting Buchanan's position in the cabinet. Polk confronted Buchanan about the article, after learning from Robert Walker that Buchanan and Nugent were "in habits of intercourse." Senator Edward Hannegan of Indiana similarly complained to Polk of Buchanan's "habits of intimacy" with Nugent, noting that the pair were often "closetted" together at the State Department and at Buchanan's home on F Street. Following the ratification of the treaty, the *Herald* published the full text of the president's message to Senate and later, the full text of the treaty itself, an action specifically prohibited by Congress. The Senate held Nugent in contempt and jailed him, but the reporter never publicly revealed the source of his information. Buchanan vehemently denied leaking the documents, but few others had access to them. In the subsequent defense of his editorials, Nugent noted how Polk's friends threatened that the president would use his "interests throughout the country" to throw "into the scale in the approaching presidential election against Mr. Buchanan, with whom I was known to be on terms of warm personal intimacy." For his part, this "warm personal intimacy" especially bothered Polk; he variously complained of Buchanan's "notorious intimacy" with this "unprincipled letter writer" and felt that it nearly cost his secretary of state's political reputation.[50]

At root, Polk seems to have condemned Buchanan's broader penchant for bosom friendship. A contemporary remembered the Irish-born Nugent, who was about twenty-seven at the time of the incident, as of "low stature, and lithe, delicate frame, with face smooth and fair as a girl's," but possessing "the spirit of a hero, and . . . every inch a man." With this manly, and unmarried youth, Buchanan enjoyed a politically dangerous intimate companionship, not unlike those formed with the younger members of the bachelor's mess. But unlike those past intimacies, he had miscalculated in attaching himself to a journalist whose loyalty could not be fully counted on in return. Indeed, as the presidential election of 1848 approached, Buchanan had neglected the one bosom friend on whose sage advice hinged his very political future— William Rufus King.[51]

* * *

The Polk years dramatically changed the political course of King and Buchanan. King's role as the American minister to France required him to support publicly the president's expansionist policy, first on Texas annexation, then on the Oregon boundary dispute, and finally on the War with Mexico. But privately, he worried about the long-term political effects of territorial acquisition from Mexico, especially regarding the slavery question. King also gleaned more worldly insights from his time abroad, which served to reinforce his already high opinion of Buchanan. Much of Europe applauded Buchanan for his cautious and skillful diplomacy in the Oregon boundary issue, and King followed suit. He likewise absolved his former messmate of responsibility for expanding the War with Mexico, even as he counseled moderation from his new position as a retired statesman in Alabama. Unlike most in the Democratic Party, he firmly believed that Buchanan would garner the presidential nomination in 1848.

For his part, Buchanan adopted the martial spirit of the times and ministered an pro-slavery and expansionist foreign policy. In the process, he evolved from a mere northern doughface in Congress to a shrewd continentalist with a viable path to the presidency. On the Oregon question, he followed King's advice and pushed for a compromise in the hope of preventing war with Great Britain. Later, in the War with Mexico, Buchanan discovered a newfound zeal for territorial expansion. As the conflict concluded, Buchanan realized that victorious generals, and not the diplomats and peacemakers, had acquired an unprecedented popular standing. In this he learned a valuable lesson: territorial conquest attracted the accolades of the Democracy.

Much had also changed in the terms of the friendship between Buchanan and King. With Buchanan's appointment as secretary of state, he had become King's immediate superior. Their relationship evolved from one of domestic intimacy to one of administrative indifference. Four years later each man, and their friendship along with it, had been exhausted by the unceasing efforts required to achieve Polk's ambitious diplomatic agenda. Yet they still hoped that their foreign ministrations would be sufficient to carry one or both of them to the White House. As the Democratic National Convention of 1848 approached, Buchanan and King shifted their attentions from ministering to the affairs of state to the internecine conflicts of partisan politics. In that charged atmosphere, all seemed possible between them once again.

6

Running, 1848–1853

THE YEAR 1848 witnessed an unprecedented series of democratic revolutions sweep across Europe. In February the French king Louis Philippe, whom William Rufus King had so admired, abdicated the throne, and the Second Republic took shape; in turn, Secretary of State James Buchanan encouraged immediate recognition of the new government. In the months ahead revolutions sprouted in the German states of Baden and Prussia, in the war for independence in Hungary, and in the Italian states of Milan and Venice, then part of the Habsburg Austrian empire. The "springtime of the peoples" engulfed nearly all the European continent. In the United States, by contrast, no grand revolution unfolded in the streets, which served to further Americans' view of themselves as an exceptional nation, and spared the country from the bitter class divisions of Europe. From the relative safety across the Atlantic, American political leaders felt secure enough to encourage self-determination abroad.[1]

Yet the country had not resolved a question of enormous consequence for its own future—how to organize the vast lands of the Mexican cession. At issue was whether slavery would be permitted in these newly acquired territories. With the settling of the Oregon boundary and the conclusion of the War with Mexico, the Polk administration had firmly established the United States as a continental power. But it had been unable to suppress the intensification of sectional differences in the process. The Wilmot Proviso, first proposed in 1846 by David Wilmot of Pennsylvania in an effort to forbid slavery in any territories acquired as a result of the war, proved popular among northern congressmen of both parties. By contrast, southern congressmen and their northern allies (Buchanan prominent among them) opposed the measure outright and insisted upon the constitutional protections to property, including enslaved people. From the west, a doctrine of popular sovereignty, in which the settlers of those territories decided the fate of slavery for themselves, took shape as a possible compromise. Stephen Douglas, then an ambitious thirty-nine-year-old politician from Illinois, championed the idea in the Senate. No immediate solutions were obvious.[2]

The pressing issues resulting from the War with Mexico, along with the many others that became the basis for the great congressional debates of 1850, shaped the partisan calculations leading to the presidential election of 1848. Traditional political issues, notably the protective tariff, still mattered to some voters, but the terms of the debate abruptly became more sectional. So too, a martial spirit afflicted both parties in their promotion of presidential nominees, which disadvantaged the more cautious ministers of the Polk administration. Brewing divisions in both parties bubbled to the surface. The "Conscience" Whigs stood in contrast to the mainline of the party, while a similar schism portended problems for the northern wing of the Democratic Party. In the ensuing months, a third-party group known as the "Free Soilers," whose core consisted of the old anti-slavery Liberty Party, organized around opposition to the expansion of slavery in the Mexican Cession. By 1848, the Democrats and the Whigs each hoped to avoid the slavery issue altogether and instead ride the less controversial campaign themes of prior election cycles to victory.[3]

Both James Buchanan and William Rufus King were thus contenders for their party's nomination in 1848. Since the early 1840s, Democratic newspapers had declared the possibility of what some editors termed a "bachelor ticket," a suggestion of their sustained influence and their political identities as unmarried men. Even as they remained linked together in the public eye, the old intimacy of their friendship, weakened by years of transatlantic neglect and the constant political conflict of the Polk presidency, had noticeably diminished. Worse, the two former bachelor messmates threatened to work at cross purposes in their individual responses to the brewing sectional conflict. King yet acted as a voice for moderation within the Senate, while Buchanan sought to stand above the fray in a dignified retirement. In 1848, they seemed to be running toward the same goal of party unity and the laurels of national office, but in opposite directions of one another. Which man would seize the main chance first?[4]

Old Maids of State

Since arriving home in the fall of 1846, King had been plotting his return to political power in Alabama. He was unanimously selected as the presiding officer at the state's Democratic Party convention in May 1847, when, as he told Buchanan, he narrowly avoided "the net, so avidly spread for me" of election to the Alabama governorship (and thus be placed out of the running for the US Senate). A sizable obstacle stood between King and his old seat in the Senate, however, in the form of Dixon Hall Lewis, a hulkingly large politician who had filled the spot in 1844. Nevertheless, he optimistically predicted to niece Catherine Margaret Ellis that "a very large proportion" supported his re-election, while to Buchanan he claimed that the people "are decidedly in favor of reinstating me in the Senate, and unless their Representatives play the people false, my election is certain." But the legislature instead chose Lewis for the seat, split as they were over the future course of the national Democratic Party: King and the administration Democrats supported the unpopular President Polk, while Lewis and the "Chivalry" faction of the party threw their substantial weight behind the radical states' rights agenda of John C. Calhoun. King's first chance for the Senate had passed.[5]

Not easily deterred, King turned his full attention to the Democratic Party nominating convention of 1848. In February, he attended the Alabama state party meeting at Montgomery, where the convention delegates unanimously recommended him for the vice presidential nomination at the upcoming national convention in Baltimore. Prior to then, King privately expressed his desire to align with President Polk's plan to extend the Missouri Compromise line to the Pacific, but he feared the possible results of declaring his public support for the measure. In turn, King's Alabama faithful George Washington Gayle wrote to Buchanan on King's behalf, "knowing the intimacy existing between you, with a hope that you will urge Col. King to consent to a publication of his views, if called upon: And, if you approve the policy, and can gain his consent, we will soon have him out." But as before, Buchanan filed away the request and does not seem to have written to King about the matter.[6]

By the spring of 1848, the political focus had shifted fully to the question of Polk's successor. From the outset of his presidency, Polk had attempted to control the aspirations of his cabinet appointees for higher office. In a circular letter to all cabinet nominees in 1845, he had insisted that should "any member of my Cabinet become a Candidate for the Presidency or Vice Presidency of the United States, it will be expected upon the happening of such an event, that he will retire from the Cabinet." He was especially concerned about Buchanan, who responded cagily to this unprecedented demand. "I cannot proclaim to the world that in no contingency shall I be a Candidate for the Presidency in 1848," he explained. But he also promised never to make any "personal exertions" for the next presidential nomination, while still serving as secretary of state. In this, Buchanan almost certainly prevaricated. Over the winter months of 1847 into 1848, he hosted regular Saturday evening dinners to gain influence with prominent members of the Democratic Party across the country. President Polk permitted the polite fiction to continue throughout his term in office for a simple reason: Old Buck was too useful an instrument of expansionist statecraft.[7]

The two major parties' nominating conventions were a comedy of politicking. Under the guidance of the "Young Indians," a group that included such notables as congressmen Abraham Lincoln of Illinois and Alexander Stephens of Georgia, the Whigs determined to pass over their aging champion Henry Clay and snag the apolitical war hero Zachary Taylor, "Old Rough and Ready," as their candidate. They consummated this odd political marriage at their convention in June. By contrast, the Democrats were without an obvious candidate, as Polk, debilitated by ill health and thoroughly exhausted by the office, had previously announced his intention not to run for a second term. For a successor, the president privately favored General Lewis Cass of Michigan—whose stale military credentials dated to the War of 1812—but he exerted little overt influence on the process. Of course, King preferred Buchanan for the nomination, lauding the secretary of state as the "Atlas of the Administration" and adding that his niece Catherine Margaret Ellis hoped to "hear you deliver your Inaugural from the front of the Capitol in 1849."[8]

In May, the Democratic National Convention met in Baltimore to decide the presidential question. On the first ballot, the frontrunner, Lewis Cass, fended off both Buchanan and Levi Woodbury of New Hampshire, an associate justice of the US Supreme Court, who, to Buchanan and King's great disappointment, carried the support of the Alabama delegation. Yet no single candidate garnered sufficient support to obtain the necessary two-thirds vote for the nomination. As the balloting continued, Cass grew in strength, absorbing the votes of minor candidates and taking some votes away from Buchanan. In the fourth round, Cass had surpassed the necessary number of delegates to obtain the nomination. The bachelor ticket fared little better in the balloting for the vice presidential nomination. King ran a distant third, behind both William O. Butler of Kentucky and John Quitman of Mississippi. By the second ballot, the convention united behind Butler, a high-ranking general in the conflict with Mexico, and made the selection unanimous. Although a Buchanan-King ticket had seemed a possibility in 1848, the Democratic convention had instead chosen two prominent war heroes as their standard bearers.[9]

What explains the failure of either half of the bachelor ticket to obtain the nomination in 1848? Certainly, the successful prosecution of the War with Mexico had left the country in a martial mood. By contrast, the careful, diplomatic style of Buchanan and King lacked comparative luster next to the buff and bluster of two war heroes. But of the pair, Buchanan had fared worse than expected. The position of secretary of state—once a natural jumping off point to higher office—no longer summoned the same electoral magic it once did. In fact, no sitting secretary of state had obtained his party's nomination since John Quincy Adams in 1824. Besides, the burdens of office under Polk had limited Buchanan's ability to secure important state-level endorsements—ironically, the president's intensive work schedule had exacted his requirement that no cabinet member should succeed him. By contrast, Lewis Cass enjoyed the public spotlight and the comparative leisure of a seat in the US Senate. Prior to the Senate, he had preceded King as the American minister to France—a point not lost on Buchanan in future years—and thus demonstrated ample diplomatic experience. While not as strong electorally as Buchanan in the ever-important Pennsylvania vote, Cass posed a decent chance of carrying the Keystone State and thus winning the presidential election in the fall.[10]

In the aftermath of the convention, King faced an even more uncertain return to national office. Worse still, the presidential balloting had precipitated a public contretemps between King and fellow Alabama politician William Yancey. The dispute stemmed from Yancey's abandonment of King's vice presidential candidacy after the first round of voting at the national convention; subsequently, Yancey published a lengthy address to the citizens of the state explaining his conduct, which considerably rankled King. In June 1848, events took an unexpectedly positive turn, however. President Polk appointed Arthur Bagby, a US senator from Alabama since 1841, as the new American minister to Russia. King's name immediately circulated as a possible replacement. "I hear nothing from Alabama but am informed that [George] Houston says the Gov. dare not give me the appointment," he wrote to Buchanan in late June. He predicted that Dixon Lewis would attempt to block his nomination, due to the "personal hostility" between the two men. Nevertheless, in early July, Governor Reuben Chapman appointed King to fill the vacancy, rounding out an ironic full circle as both King and Buchanan had earlier been removed from the scene of domestic power through similar appointments to the Russian legation. By the middle of July 1848, King, who in the interim had taken to "imprudent sea-bathing" to improve his increasingly feeble health, received notification of his appointment and headed directly to the capital.[11]

Even before his return to Washington, King's political enemies within the Democratic Party began once more to deprecate their old rival. Democratic editor Francis Preston Blair wrote to Martin Van Buren, who had recently joined the anti-slavery Free Soil Party, about King's possible reappointment to the Senate. "Bagby they tell me is to go minister to Russia & open the way for King back to the Senate," Blair reported. "The latter they say cohabits still with old Buck." Although King and Buchanan had not been messmates in over four years, Blair's use of the word "cohabits" suggested that a domestic tie still bound them together politically in the eyes of their opponents. Similarly, King's possible return must have miffed the elderly Thomas Hart Benton, who demurred that the title bestowed upon him as "Father of the Senate" would return to the more senior senator from Alabama. "But," Benton added cruelly, "I regret to add that my friend, a hopeless bachelor as he is—is father of nothing else." King's homecoming would not be an entirely happy one.[12]

Yet other politicians remembered King's cohabitation with Buchanan in a more positive light. Robert Winthrop of Massachusetts, a conservative Whig who had been elected speaker of the House of Representatives in the Thirtieth Congress, likened his own friendship with Jacob Miller of New Jersey to that of Buchanan and King. "Since my return I have taken my old friend Senator Miller into partnership," he wrote to a friend in June 1848, "& we live like Achilles & Patroclus,—or, it were more modest to say, Nisus & Euryalus." But these odes to the classical past yielded to a more contemporary analogy. "A less *anachronous* comparison would be Buchanan & King of Alabama," Winthrop continued, "who chummed together for a term of years, to the envy of all the old maids in the Metropolis." Despite this gibe at their bachelor status, Winthrop apparently admired Buchanan and King enough to strive for a similar level of intimacy with his own messmate.[13]

Once in the capital, King settled in for the short months left in the congressional session. But the question remained, in Winthrop's inimitable phrasing: where and with whom would King "chum"? One possibility was at Brown's Hotel, or another such establishment where southerners increasingly lodged during their time in Washington. Another possibility was for King to stay with Buchanan at their old lodgings on F Street. Such an arrangement would not have been out of character for the secretary of state, as he had invited numerous prominent figures as guests to his F Street home during the previous three years. Richard Rush, King's replacement as American minister to France, James Shields, a brigadier general during the Mexican War and later a US senator, and John Slidell, the American minister to Texas, had all stayed as Buchanan's guests.[14]

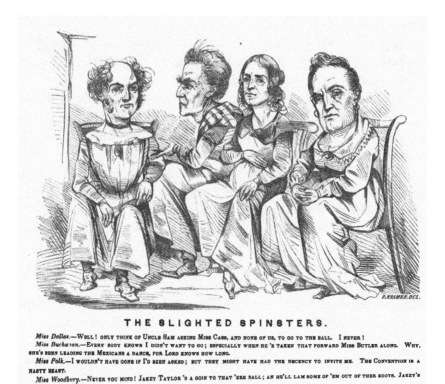

THE SLIGHTED SPINSTERS.

Miss Dallas.—WELL! ONLY THINK OF UNCLE SAM ASKING MISS CASS, AND NONE OF US, TO GO TO THE BALL. I NEVER!

Miss Buchanan.—EVERY BODY KNOWS I DIDN'T WANT TO GO; ESPECIALLY WHEN HE 'S TAKEN THAT FORWARD MISS BUTLER ALONG. WHY, SHE'S BEEN LEADING THE MEXICANS A DANCE, FOR LORD KNOWS HOW LONG.

Miss Polk.—I WOULDN'T HAVE GONE IF I'D BEEN ASKED; BUT THEY MIGHT HAVE HAD THE DECENCY TO INVITE ME. THE CONVENTION IS A NASTY BEAST.

Miss Woodbury.—NEVER YOU MIND! JAKEY TAYLOR 'S A GOIN TO THAT 'ERE BALL; AN HE'LL LAM SOME OF 'EM OUT OF THER BOOTS. JAKEY'S [illegible]

FIGURE 6.1 "The Slighted Spinsters." In the wake of the 1848 Democratic National Convention, a political cartoon lampooned the losing presidential contenders: Levi Woodbury of New Hampshire, George Dallas of Pennsylvania, James Polk of Tennessee, and James Buchanan. Published in *The John-Donkey*, vol. 1, no. 24 (June 10, 1848): 377.

Buchanan warmly welcomed King back to Washington. On July 15, 1848, he hosted another of his famous Saturday evening dinners at his home on F Street. Besides King, the guest list included a number of their Washington friends, primarily from the Whig Party: Robert Toombs of Georgia, Joseph R. Ingersoll of Pennsylvania, Samuel D. Hubbard of Connecticut, John Clayton of Delaware, Joseph Underwood of Kentucky, John M. Berrien of Arkansas, King's former messmate Willie Mangum, and the Whig newspaper editors Joseph Gales and William Seaton, leaving Ambrose Sevier of Arkansas, Buchanan, and King as the only Democrats present. King's homecoming was short-lived, however. The congressional session ended in August, after which time Buchanan and King traveled with the Washington bon vivant John T. Sullivan to the fashionable summer resort at Saratoga Springs, New York. There Buchanan reported to Richard Rush that "much agreeable

company yet remains," including King, Reverdy Johnson of Maryland, and
Postmaster General Cave Johnson. Whether in Washington or in New York,
Buchanan and King were once again reunited, albeit temporarily, in their
former domestic intimacy.[15]

In November, Zachary Taylor defeated the Democratic challenger Lewis
Cass and the Free Soil Party insurgency represented by ex-president Martin
Van Buren. A month later, the outgoing members of the Thirtieth Congress
returned for the lame-duck session. This time, King arranged to live in a mess
with other southern congressmen at a boardinghouse near Capitol Hill.
There he joined Jefferson Davis of Mississippi, whose wife Varina Davis later
remembered her husband's messmate as "a man as elegant as he was sound and
sincere," and the Louisiana Democrats Solomon Downs and Emile La Sére.
During the short session, King emerged as a warm supporter of the lame-duck
Polk administration, serving as a member of a joint congressional committee
to receive the president's annual message. One month later, King tried to re-
solve the question of slavery in the newly acquired western territories, though
to no avail. Committed more than ever to rising above the partisan fray, he
was once again on his way to assuming a leadership role in the Senate.[16]

The rising prominence of the senior King corresponded to the dwindling
status of the more junior Buchanan. Still, the former Siamese twins of the US
Senate rekindled their friendship during the short lame-duck session. The pair
attended a dinner given by President Polk for his cabinet and key Democratic
senators on December 14. On December 30, King and his southern messmates
attended another of Buchanan's Saturday evening dinners, this time with
mostly foreign dignitaries and fellow Democrats as guests. Buchanan continued to host regular gatherings at his home until the end of his term in
office. The final such dinner on February 24, 1849, was a more intimate affair
with mostly Democrats, including King, Henry Nicoll of New York, Jessie
Bright of Indiana, James Shields recently of Illinois, and Supreme Court
Justices James Wayne of Georgia, Robert Grier of Pennsylvania, and Levi
Woodbury of New Hampshire. Buchanan and King would not see each other
again for nearly a year.[17]

Until the very end, President Polk recorded his negative judgments about
his secretary of state. He found Buchanan to be at once overly worrisome about
small matters and intractably recalcitrant on larger issues. In late February 1849,
when president-elect Taylor arrived in Washington, Polk complained that
Buchanan breached protocol in calling directly on him before the appropriate
time. "Mr. Buchanan is an able man," Polk grumbled, "but is in small matters
without judgment and sometimes acts like an old maid." As this inversion of

gender norms slyly hinted, Buchanan exhibited undeniably feminine qualities, a view echoed by Lancaster editor John Forney who remembered his former political boss as a "masculine Miss Fribble" (a reference to the foppish female lead of a popular English play). Polk's old maid observation has more than a touch of irony to it, given Buchanan's worries about marrying one. But four years in Washington had brought him no closer to finding a wife.[18]

The Firmness of Friendship

At the close of 1849, America faced a panoply of crises. In distant California, gold had been discovered and thousands had hastened westward to seek their fortunes in the ground. While few actually profited from the venture, the California gold rush accelerated the need for civil government in the remote territory. By year's end Californians clamored for full statehood, without the institution of slavery permitted within its borders. Meanwhile, trouble brewed in Texas, whose western boundary necessitated careful mediation. Closer to home, northern congressmen demanded the application of the Wilmot Proviso and the end of the slave trade in the District of Columbia, while southerners equally demanded the right to carry their slaves into the lands of the Mexican Cession and the lawful return of fugitive slaves to their masters. Polk had hoped (but failed) to solve these many issues during the lame-duck congressional session; instead, to Zachary Taylor and the next Congress fell this political logjam.[19]

Back in Alabama, King once again sought a seat in the US Senate, as his appointment to the Bagby vacancy had been temporary. Dixon Lewis had died suddenly the previous summer, necessitating the Alabama state legislature to appoint two US senators. Although one Democratic opponent complained that King exhibited "a *childish overweening desire to be elected to the Senate*," he successfully obtained one of the two seats. In celebration, he hosted a party at the Exchange Hotel in Montgomery, where one legislator reported that "wine passed pretty freely." Afflicted by a "severe cold," King lingered in the state capital for days. He also inquired of a Selma neighbor about his niece Catherine Margaret Ellis. "I had expected she would have been at this place before now prepared to accompany me to Washington," he wrote. Thus delayed in Montgomery, he was on hand to witness the burning of the Alabama state capitol building on December 14. With this ill omen as a backdrop, he began the journey by stage, boat, and train to Washington.[20]

In contrast, Buchanan had already turned his attention to private life in Lancaster. By chance, the grand federal home of William Meredith, known as Wheatland and situated on a twenty-two-acre estate, had become available for purchase. Buchanan wrote directly to Meredith and began a months-long process of negotiation that ultimately led to his purchase and occupation of the new home on May 16, 1849. Once installed at Wheatland, a contemporary observed that Buchanan engaged in the "calm pleasures of country life . . . where he dispensed a Southern-like hospitality to all who came within its limits, and where he himself, always genial and agreeable, was the very life of the home circle." He enjoyed the simple pleasures of country life, especially serving libations from casks stamped with the moniker "Old J. B. Whiskey" (purchased from Jacob Baer's nearby distillery). Over time, this retreat, reminiscent of his hero George Washington, earned him a new moniker: the "Sage of Wheatland." But unlike Washington's final retirement at Mount Vernon, Buchanan utilized his position at Wheatland to build a network of political contacts with an eye toward the Democratic presidential nomination in 1852.[21]

By early 1850, the professional paths of the two former messmates had diverged. Unlike the peripheral position Buchanan had assumed at Wheatland, King found himself in the center of the many issues deadlocking the Senate. Events once more precipitated the renewal of their correspondence, highlighting how their bosom friendship had been reduced to a more

FIGURE 6.2 "Wheatland." Buchanan took ownership of this grand home built in the federal style in May 1849. Lithograph by Frederick J. Pilliner. Published in *Gleason's Pictorial Drawing-Room Companion* vol. 6, no. 12 (Mar. 25, 1854): 192.

formal relationship. Still the two men had much to discuss. For one, Thomas Hart Benton, who had split with the Polk administration over its treatment of his son-in-law John C. Frémont, had recently denounced Buchanan's past attempts to limit the organization of a territorial government in California. King offered to publish selections from their private correspondence to quell the matter, but Buchanan strongly cautioned against the idea. Somewhat taken aback at his friend's tone, King reiterated his commitment to him, writing that he hoped never to become "of such a character as would prevent me from vindicating you to the extent of my ability, whenever improperly attacked, be the consequences . . . what they may." In reply, Buchanan offered his own pledge of friendship. "I did not mean, in anything I said in my former letter to insinuate that you would not stand by me when right with the firmness of friendship," he wrote. "Such a thought never entered my mind."[22]

The "firmness of friendship" notwithstanding, the political struggle ongoing in the Senate described in King's letters genuinely concerned the Sage of Wheatland. As before, the Congress had split along sectional lines on the extension of slavery into the western territories. "To show you the state of feeling in the South," Buchanan wrote to a New York political operative, "I shall extract a few sentences from a strictly private letter from Colonel King received within the last week." He then added: "Every body who knows that gentleman is aware that he is prudent, patriotic & discreet, & has heretofore exerted all his influence to suppress excitement on this subject." Similarly, he confided to Nathan Clifford of Maine—his former clerk in the State Department—that "I have deemed it best to make Colonel King acquainted with all the facts." Once more, King had become his most important source of reliable information—now reporting news from the nation's capital itself.[23]

Yet Buchanan soon found his correspondence with King insufficient to meet the developing crisis. Earlier in the session, King had proposed that his old messmate join him in the capital. "We will however discuss the matter when I have the pleasure of seeing you in Washington. I am at Browns Hotel," he noted. King also indicated that his nieces, Catherine Margaret Ellis and Margaret William King, had joined him for the session. Evidently, Buchanan took up King's offer to visit, arriving there in the last week of January and staying for four weeks. He may well have joined King and his nieces at a mess on New Jersey Avenue, where the group reportedly boarded for the session. However, he likely missed King's first entry into the debate, when the senior senator urged "good sense and moderate counsels" to prevail in the increasingly contentious arguments over slavery. The warning did little good, as politicians on both sides of the slavery divide pushed their respective views.[24]

With the two former messmates reunited in February 1850, they once more intertwined their families in an expansive domestic intimacy. By then, King had evidently come to know Buchanan's niece Harriet Lane, for he referred to her as "my young friend Miss Harriet," and in the years ahead, he made sure to report any encounters with her back to Buchanan. For his part, Buchanan professed a sincere interest, bordering on the romantic, toward the nineteen-year-old Margaret William King. From his stay in the capital, he evidently became familiar with her, for he closed one letter: "Please to remember me in the very kindest terms to Mrs. Ellis, & give my love to Margaret." In turn, King responded with the line: "Mrs. Ellis tenders her best respects, and Margaret sends her love to you." Buchanan so implicitly trusted both Catherine Ellis and Margaret King that he even excepted them from his usual scrupulous provisions about the confidentiality of his correspondence.[25]

How serious was Buchanan's flirtation with Margaret William King? Certainly, he still complained of his bachelor status, even as he invited friends to visit him at his "bachelor's home" and "bachelor's abode" at Wheatland. Likewise, the fifty-nine-year-old Buchanan still routinely gossiped and flirted with a number of much younger women, including the coquettish twenty-seven-year-old Eliza Watterston, daughter of the former Librarian of Congress. In the case of Margaret William King, the age difference seems not to have deterred Buchanan's interest in the young woman. Equally pleasing must have been the renewed repartee such flirtation brought with his old friend. In May 1850, Buchanan invited King and his family to visit him at Wheatland: "I should be very glad indeed to see you: & still more so, if you would bring Mrs. Ellis along," he said, adding, "Miss [Margaret] King I presume has left you, as you do not mention her in your last." While the ongoing debates in the Senate prevented King from visiting, he specifically confirmed his old messmate's suspicions about his young niece: "Margaret has returned to the house of her childhood [in Alabama], where you must seek and win her." Of course, Buchanan did not seek young Margaret's hand, but remarkably the flirtation persisted in the years ahead.[26]

During his visit to Washington in February 1850, Buchanan met privately at the boardinghouses of leading politicians from both parties, including with the Whig senator Willie Mangum and the Democratic senator David Atchison of Missouri. According to one congressional observer, Buchanan attempted to broker a deal that would have extended the Missouri Compromise line to the Pacific Ocean (and promote his presidential ambitions besides). Unsuccessful in these efforts, he returned to Wheatland, where his fears for the Union only magnified. To his Virginia confidant Robert Tyler, he wrote in late

February: "No man at a distance from Washington can justly appreciate the condition of affairs there, nor can any person on the spot unless admitted behind the scenes." Buchanan also conceived of preparing a public letter on the crisis; as he wrote to Tyler, "I have been maturing a project for the settlement of the Slavery question; but the time is not yet." In March, days after Calhoun's dire sectional prognosis and just prior to Webster's thunderous reply in defense of the Union, Buchanan had settled upon the direction of his own message. "I wish you to be my Mentor," he beseeched King from Wheatland, "& I now write to you for advice." Buchanan proposed a six-point plan, which took a pro-southern tack by extending the Missouri Compromise line across the remaining territory of the Mexican Cession. "That it would add much to your existing popularity in the South, I cannot doubt," King fired back, "whether it should prevail in Congress or not." Months later, after King had read the final draft of Buchanan's proposed letter, which he deemed an "able production" and one that "takes a correct view of the disputed question," he lamented that its late appearance in print would minimize its desired effect.[27]

Although they once more accorded on domestic questions, the former messmates soon found themselves in disagreement over a significant foreign policy measure. For the Thirty-First Congress, King had been appointed chairman of the Senate's Foreign Relations Committee, which afforded him insights to the various treaties enacted during the Polk and Taylor administrations. Whereas Buchanan had evolved into an avowed expansionist during the Polk years, King sincerely regretted "our recent acquisitions on the Pacific." Now, King shouldered the responsibility of moving the Clayton-Bulwer Treaty with Great Britain through the Senate. Negotiated by Taylor's secretary of state John Clayton to obtain American canal rights in Nicaragua, the strict limitations proposed in the document much chagrined former secretary of state Buchanan. As a proponent of the treaty, King told Buchanan that he was "decidedly opposed to any further acquisition of Territory at this time in any quarter." In reply, Buchanan expressed his "regret that for the first time we differ radically upon a question which I deem of such vast importance as the Nicaragua Treaty," but unlike King, he knew territorial expansion to be a politically popular position. The two men seemed to agree to disagree on this issue.[28]

As the monotony of the winter's debates dragged into spring, King took an enlarged role in the crisis. Whereas in March he had defended Buchanan from partisan attacks made by William Seward of New York, in April he was appointed as a member of the Committee of Thirteen, chaired by old antagonist Henry Clay, whose labors eventually produced the "Omnibus Bill." On

May 6, after Vice President Millard Fillmore had temporarily vacated the seat, King was chosen president pro tempore of the Senate—a "most admirable selection for the present crisis," one newspaper reported. In June, southern radicals called for a convention at Nashville, which King loudly rejected, but the conference failed to produce its desired effect of southern unification. Next, on July 4, while observing a parade and partaking of a summer repast, President Taylor took seriously ill and died five days later. Vice President Fillmore assumed the presidency, leaving King as the permanent presiding officer just as the Omnibus Bill stalled in the Senate. But in August, Stephen Douglas emerged as the floor leader for the compromise measures. He devised a clever strategy to separate the Omnibus Bill and to hold sequential votes, in which congressmen who agreed with parts but not all of the measures in a particular bill could conveniently absent themselves on its final vote. The strategy worked.[29]

All the while, King and Buchanan kept drifting in opposite directions. King's focus remained entirely political, but Buchanan turned his attention toward more leisurely pursuits. In August, he invited King and Catherine Ellis to join him and Harriet Lane for a vacation at Bedford Springs. King regretted that he could not attend: "Mrs. Ellis and myself would be most happy to join you and Miss Harriet either at Bedford or any other point, so as to spend the summer at some place more agreeable than Washington . . . but the rejection of the Bill called the compromise . . . will effectively preclude us from joining you." By its usual custom, the Senate should have adjourned by the middle of August, but the unprecedented nature of the debates had disrupted the usual pattern. When King once more declined the invitation due to the demands of the Senate, Buchanan stopped responding to his letters. He docketed his last letter to King dated August 1850 with a telling note: "Put away 1 Sept. 1850." With that, the incipient renewal of their bosom friendship was laid to rest.[30]

Buchanan's Bosom Friend

The various bills that comprised the Compromise of 1850 passed both houses of Congress and were subsequently signed by President Fillmore in mid-September. A calm settled over Washington, but the issues that had animated the great debates of the preceding months lay just beneath the surface. The debates had claimed the lives, both in a literal and metaphorical sense, of its primary spokesmen—Calhoun had died in April after his last gasp for southern unity, Clay broke down physically due to his tireless efforts at conciliation, and Webster stood pilloried in the North for his ardent unionism.

In a tableau portrait that paid tribute to the compromise, King and Buchanan were both pictured, one standing in front of the other, alongside the "Great Triumvirate" of Calhoun, Clay, and Webster, and numerous other notables (in a historical irony, an artist reworked the same scene for republication in 1861, replacing King with Union general Benjamin Butler and Buchanan with Major Robert Anderson of Fort Sumter fame). On the national level, however, the Whig Party lay in tatters, bereft of a clear presidential candidate in 1852, while the Democrats faced the prospect of another divided convention between competing regional favorites. To both sides, the presidency seemed ripe for the picking.[31]

In the fall of 1850, King returned home to Chestnut Hill to attend to his cotton plantation and to defend his voting record. Across Alabama, he was derided for the "loose declarations" made during the compromise debates. To a fellow Democrat he cautioned against immediate southern secession, but he also revealed a limit to his unionism: "The North should be made to understand that we will bear no more, that another step taken by her to endanger our safety must and will snap the cord, which binds us together." He

FIGURE 6.3 "Union." James Buchanan is depicted standing behind the bust of George Washington and directly in front of William Rufus King, in the second row at right. Engraving by Henry S. Sadd in 1852 from the painting by Tompkins H. Matteson. Prints and Photographs Division, Library of Congress, LC-DIG-pga-02601.

took this limited approach at a meeting in the old state capitol at Cahawba, where he addressed an audience to open "the eyes of many worthy men, who had been misled by bold assertion, and exagerated statements in which the self constituted defenders of Southern rights have so constantly indulged." Ultimately, the Compromise of 1850 yielded an uneasy but significant truce among the warring factions in Alabama.[32]

Meanwhile, Buchanan, ensconced at Wheatland, began his indirect bid for the Democratic presidential nomination in 1852. In response to months of epistolary silence, King invited Buchanan to stay with him in Washington for the short congressional session set to begin in the winter of 1851. Still incensed at the snub, he wrote in January 1851: "I will however forgive all, if you come to Washington and spend a few weeks with me. I am at our old establishment on F Street, quite alone and can furnish you with tolerably good quarters." As before, Buchanan accepted the offer and took Harriet Lane with him for a fortnight's stay. When Congress recessed, however, another drought of correspondence ensued. King tried once more to engage his old friend, this time playing into the eternal wellspring of his former messmate's presidential ambitions. "Perhaps you suppose I have so little influence that my Friendship is of minor importance," he mused. "Do not be deceived. I am the only man who can beat you in Alabama; and unless you pay more attention to me, I will have the ticket." To add even more fuel to the fire, he reported that Alabama newspaper editors were proposing a ticket of King and George Mifflin Dallas, Buchanan's old Pennsylvania rival, for the Democratic nomination. The bait worked; Buchanan replied the next day.[33]

When the ensuing session of Congress gathered in December 1851, the pair turned their full attention to the presidential nomination. Ever the faithful friend, King professed his continued devotion to Buchanan's presidential ambitions. "Of one thing you may rest assured," he wrote at the start of the new congressional session, "there is no man north of Mason & Dixon's line for whom the Democracy of the South would vote in prefference to yourself." As before, Buchanan relied on King for the latest news from the capital, but recurring bouts of rheumatism often rendered correspondence difficult (Catherine Margaret Ellis served as her uncle's amanuensis during these episodes). In January 1852, King again invited Buchanan to visit with him in Washington. He implored Buchanan "to come and stay with me. I have a room at your service; and shall be much gratified if you will do me the favor to occupy it as long as your arrangements will permit." In February, Buchanan accepted the offer and made a quick visit to Washington. He considered another appearance the following month; however, King now advised him to "delay your visit for some time longer," due to ongoing congressional debates over the qualifications of prospective presidential nominees. Thus Buchanan's visit in February 1852 would be the last time the old Siamese twins ever saw one another.[34]

By May, the presidential speculation reached a fever pitch. On the Whig side, the battle lay between President Fillmore and General Winfield Scott. At the convention, Scott eked ahead after many rounds of balloting. On the Democratic side, Buchanan ran neck in neck with Lewis Cass, the party's 1848 nominee, among Democratic insiders. All the while, Stephen Douglas worked behind the scenes to secure the delegates' support as their second choice, should neither man prove able to obtain the necessary two-thirds votes. This latter development especially troubled Buchanan, who wrote candidly to Cave Johnson in Tennessee "such a letter as I have never written to any other friend except Col. King. It is the sober truth." While he doubted Cass's ability to carry Pennsylvania, others in the party questioned Buchanan's own strength there. A Washington correspondent for the New Orleans *Times* aptly named "Le Diable Boiteux" ("the Lame Devil") wrote presciently of Buchanan: "He is eminently conservative, not progressive; and would have been a great man in the earlier party of the eighteenth century." Far better, some believed, to choose a representative of "Young America," such as Douglas, than an "Old Fogy," such as Buchanan (age sixty-one) or Cass (age seventy).[35]

The vice presidency, as always, remained an afterthought. Nevertheless, King attracted favorable notice, especially among newspapers in Alabama, Mississippi, North Carolina, and Pennsylvania. Calls for a bachelor ticket, which had found voice as early as 1842, issued forth once more, with the names Buchanan and King linked publicly together in numerous papers. The Alabama *Advertiser and Gazette* boasted that "such a ticket would carry every solitary Southern State," while the Pittsburgh *Daily Post* proudly printed a banner declaring: "Democratic Ticket. For President of the United States: James Buchanan of Pennsylvania; Subject to decision of the Democratic General Convention. For Vice President: William R. King, of Alabama; Subject to the same decision." Others doubted the efficacy of the bachelor ticket. Although "exceedingly well located," the critical Le Diable Boiteux observed, the ticket was "not calculated to inspire this prolific and progressing country with any great enthusiasm." The combination of Buchanan and King, in other words, could not sufficiently convince the increasingly youthful electorate to cast their ballots for the older pair.[36]

With the convention only weeks away, Buchanan worked furiously to secure support from the various state delegations and to quell opposition from opposing factions within Pennsylvania. He considered another Washington visit to canvass as many national convention delegates as possible. To David Lynch, his long-time political operator in western Pennsylvania who had recently traveled to Richmond on Buchanan's behalf, he expressed concern that such a trip would "do far more harm than . . . good," but he also decried the rumors circulating in the capital that he was "an old decrepit man . . . [who] would not, in all probability, survive until the end of the term." In his usual tongue-in-cheek style, Buchanan boasted that he was still a "young gentleman of sixty-one who has never yet had occasion even to resort to spectacles & who is still something of a beau among the ladies." Although an "Old Fogy" in the eyes of many, Buchanan stubbornly clung to a sense of his own allure to women of fashionable society.[37]

For his part, King encouraged the trip to Washington. He observed that "your presence here ten or fifteen days before the meeting of the Convention could certainly do no harm, and would probably be beneficial." He also rebuffed Buchanan's self-effacement by passing along a comment from his niece Catherine Margaret Ellis. "Mrs. Ellis is quite indignant that you should labor under the imputation of being an old man," he remarked and added saucily: "If all the Ladies of our country were as warm in your cause as are those of Washington, and had the right to vote, your election would be beyond all question." Despite these warm affectations from King and his family, Buchanan's proposed visit to Washington would require him to lodge at a hotel, since the previously proffered room was now occupied by a "fair Lady." After much back and forth, Buchanan determined to stay at Wheatland. King deeply regretted the necessity of his friend's choice, but as he stated in the week before the Democratic Convention in Baltimore: "Washington is now no place for a high minded and honorable man, whose name is before the country for the Presidency." A false step could be magnified one hundred fold in such an environment.[38]

Expectations ran high as the convention finally got underway on June 1. On the first round of balloting, Cass received 116 votes to Buchanan's 93 votes, with William Marcy of New York, Stephen Douglas, and numerous others obtaining handfuls of votes. No candidate yet neared the required 198 votes to achieve the necessary two-thirds majority for victory. After twenty ballots, however, Buchanan emerged as his party's leading contender for the first time in his long political career. He remained the top vote-getter for fully ten rounds of balloting, until he began to lose ground first to Douglas and then to Cass. By then, thirty-four rounds had passed with no clear selection in sight. Then, on the thirty-fifth ballot, a new candidate, Franklin Pierce of New Hampshire, received his first votes. The Pierce delegation had quietly followed the "dark horse" strategy pioneered by James Polk in 1844, and like him, they eventually secured enough support for their candidate's nomination. It had taken forty-nine ballots, but Franklin Pierce would be the Democratic nominee in 1852.[39]

The convention next considered the selection of a running mate. The party leaders recognized the necessity of a southern man to balance the ticket. On the first ballot, King was accordingly nominated and received 125 votes, while his former messmate Solomon Downs of Louisiana ran a distant second with numerous others further behind. Given King's connection to Buchanan, many Democratic insiders hoped the Alabamian's nomination would unite the fractured party. Edmund Burke of New Hampshire, Pierce's convention manager, thought as much. "I think we did right in putting King on the ticket," he told Pierce. "You know he is Buchanan's bosom friend and thus a great and powerful interest is conciliated." The support of Buchanan and King's many political friends could not be ignored.[40]

A pair of questions emerges from the selection process: why had the bachelor ticket failed to gain traction in 1852, and equally significant, why had King, rather than Buchanan, been chosen of the two bosom friends? At the heart of the problem lay King's old two-thirds rule, which by then reflected the divisions in the northern, southern, and western wings of the Democratic Party. Southern votes were especially critical to the party's electoral strategy in 1852, which meant that the ticket needed to include a candidate from each section. To overcome this high parliamentary bar, the Democrats had since 1844 taken a strategy of selecting northerners and westerners for the top of the ticket and southerners for the second spot. However, southern and western Democrats rejected Buchanan as having too much political baggage; instead, the dark horse Pierce seemed the safer northern choice. By contrast, King, who following Taylor's death already functioned as the de facto vice president, had earned his party's loyalty by supporting the compromise measures of 1850. In addition, the selection of King mollified Buchanan's ardent supporters in the North. In short, King had proven more appealing than Buchanan in the unsettled political climate of 1852.

The outcome of the convention precipitated an outpouring of the blandest variety of platitudes from Buchanan. In private, he barely mustered lukewarm support for the Pierce and King ticket. To Virginia ally Robert Tyler, he predicted that King "would make a safe and excellent president," while to another correspondent, he stated more coolly: "Col. King is every thing he ought to be & I shall give the ticket a cordial support." To Cave Johnson he wrote with hardly more enthusiasm: "Both personally and politically General Pierce and Colonel King are highly acceptable to myself." Publicly, though,

Buchanan was more effusive, proclaiming "the warmest feelings of friend-ship" for King. "Of Colonel King," he wrote to a delegation of Pennsylvania Democrats, "I can say emphatically, that he is one of the purest, the best and the most sound judging Statesman, I have ever known." Likewise, a "purer, a better, or a sounder judging man does not live," as he wrote to the editor of the Washington *Daily Union*.[41]

In contrast, King deplored the decision of the convention to pass over Buchanan. Even as he publicly supported Pierce's nomination, King made his opinions known privately. "I would have greatly preferred our Friend Buchanan," he confided to Robert Tyler, but "he was set aside." To Buchanan himself, King penned a heartfelt letter. "No Friend of yours could feel more mortification at your failure to obtain the nomination of the Baltimore convention than I did," he effused. The convention had disgusted him; Catherine Ellis, he said, "mourned over your defeat." Buchanan waited a week to issue his own reply, which effectively ended their correspondence for many more months. With little interest in campaigning for the ticket, Buchanan tried to escape from his problems by summering in Saratoga Springs. In the fall, he hunkered down at Wheatland to await the results of the election.[42]

Even as the Democratic Party appeared to be poised for victory, all was not well physically with the man who occupied the bottom half of its ticket. By the summer of 1852, King's health had deteriorated to the point where he could no longer easily travel, afflicted as he was by a worsening tubercu-losis. Buchanan lamented King's decline, writing in response to a dire report from their mutual friend, Rose O'Neal Greenhow. "I am sorry to hear that Col. King is looking badly," he wrote and effused praise: "He is a man of a thousand. He has always been my friend, through good & through evil re-port. He . . . is ever the same faithful, correct & honorable gentleman of the Old School." In August, King was invited to attend a campaign rally sched-uled in North Carolina, but he regretfully declined, as he had been advised by physicians and friends alike "to seek some quiet watering place in the moun-tains, where pure air and rest would, it is hoped, speedily restore me to my usual health." In the fall months, the vice presidential candidate spent his time doing just that, but no healthful respite could cure his condition. William Rufus King was dying.[43]

A Northern Man with Southern Principles

On the surface, the presidential election of 1852 was politics as usual. It fea-tured the two long-standing national parties, each with its respective set of candidates, trying to convince the American people that they represented the best hope for the Union (the third-party Free Soilers also contended for northern votes). "We Polk'ed you in '44, and we shall Pierce you in '52!" memorably exclaimed the Democrats; Pierce was the victor of "many a hard-fought bottle," retorted the Whigs. In fact, the respective candidates, Franklin Pierce and Winfield Scott, had both fought in the War with Mexico, with Scott the superior to Pierce in military rank and physical stature. But in the election the roles reversed, with the voters elevating the junior officer above his senior. Pierce carried an astounding twenty-seven of thirty-one states, including Alabama and Pennsylvania. Though few at the time understood its full implications, the election of 1852 had signaled the death knell of the Second Party System of Democrats and Whigs.[44]

While Pierce and Scott received the majority of public attention during the campaign, King also attracted notice from journalists across the spectrum. Two themes tended to predominate the coverage of King: his bachelorhood and his many years of public service. Typical was the commentary from the pro-Democratic Brooklyn *Daily Eagle*: "Mr. King is a man of fortune and a bachelor; but he is so mature in years, that we suspect he will not be carried off by the ladies, should he be elevated to the dignified position to which his party has named him." As the campaign wore on, biographies of the candidates repeated this focus. At rallies, King's numerous contemporaries continued their warm, if tongue-in-cheek, support of their vice presidential candidate. "I know him well, love him dearly, and am proud to be called one of his friends," said the irascible former Virginia governor William "Extra Billy" Smith, at a September meeting in San Francisco. "To be sure, he has never brought a woman to his bosom (laughter), but he is nonetheless kind and attractive in his disposition." As always, King's supporters mixed their praise with ribald humor.[45]

If King's Democratic friends huzzahed his name, his enemies among the Whigs and southern states' rights extremists protested it. Critics attacked his perceived effeminacy by commenting about his waning manhood. King was "distinguished, because he has the smallest foot of any man in the United States Senate," said one newspaper editor, while another complained that he was of that "flimsy, tinsely sort of stuff that is intended rather to be admired than handled." Not to be outdone, the *New York Times* purported that many years earlier John Randolph of Roanoke had responded to a woman's inquiry about King with the exasperated reply: "Mr. King? Why madam, Mr. King is—is—in fact Madam, Mr. King wears the handsomest pair of boots in Washington." King took all these assaults in stride, dismissing them as "puerile and illiberal." As he well knew, such gendered insults were part and parcel of political contests in nineteenth-century America.[46]

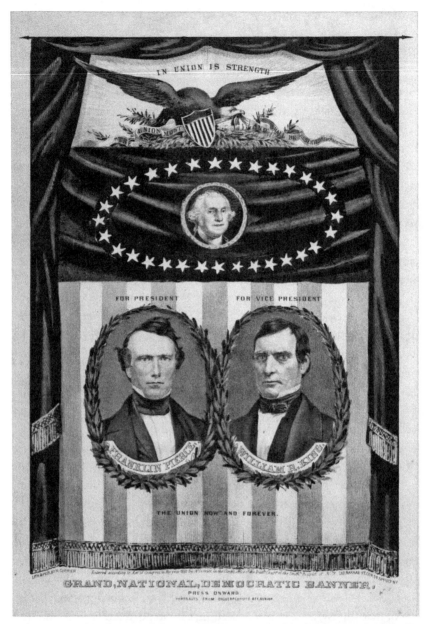

FIGURE 6.4 Grand National Democratic Banner, 1852. The banner at top reads, "In Union is Strength," with Franklin Pierce for President and William R. King for Vice President. The scroll at bottom proclaims: "The Union Now and Forever." Lithograph by Nathaniel Currier, 1852. Prints and Photographs Division, Library of Congress, LC-DIG-pga-08998.

The triumphant election of Pierce and King in November reactivated Buchanan's political instincts. To the president-elect, he reiterated his view of King as "among the best, purest and most consistent public men I have ever known, and is also a sound judging and discreet counsellor." He then added: "You might rely with implicit confidence upon his information, especially in regard to the Southern states." But Pierce ignored both Buchanan's letter and King himself, a common pattern between a president-elect and his running mate in the nineteenth century. In early December, Pierce offered a glimmer of hope to Buchanan. "An interchange of thoughts with Colo. King (whose returning health is a source of great joy to me) would also be peculiarly pleasant & profitable, but here again there are obstacles in the way," Pierce wrote. At issue, King's illness prevented travel from Washington, while Pierce's schedule required him to remain in New Hampshire. Thus shut out from the confidence of the president-elect, Buchanan predicted to a friend in New York that he would "gracefully & gradually retire from public view."[47]

Like Buchanan, the vice president-elect felt little excitement over the new president-elect. "I am not one of those whom he takes into his confidence, for not a single line have I received from him since his nomination," he told Buchanan. Although Pierce passed over Buchanan for secretary of state, a position which King had hoped his old messmate would be offered, the vice president-elect approved of Buchanan's efforts to secure patronage appointments for his political friends. In response, Buchanan praised his old messmate's "enlightened & experienced judgment & his sense of self respect." Still, King held "little confidence" in the men advising the new president-elect. Neither man had fully accepted the outcome of the previous national convention. Reflecting on Pierce's nomination the previous June, King warned of the president-elect's apparent kowtowing to the northern enemies of southern interests. "Let us again be deceived and all the powers of earth will never be able in future to secure the Southern vote for a *Northern man* with *Southern principles*," he declared. In this dire final statement, King accurately prognosticated something of his friend's political future. Only a "safe northern man," approved by the majority of the South, would be acceptable in 1856.[48]

The final months of King's life were marked by sickness and failing health. Back in Washington, his weakened state prevented him from resuming his seat in the Senate. On December 20, he passed the gavel as president pro tempore of the Senate to the more radical David Atchison, to whom he also confided his fears about the dissolution of the Democratic Party. By January 1853, King was so enfeebled that he relied on his niece Catherine Margaret Ellis not only to transcribe but also to compose letters on his behalf. "He requests me to inform you of his proposed departure, and of his sincere desire to see you before he leaves," Ellis wrote Buchanan on New Year's Day 1853, adding, "Uncle desires me to give you his affectionate remembrances." But Buchanan did not visit Washington to send off his old messmate.[49]

On January 22, having officially resigned from the Senate, King boarded the American warship *Fulton*—kindly placed at his disposal by President Fillmore—for Cuba. Like his friend Israel Pickens before him, King hoped to find more salubrious air among the island's sugar cane plantations. As he appeared unlikely to return in time for the inaugural proceedings, Congress granted the vice president-elect a special dispensation to take the oath of office abroad. On March 24, on the grounds of La Ariadne plantation, near Matanzas, William Sharkey, the American consul general at Havana, inaugurated King as the thirteenth vice president of the United States, making him the only American executive ever to have taken the oath of office on foreign soil. One observer noted that the inaugural ceremony, "although simple, was very sad and impressive and will never be forgotten by any who were present." Nevertheless, Consul Sharkey advised Secretary of State William Marcy, there was "but little ground to hope for a recovery." The change of climate could hardly stop King's incurable tuberculosis from worsening.[50]

Following the inauguration, Catherine Margaret Ellis updated Buchanan on her uncle's condition. "I should have written to you before this," she apologized, "but for the unsettled life we have led since our arrival in Cuba." Ellis reported that "Uncle spends two hours a day in the Sugar House, the vapor of which is highly recommended in pulmonary affections." To the last, Ellis acted as a proxy to King's wishes, even when they concerned Buchanan's quixotic pursuit of his twenty-two-year-old niece Margaret William King. "Maggie sends her love," she wrote, "and reminds you of an engagement existing between you and herself, and says, she will expect its fulfillment, if you go to England." Buchanan made no such effort. The unfulfilled courtship of Margaret William King thus fit a long-standing pattern in their friendship: King continued to give fully of himself and his family, but Buchanan did not reciprocate in turn.[51]

In April, King at last determined to return to the United States. On April 7, he boarded the USS *Fulton* for the four-day journey to Mobile, where he recuperated at the Battle House Hotel for several days. From Mobile, the party boarded a river boat to ferry them to King's home at Chestnut Hill, where they arrived on April 17. In the glow of an early Alabama spring, King reportedly remarked that his cotton fields never looked greener. On April 18, 1853, having not even served one month in office, he died at the age of sixty-seven.

His last words were a simple admonition to those present: "Hush, let me pass quietly." Among the many memorial notices, obituaries, and eulogies, the one by his fellow senator from Alabama, Arthur Bagby, while slightly massaging the truth of his political life, perfectly captured the essence of the man: "For forty years . . . neither envy, nor hate, nor malice, nor any manner of unchar-itableness ever whispered a tale of dishonor against him or attempted to cast the slightest shade of suspicion upon the spotless purity of his character." Following a funeral held at the St. John's Episcopal Church in Selma, he was buried in the King family cemetery at Pine Hill.[52]

As the nation mourned for the fallen vice president, Buchanan neither eulogized King nor issued any kind of public statement from Wheatland. Instead, he shared his emotions privately with their mutual political friends, relying upon the same stale language that he had used to describe King during the presidential campaign. To Francis Pickens of South Carolina, he wrote: "I have never known a purer or a better man." In a summation of their years to-gether in Washington, he recounted how he "lived with him for many years as a brother," where King was "always the same amiable, kind-hearted, sound-judging and consistent gentleman." He had known many men in politics, but he "would rather have taken [King's] advice upon any subject, personal or po-litical" than that of any other man. For Buchanan, the memory of his fraternal bond with King, founded in the domestic intimacy of bygone years, was all that remained of their bosom friendship.[53]

Although King was gone, Buchanan felt his influence in other ways during the spring of 1853. In the transition to the new administration, Buchanan urged Pierce to appoint a variety of Pennsylvanians, though never himself, to public office. The president-elect ignored these requests and instead offered Buchanan the desirable post of the American minister to the Court of St. James in London. Ministerial posts had long been the prize possessions of pres-idential patronage appointments, but as Buchanan well knew, they could also set back, or even end, a political career. Might Pierce, who was nicknamed the "Young Hickory of the Granite Hills," be borrowing from the old Jacksonian playbook by thus removing a powerful rival within the Democratic Party? Possibly. Equally so, might Buchanan not profit by following the example of past Democratic nominee Lewis Cass, or for that matter his messmate King, and go abroad to a respectable ministerial post? Again, possibly so. In what amounted to a twenty-five-page defense of his actions, Buchanan concluded in early July 1853: "After mature reflection, I had determined to reject the mis-sion, if I found this could be done without danger of an open breach with the administration; but if this could not be done, I was resolved to accept it, however disagreeable." Accept he did, and with that, he prepared for one last foreign mission.[54]

* * *

As Buchanan set sail for England, he might have reflected on the sequence of events that had removed him from the scene of domestic politics by the summer of 1853. In 1849, having been once again passed over for his party's nomination, he had retired as a private citizen to the tranquility of his country estate at Wheatland. Yet Old Buck could not resist the allure of politics—his reconnection with King during the congressional crisis of 1850 reanimated his hopes for a presidential nomination in 1852. His reengagement with King, while promising both personally and politically, ultimately proved fleeting. Instead, he practiced the life of a gentleman farmer and cultivated a national reputation as the "Sage of Wheatland." This strategy of removal failed to obtain him the presidential nomination in 1852 and ostensibly ended his prospects for public office.

While the bachelor ticket had not come to pass in 1852, the combination of Pierce and King had emerged as an acceptable pairing for a party perpetually warring among its competing sectional and ideological wings. The triumphant election of Pierce and King reaffirmed the political wisdom of the moderate unionism embraced by the national Democratic Party. The year 1852 found both men to be running: King toward the needs of the nation, and on to the vice presidency, and Buchanan toward Wheatland and away from the responsibilities of national leadership. In the breach, their active political and personal partnership permanently ran its course.

By the time of King's death the Siamese twins of the Tyler years had already long been separated, their bosom friendship withered on the political vine. Of the pair, King's approach resulted in the more immediate electoral reward. His moderate unionism possessed a wider appeal to both sections of the party. Although taunted as a hopeless bachelor on the campaign trail by both friends and foes, he managed to minimize these attacks and backhanded compliments through a dignified silence. He masterfully played the national political game until his death. In contrast, Buchanan's prospects for higher office had never been more dismal than in the summer of 1853. By then he had thrice tried for the Democratic presidential nomination, each time without gaining the necessary support from the southern states. If he ever hoped to achieve his lifelong ambition of the presidency, a complete reversal of the winds of political fortune would be required.

7

Presiding, 1853–1868

THE SECTIONAL DIVISIONS afflicting the nation subsided following the death of William Rufus King. The new president, Franklin Pierce, was charismatic and amiable, even as social life in the White House suffered under the dark gloom of recent deaths in his family. But discord was arising in other ways that subtly eroded the harmony engendered by the 1852 Democratic convention. With the Democrats out of power for four long years, the Pierce administration labored to divide federal patronage appointments among the party faithful. The cabinet and ministerial posts having been split more or less equally across sections, the colossal task of distributing the lesser jobs beguiled. In the key state of New York the administration attempted to reunify the party, which had previously split over the question of whether to cooperate with the "Barnburner" faction that had broken away in support of a Free Soil platform. As events played out, the Pierce administration's assignment of federal jobs heavily favored the "Softshells," or moderate faction at the expense of the "Hardshell Hunkers," or conservative faction, leaving a lasting schism. The process repeated itself elsewhere, such that the Pierce administration was internally divided after its first six months in office.[1]

Those same opening months of the Pierce administration found the national economy booming and its expansionist foreign policy thriving. But the congressional session that opened in December 1853 proved one of the most disastrous in American history. Previously, Democrats Stephen Douglas and David Atchison had argued bitterly over the organization of the Nebraska territory, a vast swath of land carved from the eastern third of the Louisiana Purchase, with little progress made. To break the political logjam, the two men crafted a compromise solution. The resulting proposal was nothing short of political dynamite: to organize Nebraska, the bill's proponents proposed to repeal the Missouri Compromise and to substitute in its place the doctrine of popular sovereignty, which permitted the settlers of the various territories to decide the slavery question for themselves. By application of direct pressure on President Pierce, the terms of the bill quickly became an administration mandate. The resulting Kansas-Nebraska Act, passed into law in May 1854, sent political shockwaves across the nation.[2]

The Kansas-Nebraska Act also upended the existing two-party system. Its passage broke the unity of the old Whig coalition and resulted in a partisan realignment marked by new political factions. The anti-slavery Republican Party was the most important of these groups, while a nativist coalition that organized under the banner of the American Party, and whose members were commonly derided as the "Know Nothings," also clamored for attention. The Democratic Party was seriously weakened, too. Prior to 1854, Democrats expressed confidence in both the leadership of Franklin Pierce and the policies of Stephen Douglas, but just two years later, both men found a hostile climate toward their presidential ambitions. Worse still, the repeal of the Missouri Compromise permitted slavery in all federal territories hitherto unorganized. In 1856, the caning of Charles Sumner at the hands of congressman Preston Brooks of South Carolina and the skirmishes among pro-slavery and anti-slavery forces in the Kansas territory epitomized the new factionalism rendered by the act. The political stakes had been violently and irrevocably raised.[3]

From his ministerial post in London, James Buchanan followed political developments at home with great interest. Still, he remained publicly silent as the dramatic events unfolded in Congress. "I have expressed no opinion to any person on the Nebraska Bill," he wrote to a Lancaster friend in May 1854, as "I have thought that in a foreign land & with a desire to part from public life in peace with all my friends, I might be justified in my silence." But even as he shied away from active engagement with domestic political questions, he could not forever cling to his stance as a neutral observer. Moreover, his many political friends back home, sensing that Old Buck had once more become a presidential contender, beseeched him to return to the United States as soon as possible. The ticket of Franklin Pierce and William Rufus King, which had promised to unify the Democratic Party and steer the nation past the shoals of sectional partisanship, had instead foundered on those very same treacherous rocks. As American party politics shifted yet again, the door had been opened for a change in political leadership. Who would be thrust into the void?[4]

Who Did Not Love Him?

The new American minister to England was well-prepared for the assignment. Once in London, Buchanan incorporated his legation staff into an unofficial family. Like most families, his was not without its problems—he especially came to detest his legation secretary, the flamboyant and at times reckless Daniel Sickles of New York. The rift with Sickles cost him a "very intimate" friendship with George Peabody, the famous American philanthropist and a fellow bachelor. In counterbalance he grew closer to his niece Harriet Lane, who persuaded Buchanan to permit her to travel to England. Once there, Queen Victoria formally bestowed the standing of a ministerial consort upon Lane. Unsurprisingly, she also attracted numerous suitors, but in compliance with her uncle's wishes, Lane dutifully refused all marriage offers while she served as his official hostess.[5]

At the start of the Pierce administration, the tenuous state of Anglo-American affairs required both sides to tread carefully. Buchanan initially focused his attention on the area along the Mosquito Coast (the present-day basin centered on Honduras and Nicaragua), where both countries claimed a territorial interest. Under the terms of the Clayton-Bulwer Treaty—a measure King had favored but detested by Buchanan—America gained a path to build a canal to the Pacific Ocean, while Great Britain delimited future American expansion in the Caribbean basin. Yet conflicts in the region persisted in the 1850s, fueled by southern filibusterers and an unquenchable American desire to acquire the island of Cuba. The crown jewel of the Caribbean had long fascinated the new American minister. During his time as secretary of state, he formally inquired to Spain about acquiring the island, but was rebuffed in no uncertain terms. By 1853 the news of a possible purchase led to unauthorized filibustering across the Caribbean, the continued fallout of which Buchanan managed as American minister to England.[6]

From early on, Buchanan urged Pierce to pursue a policy favorable to the acquisition of Cuba. In 1854 the president directed that the three top American ministers abroad—Pierre Soulé (Spain), John Y. Mason (France), and Buchanan (England)—meet and prepare a statement of intent to present to Spain. Although reluctant to play the American hand so overtly, Buchanan traveled with Lane to Ostend, along the Belgian coast, before the combined party decamped to the more secluded Aix-Chappelle, along the French-Prussian border. At these meetings the cautious Buchanan acted as a counterweight to the more hot-headed Soulé. In the final document, written in Buchanan's inimitable hand, the American ministers boldly asserted that pending a hostile threat from Spain, the United States was "justified in wresting [Cuba] from Spain, if we possess the power." Northern outrage ensued when word leaked to the press of the mislabeled "Ostend Manifesto." Nevertheless, Buchanan persisted in his course. In so doing, he implicitly hoped that the acquisition of Cuba might appease southern demands to expand into the western territories acquired as part of the Mexican Cession. Cuba could be a relief valve for slavery's expansion.[7]

After the meeting at Ostend, Buchanan quietly moved to curtail his English mission. Once more, the possibility of a presidential nomination motivated him. Although he categorically denied any interest in running, often underlining his disavowal to his many correspondents, the political fallout from the passage of the Kansas-Nebraska Act seems to have activated his presidential instincts once again. By early 1855 he began to demur less loudly at his friends' entreaties about the upcoming presidential election, and by the end of the year, he more firmly insisted to Secretary of State Marcy for his release from his ministerial post. Before leaving England, Buchanan strategically cultivated the Irish Catholic vote back home, when he hosted a public dinner for Cardinal Nicholas Wiseman. Thurlow Weed remarked years later "that dinner party made Mr. Buchanan President of the United States!" Finally, in March 1856, Buchanan received his formal notice of recall and prepared to return home.[8]

When James Buchanan boarded the steamship *Atlantic* for England in August 1853, he probably had little idea that he would return to the United States four years hence as a serious presidential contender. Fewer than three years later, the public greeted Buchanan as a returning hero and as the presumptive presidential candidate of the Democratic Party. Across the country, "Wheatland Clubs" had sprouted up to promote his candidacy. Upon arrival in the United States, Buchanan traveled from New York to Philadelphia and then on to Lancaster, where the local Wheatland Club fired the inaugural shots from the "Old Buck Cannon." Almost immediately, Buchanan opened his doors and poured copious amounts of alcohol to political friends, journalists, and well-wishers. By the end of April he had devoted himself entirely to securing the presidential nomination, spending hours in answering letters and meeting with his campaign managers. With the Pennsylvania Democracy finally united behind its favorite son, he must have looked optimistically to the national convention scheduled for early June.[9]

In opposition to the Democrats stood the nativist American Party and the anti-slavery Republican Party. The American Party met in February at National Hall in Philadelphia, where they nominated former president

Millard Fillmore as its standard-bearer. If the nativist American Party was more flash than substance, the Republican Party posed a more serious challenge. The Republicans had recently emerged as an anti-slavery party comprised of northern Whigs, Free Soilers, and disaffected Democrats. Meeting at the newly constructed Musical Fund Hall in Philadelphia, they chose John C. Frémont, nicknamed the Pathfinder to the West, as their candidate. In turn, the anti-slavery northern Know Nothings, who had earlier bolted from the party, independently settled on Frémont, hoping for a "fusion" ticket with the Republicans. Finally, the remnants of the Whig Party endorsed the southern-leaning American ticket. The contest in 1856 had become a three-way, largely sectional race.[10]

By comparison, the old Jacksonian coalition that comprised the national Democratic Party held steadfast. Breaking with past tradition, they met in Cincinnati, where the delegates caroused, shouted, and smoked their way through the usual litany of candidates. But for the first time, Buchanan entered as the convention's front-runner; on the first ballot, he received more votes than any of the other three candidates—Franklin Pierce, Stephen Douglas, and Lewis Cass—though he remained well short of the 198 votes needed for a two-thirds majority. With each additional ballot Buchanan gained strength, while Douglas sapped delegates from Pierce. On the fifteenth ballot, the incumbent president's name was withdrawn—the first and only such occurrence in the history of nominating conventions—which sent Buchanan and Douglas surging to new heights. Finally, on the seventeenth round of ballots, the Douglas delegates withdrew their support for the Little Giant and unanimously switched to Old Buck. Buchanan had won. To balance the ticket, the assembly chose one of its own delegates, John C. Breckinridge of Kentucky, for vice president. From there, the alliterative chant of "Buck and Breck" resounded from the convention hall to the front pages of newspapers across the nation.[11]

What explains the strength of Buchanan's candidacy in 1856? Simply put, he had broadened his electoral appeal in the North, while maintaining support in key southern states. Whereas in 1852 he had received votes from ten states—up from just a handful of states in 1848—he drew votes from some fourteen states in 1856. In order of votes cast on the first ballot, these were Pennsylvania, New York, Virginia, Ohio, Indiana, Michigan, Wisconsin, New Jersey, Maryland, Louisiana, Maine, Massachusetts, Kentucky, and Delaware. Of these states, the Pennsylvania–Virginia axis, so assiduously cultivated through his friendships with Robert Tyler and more recently with Henry Wise, formed the core of his electoral strength. Aside from steadfast

FIGURE 7.1 Grand National Democratic Banner, 1856. The banner at top reads, "One Country, One Constitution, One Destiny," while the scroll at bottom proclaims: "James Buchanan and John C. Breckenridge [*sic*], the Democrats Choice for President and Vice President from 1857 to 1861." Lithograph by Nathaniel Currier, 1856. Courtesy Falvey Memorial Library, Villanova University.

Louisiana, Buchanan received almost no support from the Deep South, including Alabama. For the past decade he had heeded the advice of his old messmate in currying those delegates, but in the end, it proved to be a poor convention strategy. In 1856, Buchanan obtained the Democratic nomination from the votes of mostly free states and only a scattered handful of southern states.[12]

If Buchanan had not followed King's southern strategy to the nomination, he had heeded his advice in other ways. Foremost among these, he had presented himself as a "safe" candidate to the slaveholding South. While Pierce initially received the backing of most southern Democrats, Buchanan eventually merited similar support. After all, as a senator, secretary of state, and American minister to England, he had protected the expansion of slavery in the western territories and steadfastly worked to acquire Cuba. Equally, his expressions of conservativism worked to his advantage in 1856. The unprecedented feeling of national tumult cried out for the political stability of an earlier era. With his white necktie, plain republican clothing, and a Newfoundland dog named Lara at his side, the elderly Buchanan projected the image of a gentleman farmer. From the tranquility of Wheatland, he declared the Democracy to be "the only surviving conservative party of the country." He was, without a doubt, the conservatives' choice in 1856.[13]

Like King before him, Buchanan faced the lingering issue of his lifelong bachelorhood. Partly, he benefited from changing views about the unmarried across American society. At the party convention, ally Samuel Black of Pennsylvania spun Buchanan's bachelorhood into a positive, if tongue-in-cheek, good, declaring "as soon as James Buchanan was old enough to marry, he became wedded to the Constitution of his country, and the laws of Pennsylvania do not allow a man to have more than one wife." He equally profited from the echo of the love story with Ann Coleman. His advanced age also helped; at sixty-five, Buchanan was not the oldest man ever to run for president—that distinction belonged to William Henry Harrison—but his white mane of hair certainly lent an impression of dignity and equally mitigated the marriage question. Finally, his close connections to female relatives aided his cause. One visitor to Wheatland described the candidate as "about sixty-five years of age and has never married," adding that his "family consists of himself and niece, whose . . . knowledge and sense, derived from books, study and reflection, peculiarly qualify her to grace and cheer the fireside of the Sage of Wheatland." Although unwed, the Democrats asserted, their candidate was an intellectually refined family man.[14]

FIGURE 7.2 "A Serviceable Garment, Or Reverie of a Bachelor." Buchanan, a Cheshire cat at his feet, sews a coat with a patch marked "Cuba" onto the lapel and thinks: "My Old coat was a very fashionable Federal coat when it was new, but by patching and turning I have made it quite a Democratic Garment. That Cuba patch to be sure is rather unsightly but it suits Southern fashions at this season, and then (If I am elected,) let me see, $25,000 pr. annum, and no rent to pay, and no Women and Babies about, I guess I can afford a new outfit." Lithograph by Nathaniel Currier, 1856. Courtesy American Antiquarian Society.

His supporters also touted his many close political friendships through the years. Rushmore Horton, a New York propagandist hired to write a campaign biography of the Democratic candidate, presented his relationship to King as emblematic of the cross-sectional friendship of a bygone era. Buchanan, he noted, was "the friend of Levi Woodbury, the companion of Wm. R. King, of Roane, of Silas Wright, of John C. Calhoun, of Felix Grundy, and of all that sterling race of men who adorned the era in which he was an actor." In the same tract,

Horton added another touching detail about Buchanan's relationship with King when quoting a letter from an anonymous visitor to Wheatland: "I was much gratified in finding in his library a likeness of the late Vice-President King, whom he loved (and who did not?)" To this same unnamed visitor, Buchanan echoed his characterization of King from years earlier, calling his former messmate "the purest public man that he ever knew, and that during his intimate acquaintance of thirty years he had never known him to perform a selfish act." Even from the grave, King aided his old friend as a rhetorical touchstone.[15]

As fall arrived, the three-way race of 1856 remained as uncertain as any in recent memory. By October the favorable results from Pennsylvania, which voted early, boded well for the Democracy. In November, the Democrats carried thirteen southern states, the critical battleground states of Illinois, Indiana, and New Jersey, and the new state of California. By contrast, the Republicans took only northern states, including electorally rich Ohio and New York, but they did not receive any votes from south of the Mason-Dixon Line (the badly split American Party carried only Maryland). In total, Buchanan easily won the Electoral College, taking 174 votes to Frémont's 114 and Fillmore's 8, and gained the highest count in the popular vote, with an overall 45.3 percent as compared to 33.1 percent for Frémont and 21.6 percent for Fillmore. Although a win for the Democracy, Buchanan's margin of victory was worrisomely smaller than those of James Polk and Franklin Pierce.[16]

The Gayest Administration

After the election of 1856, much of the country breathed a collective sigh of relief. "Better tidings from Kansas, the cooling of tempers, and, no doubt, the magic of the season," one historian has written of this period, brightened the American popular mood and cheered the incoming presidential administration to start the new year of 1857. Despite paeans from hopeful conservatives, the president-elect faced a country hopelessly divided over the issue of slavery. The prior year's events in "Bleeding Kansas" further escalated, and tempers flared hotter on both sides. Nevertheless, Buchanan clung faithfully to his conception of cross-sectional friendship in his appointment of cabinet officers, in the social life administered by his White House, and across the councils of a dividing Democratic Party. To save the Union, President Buchanan prescribed pure and unselfish patriotism—exemplified best by the course of his old friend King—as the cure for the ailing nation.[17]

Even as historians have condemned his presidency, the scholarly consensus still holds that Buchanan was among the best prepared men ever elected to the office. He first demonstrated the wisdom of past experience in the selection of his cabinet. Like Polk, whose course he followed throughout his presidency, Buchanan attempted to balance sectional and ideological interests across the badly fractured Democratic Party. And like Polk, he intended to control much of the foreign policy of his administration; accordingly, he chose his former presidential rival, Lewis Cass of Michigan, to head the State Department. For the treasury, he picked Howell Cobb of Georgia, a forty-one-year-old former congressman; for war, the politically connected John Floyd of Virginia; for navy, Isaac Toucey of Connecticut, attorney general under Polk; for postmaster general, former antagonist Aaron Brown of Tennessee; for attorney general, Jeremiah Black of western Pennsylvania; and finally, to head the new department of the interior, Jacob Thompson from Mississippi. Even more than Polk, however, Buchanan came to regret deeply the later actions of many of these cabinet officers.[18]

The ordeals of office began earlier than usual. While staying at the National Hotel in the days before his inauguration, the president-elect, his nephews Eskridge Lane and James Buchanan Henry, and several other hotel guests fell violently ill. Some suspected poisoning by arsenic, but the actual cause seems to have been unsanitary drinking water. According to a later report of his southern confidante Rose O'Neal Greenhow, Buchanan remained "in a very critical condition." Thus weakened, Buchanan roused himself for his inauguration on the morning of March 4, 1857. Per custom, outgoing president Franklin Pierce met the president-elect for a ride in an open carriage to the Capitol. Perhaps forty thousand people gathered to witness the ceremony, making it the largest crowd ever gathered for a presidential inaugural to that time. The customary inaugural ball followed, with massive quantities of food consumed, including memorably a "pyramid of cake four feet high, ornamented with a flag bearing the arms of every State and Territory." The presence of Harriet Lane, adorned in a white lace dress with a low bertha topped by a garland of flowers, added to the perception that the Buchanan White House would be a festive one.[19]

As the celebrations died down, newspapers reported the president's inaugural address. Buchanan covered the usual litany of Democratic issues, deplored the evils of sectionalism, and addressed the conflict over territorial expansion, especially in Kansas. To a perceptive reader, one line may have stood out; speaking of the question of slavery in the territories, he said, "Besides, it is a judicial question, which legitimately belongs to the Supreme Court of the United States, before whom it is now pending, and will, it is understood, be speedily and finally settled." Indeed, two days later, Chief Justice Roger Taney read his decision in the case of *Dred Scott v. John F. A. Sanford*, in which he not only ordered Scott back into slavery, but declared that African

FIGURE 7.3 Inauguration of James Buchanan, March 4, 1857. The crowd was the largest assembled theretofore for a presidential inauguration. Daguerreotype by John Wood. Montgomery C. Meigs Papers, Prints and Photographs Division, Library of Congress.

Americans did not (and could not) possess the same rights of citizenship as white Americans. The timing of Buchanan's message was no coincidence: he had spent the previous months in correspondence with at least two separate justices of the court, including Pennsylvanian Robert Grier and former messmate John Catron of Tennessee. In these missives, he had urged that the court render a definitive legal judgment on the question of slavery in the western territories. With *Dred Scott* the president got his wish, though at a substantial political price in the years ahead.[20]

From the outset, President Buchanan steadfastly projected his administration's program based on strict Democratic principles. Overwhelmed by the usual requests for patronage appointments, the new president almost exclusively rewarded those who had proved loyal to him in the past. In many respects, he was an effective chief executive in his first year in office. His initial annual message—delivered to the incoming members of the Thirty-Fifth Congress in December 1857—reported on the dire state of the economy, relations with Central American nations, the situation in Kansas, and the military expedition that precipitated a conflict with the Mormon settlers in Utah. Of all the issues, the Panic of 1857, brought on by a stock market sell-off in response to the news of railroad and bank failures, threatened to shake the creditworthiness of the nation. Although he acknowledged the practical necessity of paper money, the president cautioned against the establishment of a new national bank. In a paean to the old Jacksonian wisdom, he declared: "After all, we must mainly rely upon the patriotism and wisdom of the States for the prevention and redress of the evil." The depression continued for nearly two years.[21]

Neither the *Dred Scott* case nor the faltering economy sank the Buchanan administration. Instead, much as the Kansas-Nebraska Act had railroaded the presidency of Franklin Pierce, Buchanan foundered over the issue of slavery in "Bleeding Kansas." The violence between conflicting pro- and anti-slavery forces had been accompanied by a pro-slavery constitutional convention that met under dubious circumstances at Lecompton. An ensuing vote, the results of which were almost certainly fraudulent, produced the Lecompton Constitution, which was sent on to Congress for approval. The territorial governor, former Polk cabinet member Robert Walker of Mississippi, protested that the document had been begotten by undemocratic methods, but President Buchanan, who had already determined to admit Kansas along pro-slavery lines, sent along a lengthy message to Congress in support of its ratification. The Senate dutifully accepted the Lecompton constitution, but the House added conditions to the bill that required further compromise. Stephen Douglas and his supporters, who had already broken with Buchanan, declared the Lecompton Constitution to be a fraud. Douglas's public betrayal infuriated Buchanan and led to a permanent rift between them. From then on, the nation's two most powerful Democrats openly opposed one another.[22]

While the fallout over the Lecompton Constitution derailed the administration's political program, the social life at the White House prospered under the careful management of First Lady Harriet Lane. She followed in the style of Dolley Madison and Sarah Childress Polk, and, for that matter, the president's southern cabinet officers. "Washington was never gayer than during this administration," remembered Sara Agnes Rice Pryor, wife of a southern senator. The entertainment included "morning receptions, evening receptions, dinners, musicales, children's parties, old-fashioned evening parties with music and supper, and splendid balls." So many functions vied for attention that Washington socialites often "attended three balls in one evening." At one notable costume ball given by Senator William and Mary Bell Gwin of California, even the scrupulous Buchanan participated in the receiving line. Decades later, one observer still remembered antebellum Washington as "a mixture of Arlington grandeur, Jeffersonian simplicity, Dolly-Madisonism, Fillmore primness and the gracious chill of Miss Harriet Lane." Notwithstanding these social delights and the construction of the first permanent greenhouse, the legacy of the Buchanan years among White House historians has been one of shabby living quarters overrun by a swarm of southern sympathizers, most notably Rose O'Neal Greenhow. Although many of these social connections were long-standing, the subsequent events of the Civil War years have made them appear suspect in retrospect.[23]

FIGURE 7.4 Harriet Lane. Her skillful arrangement of the White House social calendar and status as President Buchanan's niece merited her the title of "First Lady." Daguerreotype, ca. 1857. Courtesy Brady-Handy Photograph Collection, Prints and Photographs Division, Library of Congress, LC-DIG-cwpbh-00692.

First Lady Harriet Lane invigorated the capital's social life, but she did not always agree with her uncle's strict prerogatives. For example, after Lane arranged for a pleasure cruise along the Potomac River on the Coast Guard revenue cutter *Harriet Lane*, the president forbade future outings and ordered the treasury department to pay for the use of the ship. The friction worsened as Lane continued to attract suitors, including southerners William Porcher Miles of South Carolina and Thomas Clingman of North Carolina. Her uncle again discouraged any match until his term of office had concluded. Following these family quarrels, Lane often visited with friends away from Washington, such as with Cornelia Van Ness Roosevelt in New York. "I do not care how long she stays," Buchanan said of her absences. "I can do very well without her." With the close of the congressional session in June 1858, the social season in Washington ended and the president decamped alone to a cottage on the grounds of the Old Soldiers' Home, some three miles away in the countryside.[24]

As he had done during his ministerial posts, Buchanan treated his cabinet subordinates as his official family. In turn, they bestowed upon him an affectionate nickname: "the Squire." Buchanan grew especially intimate with treasury secretary Howell Cobb, owing to the frequent absence of his wife, Mary Ann Lamar Cobb. At Cobb's Washington home, dubbed the "Widower's Den," the president regularly called on his treasury secretary to play cards, especially euchre (the games became so frequent that the neighborhood acquired the nickname of "Euchre Circle"); in turn, Cobb dined with the president for weeks at a stretch and received the supervisory duties of the government during presidential absences. The Buchanan–Cobb bosom friendship resembled those formed with King and the others in the bachelor's Mess decades earlier. While Cobb proved a suitable substitute for King on a personal level, his friendship with Buchanan was not one of political equals. Moreover, Cobb's strongest personal connection remained to his family rather than to the bachelor president.[25]

Buchanan continued to enjoy romantic flirtations, now exclusively with southern widows. Even before returning to the United States, a rumor had circulated that he intended to court the stately widow Sarah Childress Polk, though both parties categorically denied this. As president he first attached himself to widow Elizabeth Church Craig, a daughter of the president of the University of Georgia and an intimate friend of the Cobbs, who once declared to them that "nothing short of the first man will answer" her plans for a second husband. In the winter of 1858, Craig visited the capital and resided by invitation of the president at the White House. When she departed Washington the following spring, the Old Buck kept up a polite, if not petty, interest in her personal affairs, but he subsequently snubbed her new husband at a social event. By then, Buchanan had moved on to his next dalliance. In the summer of 1859, he became attached to Eugénie Bate Bass of Mississippi, a wealthy thirty-three-year-old widow and mother of three. When Bass visited Buchanan at the cottage, the president reportedly rushed out of the parlor to change clothes, returning "dressed in an inch of his life" as Kate Thompson, wife of the interior secretary, recollected to Mary Ann Lamar Cobb. In August 1859, the president "squired" Bass and her three children with him to Bedford Springs. But these flirtations aside, Buchanan remained incorrigibly a bachelor.[26]

As the president frolicked and socialized through the congressional recess, the Democratic Party deteriorated during the fall of 1858. The open rift between Douglas and Buchanan festered in the northern states, where the Republicans gained ground during the midterm congressional elections

FIGURE 7.5 Eugénie Patience Bate Bass. The wealthy widow and mother of three was a social favorite of the Buchanan White House. Courtesy Bate Family Papers Collection, Tennessee State Library and Archives.

of 1858. The president heard the dismal election results from Pennsylvania while attending a dinner party with fellow Democrats. "We had a merry time of it," he reported to Harriet Lane, "laughing among other things over our crushing defeat. It is so great that it is almost absurd." In his second annual message, however, Buchanan boostered the state of national affairs, and, among other foreign policy measures, reiterated his request to consider the purchase of Cuba. The lame-duck Congress dutifully debated the purchase, even going so far as to propose putting thirty million dollars at the president's disposal, but the Senate delayed action on the controversial measure, tabling the bill indefinitely. Its failure signaled Buchanan's last serious effort at territorial expansion—a project that had churned since the days of Polk—and further antagonized southern legislators. The short session of the Thirty-Fifth Congress concluded in March 1859 with little accomplished.[27]

Despite legislative false starts and worsening sectionalism, the prospects for the remainder of 1859 appeared good. Following in the footsteps of Polk, President Buchanan accepted the invitation of the University of North Carolina to deliver its annual commencement address that June. Buchanan understood that the success of a southern secession movement would depend on attracting the populous states of Virginia and North Carolina, his old messmate's birthplace. On the way south, the president and his entourage attracted large, friendly crowds, where one newspaper reported that he appeared as "gay and frisky as a young buck." Ever chivalric, he "kissed hundreds of pretty girls"—at one point veritably jumping from off the speakers' stage to greet a crowd of women—"which *made his mouth water*," Kate Thompson gossiped. At Raleigh and then at Chapel Hill, the president addressed the citizens and gladly accepted an honorary membership into the Philanthropic Society; he may well have seen King's portrait hanging in the society's meeting room. Buchanan declared to an assembled crowd at Wilmington: "[King] was my most intimate friend, for I was more intimate with him than I ever was with any other man in my life, and he was as pure and patriotic and honorable as any man that ever lived." Their association continued to prove useful.[28]

Mr. Buchanan's War

In retrospect, the halcyon days of the summer of 1859 were the calm before the storm. On October 16, the militant abolitionist John Brown led a group of nearly two dozen armed men into western Virginia, where they seized the arsenal at Harpers Ferry in an effort to foment an armed rebellion among the enslaved people of the region. When word of the raid reached the president, he ordered federal troops under the command of Col. Robert E. Lee to subdue Brown and his posse—all told, ten of Brown's men were killed and another seven captured, including Brown himself. The Thirty-Sixth Congress convened only days after the execution of John Brown that took place on December 2. From the outset, the sectional divisions crippled the ability of the Congress to organize (nearly two months passed before the House agreed upon a compromise candidate as its speaker). In this divided atmosphere, President Buchanan delivered his third annual message. He immediately decried the raid on Harpers Ferry as "but symptoms of an incurable disease in the public mind, which may break out in still more dangerous outrages, and terminate, at last, in an open war by the North to abolish slavery in the South." Yet as before, Buchanan primarily updated the Congress on his progress in foreign affairs, reviewed the record of legislation from the previous term, and opined on the state of fiscal affairs in the nation. All the same, his

FIGURE 7.6 Cabinet of James Buchanan, ca. 1859. The photograph shows President Buchanan standing, surrounded by his cabinet including (from left to right) Jacob Thompson, secretary of the interior; Lewis Cass, secretary of state; John B. Floyd, secretary of war; Howell Cobb, secretary of the treasury; Isaac Toucey, secretary of the navy; Joseph Holt, postmaster general; and Jeremiah S. Black, attorney general. Brady-Handy Photograph Collection, Prints and Photographs Division, Library of Congress, LC-BH8277- 537.

steadfast belief in the power of the Union and an unshakable equanimity in the face of growing calamity could not alleviate the palpable tensions felt across the nation.[29]

Unlike the great debates that followed in 1850, neither side wished to compromise in 1860. The Democratic-controlled Senate initiated an investigation into the raid on Harpers Ferry, with an eye toward implicating the Republicans (no evidence was found to establish a link). In turn, the Republican-controlled House formed a committee under the leadership of Pennsylvania Republican John Covode to investigate possible corruption in the Buchanan administration. In reply, the president issued a formal rebuke of the committee along constitutional and historical lines. "Since the time of the Star Chamber and of general warrants there has been no such proceeding in England," he protested. Although the committee sought evidence of impeachable offenses, the final report, split into competing Republican and Democratic sections, failed to produce a vote for impeachment. Once more, Buchanan rebuked the committee and even attempted to engage newspaper editor James Gordon Bennett of the *New York Herald* directly on his behalf. But the effect of the Covode Committee was irreversible: the majority of Americans no longer trusted the integrity of their chief executive.[30]

Meanwhile, the presidential election of 1860 loomed. In late April, the Democratic Party convened at Charleston, a concession to its southern base. The strategy backfired when delegates from the same seven Deep South states that later seceded from the Union walked out of the convention. Throughout the balloting front-runner Stephen Douglas consistently received the majority of the votes, but he failed to achieve the required two-thirds. In an unprecedented move, the delegates adjourned without selecting a candidate, agreeing to return to more familiar ground in Baltimore the following month. Meanwhile, a Constitutional Union Party met and put forward John Bell as its nominee, while the anti-slavery Republicans selected Abraham Lincoln as its standard-bearer. Once in Baltimore, the Democrats again split into two factions, with the northern camp selecting Douglas as its nominee and the southern wing choosing Vice President John C. Breckinridge. By the end of June, the fractured presidential contest had become a four-way race.[31]

Buchanan remained publicly quiet about the troubling events taking place within his party. However, he delivered an impromptu address from the front portico of the White House on the evening of July 9. The president offered an incisive historical review of the events that had led to the splintering of the Democratic Party, noting especially the origins of the two-thirds rule. "It was believed that under this rule no candidate could ever be nominated without embracing within two-thirds the votes of a decided majority of the Democratic States," he declared. Though he did not mention King, Buchanan tacitly supported his old messmate's part in the rule's early development. But he did not remain above the political fray; instead, he fingered the actions of Douglas and his supporters at the Baltimore convention as having caused the break-up of the Democratic Party. He then formally endorsed Breckinridge and further recounted how the tumultuous events of his presidency had led the nation to its current predicament. He still believed that a "united Northern Democracy" could stop the "Northern agitation and fanaticism" that endangered the Union. His faith in the old Jacksonian coalition, even after it had so clearly disintegrated, was myopic.[32]

As the presidential race heated up, Washington entered its usual summer lull. For his part, Buchanan's attention drifted to more pleasant memories of days gone by. In September, Harriet Lane received word from her uncle that Catherine Margaret Ellis, recently returned from a European sojourn, had been invited to visit the White House. "Mrs. E. is bright & attractive," observed Sophie Plitt, a friend of Lane's, "& it seems to me you could not have a more agreeable person." As a token of her affection, Ellis presented Lane with a gift of "a gold belt from Tiffany's." Over the next several weeks, the two women quickly reaffirmed their intimate bond of affection and publicly socialized together, often as the only two ladies among groups of men. Before the close of the congressional session, each woman also attracted the notice of eligible men in the capital. The diarist Mary Chesnut recorded that Lane entertained eleven suitors, mostly southerners, while Ellis refused at least one proposal. Yet both remained unmarried through the end of the Buchanan administration.[33]

Meanwhile, Buchanan focused his executive authority on his preferred arena of diplomacy. In May 1860, the White House had hosted a delegation of Japanese officials, who greeted the president wearing traditional garb and equipped with samurai swords. The stir created by the Japanese visitors was only surpassed by the royal visit of Prince Albert Edward (the future King Edward VII) in October. The president extended the official courtesies of office, but Harriet Lane, who along with Catherine Ellis first greeted the prince in the Blue Room, most impressed the young royal. "I thought Miss Lane a particularly nice person and very pretty," Prince Albert Edward wrote to his mother, Queen Victoria. On the following day a large contingent, including Buchanan and the prince, cruised aboard the *Harriet Lane* on a visit to the tomb of George Washington at Mount Vernon. A portrait from the event depicted some three dozen dignitaries, including Harriet Lane and Catherine Ellis, the latter of whom "made a most agreeable impression upon our guests."[34]

FIGURE 7.7 *Visit of the Prince of Wales, President Buchanan, and Dignitaries to the Tomb of Washington at Mount Vernon, October 1860.* Harriet Lane, holding a parasol, and Catherine Margaret Ellis, wearing a black shawl with her back to the viewer, stand to the left of President Buchanan and Prince Albert Edward. Oil on canvas by Thomas Rossiter, 1861. Bequest of Harriet Lane Johnston, Smithsonian American Art Museum.

Try as it might, the Buchanan administration could not retreat into so- cial pleasantries. The election of Abraham Lincoln produced tremors that cracked the foundations of the national union. Its aftershocks were even worse. In the North, the Republican Party celebrated the triumph of its plat- form of "free soil, free labor, and free men," while in the South, many doubted the continuation of a Union under the first avowedly anti-slavery president. As with the nullification crisis thirty years earlier, South Carolina led the way. On December 11, 1860, secession delegates convened in Charleston to vote the Palmetto State out of the Union. Not long thereafter, Georgia, Alabama, Mississippi, Louisiana, Arkansas, and Texas followed suit. Still, the border states of the Upper South clung to the Union. To President Buchanan and the lame-duck session of the Thirty-Sixth Congress fell an impossible chal- lenge: stabilize the political fallout, preserve the integrity of federal property in the seceded states, and prevent further secession of the border states.[35]

President Buchanan sent his fourth annual message to Congress on December 3, 1860. At times, the document assumed an almost apocalyptic tone. He meditated at length about the constitutional crisis precipitated by South Carolina's proposed ordinance of secession and concluded that neither the president nor the Congress possessed the power to enforce the preserva- tion of the Union. "The fact is, that our Union rests upon public opinion," he declared, "and can never be cemented by the blood of its citizens shed in civil war." Ever the strict interpreter of the Constitution, he proposed that the Congress pass a constitutional amendment for the express purpose of protecting slavery and returning fugitive slaves. Once more, his policies stood out of alignment with many in the Republican-controlled House; however, his message found willing listeners in the more conservative Senate. John Crittenden, taking a page from the playbook of his Kentucky predecessor Henry Clay, attempted to steer six constitutional amendments through the Congress. But president-elect Lincoln, in conjunction with members of his new cabinet, opposed the measures. A final "Peace Conference," led by ex-president John Tyler, similarly failed to find a solution to the constitutional crisis, despite repeated and deeply emotional protests from Buchanan urging the delegates to avoid a "bloody, fratricidal war." By the end of the congressional session, disunion had achieved a semipermanent status.[36]

Well before then, the challenges of the secession winter overwhelmed the president. He was fast losing the support of southerners in Congress. For example, the formerly friendly Robert Toombs and Alexander Stevens, described by one newspaper as "the Siamese Twins of Georgia," now declared their support for southern secession. When a group of delegates from South Carolina demanded an interview to discuss secession, Buchanan attempted to ignore them. Finally, he acceded to their request, after which the commissioners mistakenly maintained the impression that the president would allow for their state's peaceful separation from the Union. The confusion arose, one historian has written, as "Buchanan was facile at such interviews, bestowing no stern rebukes." The president soon disappointed them, as his strict interpretation of his constitutional prerogatives demanded that he protect all federal installations. The failed attempt of the ship the *Star of the West* to reinforce Fort Sumter in Charleston harbor signaled his unwillingness to comply entirely with southern demands.[37]

Meanwhile, his official family was disintegrating. For weeks, the "Old Chief" had publicly disagreed with nearly every member of the cabinet—the southern members demanding that the president remove all troops from Fort Sumter, while the northern members insisting that he reinforce them. Secretary of State Lewis Cass submitted his resignation first, citing disagreements over the president's decision not to reinforce the fort. Secretary of war John Floyd resigned his office in December, under protest that the president meant to back up Major Robert Anderson at Fort Sumter. So too went Buchanan's intimate friends Howell Cobb and Jacob Thompson. Jeremiah Black remained ever steadfast, as did Joseph Holt (who had replaced Aaron Brown as postmaster general upon the latter's death). Accordingly, Buchanan promoted Black to head the State Department and subsequently appointed Edwin Stanton, another Pennsylvania Democrat, to the vacancy in the attorney general's office. Thus abandoned by his southern friends, Buchanan turned to the class of men whom he had trusted deepest and longest, his fellow northern Democrats.[38]

Despite the many defections, the president persisted in fostering amical personal relations with the departing members of his cabinet. On February 3, Buchanan hosted a farewell dinner for Jacob and Kate Thompson. Also in attendance were Catherine Ellis and the new treasury secretary General John Adams Dix, both of whom were staying at the White House. "The President asked me at dinner who was to be *our President*," Kate Thompson wrote Mary Ann Lamar Cobb, adding that "Mrs. Ellis did not think either—Cobb or Toombs would do—but she claims to be a great secessionist." Buchanan and his remaining White House family soon had an answer, for on February 9 a convention of secessionist delegates met at Montgomery, the state capital of Alabama, and chose Jefferson Davis as president of the Confederate States of America. One week later, Catherine Ellis prepared to depart the White House for the final time.[39]

The presence of Catherine Margaret Ellis during the waning days of the Buchanan administration made for a fitting symbol of the breakdown of the American political experiment. Gone was the moderating force of her uncle William Rufus King, replaced by a sectional politics that had divided the nation over the question of slavery. Yet like Buchanan's sympathetic attitude toward the peculiar institution, the basis of his political unionism necessarily meant the continued enslavement of more than four million people. Buchanan later famously proclaimed himself to be the last president of the United States (given that the South had seceded). In many ways, he was just that—the final president of a union pioneered by the Democratic Party of Andrew Jackson more than three decades earlier. And like its last president, the old union was politically exhausted by ideas and policies that could no longer contain the political, social, and moral forces that was pulling it apart at its seams.

Most Devotedly Attached

The morning of March 4, 1861 dawned clear and bright but blustery, an accurate reflection of the national mood. President Buchanan, who had the night before stationed himself at the Capitol to sign any final legislation, returned to the White House early that morning. Around eleven o'clock he greeted president-elect Lincoln at Willard's Hotel, where the pair proceeded, arm in arm, to an open barouche carriage. The two presidents rode silently down Pennsylvania Avenue, lined by hundreds of armed soldiers, to the Capitol, where they repaired to the East Portico for the inauguration. "If you are as happy, my dear sir, on entering this house as I am in leaving it and returning home," Buchanan told Lincoln on the ride back to the White House, "you are the happiest man in this country." Following the event, Buchanan, who politely refused to attend the inaugural ball, blithely advised Lincoln on the drinking water at the White House. The next day, having convened the remaining members of his cabinet for a final time, the ex-president and his retinue traveled by train to Baltimore, Philadelphia, and finally on to Lancaster.[40]

The inauguration of Abraham Lincoln also concluded Buchanan's time as a decades-long resident of Washington. Despite his professed happiness upon leaving the capital, he soon regretted his exclusion from its society. "Had it not been for the troubles of the times, I should have passed some months every year of my life in Washington," he wrote former mayor William Seaton in 1862. "Its society was more agreeable to me than that of any other city I have ever known." The feelings were hardly mutual—the Republican-controlled Congress revoked the ex-president's franking privilege, which had given him free usage of the mails, and refused to pay artist George Healey for Buchanan's official presidential portrait. Former friends also grumbled for money owed to them. White House physician Dr. Foltz, who had turned

FIGURE 7.8 "President Buchanan and Lincoln Entering the Senate Chamber before the Inauguration." Buchanan reportedly said to Lincoln: "If you are as happy, my dear sir, on entering this house as I am in leaving it and returning home, you are the happiest man in this country." Published in *Harper's Weekly*, March 16, 1861, p. 165. Prints and Photographs Division, Library of Congress, LC-USZ6-175.

against Buchanan over being denied a patronage appointment, sent the ex-president a belated bill for eleven years of "Medical Services rendered" totaling $1,000 (Buchanan, and later his estate, disputed the matter). But despite it all, Buchanan cherished his retirement at Wheatland. He attended closely to his financial affairs, at one point estimating his net worth to be approximately $250,000 (or just over four million in today's dollars). He formally made communion with the Presbyterian Church, served on the board of trustees for Franklin & Marshall College, took the mineral waters at Bedford Springs, and continued to enjoy libations from barrels labeled "Old J. B. Whiskey."[41]

Throughout his retirement, Buchanan stayed attuned to Pennsylvanian politics and national affairs. When the war concluded he was one of three ex-presidents still living. Nearing seventy-five, his mind dwelled not in the political present or future but in the antebellum past. He spent much of the war years laboring to complete a defense of his presidency, famously written in the third person and published in 1866 as *Mr. Buchanan's Administration on the Eve of Rebellion.* Part history of the causes of the Civil War and part memoir of his administration, he presented himself as a constitutionally prudent executive and a peacemaker. As such, he mostly assigned blame to others: he blasted the Congress for refusing to act, lamented the sectional politics of the Republican Party, bemoaned his cabinet for abandoning him in his hour of need, questioned the judgment of Major Anderson at Fort Sumter for not requesting reinforcements sooner, and ridiculed General Winfield Scott for reversing his policy toward the seceding states. Until his dying day, he held steadfast to the misguided belief that the crisis could have been settled peacefully and, even more naively, that "history would vindicate my memory."[42]

All the same, politics, even those of the recent past, slowly receded as his primary avocation. Instead, he enjoyed the company of his many family members and friends who visited him for extended periods at Wheatland, especially his niece Harriet Lane. Per his wishes, she had remained unmarried while the war raged. Unlike her uncle, Lane traveled around the country during the war years, including visits to the fashionable summer resorts at Saratoga Springs and Bedford Springs. At Bedford Springs, she met her future husband Henry Elliot Johnston, a banker from Baltimore. The couple became engaged, and on January 1, 1866, Lane, then thirty-six, married Johnston in a private ceremony officiated by her uncle Edward Buchanan in the front parlor of Wheatland. The newlyweds traveled to Cuba for their honeymoon, a fitting choice given Buchanan's (and King's) enduring interest in the island.[43]

The announcement of the marriage of Harriet Lane and Henry Elliot Johnston reinitiated an unexpected correspondence with Catherine Margaret

Ellis. "By a happy chance, the cards with your new name found me at last," Ellis wrote the new Mrs. Johnston in April 1866, "and altho I had heard of your marriage, the reality of the event impressed me deeply." Ellis immediately precluded "any mention of the past four years," but she assured "my own dear friend... that I love you as I ever did." In June, Ellis traveled to Saratoga Springs, where she wrote of her arrangements to Buchanan. In reply, he expressed his relief. "Miss Lane & myself were anxious to hear from you during the late civil war & a thousand times wished you were with us; but all in vain," he declared. Buchanan noted that Lane had tried to reach Ellis through their mutual friend General John Adams Dix, but to no avail. "You were certainly well aware of the warm affection and respect for you which I have never attempted to disguise," he wrote. In response to the troubling news that the land containing her uncle's grave was now owned by "strangers to the name of King," he reflected once more: "Of all the men I have ever known, I was the most devotedly attached to him, and I have often thought it may have been a kind dispensation of Providence to take him from earth before the commencement of the war." His old paeans to King did not easily fade.[44]

In their correspondence, Catherine Margaret Ellis poured out her inner thoughts and feelings to Harriet Lane Johnston. Like the nation as a whole, the Civil War had temporarily separated, but not permanently broken, the bonds of their friendship. To "my dearest friend," she struggled to "find words, to express my gratitude for the friendship you offered me at a time when it was *so much* needed. Under no circumstances can I ever be unmindful of the obligation, or cease to love you with a sister's love. My affection for you, has not been tried, yours for me has been tested, and proved." Thus rebound in emotional sisterhood with Johnston, Ellis detailed the calamities that befell her as a result of the conflict. "My experiences during the war were sad indeed; independent of the loss of many relations, and friends, I witnessed scenes which I cannot think of calmly," she wrote. In Camden, Alabama, where she had relocated to tend to the children of her nephew Franklin Beck King while he fought in the war, Ellis watched as a "Brigade of Negroes overrun the neighborhood I lived in. They broke into my house and committed outrages in my sight. I was protected by an officer, but others were not." Before the war, she had been quite prosperous—the census recorded ownership of seventy-four enslaved people. Following emancipation and the destruction of her cotton fields by the Union Army, she possessed little prospect for future material wealth.[45]

With the memory of King thus invoked, Buchanan expressed a firm determination to see Ellis once more. "*We must meet again, God willing*," he declared. At age seventy-five and in chronically uncertain health, he avoided all unnecessary travel; nevertheless, he considered joining Ellis in Saratoga Springs. As he told Harriet Lane Johnston, "I had only thought of going to Saratoga to meet her." But ill health prevented further communication. When he learned that Ellis had already left Saratoga for New York, he proposed that she visit his home. After several months of travel without further word, Ellis finally updated Johnston about her plans to return to Alabama by way of Baltimore. "I must see Mr. Buchanan," she wrote with equal determination in early October 1866, "and if he cannot meet me at your house, I shall go to Wheatland for two, or three, days, en route to Alabama."[46]

Later that month Ellis made the promised visit to Wheatland, where she spent a week with Buchanan, housekeeper Miss Hetty, and other relatives. One Buchanan family friend described her as "looking fat & well." Old Buck found her "agreeable as ever" and "charming." To Harriet Lane Johnston, he wrote: "She is sensible concerning the war & has suffered much; she will give you a great deal of information in a most agreeable manner." From there, Buchanan and Ellis traveled together to see the Johnstons in Baltimore, where they visited with a heavily pregnant Harriet. Only after his arrival back at Wheatland did Buchanan learn that Ellis had "without my knowledge carried away her picture that hung in the big dining room," as few personal effects remained to her. Ellis promised another visit to Buchanan the following summer, but her picture never returned to Wheatland, with the result that no individual likeness of William Rufus King's favorite niece has survived.[47]

About the same time as Ellis's visit to Wheatland, Buchanan received an unusual request from Harrison Wright, a budding young autograph collector and son of a political friend from Wilkes-Barre. The young Wright hoped that the ex-president might be able to send him an original autograph of former Vice President King. But Buchanan disappointed him: "I have preserved none of his letters except two or three upon important subjects which I should be unwilling to mutilate." He added further: "I should be glad to oblige you, and had you asked me for his autograph a month ago, before I had completed the task of arranging my papers & destroying all useless letters this would have been in my power." Of course, Buchanan had actually saved far more than "two or three" of King's letters.[48]

Two weeks later, he conducted a more thorough search of his personal papers and clipped not only the signature, but the entire bottom portion of King's lengthy letter of May 14, 1844. As such, he amended the now infamous letter to end with its equally notorious closing lines: "I am selfish enough to hope you will not be able to procure an associate, who will cause you to feel no regret at our separation. For myself, I shall feel lonely in the midst of Paris, for there I shall have no Friends with whom I can commune as with my own thoughts." Not content to let the excision go undocumented, he noted it on the docket of the letter: "Nov. 30, 1866. The conclusion & signature cut off & sent as an autograph to Master Harrison Wright of Wilkesbarre."[49]

Was there more to King's letter of May 14, 1844? That Buchanan chose this particular letter out of the several dozens in his collection to cut off as a memento for Wright perplexes. Perhaps King's prose continued in the same intimate vein as the previous lines—conceivably the clipped conclusion hid from view an embarrassing emotional expression. Or maybe it contained nothing of significance, it being the first letter that came to hand and cut at a convenient crease in the page. The latter case seems more likely; for if Buchanan actually sent along the clipped signature to Wright, he must not have found its contents to be particularly troubling. After all, with the actual letter in his hands once more, he could have easily destroyed it and thus sent another King autograph to Wright. Instead, as with so much of his correspondence, he dutifully annotated this minor act of erasure and filed the letter away once more for future safe-keeping.[50]

In his final years, Buchanan immersed himself fully in memories of the political past. He learned that Catherine Ellis had returned to Camden, where she encountered an "annoying situation," probably related to the depleted state of her cotton plantings. "I have ever, since our first acquaintance, felt for you a warm affection and a high respect," he reflected. He then added a reference to King, using the same language that had marked his correspondence about him for decades: "Your conduct has always been worthy of your uncle who was one of the purest and best men that ever lived." Ironically, given his own checkered history of correspondence with King, Buchanan faulted Ellis for not writing often enough to him. Never content to stick exclusively to personal affairs, he reported approvingly on the "hostility to negro suffrage" in the North. Much as the continuation of the slave system had once been a foundational part of his friendship with her uncle, his relationship with Ellis relied on the continued subjugation of African Americans. It was a fitting last letter in a lifetime of friendship with William Rufus King and, by extension, with the slaveholding South.[51]

Much as his political reputation had dimmed, so too had Buchanan's robust physical vigor declined. His carefully managed outward appearance deteriorated; he even allowed sideburns to grow unchecked. In these final years his personal doctor, Henry Carpenter, made constant house calls. For several years Buchanan had suffered from a painful rheumatic gout, which left him immobilized for days and weeks at a stretch. By the spring of 1868, this condition had worsened due to respiratory complications; it was followed by heart failure and finally pneumonia. Buchanan was dying. Having recently professed membership in the Presbyterian Church, his last words reflected an increased religious conviction: "Oh, Lord God Almighty, as thou wilt!" He died at Wheatland on the morning of Monday, June 1, 1868.[52]

The nation widely noticed—though little mourned—the passing of James Buchanan. Many newspapers, including even the Democratic organ of Lancaster, dismissed him as a "traitor" or a "political idiot." Most commentators condemned Buchanan as a northern collaborator with the defeated southern wing of the Democratic Party. All the same, the city of Lancaster prepared for an unprecedented public tribute. Although Buchanan had instructed executor Hiram Swarr to avoid "pomp and parade," over twenty thousand citizens paid their respects to their most famous townsman, as nearly two dozen pallbearers escorted Buchanan's body from Wheatland along the two-mile funeral route. Nearly every public official and organization, including the brothers of Masonic Lodge no. 43, the members of the Union Steam Fire Engine Company, the trustees of Franklin & Marshall College, and elected officials of every kind, marched in the procession. President Buchanan was laid to rest at Woodward Hill Cemetery, a plain stone monument marking the spot.[53]

* * *

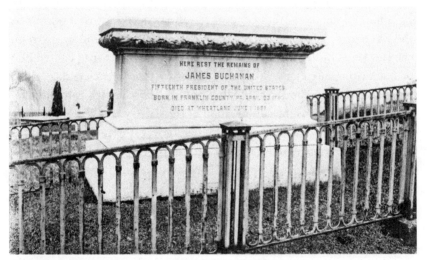

FIGURE 7.9 Tomb of James Buchanan in Woodward Hill Cemetery, Lancaster, Pennsylvania, ca. 1908. Courtesy Prints and Photographs Division, Library of Congress, LC-USZ62-107072.

The rise and fall of the administration of James Buchanan mirrored that of the United States of America. It also sounded the swan song of cross-sectional friendship in the Democratic Party and of the kind of wooing that a bachelor president attempted with the southern members of his cabinet and southern Democrats in Congress. Beyond the official realm of party politics, his gossipy flirtation with the southern belles of Washington mirrored his long-standing political wooing of southern women. But like the lifelong bachelor that he was, he failed to marry the fortunes of his party with those of the nation. His presidency had relied upon the bonds of patriotism, as constituted in the many cross-sectional friendships cultivated through a lifetime of politicking, to save the imperiled Union. His trust in the power of that alchemical combination of personal and political friendship ran deep, from his earliest days as a Pennsylvania politician to his final days as president. He lived and died by his commitment to the idea.

All along, Buchanan and King's version of bosom friendship was predicated on partisan politics that suppressed the question of slavery. From their shared reliance on enslaved people in their Washington mess and at home to their support for the gag rule in the Senate to Buchanan's undying support for the *Dred Scott* case during his presidency, they had built their career on the back of America's peculiar institution. It was only fitting then that Buchanan's presidency brought about not only the disintegration of the old American union of slaveholding states, but also the very economic, social, and political conditions that had enabled his friendship with William Rufus King. In time the war fought over the secession of southern states expanded into a war to end slavery, and as a result, Buchanan witnessed the devastation of his beloved Democratic Party as the Republican Party ascended to power in the decades ahead. In hindsight—and not without justification—the Buchanan presidency, along with many of the administrations before the Civil War, have been judged failures.

But what of the bosom friendship of Buchanan and King itself? An interesting hypothetical question remains. What would have happened to their friendship had King lived beyond 1853? Undoubtedly, King would have counseled moderation in the Senate and might even have averted the repeal of the Missouri Compromise as part of the Kansas-Nebraska Act. The election of his old friend in 1856 equally would have pleased him, as might Buchanan's stance on the Lecompton Constitution and the raid on Harpers Ferry; less clear is how King would have viewed Buchanan's foreign policy initiatives. In the disintegration of the Democratic Party into its sectional wings, King, like Buchanan, would have supported Breckinridge in 1860. While he might not have counseled secession following the election of 1860, he certainly would have followed Alabama into the Confederacy. Indeed, his own nieces and nephews were ardent Confederates during the war years. Buchanan implicitly understood as much in his comment that he was glad King had not lived to see the calamities of the war years. Like their shared political commitment to sustaining a union based on slavery, the Siamese twins of old would have been fatally separated.

Epilogue

PRESERVING

JAMES BUCHANAN NEVER seemed quite able to let go of William Rufus King. Certainly, the similarities of their early political lives, the intimacy of their Washington boardinghouse, the commonalities of lifelong bachelorhood, and their unceasing desire for elected office contributed to the lasting power of their relationship. But its ultimate longevity may be attributed to another factor altogether: their nieces, Harriet Lane Johnston and Catherine Margaret Ellis. Indeed, the enduring bond between these two women explains why more than sixty private letters exchanged between their uncles, and also those traded among themselves, yet survive. Despite the trials of civil war, the friendship of Harriet Lane Johnston and Catherine Margaret Ellis persisted into the decades of the 1870s and 1880s, as each woman presided over the preservation of the memory of their uncles and their bosom friendship. The particulars of this postbellum connection, itself part of an ongoing, symbolic reunification of North and South, provides a final key to understanding the legacy of the Siamese twins of the Tyler years.[1]

The death of James Buchanan began a new phase in the life of Harriet Lane Johnston as protector of her uncle's legacy. In preparation for a proposed biography by William Reed, Johnston began to reassemble Buchanan's papers from his many far-flung correspondents. In August 1868, she wrote Catherine Ellis with the news of Buchanan's passing and requested the return of all his outgoing correspondence to King. In reply, Ellis regretted that her own poor health had not permitted her to see Buchanan before his death, but she attested that the memory of her recent visit to Wheatland still possessed a talismanic hold over her. In "imagination," she wrote, "I often transport myself to Wheatland, as it *was* and as it *is*." Since her removal to Camden, Alabama, Ellis was unsure of the state of William Rufus King's papers left behind at the

King's Bend plantation. Still, she reported: "There was at King's Bend a large package of letters from Mr. Buchanan to my Uncle, and I hope they may not have been destroyed in the raid which was made on the place at the surrender." Ellis promised to write to Evelyn Hewett Collier King, the widow of her cousin William Thomas King, to inquire further. She further noted: "Among my *souvenirs*, I have two, or three, letters given to me, by my cousin, and which belonged to the package above named. These, I will send to you as soon as I return to Ala." There ends the trail of correspondence about the matter.[2]

The near complete lack of letters from Buchanan to King continues to mystify modern observers, but clues as to their fate can be gleaned from the surviving correspondence in the other direction. Although Ellis noted "a large package of letters," that same bundle already included fewer letters than had been exchanged between the pair over their lifetimes. The reason for the mismatch stemmed from the "confidential" and "private" nature of their correspondence; indeed, those very same words marked many of their letters. Occasionally, each instructed the other to burn a letter after reading it. For example, King closed one letter with the command: "Do not condemn this long letter to the flames without reading it." Obviously, Buchanan failed to destroy this particular note, but other evidence suggests that he commanded King to destroy his own letters with some regularity. In one letter from 1846, King noted: "I read your kind letter attentively and then committed it to the flames, as you requested." In another letter from 1852, he felt compelled to add in a postscript: "Your letter is in ashes." As with other aspects of their relationship, King was more faithful in following the wishes of his friend than Buchanan proved in turn.[3]

Other letters from Buchanan never reached King. After King's election to the vice presidency, Buchanan's concerns about the privacy of their correspondence intensified. Previously, he had requested King "not [to] suffer this letter to lie about on your table for the inspection of those who may come into your room." In March 1853, with King and Ellis gone to Cuba, he instructed William W. King—possibly a former messmate, of no relation to William Rufus King—to burn an unopened letter directed to the vice president-elect. William W. King promptly obeyed the request. "The letter addressed to Mr. K. has been *disposed* of according to your *direction*," he reported. Might this final letter have contained sensitive information? Almost certainly. But it likely was of a political rather than of a personal nature, concerning the prospects for political appointments in the new Pierce administration. As always, the cautious and meticulous Buchanan insisted that his private statements to King did not become public knowledge.[4]

Still, just what happened to the large package of letters at King's Bend? Assuming that it survived the Civil War, it is possible that Ellis instructed her cousin to locate the package and then sent the letters on to Johnston, as promised. Had they arrived in time, Johnston would most likely have passed them along to the first Buchanan biographer, William Reed, who might have made copies of the correspondence; subsequently, the letters or copies would have been passed on to later Buchanan biographers John Cadwalader and George Ticknor Curtis. If so, it is then possible that their letters were among those later destroyed in a warehouse fire during the late 1890s. Editor John Bassett Moore noted this conflagration in the preface to his first volume of the *Works of James Buchanan* (1908): "Some years ago, before the Buchanan materials were placed in the Historical Society of Pennsylvania, those used by Curtis passed through a fire in a storage warehouse in New York, and some of them, doubtless, were destroyed." Although Curtis included six letters from King to Buchanan in his two-volume biography—all of which survive today at the Historical Society of Pennsylvania—he did not include any outgoing correspondence from Buchanan to King. The same goes for biographers William Reed and John Cadwalader, neither of whose own papers make any mention of Buchanan's correspondence with King.[5]

Then there is the possibility that the package of Buchanan's letters never left Alabama. Possibly Catherine Margaret Ellis, whose health had declined in later years, did not arrange for the package to be sent north to Johnston. However, the five surviving letters from Buchanan to King written in the spring of 1850 hint that she may have sent along these "souvenirs" to Johnston (though these letters may well have been copies specially prepared by Buchanan for his own records). Given Ellis's commitment to her uncle's memory and her friendship with Harriet Lane Johnston, it is unlikely that she ignored Johnston's request to locate the package. Still, the letters could have easily been lost in the tempest of war. On April 2, 1865, in the closing days of the Civil War, Union and Confederate forces met at Selma in what turned out to be one of the final battles of the conflict. In the days that followed, the Union Army raided and burned numerous plantations in the area, including King's Bend. A bundle of letters might easily have been destroyed in the mayhem.[6]

But even if the package of letters had survived the war years, it still might have been temporarily misplaced or removed or lost in the ensuing decades. Natural disasters may well have played a role in its demise. In the years 1886, 1888, and 1961, the Alabama River severely flooded and reached such heights that the low-lying plantation house at King's Bend stood highly susceptible to damage. Relatively few letters written to William Rufus King have survived overall, and much of King's personal papers seem to have been lost over the years. The William R. King Family Papers at the Alabama Department of Archives and History, for example, contains just one box of personal letters, while related collections only hold a handful more. The ravages of war and weather seem to have done their devastating work not only to letters from James Buchanan and Harriet Lane Johnston, but to a lifetime of correspondence pertaining to both William Rufus King and Catherine Margaret Ellis.[7]

FIGURE E.I Harriet Lane Johnston, ca. 1895. Her careful efforts preserved the personal papers of James Buchanan, as well as her own correspondence, for future researchers. Courtesy James Buchanan Foundation Photograph Collection, LancasterHistory.org, Lancaster, Pennsylvania.

Of course, there is the possibility that Buchanan's letters to King were destroyed by prearrangement between Ellis and Johnston. Yet of all the imaginable scenarios, this one seems highly unlikely for two reasons. First, many letters written from King to Buchanan do indeed survive. Throughout his lifetime, Buchanan methodically labeled and filed nearly every letter that he received. He threw very little away, and as such few, if any, of King's letters written to him appear to be missing. Those letters that do survive have not been overlined, mutilated, or in any way censured (with the exception of the Harrison Wright autograph request noted earlier). These letters from King, Buchanan surely recognized, would be valuable to future biographers. Second, both nieces were deeply committed to the preservation of their uncle's respective papers. At the very least, Ellis had ensured that Buchanan's letters at King's Bend survived for more than a decade after her uncle's death, while Johnston carefully preserved her uncle's correspondence, whatever the cost. In the years ahead she even sued her own uncle, the Rev. Edward Buchanan, for improperly removing some letters from Wheatland, with the resulting case estranging the family for decades to come. That either Harriet Lane Johnston or Catherine Margaret Ellis would counsel the burning of any of her respective uncle's letters seems highly improbable. On the contrary, each niece spent their remaining years as stewards of their uncles' legacies (see Appendix C).[8]

* * *

The latter-day preservation efforts of these nieces provide one last insight into the origins of the phrase "Siamese twins" that has become associated with Buchanan and King. Historian Elizabeth Ellet sourced the material for her later histories from the accounts of contemporaries, including several people related to the pair. In the *Queens of American Society* (1867), Ellet prominently featured Buchanan and Johnston's intimate friend Cornelia Van Ness Roosevelt, even using an engraving of her portrait for the frontispiece. For the *Court Circles of the Republic* (1869), Ellet's assistant contacted Harriet Lane Johnston to request recollections about her uncle's administration. Ever careful of whom she could trust, Johnston first turned to Roosevelt, knowing of the latter's connection to Ellet, for advice. "I know Mrs. Ellet very well," Roosevelt replied, and noted that Ellet, "being very intimate with Mrs. [Elizabeth Moss] Crittenden . . . has spoken to her often about you." Meanwhile, Roosevelt suggested that Ellet write directly to Johnston, which she did.[9]

Eventually, the historian and the former first lady began a correspondence in early 1869. Johnston sent along a memoir written by Jane Findlay Shunk, daughter of Buchanan's old Pennsylvania rival William Findlay, which included a reminiscence of the visit of Prince Albert Edward to the United States in 1860. Ellet ultimately decided not to use the memoir, since, as she told Johnston, the "slightest tone of 'friendship' in a biography spoils it for the general and indifferent reader." She further elaborated on the difficulty of obtaining source material for this new book, noting how she had "found the labor of seeking original material so great that I have as yet received only one sketch, that of Mrs. [Julia Gardiner] Tyler," the widow of President Tyler. This last comment was telling. Since Ellet placed the description of Buchanan and King as "the Siamese twins" in her section on the Tyler administration, she almost certainly lifted it from Julia Gardiner Tyler's sketch. Just who applied the phrase to Buchanan and King remains unclear, but by then, it had even entered into popular literature; for example, Mark Twain used it for the title of a short story published in 1868. In passing along this recollection to Ellet, Tyler, like so many others who participated in early American politics, ensured its permanency in the historical record. For her part, Harriet Lane Johnston graciously agreed to correct Ellet's manuscript about the social life of the Buchanan administration, but she refused to permit her own picture to appear in the final volume. She acted the part of the dutiful niece to a fault.[10]

In the years that followed, the friendship of Harriet Lane Johnston and Catherine Margaret Ellis endured. In July 1869, Ellis joined the Johnston family for a summer holiday in Cape May, New Jersey, and there met little James Buchanan Johnston (born November 21, 1866). But the years ahead proved especially difficult for Johnston. Between 1881 and 1882, she lost both her young children to rheumatic fever, and in 1884, she lost her husband to pneumonia. Likewise, as Ellis grew older, poor health and dwindling finances afforded her less time to travel outside the South. She lived out her remaining days at the Beck House in Camden, where she died in 1890. Following Ellis's death, Harriet Lane Johnston continued to think fondly of her friend. In 1899, for example, she gratefully accepted a photograph of Ellis from a family friend. Johnston, who spent many of her final years traveling across Europe, relocated from Baltimore to Washington, DC, where she lived in a townhouse with her cousin May Kennedy. She also ensured the preservation of her uncle's voluminous personal papers and provided in her will for their eventual publication. She died on July 3, 1903, at Narragansett Pier, Rhode Island, and she was buried south of the Mason-Dixon Line at Baltimore's Green Mount Cemetery, alongside her husband and two children.[11]

The succeeding generations of King relatives kept alive the memory of William Rufus King. In 1882, King's remains were removed from the family's burial site at King's Bend and reinterred at Live Oak Cemetery in Selma (a move supported by Buchanan, who agreed many years earlier that his "remains, undoubtedly, ought to be removed to Selma"). Other forms of recognition have been slowly forthcoming: the US Senate commissioned a marble bust of King in the 1890s; in 1920, Congress paid for a bronze bust of King, which still stands guard over the courthouse in Clinton County, North Carolina; and the plantation on which King was raised in the town of Newton Grove, North Carolina, was renamed William Rufus King Road. To mark the centennial of his inauguration as vice president, a contingent of Alabama citizens traveled to Matanzas, Cuba, to install a historic marker at the site. In Selma, the Old Depot Museum, the Vaughan-Smitherman Museum, and the Selma Public Library all bear tribute to King's legacy. As King's plantation home at Chestnut Hill burned to the ground in the 1930s, the William Rufus King room at the Alabama Department of Archives and History in Montgomery remains the only physical site dedicated to his memory. And in a historical irony, the land that once formed the King's Bend plantation is today owned by Buchanan Lumber Mobile, Incorporated, of Mobile, Alabama.[12]

Memorials to James Buchanan have been more prevalent, largely due to the generous behests of Harriet Lane Johnston. Following the death of her children and husband, Johnston sold Wheatland to George Wilson, whose family kept possession of the home through the 1930s. The newly formed James Buchanan Foundation for the Preservation of Wheatland (today President James Buchanan's Wheatland) purchased the site, designating it as a national shrine, and began to operate the home as a living museum. At the crossroads of Stony Batter, near what is today Cove Gap, Pennsylvania, a memorial shrine marks the place where the Young Buck spent his early childhood. In Washington, DC, the James Buchanan memorial in Meridian Hill Park (later Malcolm X Park), completed in 1930 and dedicated by President Herbert Hoover, bears silent testimony to his statecraft. Statues of Buchanan, such as the one in Buchanan Park in Lancaster and more recently in Mercersburg, have been erected. Slowly but surely, the people and places associated with James Buchanan have paid tribute to his memory.[13]

* * *

As individuals, Buchanan and King have received comparatively little notice from historians or the public. But the changing consensus about their relationship has triggered an outpouring of speculation about the pair in recent years. Of course, the idea of a sexual relationship between them, so intriguing to observers in the late twentieth and early twenty-first centuries, lays at the heart of this renewed interest. That the subject of their friendship has become the cause of so much attention likely would not have surprised Buchanan, King, or their nieces. In their own day, gossip regularly circulated about the two men in the parlors of the Washington community and across the correspondence of their political rivals. As this book has argued, theirs was a bosom friendship begun in the domestic world of the boardinghouse, transformed by the rigors of public service and the powerful forces of partisanship, and continued, metaphorically at least, through familial relations in the decades that followed. Less clear, given the particularities of their historical moment, are other questions about the continuation of bosom friendship itself: what happened to these intimate friendships after the Civil War? Do they survive in Washington politics today? And, if so, might these later examples offer a contemporary analogy to understand this relationship from long ago?

The public perception of bosom friendships among politicians remained contested terrain in the years following the Civil War. By the 1880s, the end of Reconstruction and the return of a robust two-party system between Democrats and Republicans yielded comparable intimacies among political cronies. In 1884 the country elected a second bachelor to the White House, Grover Cleveland of New York, who in turn was unseated by Republican challenger Benjamin Harrison four years later. Of note, Harrison's fellow Indiana Hoosier William Dudley dedicated himself to his party chief in the language of bosom friendship. "I love you as a brother and will stand by you as long as I live," Dudley wrote. When Dudley also purportedly proposed to buy off voters in Indiana for the Harrison cause, Democratic newspapers mocked his relationship with the Republican candidate as that of a pair of Siamese twins. At around the same time, a Republican cartoonist ridiculed the political conjunction of the mustachioed David Hill of New York and the Populist William Peffer of Kansas as Siamese twins. Mark Twain once more mediated on the idea of a conjoined pair for his book *Pudd'nhead Wilson and Those Extraordinary Twins* (1894); of note, he also used the phrase "bosom friend" to refer to the relationship between his iconic characters Tom Sawyer and Joe Harper. The use of "the Siamese twins" to describe political friendships persisted well into the twentieth century.[14]

The importance of bosom friendships of the earlier kind endured, if in modified form. In fact, personal friendships, even across the deepest of party

FIGURE E.2 "The Siamese Twins of Statesmanship." Democratic senator David Hill of New York and Populist senator William Peffer of Kansas pictured as a pair of political Siamese twins. Drawing by George Yost Coffin, 1893. Courtesy Prints and Photographs Division, Library of Congress, CD 1 - Coffin (G.Y.), no. 154 (B size).

lines, have formed a constitutive part of modern politicking. The congressional partisans John F. Kennedy and Richard Nixon shared an unexpected friendship in the 1940s and early 1950s. Likewise, Republican senator George Aiken of Vermont and Democratic senator Mike Mansfield of Montana daily breakfasted together, while the long-time Democratic speaker of the House Tip O'Neil was famously chummy with President Ronald Reagan. The same could be said for Democrat George Mitchell of Maine and his Republican counterpart Bob Dole of Kansas, or for that matter, Democrat Ted Kennedy of Massachusetts and his Republican colleague Orrin Hatch of Utah. In recent years, Democrat John Kerry of Massachusetts and Republican John McCain of Arizona valued their close personal friendship, as did Republican Jeff Flake of Arizona and Democrat Chris Coons of Delaware. These many later relationships, some within the boundaries of party and some outside of those strictures, suggest the continued valence of intimate male friendship among politicians from different parties and sections of the country.[15]

As was the case with Buchanan and King, living arrangements in Washington have recently fostered the growth of personal and political friendships among congressmen. During the 2000s, six congressmen affiliated with a nondenominational Christian "Fellowship"—Tom Coburn of Oklahoma, Zach Wamp of Tennessee, Heath Shuler of North Carolina, Bart Stupak of Michigan, Mike Doyle of Pennsylvania, and John Ensign of Nevada—decided to live together in a nineteenth-century row house on C Street. The six men spoke of "deeply personal" subjects and considered themselves the most intimate of friends, which made the unanticipated revelation that Senator Ensign was having an affair with the wife of an aide on Senator Coburn's staff that much more troubling. As was the case with Buchanan and King, romantic pursuits still carry the potential to disrupt male friendship. Politics continues to make not only for strange but intimate bedfellows.[16]

Indeed, America is in the midst of a renaissance of bosom friendship. New ways to describe male intimacy enter the lexicon with insistence. Many such words, including the concept of the "bromance," originated from the domestic confines of college life. With the bromance of today, however, the bosom friendships of old have been reconfigured as avowedly de-eroticized. Even politicians now seem to enjoy an occasional bromance: the friendship of President Barack Obama and Vice President Joe Biden earned them the conjoined nickname of "Jobama." Photographs of the two men walking side by side or embracing arm and arm hearkened back to depictions of the political Siamese twins of an earlier era. Intimate friendships, especially among men, continue to exert an undeniable influence on the current political culture.[17]

Beyond the bromance, the widespread acceptance of same-sex oriented people in the United States has also changed the parameters of intimate male friendship. Indeed, people of all sexual orientations, and increasingly gender expression, are becoming friends. In 2016, a *New York Times* correspondent noted that "bromosexual" relationships—those friendships formed between straight men and gay men—had become an accepted part of popular culture. "Obviously, there have always been friendships between gay men and straight men," the reporter observed, "but only recently have they become more prominently, and comfortably, represented in TV shows, movies, books and blogs." The confluence of gendered performance and sexual orientation in the construction of modern male dyads reveals much—American men are interested more than ever in exploring the many, sometimes complicated, possibilities of friendship with one another.[18]

Does figuring Buchanan and King as part of a "bromantic" or even "bromosexual" relationship clarify the interpretation of the pair? Perhaps so, even as the categories of historical sexuality do not easily conform to modern understandings and practices. Whether more profitably figured as bromantic or perhaps bromosexual, one thing is certain: Buchanan and King, like their twenty-first century counterparts, took great satisfaction in their personal and political association. As bosom friends, they navigated the shoals of bachelorhood and American politics alike; they confided and commiserated as messmates and transatlantic correspondents; and finally, they obtained the highest echelons of elected office. In retrospect, their example helps to define the possibilities for male intimacy in nineteenth-century America.

Their friendship epitomized the inherent paradox of American politics during the antebellum years. To advance politically, each embraced the other: Buchanan oriented his political and personal worldview toward the South, and King moderated his course toward the preservation of the Union. Begun as mere expedient, their connection evolved over time into a far more intimate political and personal relationship, one that included members of their extended families as well. That they hoped to forge a cross-sectional partnership and together obtain the presidency and vice presidency revealed their rawest political ambitions. That they did so primarily to maintain the Union underscored their greater commitments to the patriotic aims of the second generation of Americans. That their bosom friendship ultimately required both men to preserve a union of slaveholders has not been, and should not be, ignored. In their perpetual dismissal, both then and now, the judgment of history upon them weighs heavy still.

Washington Residences of James Buchanan and William Rufus King (1834–1853)

Congressional Session	Boardinghouse and Messmates
23rd Congress, 2nd Session (December 1, 1834, to March 3, 1835)	*Saunder's, E St, near the General Post Office* Bedford Brown (S), NC James Buchanan (S), PA William R. King (S), AL Edward Lucas, VA
24th Congress, 1st Session (December 7, 1835, to July 4, 1836)	*Mr. Saunder's, 7th St.* William R. King (S), AL Edward Lucas, VA *Mr. Guest, Tenth St., near F St. (private residence)* James Buchanan (S), PA
24th Congress, 2nd Session (December 7, 1836, to March 3, 1837)	*Mrs. Galvin, No. 2, C St.* James Buchanan (S), PA William R. King (S), AL Robert C. Nicholas (S), LA Edward Lucas, VA
25th Congress, 1st Session (September 4 to October 16, 1837)	*Mr. Ironside, 7th St.* James Buchanan (S), PA William R. King (S), AL John P. King (S), GA Robert C. Nicholas (S), LA

Congressional Session	Boardinghouse and Messmates
25th Congress, 2nd Session (December 4, 1837, to July 9, 1838)	*Mr. Ironside, 7th St.* James Buchanan (S), PA William R. King (S), AL Robert C. Nicholas (S), LA
25th Congress, 3rd Session (December 3, 1838, to March 3, 1839)	*Mrs. Ironside, E between 9th and 10th St.* James Buchanan (S), PA Robert C. Nicholas (S), LA William R. King (S), AL
26th Congress, 1st Session (December 2, 1839, to July 21, 1840)	*Mrs. Ironside, E St., between 9th and 10th St.* James Buchanan (S), PA William R. King (S), AL Robert C. Nicholas (S), LA William S. Ramsey, PA
26th Congress, 2nd Session (December 7, 1840, to March 3, 1841)	*Mrs. Ironside, E between 9th and 10th Streets* James Buchanan (S), PA William R. King (S), AL Robert C. Nicholas (S), LA William H. Roane (S), VA
27th Congress, 1st Session (May 31 to September 13, 1841)	*Mr. Beale's, Capitol Hill* James Buchanan (S), PA William R. King (S), AL Clement C. Clay (S), AL
27th Congress, 2nd Session (December 6, 1841, to August 31, 1842)	*Mrs. Dashiell's, C Street* James Buchanan (S), PA William R. King (S), AL John Catron (Supreme Court), TN
27th Congress, 3rd Session (December 5, 1842, to March 3, 1843)	*Mrs. Miller's, F Street between 13th and 14th Streets* James Buchanan (S), PA William R. King (S), AL
28th Congress, 1st Session (December 4, 1843, to June 17, 1844)	*Mrs. King's, F, bet. 13th and 14th Streets* James Buchanan (S), PA William R. King (S), AL
28th Congress, 2nd Session (December 2, 1844, to March 3, 1845)	*Mrs. King's, F, bet. 13th and 14th Streets* James Buchanan (S), PA (†)

Congressional Session	Boardinghouse and Messmates
30th Congress, 2nd Session (December 4, 1848, to March 3, 1849)	*Mrs. Duvall's, corner 4 ½ Street and Missouri Ave.* Jefferson Davis (S), MS Solomon W. Downs (S), LA William R. King (S), AL Emile La Sère, LA
31st Congress, 1st Session (December 3, 1849, to September 30, 1850)	*Mr. North's, New Jersey Avenue, Capitol Hill* William R. King (S), AL (§)
31st Congress, 2nd Session (December 2, 1850, to March 4, 1851)	*Mrs. King's, F, bet. 13th and 14th Streets* William R. King (S), AL (§)
32nd Congress, 1st Session (December 1, 1851, to August 31, 1852)	*Private, south side C bet. 3rd and 4 ½ Streets* William R. King (S), AL (§)
32nd Congress, 2nd Session (December 6, 1852, to March 4, 1853)	*Private, south side C bet. 3rd and 4 ½ Streets* William R. King (S), AL (§)

(*) indicates married ladies present in the boardinghouse
(§) indicates single ladies present in the boardinghouse
(†) Buchanan remained in this house during his term as secretary of state (1845–1849)

Sources: Goldman and Young, eds., *United States Congressional Directories; Congressional Directories* (27th to 31th Congresses); and various manuscript collections.

Percentage Correlation of Roll Call Votes of James Buchanan with Senators in the Bachelor's Mess, 23rd to 28th Congresses (1834–1844)

	23rd Congress (1834–1835)	24th Congress (1835–1836)	25th Congress (1837–1839)	26th Congress (1839–1841)	27th Congress (1841–1843)	28th Congress (1843–1844)	Total Average % Correlation (weighted)
William Rufus King	80.0%	78.4%	87.4%	84.5%	91.2%	100%	**87.9%**
Bedford Brown	75.8%	n/a	n/a	n/a	n/a	n/a	**75.8%**
Robert Carter Nicholas	n/a	83.5%	83.6%	75.6%	n/a	n/a	**80.9%**
John Pendleton King	n/a	n/a	88.0%	n/a	n/a	n/a	**88.0%**
William Henry Roane	n/a	n/a	n/a	83.3%	n/a	n/a	**83.3%**

	23rd Congress (1834– 1835)	24th Congress (1835– 1836)	25th Congress (1837– 1839)	26th Congress (1839– 1841)	27th Congress (1841– 1843)	28th Congress (1843– 1844)	Total Average % Correlation (weighted)
Clement Comer Clay Sr.	n/a	n/a	n/a	n/a	92.5%	n/a	**92.5%**
Total Average % Correlation by Session (weighted)	77.9%	81.0%	85.6%	80.6%	91.6%	100%	

Methodology: I tabulated the total number of "yes" and "no" roll call votes of each messmate and correlated them to the votes of James Buchanan (excluding abstentions by one or both parties). I then calculated the percentage of votes exactly in common (either "yes" or "no" votes), and likewise those during which Buchanan was not a messmate (indicated by "n/a"). For the total average by messmate, I weighted the average across all relevant sessions (23rd to 28th Congresses), and for the total average by session, I weighted the average for all the relevant members of the mess. Thus, the total averages reveal both how messmates voted with Buchanan in a given congressional session and how they voted with Buchanan across the period living together as messmates.

Source: Keith T. Poole, NOMINATE Roll Call Data (revised from Interuniversity Consortium for Political and Social Research data set), http://www.voteview.com.

Calendar of Correspondence of James Buchanan | Harriet Lane Johnston and William Rufus King | Catherine Margaret Ellis (1837–1868)

Date	From	To	Place	Status of Original	Notes
October 5, 1836	WRK	JB	Selma, AL	HSP	
June 2, 1837	WRK	JB	Selma, AL	HSP	
June 29, 1837	JB	WRK	Lancaster, PA	Lost	Referenced in docket of WRK to JB, June 2, 1837
June 20, 1839	WRK	JB	Selma, AL	HSP	
August 31, 1839	JB	WRK	Lancaster, PA	Lost	Referenced in docket of WRK to JB, June 20, 1839
May 10, 1844	WRK	JB	New York	HSP	
May 14, 1844	WRK	JB	New York	HSP	Docket: "Nov. 30 1866. The conclusion & signature cut off & sent as an autograph to Master Harrison Wright of Wilkesbarre."

Date	From	To	Place	Status of Original	Notes
May 1844	JB	WRK	Washington, DC	Lost	Referenced in docket of WRK to JB, May 10, 1844
July 1, 1844	WRK	JB	Paris	LC	
November 14, 1844	WRK	JB	Paris	HSP	
January 28, 1845	WRK	JB	Paris	HSP	
March 25, 1845	JB	WRK	Washington, DC	NA	Diplomatic Instructions of the Department of State, France, no. 18; Moore, ed., *Works*, 6:127, no. 18; Manning, ed., *Correspondence*, 6:351
April 16, 1845	WRK	JB	Paris	LC	Private; Thomas Sidney Jesus Papers
April 29, 1845	WRK	JB	Paris	NA	Despatches from US Ministers to France, no. 13; Manning, ed., *Correspondence*, 6:548
April 30, 1845	WRK	JB	Paris	HSP	Confidential
May 6, 1845	JB	WRK	Washington, DC	LC	Diplomatic Instructions of the Department of State, France, no. 19; Moore, ed., *Works*, 6:154
n.d. (ca. late May 1845)	WRK	JB	Paris	HSP	First part of letter missing
June 16, 1845	WRK	JB	Paris	NA	Despatches from US Ministers to France, no. 14; Manning, ed., *Correspondence*, 6:549
June 20, 1845	JB	WRK	Washington, DC	NA	Diplomatic Instructions of the Department of State, France, no. 20

Date	From	To	Place	Status of Original	Notes
June 30, 1845	WRK	JB	Paris	NA	Despatches from US Ministers to France, no. 15
June 30, 1845	WRK	JB	Paris	HSP	Private
August 1, 1845	WRK	JB	Paris	NA	Despatches from US Ministers to France, no. 16
August 15, 1845	WRK	JB	Paris	NA	Despatches from US Ministers to France, no. 17
September 4, 1845	JB	WRK	Washington, DC	NA	Diplomatic Instructions of the Department of State, France, no. 22
September 29, 1845	WRK	JB	Paris	HSP	Private
October 14, 1845	WRK	JB	Paris	NA	Despatches from US Ministers to France, no. 18
October 29, 1845	JB	WRK	Washington, DC	NA	Diplomatic Instructions of the Department of State, France, no. 23
October 31, 1845	WRK	JB	Paris	NA	Despatches from US Ministers to France, no. 19; Manning, ed., *Correspondence*, 6:554
November 10, 1845	JB	WRK	Washington, DC	NA	Diplomatic Instructions of the Department of State, France, no. 24
November 14, 1845	WRK	JB	Paris	NA	Despatches from US Ministers to France, no. 20; Manning, ed., *Correspondence*, 6:555

Date	From	To	Place	Status of Original	Notes
November 28, 1845	WRK	JB	Paris	HSP	Private
January 1, 1846	WRK	JB	Paris	NA	Despatches from US Ministers to France, no. 21
January 1, 1846	WRK	JB	Paris	HSP	
January 27, 1846	WRK	JB	Paris	NA	Despatches from US Ministers to France, no. 22; Manning, ed., *Correspondence*, 6:559
January 27, 1846	WRK	JB	Paris	HSP	Private
January 29, 1846	WRK	JB	Paris	NA	Despatches from US Ministers to France, no. 23
January 29, 1846	WRK	JB	Paris	NA	Despatches from US Ministers to France, no. 24; Manning, ed., *Correspondence*, 6:560
January 30, 1846	WRK	JB	Paris	NA	Despatches from US Ministers to France, no. 25; Manning, ed., *Correspondence*, 6:562
February 5, 1846	JB	WRK	Washington, DC	NA	Diplomatic Instructions of the Department of State, France, no. 25
February 6, 1846	JB	WRK	Washington, DC	NA	Diplomatic Instructions of the Department of State, France, no. 26
February 19, 1846	JB	WRK	Washington, DC	NA	Diplomatic Instructions of the Department of State, France, no. 27

Date	From	To	Place	Status of Original	Notes
February 26, 1846	JB	WRK	Washington, DC	Destroyed	Referenced in docket of WRK to JB, Jan. 27, 1846; destroyed by WRK as referenced in letter to JB of Feb. 28, 1846
February 28, 1846	WRK	JB	Paris	NA	Despatches from US Ministers to France, no. 26; Manning, ed., *Correspondence*, 6:564
February 28, 1846	WRK	JB	Paris	HSP	
March 27, 1846	JB	WRK	Washington, DC	NA	Diplomatic Instructions of the Department of State, France, no. 28; Manning, ed., *Correspondence*, 6:566
March 28, 1846	WRK	JB	Paris	HSP	Confidential
March 29, 1846	JB	WRK	Washington, DC	Lost	Referenced in docket of WRK to JB, Feb. 28, 1846
April 4, 1846	JB	WRK	Washington, DC	NA	Diplomatic Instructions of the Department of State, France, no. 29
April 18, 1846	JB	WRK	Washington, DC	NA	Diplomatic Instructions of the Department of State, France, no. 30
April 30, 1846	WRK	JB	Paris	NA	Despatches from US Ministers to France, no. 27
April 30, 1846	WRK	JB	Paris	HSP	Received May 23, 1846

Date	From	To	Place	Status of Original	Notes
May 4, 1846	JB	WRK	Washington, DC	NA	Diplomatic Instructions of the Department of State, France, no. 31
May 14, 1846	JB	WRK	Washington, DC	NA	Diplomatic Instructions of the Department of State, France, no. 32; Manning, ed., *Correspondence*, 6:452
May 20, 1846	JB	WRK	Washington, DC	NA	Diplomatic Instructions of the Department of State, France, no. 33
June 1, 1846	WRK	JB	Paris	NA	Despatches from US Ministers to France, no. 28; Manning, ed., *Correspondence*, 6:566
June 1, 1846	WRK	JB	Paris	HSP	
June 6, 1846	WRK	JB	Paris	HSP	Letter of introduction
June 23, 1846	JB	WRK	Washington, DC	HSP	Extract included with letter of WRK to JB, June 1, 1846
June 27, 1846	WRK	JB	Paris	HSP	
June 30, 1846	WRK	JB	Paris	NA	Despatches from US Ministers to France, no. 29; Manning, ed., *Correspondence*, 6:568
July 3, 1846	WRK	JB	Paris	HSP	
July 15, 1846	WRK	JB	Paris	NA	Despatches from US Ministers to France, no. 30
July 15, 1846	WRK	JB	Paris	HSP	
July 20, 1846	WRK	JB	Paris	NA	Despatches from US Ministers to France, no. 31; Manning, ed., *Correspondence*, 6:570

Date	From	To	Place	Status of Original	Notes
July 31, 1846	JB	WRK	Washington, DC	NA	Diplomatic Instructions of the Department of State, France, no. 34
August 12, 1846	JB	WRK	Washington, DC	NA	Diplomatic Instructions of the Department of State, France, no. 35
September 15, 1846	WRK	JB	Paris	NA	Despatches from US Ministers to France, no. 35
October 1, 1846	WRK	JB	Liverpool	HSP	Received Oct. 23, 1846
February 10, 1847	WRK	JB	Selma, AL	HSP	
May 16, 1847	JB	WRK	Washington, DC	Lost	Referenced in WRK to JB, June 11, 1847
June 11, 1847	WRK	JB	Selma, AL	HSP	Private
October 5, 1847	WRK	JB	Selma, AL	HSP	
June 28, 1848	WRK	JB	New York	HSP	
July 1848	JB	WRK	Washington, DC	Lost	Referenced in docket of WRK to JB, June 28, 1848
January 6, 1850	WRK	JB	Washington, DC	HSP	
January 8, 1850	JB	WRK	Lancaster, PA	Lost	Referenced in docket of WRK to JB, Jan. 6, 1850
January 13, 1850	WRK	JB	Washington, DC	HSP	
January 18, 1850	JB	WRK	Lancaster, PA	HSP	
March 6, 1850	JB	WRK	Lancaster, PA	HSP	Moore, ed., *Works*, 8:369
March 11, 1850	WRK	JB	Washington, DC	HSP	
March 15, 1850	JB	WRK	Lancaster, PA	HSP	Moore, ed., *Works*, 8:370

Date	From	To	Place	Status of Original	Notes
March 20, 1850	WRK	JB	Washington, DC	HSP	Moore, ed., *Works*, 8:374
March 20, 1850	JB	WRK	Lancaster, PA	HSP	Moore, ed., *Works*, 8:374
May 8, 1850	WRK	JB	Washington, DC	HSP	Moore, ed., *Works*, 8:381
May 13, 1850	JB	WRK	Lancaster, PA	HSP	Moore, ed., *Works*, 8:383-85
June 8, 1850	WRK	JB	Washington, DC	HSP	
June 11, 1850	WRK	JB	Washington, DC	HSP	
June 13, 1850	JB	WRK	Lancaster, PA	Lost	Included copy of letter on Missouri Compromise; referenced in docket of WRK to JB, June 11, 1850
June 19, 1850	WRK	JB	Washington, DC	HSP	
August 4, 1850	WRK	JB	Washington, DC	HSP	Confidential
August 10, 1850	JB	WRK	Lancaster, PA	Lost	Referenced in docket of WRK to JB, Aug. 4, 1850
August 26, 1850	WRK	JB	Washington, DC	HSP	Docket: "Put away 1 Sept. 1850"
January 12, 1851	WRK	JB	Washington, DC	HSP	
January 15, 1851	WRK	JB	Lancaster, PA	Lost	Referenced in docket of WRK to JB, Jan. 12, 1851
March 13, 1851	WRK	JB	Washington, DC	HSP	

Date	From	To	Place	Status of Original	Notes
March 26, 1851	JB	WRK	Lancaster, PA	Lost	Referenced in docket of WRK to JB, Mar. 13, 1851
October 14, 1851	WRK	JB	Selma, AL	HSP	Confidential
October 1851	JB	WRK	Lancaster, PA	Lost	Referenced in docket of WRK to JB, Oct. 14, 1851
December 12, 1851	WRK	JB	Washington, DC	HSP	
January 16, 1852	WRK	JB	Washington, DC	HSP	
January 20, 1852	JB	WRK	Lancaster, PA	Lost	Referenced in docket of WRK to JB, Jan. 16, 1852
March 6, 1852	WRK	JB	Washington, DC	HSP	
March 10, 1852	JB	WRK	Lancaster, PA	Lost	Referenced in docket of WRK to JB, Mar. 10, 1852
March 24, 1852	WRK	JB	Washington, DC	HSP	In handwriting of CME
March 26, 1852	JB	WRK	Lancaster, PA	Lost	Referenced in docket of WRK to JB, Mar. 24, 1852
March 31, 1852	WRK	JB	Washington, DC	HSP	In handwriting of CME
May 13, 1852	WRK	JB	Washington, DC	HSP	
May 15, 1852	JB	WRK	Lancaster, PA	Lost	Referenced in docket of WRK to JB, May 15, 1852
May 17, 1852	WRK	JB	Washington, DC	HSP	
May 20, 1852	WRK	JB	Washington, DC	HSP	Moore, ed., *Works*, 8:451

Date	From	To	Place	Status of Original	Notes
May 21, 1852	JB	WRK	Lancaster, PA	Lost	Referenced in docket of WRK to JB, May 20, 1852
May 24, 1852	WRK	JB	Washington, DC	HSP	
May 26, 1852	WRK	JB	Washington, DC	HSP	With rejected letter to Robert G. Scott enclosed
June 12, 1852	WRK	JB	Washington, DC	HSP	In handwriting of CME
June 21, 1852	JB	WRK	Lancaster, PA	Lost	Referenced in docket of WRK to JB, June 12, 1852
December 1852	JB	WRK	Lancaster, PA	Destroyed	Destroyed by WRK as referenced in letter to JB of Dec. 13, 1852
December 13, 1852	WRK	JB	Washington, DC	HSP	
December 14, 1852	JB	WRK	Lancaster, PA	Lost	Referenced in docket of WRK to JB, Dec. 13, 1852
January 1, 1853	CME	JB	Washington, DC	HSP	
January 1853	JB	WRK	Lancaster, PA	Destroyed	Destroyed by William W. King as referenced in letter to JB of Dec. 13, 1852
March 9, 1852	CME	JB	Matanzas, Cuba	HSP	
September 17, 1855	CME	JB	Newport, RI	HSP	Letter of introduction
April 13, 1866	CME	HLJ	Camden, AL	LC	
June 28, 1866	CME	JB	Saratoga Springs, NY	Lost	Referenced in letter of JB to CME, June 30, 1866

Date	From	To	Place	Status of Original	Notes
June 30, 1866	JB	CME	Lancaster, PA	DCL	
July 1866	CME	JB	Saratoga Springs, NY	Lost	Referenced in letter of JB to HLJ, July 18, 1866
July 1866	HLJ	CME	Baltimore	Lost	Referenced in letter of CME to HLJ, Oct. 4, 1866 [Moore, ed. *Works of James Buchanan*, 11:421-22]
October 14, 1866	CME	HLJ	New York	LC	
December 14, 1867	JB	CME	Lancaster, PA	LC	Acquired separately by LC in 1911; microfilm version incomplete
August 20, 1868	HLJ	CME	Baltimore	Lost	Referenced in letter of CME to HLJ, Sept. 16, 1868
September 16, 1868	CME	HLJ	Saratoga Springs, NY	LC	

Note: "Lost" indicates that the letter existed, but it has not survived. "Destroyed" indicates that the letter can be verified as having been disposed of. Excepting circular instructions, Buchanan's instructions and King's official despatches are included in the above calendar.

Abbreviations

People

CME	Catherine Margaret Parish Ellis (1816–1890)
HL/HLJ	Harriet Rebecca Lane Johnston (1830–1903)
JB	James Buchanan (1791–1868)
WRK	William Rufus King (1786–1853)

Places

AAS	American Antiquarian Society, Worcester, Massachusetts
ADAH	Alabama Department of Archives and History, Montgomery
DCL	Archives & Special Collections, Dickinson College
DUL	David M. Rubenstein Rare Book & Manuscript Library, Duke University
F&M	Archives and Special Collections, Franklin & Marshall College
GLC	Gilder Lehrman Collection, New-York Historical Society
HA	Heritage Auctions, Dallas, Texas
HSP	Historical Society of Pennsylvania, Philadelphia
HUL	Houghton Library, Harvard University
LC	Manuscript Division, Library of Congress, Washington, DC
LCHS	Lancaster County Historical Society, Pennsylvania
NA	National Archives, College Park, Maryland
NJHS	New Jersey Historical Society, Newark
N-YHS	New-York Historical Society, New York
NYPL	Manuscripts and Archives Division, New York Public Library
PSU	Eberly Family Special Collections Library, Pennsylvania State University

PUL   Rare Books and Special Collections, Princeton University
SHC   Southern Historical Collection, University of North Carolina
TSLA   Tennessee State Library and Archives, Nashville
UGA   Hargrett Rare Book & Manuscript Library, University of Georgia
VHS   Virginia Historical Society, Richmond

Notes

INTRODUCTION

1. Ellet, *Court Circles of the Republic*, 332. This is the first known reference in print to Buchanan and King as "the Siamese twins." On Ellet, see Linda K. Kerber, "'History Can Do It No Justice': Women and the Reinterpretation of the American Revolution," in *Women in the Age of the American Revolution*, eds. Hoffman and Albert, 3–42; Casper, "An Uneasy Marriage of Sentiment and Scholarship"; Mattingly, "Elizabeth Fries Lummis Ellet"; and Murphy, *Citizenship and the Origin of Women's History in the United States*, 150–61.

2. On the origin of the phrase "Siamese twins," see the entry in the *Oxford English Dictionary*; Wallace and Wallace, *The Two*, esp. 88; and Orser, *Lives of Chang & Eng*, esp. 22. For its evolution, see Edward Bulwer Lytton's poem "The Siamese Twins" (1831); the cartoon, "The Siamese Twins or the Unnatural Alliance!" (1832), BL; and Grand Gulf *Advertiser*, Sept. 12, 1837, reprinted in the *Weekly Arkansas Gazette*, Oct. 24, 1837 (quoted). Although scholars argue that the phrase later obtained a more overtly sexual connotation, if the historical example of Chang and Eng offers any insights, both married women and produced children by their respective wives, which makes the usage of the phrase not immediately obvious as slang for two same-sex attracted men. See also Katz, *Invention of Heterosexuality*, 65; and Allison Pingree, "America's 'United Siamese Brothers': Chang and Eng and Nineteenth-Century Ideologies of Democracy and Domesticity," in *Monster Theory*, ed. Cohen, 92–114.

3. For the newspaper articles cited, see *Detroit Free Press*, Feb. 28, 1840; New York *Tribune*, Aug. 19, 1844; *Portage Sentinel*, Oct. 2, 1856; *Baltimore Sun*, Jan. 9, 1890. For the partisan illustrations of "Siamese twins," see "A Globe to Live on!" (1840), LC; and "The Political 'Siamese' Twins: The Offspring of Chicago Miscegenation" (1864), AAS.

4. On William Rufus King, the most important scholarly work remains the un-published dissertation by Martin, "William Rufus King." For other helpful accounts, see Jackson, *Alabama's First United States Vice-President*; Martin, "William R. King"; Martin, "William R. King and the Compromise of 1850"; Martin, "William R. King and the Vice Presidency"; Johnston, *William R. King and His Kin*; Hatfield, "Vice Presidents of the United States, 1789–1993"; Saum, "'Who Steals My Purse'"; and Brooks, "The Faces of William R. King."

5. On James Buchanan, the essential works are Curtis, *Life of James Buchanan*; Moore, ed., *Works of James Buchanan*; Auchampaugh, *James Buchanan and His Cabinet on the Eve of Secession*; Klein, *President James Buchanan*; and Smith, *Presidency of James Buchanan*. For recent scholarship, see Birkner, ed., *James Buchanan and the Political Crisis of the 1850s*; Baker, *James Buchanan*; Horrocks, *President James Buchanan and the Crisis of National Leadership*; and Quist and Birkner, eds., *James Buchanan and the Coming of the Civil War*.

6. For the landmark study of early congressional boardinghouses, see Young, *Washington Community*. For subsequent studies of boardinghouse culture, see Bogue and Marlaire, "Of Mess and Men"; Earman, "Boardinghouses, Parties, and the Creation of a Political Society"; Earman, "Messing Around: Entertaining and Accommodating Congress, 1800–1830," in *Establishing Congress*, eds. Bowling and Kennon, 128–47; and Radomsky, "Social Life of Politics." On the later period, see Shelden, *Washington Brotherhood*; and Balcerski, "'A Work of Friendship.'"

7. On the timing of congressional elections, see Walton, "Elections for the Thirtieth Congress and the Presidential Candidacy of Zachary Taylor," 1–2.

8. On travel times to Washington, see plate 138, *Atlas of the Historical Geography of the United States*, eds. Wright; and Cullen, "Coming of the Railroads to Washington, D.C." On rotation in office, see Struble, "House Turnover and the Principle of Rotation." For other reasons, see Zagarri, "Family Factor"; and Riley, "Lonely Congressman." On the "yearling policy," see Richards, *Slave Power*, 206; and on the pay of the early Congress, see Skeen, "'Vox Populi,'" 256.

9. On Washington boardinghouses and hotels, see Shelden, *Washington Brotherhood*, esp. 102–10; Earman, "Messing Around"; and Young, *Washington Community*, 87–109.

10. On boardinghouse culture, see Gamber, *Boardinghouse in Nineteenth-Century America*; and Faflik, *Boarding Out*. See also Allgor, *Parlor Politics*, esp. 102–46.

11. For a recent historiographic overview of James Buchanan's congressional career, see Jean H. Baker, "James Buchanan: The Early Political Life," in *Companion to the Antebellum Presidents, 1837–1861*, ed. Silbey, 397–419. About King, see Martin, "William R. King."

12. For the earliest application of the "grammar of" concept, see Kann, *A Republic of Men*, 1–4; and for the "grammar of political combat," see Freeman, *Affairs of Honor*. On the concept of political gossip more generally, see Sparks, *Gossip*.

13. JB to Cornelia Roosevelt, May 13, 1844, in Curtis, *Life of James Buchanan*, 1:519; and ibid., *Works of James Buchanan*, ed. Moore, 6:1–3. See also Blaine, *Twenty Years in Congress*, 1:223–24; and Irelan, *The Republic*, 15:65–66. When quoting directly from either Buchanan or King in this book, I have preserved their original spelling and punctuation wherever possible.

14. For references to the pair as "the Siamese twins," see Auchampaugh, "James Buchanan, the Bachelor of the White House," 64fn8; Klein, *President James Buchanan*, 111; and Sellers, *James K. Polk, Continentalist*, 34. See also the memorable characterizations of King in Nichols, *Democratic Machine*, 54 and 144. On the question of Buchanan's sexuality, see Auchampaugh, "James Buchanan, the Squire from Lancaster," 29; and Klein, "Bachelor Father and Family Man," 214. For Klein's expanded view of the phrase "Siamese twins," see page 289 in copy 2 of the typescript in the Klein Papers, box 1, PSU. Later scholars followed Sellers's interpretation; see esp. Barzman, *Madmen and Geniuses*, 93–94.

15. Churcher, "First Gay President?"; Ross, *Fall from Grace*, 86–91 and 302, here 87; and Anthony, *First Ladies*, 136.

16. Updike, *Buchanan Dying*, esp. 183–262; Updike, *Memories of the Ford Administration*, esp. 224–43, here 234 and 314; and Boyer, "Notes of a Disillusioned Lover," here 66. For evidence of the friendly relations between Klein and Updike, see Birkner, "Conversation with Philip S. Klein," 244–45; and the surviving correspondence in the Updike Papers, HUL, and Klein Papers, PSU, respectively.

17. For the studies quoted, see Watson, *Affairs of State*, esp. 227–55, and 441–45, here 445; and Loewen, *Lies Across America*, esp. 367–70, here 370. For other studies that variously imply or insist upon a sexual relationship between Buchanan and King, see Cawthorne, *Sex Lives of the Presidents*, 91–95; Kramer, *American People, Volume 1*, 244; Cleves, "'What, Another Female Husband?,'" 1071; and Strauss, *Worst. President. Ever.*, 85–94. For recent examples of the popular view of Buchanan's sexuality, see Nile Cappello, "Are We Ready For A Gay President? Well, We May Have Already Had One," *Huffington Post*, June 9, 2016, http://www.huffingtonpost.com/entry/are-we-ready-for-a-gay-president-well-we-may-have_us_5759e5bae4b052f656ef5ef1; and Mo Rocca, "Worst President Ever: The Ignominy of James Buchanan," *CBS News*, Nov. 6, 2016, http://www.cbsnews.com/news/worst-president-ever-the-ignominy-of-james-buchanan.

18. On same-sex romantic and sexual intimacies among men in early America, see variously Katz, *Love Stories*; Godbeer, *Overflowing of Friendship*; and Benemann, *Male–Male Intimacy in Early America*. By comparison, same-sex unions among women could often be accepted locally; see Cleves, *Charity and Sylvia*. On LGBT history, see esp. D'Emilio, "Afterword," in *Long Before Stonewall*, ed. Foster, 384–90. For other mediations on the "essentialist" versus "social constructionist" debate, see Duberman, *About Time*; Tripp, *Intimate World of Abraham Lincoln*; Robb, *Strangers*, esp. 1–14; Halperin, *How to Do the History of Homosexuality*,

1–25; and Greven, *Gender Protest and Same-Sex Desire in Antebellum American Literature*, 1–42.

19. JB to James W. Wall, Jan. 16, 1863, JB Papers, box 52, folder 2, HSP. This framework of intimate male friendships by no means excludes a queer reading of past friendships; see esp. D'Emilio and Freedman, *Intimate Matters*, esp. 55–167.

20. For the etymology of the phrase "bosom friendship," see Johnson's *Dictionary of the English Language* (1755) and the *Oxford English Dictionary*. For the kinds of romantic friendships possible among women, see variously Faderman, *Surpassing the Love of Men*; Marcus, *Between Women*; and Vicinus, *Intimate Friends*. On the concept of bosom friendship in Melville, see for example Martin, *Hero, Captain, Stranger*, 67-94; Hardwick, *Herman Melville*, 68-97; Herrmann, "Melville's Portrait of Same-Sex Marriage in *Moby-Dick*," 71; and Laurie Robertson-Lorant, "Mr. Omoo and the Hawthornes: The Biographical Background," in *Hawthorne and Melville*, eds. Argersinger and Person, 32.

21. Godbeer, *Overflowing of Friendship*, 13; and Schweitzer, *Perfecting Friendship*, 141. On the construction of male political friendships at the exclusion of women, see Zagarri, *Revolutionary Backlash*, 148–80. For an overview of the study of early American friendship, see Lindman, "Histories of Friendship in Early America." For examples of male friendships in politics, see Stowe, *Intimacy and Power in the Old South*; Marzalek, *The Petticoat Affair*; Donald Yacovone, "'Surpassing the Love of Women,'" in *A Shared Experience*, eds. McCall and Yacovone, 195–221; Crain, *American Sympathy*; Jabour, *Marriage in the Early Republic*; Good, *Founding Friendships*; and Strozier, *Your Friend Forever*. For useful historiographic treatment of the studies of early American manhood, see Rindfleisch, "'What It Means to Be a Man'"; and Ditz, "The New Men's History and the Peculiar Absence of Gendered Power." For important studies of manhood during this period, see Rotundo, *American Manhood*; Donald Yacovone, "Abolitionists and the 'Language of Fraternal Love,'" in *Meanings for Manhood*, eds. Carnes and Griffen, 85–95; Nelson, *National Manhood*; and Williams, *Intellectual Manhood*. On the concept of "political culture," see Gendzel, "Political Culture"; and see also Freeman, *Field of Blood*, 3-20.

22. For various mentions of bosom friends in the contemporary record, see the obituary of Nathaniel Macon, *Detroit Free Press*, July 13, 1837; "The Ball Opening," *Weekly Ohio State Journal*, Nov. 2, 1842; "Review: Of the Claims and Qualifications of James K. Polk for the Presidency," *Daily National Intelligencer*, Oct. 5, 1844; "Democratic Ratification Meeting at Philadelphia," *New York Daily Times*, June 8, 1852; and "Van Buren and Buchanan," *Republican Banner*, Oct. 18, 1856.

23. For studies of the coming of the Civil War that highlight friendships among political actors, see Potter, *Impending Crisis*; Summers, *Plundering Generation*; Shelden, *Washington Brotherhood*; and Landis, *Northern Men with Southern Loyalties*.

24. Since the first poll conducted by Arthur M. Schlesinger Sr. in 1948, not a single one has ranked Buchanan above the bottom quartile. See also Merry, *Where They Stand*, 99–103; and Barzman, *Madmen and Geniuses*, 91–95.

CHAPTER 1

1. For general studies about the generation born after the American Revolution, see Appleby, *Inheriting the Revolution*; and Wood, *Empire of Liberty*. For the part played by women, see esp. Norton, *Liberty's Daughters*.
2. On declining fertility rates in this period, see Klein, *A Population History of the United States*, 68; Klepp, "Revolutionary Bodies," esp. 915-17; and Klepp, *Revolutionary Conceptions*, esp. 1–55. For the effects of higher education on the later development of young men in this period, see Sumner, *Collegiate Republic*; Pace, *Halls of Honor*; and Williams, *Intellectual Manhood*. For the prevalence of bachelorhood in the earlier period, see McCurdy, *Citizen Bachelors*, esp. 198–202; and see also Hartog, *Man and Wife in America*, 1–6.
3. Essential to establishing the King family's genealogy is the King Family Bible, Family Bibles Genealogical Collection, ADAH. On the King family, see "King Family of Virginia"; Grubbs, *Martin and Allied Families*, 258–68; King, *Our King Family*, 77–82; and Claude H. Moore, "King Family," in *Heritage of Sampson County*, ed. Bizzell, 463–64. On the DeVane family, see Thornton, "North Carolina's Own Huguenot Families"; Wilson and Glover, *Lees and Kings of Virginia and North Carolina*, 122–23; and Moore, "DeVane Family," in *Heritage of Sampson County*, ed. Bizzell, 395–96. On King's birthplace, see also J. D. Ezzell, "The Birth-Place of Vice-President William R. King," Fayetteville *Weekly Observer*, Aug. 3, 1893.
4. For the reminiscence of Bessie Hogan Williams, see Johnston, *William R. King and His Kin*, here 283.
5. For Dickson's recollection, see "Twelve North Carolina Counties," ed. Newsome, here 441. On the agricultural practices in early North Carolina, see also Morris and Morris, "Economic Conditions in North Carolina"; and Clarence L. Warren, "Evolution of Sampson Agriculture," in *Heritage of Sampson County*, ed. Bizzell, 115–27.
6. On William King Sr., see Martin, "William Rufus King," 3–22; and on the King family ownership of enslaved people, see *Stated Records of North Carolina*, ed. Clark, 26:1089.
7. For the record of King's activities at the University of North Carolina, see "Philanthropic Society Minutes," Vol. 3, Philanthropic Society Records, SHC; King's signature on a petition to the president, "Minutes of General Faculty and Faculty Council, 1799–1814," 77–78; and Archibald Henderson, "William Rufus King," in *Heritage of Sampson County*, ed. Bizzell, 207–209. See also WRK to Philanthropic Society, Oct. 10, 1837, April 4, 1838, and Sept. 29, 1851, Philanthropic Society Records, SHC.

8. On King's legal training, see Oates, *Story of Fayetteville*, 844–45. For King's earliest public duties in Sampson County, see the various entries in *Sampson County Court Minutes, 1800–1810*, eds. Bizzell and Bizzell, 81, 91, 136, 160, 182.

9. I obtained the dates of King's Masonic degree work from Nick Yakas, Phoenix Lodge No. 8. For the two recollections quoted, see WRK to John McRae, Sept. 2, 1852, WRK Papers, DUL; and WRK to Pierce and King Club Committee, Sept. 3, 1852, in Fayetteville *North-Carolinian*, Sept. 11, 1852.

10. On King's congressional campaign, see Claude H. Moore, "Old Clinton to Warsaw Road is Rich in History," in *Heritage of Sampson County*, ed. Bizzell, 4; and for the remembrance of Robert Strange, see "Eulogy on the Life and Character of William R. King," 8.

11. Earman, "Messing Around," 138. For King's early congressional messes, see Goldman and Young, eds., *Congressional Directories*, 50–51, 53, 59, 61, 66–71, and 75; and for their significance during the War of 1812, see Young, *Washington Community*, 182–86. For King's wartime vote, see *Annals of Congress*, 12th Congress, 1st session, 1637–38.

12. For the reminiscence of Sarah Weston Gales Seaton, see the diary entry of Nov. 12, 1812, in Seaton, *William Winston Seaton*, 84; and for Roberts, see "Memoirs of a Senator from Pennsylvania," ed. Klein, 236.

13. On this period, see Wood, *Empire of Liberty*, 659–700. On King's relationship with Elbridge Gerry, see his speech of June 25, 1841, in *Congressional Globe* 10, 27th Congress, 1st session, 119. On Gerry's short term as vice president, see Billias, *Elbridge Gerry*, esp. 322–30; and Kramer, "The Public Career of Elbridge Gerry," esp. 177–78.

14. On the early life of James Buchanan, see his "Autobiographical Sketch, 1791–1828," in *Works*, ed. Moore, 12:289–315, here 290–91. On the family of James Buchanan Sr., see Buchanan, *Buchanan Book*, esp. 453–54; Clemens, *Buchanan Family Record*; JB to W. E. Robinson, Feb. 6, 1844, JB Family Papers, part 1.1.1, folder 16, LCHS; and the helpful chart, "Descendants of James Buchanan, Father of President Buchanan," JB Family Papers, LCHS.

15. On life in early Mercersburg, see John L. Finafrock, "Mercersburg," in *A History of the Cumberland Valley in Pennsylvania*, ed. Donehoo, 1:347–78; William Findlay quoted in Day, *Historical Collections of the State of Pennsylvania*, 354–55; Appel, *Recollections of College Life*, 56–59; and Rev. Jacob Hassler to Editor, April 1893, in Chambersburg *Public Opinion*, May 5, 1893.

16. For the reminiscence, see John L. Finafrock, "Stony Batter," address given at Wheatland, April 7, 1940, quoted 3, in JB Correspondence, PSU. See also Klein, *President James Buchanan*, 36.

17. JB, "Autobiographical Sketch," 291–93. On John King, see Creigh, *History of the Presbyterian Church in Mercersburg*, 12–19; and for the baptismal records and for Buchanan's attitude toward King, see JB to Thomas Creigh, both in the records of Upper West Concocheague Presbyterian Church, Mercersburg. For the

question and answer book, see the uncatalogued Question/Answer Book James Buchanan (B 96.174.1), JB Family Papers, LCHS. On Buchanan's college years, see Philip S. Klein, "James Buchanan at Dickinson College," *John and Mary's College*, ed. Catton, 157–80; and for a general history of the college during his years, see Morgan, *Dickinson College*.

18. For Buchanan's records as society treasurer, see JB Receipt and Letter, Rare and Manuscript Collection, Cornell University; and JB, "Autobiographical Sketch," 293.

19. James Buchanan Sr., to JB, Sept. 6, 1809, JB Family Papers, part 5.1.2, folder 1, LCHS. See also Klein, "James Buchanan at Dickinson College"; and on his honorary degree from Franklin & Marshall College, see Klein, *Century of Education at Mercersburg*, 310.

20. JB, "Autobiographical Sketch," 293; and copies of James Buchanan Sr., to JB, Mar. 12, 1810, April 19, and July 4, 1811, JB Family Papers, part 5.1.2, folder 1, LCHS (the originals do not survive). On Lancaster during these years, see Day, *Historical Collections of the State of Pennsylvania*, 395; Harris, *Biographical History of Lancaster County*; Klein, *Lancaster's Golden Century*; and Auchampaugh, "James Buchanan, the Squire from Lancaster."

21. James Buchanan Sr., to JB, Mar. 12, 1812, JB Family Papers, part 5.1.2, folder 1, LCHS. On Buchanan's Kentucky travels, see McMurtry, "James Buchanan in Kentucky, 1813." On Buchanan's legal training and practice, see Hensel, "James Buchanan as a Lawyer"; and Klein, *President James Buchanan*, 433fn14.

22. James Buchanan Sr., to JB, Mar. 26, 1813, JB Family Papers, part 5.1.2, folder 1, LCHS. On Buchanan's association with the Union Fire Company No. 1, see Sanderson, *Historical Sketch of the Union Fire Company*, quoted 40; and Ellis and Evans, *History of Lancaster County*, 388. On the fraternal tradition of fire companies in this period, see Greenberg, *Cause for Alarm*.

23. For Buchanan's wartime service, see Worner, "Military Activities in Lancaster during the War of 1812"; and Klein, *President James Buchanan*, 17–18. See also James Buchanan Sr., to JB, Sept. 22, 1814, JB Family Papers, part 5.1.2, folder 1, LCHS.

24. Edward Y. Buchanan, "Buchanan, James, the Hon.," in Mombert, *Authentic History of Lancaster County in the State of Pennsylvania*, quoted 391; and James Buchanan Sr., to JB, Sept. 22, Oct. 21, 1814, and Jan. 20, Feb. 24, June 23, July 14, Sept. 1, and Oct. 19., 1815, JB Family Papers, part 5.1.2, folder 1, LCHS. On this period see, JB, "Autobiographical Sketch, 1791–1828" in *Works*, ed. Moore, 12:294–98; and for Buchanan's Fourth of July speech, see JB, "Fourth of July Oration," in *Works of James Buchanan*, ed. Moore, 1:2–9, and 12:316–20. See also Auchampaugh, "James Buchanan, the Squire from Lancaster," 289–312; Worner, "The Washington Association of Lancaster"; and Klein, *President James Buchanan*, 16–22, 35–37.

25. Klein, *Pennsylvania Politics*, quoted 50. On the political significance of July 4 orations, see Travers, *Celebrating the Fourth*.

26. Private Journal of WRK, WRK Papers, box 2, folder 11, ADAH. On the Compensation Act of 1816, see Skeen, "'Vox Populi.'" On Pinkney's mission to Naples, see Marraro, "William Pinkney's Mission to the Kingdom of the Two Sicilies, 1816."

27. On King's departure date and location and concerns over his expenses, see WRK to James Monroe, June 2 and Aug. 24, 1816, Despatches from U.S. Ministers to Russia, NA, reel 6. For Pinkney's view of King, see William Pinkney to Levitt Harris, Sept. 17, 1816, in *Some Account of the Life, Writings, and Speeches of William Pinkney*, ed. Wheaton, 152–54, quoted 154; and William Pinkney to James Monroe, Jan. 28, 1817, Despatches from U.S. Ministers to Russia, NA, reel 6. On the American legations to Russia, see Saul, *Distant Friends*, esp. 81–86; and Hildt, *Early Diplomatic Negotiations of the United States with Russia*, esp. 108–45.

28. On the royal wedding, see William Pinkney to John Q. Adams, July 5, 1817, Despatches from U.S. Ministers to Russia, reel 6, NA. See also Saul, *Distant Friends*, 80–83; and Lincoln, *Nicholas I*, 65–72.

29. For the family tradition of King's encounter with the czarina, see Bessie Hogan Williams, "The King Family" in Johnston, *William R. King and His Kin*, 70, 298. For echoes of the love story, see Oates, *History of Fayetteville and the Upper Cape Fear*, 845; and Octavia S. Wynn, "William Rufus King, Statesman, and Empire Builder," Selma *Times-Journal*, June 10, 1923. The love story persists among many residents of Selma, Alabama.

30. For King's original, damaged letter, see WRK to Israel Pickens, Dec. 8, 1824, Alabama Governor Administrative Files (Pickens), box 1, folder 4 (see also "Letter of Condolence"). The two poems alluded to are Thomas Gray, "Elegy Written in a Country Churchyard" (1751); and James Thomson, "The Seasons: Spring" (1730). On homosexual repression in Gray's "Elegy," see Summers, "Introduction," *Homosexuality in Renaissance and Enlightenment England*, ed. Summers, here 6.

31. Craig T. Friend, "Belles, Benefactors, and the Blacksmith's Son: Cyrus Stuart and the Enigma of Southern Gentlemanliness," in *Southern Manhood*, eds. Friend and Glover, 92–122, here 105; and Mayfield, "'The Soul of a Man!'," 481. See also Craig T. Friend, "Sex, Self, and the Performance of Patriarchal Manhood in the Old South," in *Old South's Modern World*, eds. Barnes, Towers, and Schoen, 246–68.

32. On Romantic alienation, see Faust, *A Sacred Circle*, 43.

33. Greven, *Gender Protest and Same-Sex Desire in Antebellum American Literature*, 4; and Strozier, *Your Friend Forever*, 40. For an example of the gradual diminution of punishment for sodomy, see Mark E. Kann, "Sexual Desire, Crime, and Punishment in the Early Republic," in *Long Before Stonewall*, ed. Foster, 279–302.

34. For examples of a similarly intimate correspondence among southerners, see Jabour, "Male Friendship and Masculinity in the Early National South."

35. William Pinkney to John Q. Adams, Aug. 1, 1817, Despatches from U.S. Ministers to Russia, reel 6, NA. For King's recommendation of Israel Pickens, see WRK to J. Meigs, et al., Feb. 16, 1816, Gratz Collection, case 2, box 9, folder 4, HSP. On

the death of William King Sr., see Johnston, *William R. King and His King*, 53, 104–106; and the Sampson County Court minutes for Feb. 17, 1817, in *Portrait of Nineteenth Century Sampson County*, eds. Bizzell and Bizzell, 3:151.

36. Klein, *Lancaster's Golden Century*, 45. On Passmore, see Sener, "Mayor John Passmore"; and Riddle, *Story of Lancaster*, 123. For Buchanan's estimation of his legal earnings, see JB, "Autobiographical Sketch, 1791–1828" in *Works of James Buchanan*, ed. Moore, 12:300. See also Harris, *Biographical History of Lancaster County*, 98; and Klein, *President James Buchanan*, 16, 433fn14.

37. On Rogers, see Klein, *Pennsylvania Politics*, 215; and Klein, *President James Buchanan*, 16–28. On Buchanan's masonic connections, see Welchans, *History of Lodge No. 43*; and for his views on anti-masonic feeling, see JB to Samuel H. Thomas, June 6, 1828 (typescript), JB biographical file, Pennsylvania Masonic Temple & Library.

38. On Robert Coleman's membership in Union Fire Company No. 1, see Sanderson, *Historical Sketch*, 42, 143. On the Buchanan and Coleman connections to St. James Church, see Klein and Diller, *History of St. James' Church*, 88, 102–103; and Klein, "Robert Coleman." For Buchanan's poetic verse, see the article by Isaac R. Sherwood, "James Buchanan's Blighted Romance," *Washington Post*, April 12, 1914. See also Bomberger, *Twelfth Colony Plus*, 138–39 and 183; Klein, "James Buchanan and Ann Coleman"; and Klein, *President James Buchanan*, 27–33. Ann Coleman's first name is variously spelled with and without the final "e."

39. Sherwood, "James Buchanan's Blighted Romance"; for the "trivial" quote, see George T. Curtis, *Life of Buchanan*, 1:20; for the "coolness" quote, see Hannah Cochran to Samuel Cochran, Dec. 14, 1819, quoted in Slaymaker, *Captives' Mansion*, 136 (the original letter is uncatalogued in the Slaymaker Collection, LCHS); and JB to Robert Coleman, Dec. 10, 1819, JB Papers, box 45, folder 1, HSP. See also "The Hubleys of Lancaster County," in *Historical Register*, 1:75–76; and the various entries for Mary F. Jenkins, Ann Coleman, and Grace P. Hubley in Landis, "Who Was Who in Lancaster One Hundred Years Ago," 382–83. For another account of the breaking of the engagement, see the Coleman family tradition in the letter from William Houghton to Frank W. Leach, Mar. 11, 1914, Leach Papers, box 1, folder Buchanan, James, HSP; and the article by Blanche Nevin, daughter of John Williamson and Martha Jenkins Nevin (who was the daughter of Robert Jenkins), as quoted in the now missing John Lowry Ruth Scrapbook by Klein, *President James Buchanan*, 31. See also Holler, "Some Rare Items Regarding James Buchanan and Thaddeus Stevens."

40. For the diary of Thomas Kittera, which does not survive, see the extracts made by George T. Curtis, JB Papers, box 60, folder 5, HSP; and for the observation about Coleman catching a cold, see Samuel Dale to Jacob Hibshman, Dec. 16, 1819, Hibshman Papers, box 2, folder 3, PSU. See also Clark, "Who Was Jacob Hibshman"; Klein, "James Buchanan and Ann Coleman"; Klein, *President James Buchanan*, 27–33; and Updike, *Buchanan Dying*, 151–58. The view of a possible

suicide has persisted among historians; see Klein to Updike, Aug. 1, 1968, Updike Papers, box 249 (item 4686), HUL.

41. Hannah Cochran to Samuel Cochran, Dec. 14, 1819, as quoted in Slaymaker, *Captives' Mansion*, 136; JB to Robert Coleman, box 45, folder 1, Dec. 10, 1819, JB Papers. For the obituary notice of Ann Coleman, see "Obituary," Lancaster *Journal*, Dec. 14, 1819.

42. On Buchanan's later courtships, see Klein, "Bachelor Father," here 202. On the destruction of papers related to the affair, see Curtis, *Life of James Buchanan*, 1:20–21. See also Tripp, *Intimate World of Abraham Lincoln*, 67–90; and Strozier, *Your Friend Forever*, 59–78.

43. *Harper's Magazine* 75, no. 13 (Aug. 1856): 421–22; the article by the Philadelphia correspondent, "Died in the Almshouse," *Boston Herald* Aug. 28, 1883; George T. Curtis to Hiram B. Swarr, Sept. 5, 1883, JB Family Papers, part 8.1, folder 19, LCHS; and the public letter from Curtis, dated Sept. 12, 1883, reprinted in the *Boston Post*, Sept. 18, 1883. On Emma Jacobs Thompson, see also the piece in the *Lancaster Daily Intelligencer*, Aug. 31, 1883. See also Klein, "James Buchanan and Ann Coleman." For mention of a spurious love affair with one Letitia Duncan, see Witt Kenneth Cochran, "A President's Love," *St. Paul Daily Globe*, Jan. 17, 1888; and Updike, *Buchanan Dying*, 185.

44. Samuel M. L. Barlow to George T. Curtis, Oct. 17, 1881, JB Family Papers, part 8.1, folder 19, LCHS. On this period, see Klein, *President James Buchanan*, 35–37.

45. For the relevant newspaper articles, see "Investigator," Harrisburg *Republican*, July 21, 1820; James Buchanan Sr., to JB, July 26, 1820, JB Papers, box 60, folder 5, HSP; the copy of "Colebrook" to JB [ca. July 1820], JB Family Papers, part 1.2, folder 1, LCHS; and the editorials and letters in the Lancaster *Journal* for the months of July and August, 1820. See also Weatherman, "James Buchanan on Slavery and Secession."

46. On the death of James Buchanan Sr., see Klein, *President James Buchanan*, 37; on William Speer Buchanan, see *Baltimore Patriot*, Dec. 23, 1826, p. 3; and on Sarah Buchanan Huston, see Klein, *President James Buchanan*, 101.

CHAPTER 2

1. On the broad cultural transformations of the early republic, see Bushman, *Refinement of America*; Zakim, *Ready-Made Democracy*; and Kelly, *Republic of Taste*. On their implications in Washington politics, see Freeman, *Affairs of Honor*; Kaplan, *Men of Letters in the Early Republic*; Baker, *Affairs of Party*; Zagarri, "The Family Factor"; and Riley, "The Lonely Congressmen."

2. On the Era of Good Feelings, see Dangerfield, *Era of Good Feelings*; and Howe, *What Hath God Wrought*, 91–124. On the presidential election of 1824, see Ratcliffe, *The One-Party Presidential Contest*.

3. For King's visit to the capital, see the blurb in the *National Intelligencer*, Feb. 2, 1818. On King's initial land purchases in Alabama, see the relevant entries in Barefield, ed., *Old Cahaba Land Office Records & Military Records*; and on his involvement with the Selma Land Company, see Selma Land Company account book, ADAH. See also Hardy, *Selma*, 8–10; and Fitts, *Selma*, 1–22. The work of "Ossian" was supposedly collected and published by Scottish poet James Macpherson.

4. For more on this period, see the letter of Louisa King Kornegay, ca. 1880s, in "Personal Belongings of King Still Owned Here," Selma *Times-Journal*, Nov. 23, 1952, King Family Papers, box 5, folder 7, ADAH; and the reminiscence by Bessie Hogan Williams, "The King Family," in Johnston, *William R. King and His Kin*, 283–310.

5. WRK to Eliza R. Beck, Feb. 16, 1826, box 1, WRK Papers, ADAH. See also WRK to Thomas DeVane King, June 22, 1844, WRK Papers, ADAH; and Johnston, *William R. King and His Kin*, 109–10. On the effect of migration on kinship ties across the South, see Billingsley, *Communities of Kinship*. On King's legal guardianship over the children of his sister, see the court citation in Patterson, *Kennard, King, Knight, Hardin, Goodin*, 92.

6. For the announcement of the marriage of Harvey W. Ellis and Catherine M. Parish (sometimes spelled Parrish), see Nashville *Daily Advertiser*, in *Marriages from Early Tennessee Newspapers*, ed. Lucas, 146. On Harvey W. Ellis, see Garrett, *Reminiscences of Public Men in Alabama*, 210–11. For King's observation about youth, see WRK to Thomas W. White, Jan. 10, 1827, WRK Papers, DUL.

7. For records on the King family land holdings and slave ownership, see Johnston, *William R. King and His Kin*, 109–11; "Register used by Thomas D. King to record an inventory of his property in Dallas County and Tuscaloosa County, Alabama," WRK Papers, box 6, ADAH. For King's slave ownership, see 1820 State Census, Dallas County, Alabama, p. 16. On King's treatment of slaves and his assets at the time of his death, see also "Illness of Hon. Wm. R. King," *Wheeling Daily Intelligencer*, Jan. 13, 1853.

8. For the remembrance of King, see Pickett, *History of Alabama*, 1:647. For the proceedings of the territorial constitutional convention, see *Journal of the Convention of the Alabama Territory*.

9. John Campbell to David Campbell, Aug. 11, 1819, Campbell Family Papers, box 4, DUL; and see the Campbell letters quoted in McMillan, "The Alabama Constitution of 1819," esp. 78.

10. For an overview of Alabama politics during this time, still helpful is Abernethy, *Formative Period in Alabama*; and on the "Broad River Group," see Thornton, *Politics and Power in a Slave Society*. On Crawford, see Brewer, *Alabama*, 392; on Tait, see Moffat, "Charles Tait"; on Walker, see Bailey, *John Williams Walker*; on Pickens, see Bailey, "Israel Pickens"; and on Chambers, see Brewer, *Alabama*, 350–51.

11. William H. Crawford to Charles H. Tait, Nov. 7, 1818, June 3, 1822, Sept. 11, 1822, and Feb. 16, 1823, Tait Family Papers, box 1, folders 8–12, ADAH. On McKee, see "Colonel John McKee"; and on Kelly, see Watson, *Alabama United States Senators*, 23–24.

12. For King's efforts to provide greater credit to the Bank of Alabama, see WRK to Bolling Hall, May 17, 1824, Bolling Hall Papers, box 1, folder 16, ADAH; and for his efforts to prevent the Bank of the United States from entering Alabama, see WRK to Nicholas Biddle, May 19, 1824, Etting Collection, box 30, vol. 16, HSP. For King's remarks on the substitute Treaty of Washington, see *Register of Debates*, 19th Congress, 2nd session, May 19, 1826, 781; and for its final vote, see also *Journal of the Executive Proceedings of the U.S. Senate*, Vol. 3, April 21, 1826, 531–33.

13. WRK to Israel Pickens, Oct. 1, 1824, Alabama Governors Correspondence, box 1, folder 4, ADAH; Nathaniel Macon to Bartlett Yancey, May 6, 1824, in *Letters of Nathaniel Macon*, ed. Battle, 80; and WRK to Israel Pickens, Feb. 10, 1827, Pickens Family Papers, box 1, folder 10, ADAH.

14. On this period see esp. Allgor, *Parlor Politics*, here 110; and Green, *Washington*, 81–118.

15. On Dowson's mess, see Brown, *Washington*, 137; and Bailey, *John Williams Walker*, 173–74. On the messmates' support of Dowson, see Willie P. Mangum to Joseph Gales Jr., Dec. 17, 1831, in *Papers of Willie Person Mangum*, ed. Shanks, 1:428. For King's various messes during these years, see Goldman and Young, eds., *Congressional Directories*. On Mangum, see Thompson, "Willie Person Mangum"; and on Smith, see Cassell, *Merchant in Congressman in the Young Republic*.

16. For the description of Buchanan, see Royall, *Black Book*, 3:134.

17. For the comment about being an "instruction man," see JB to Thomas Elder, Feb. 24, 1836, JB Papers, box 52, folder 30, HSP; see also JB to Jacob Kean, Dec. 8, 1834, in the *Pennsylvania Reporter*, reprinted in the *Washington Daily Globe*, Jan. 17, 1835. See also the draft of a letter, most likely written to Sarah Olcott Murdock Blake, wife of messmate George Blake of Massachusetts, cataloged as JB to "Dear Madam," ca. 1823, JB Papers, box 45, folder 2, HSP. See also Goldman and Young, eds., *Congressional Directories*, 127, 139–40.

18. On McDuffie, see Green, *George McDuffie*, esp., 27–36; Edmonds, *George McDuffie*, esp. 24–33; and O'Neall, *Biographical Sketches of the Bench and Bar of South Carolina*, 2:463–68. On slavery in the capital, see Finkelman and Kennon, eds., *In the Shadow of Freedom*. For the knapsack quote, see Hensel, "Attitude of James Buchanan," 7; and "Mission to Panama," *Register of Debates*, 19th Congress, 1st session, 2512.

19. On Buchanan's relation to Lowndes, see JB, "Autobiographical Sketch," in *Works of James Buchanan*, ed. Moore, 12:310–11; Klein, *President James Buchanan*, 38–39; Vipperman, *William Lowndes and the Transition of Southern Politics*, 252–64; and for the "Lowndes formula," see Campbell, "James Buchanan," esp. 52–91.

20. Henry R. Warfield to Henry Clay, Dec. 18, 1821, *Papers of Henry Clay*, eds. Hopkins et al., 3:147–50; George McDuffie to JB, Mar. 28, 1823, JB Papers, box 1, folder 3, HSP. See also Klein, *President James Buchanan*, 49.

21. For Buchanan's part in the election, see Klein, *President James Buchanan*, 50–53; Klein, *Pennsylvania Politics*, 177–81; and Stenberg, "Jackson, Buchanan, and the 'Corrupt Bargain' Calumny."

22. For the newspaper articles and correspondence from the summer of 1827, see the various letters in Moore, ed., *Works*, 1:260–71 (quoted JB to Andrew Jackson, Aug. 10, 1827); and the letters in *Papers of Andrew Jackson*, eds. Moser et al., 6:359–60. See also JB to Samuel D. Ingham, Aug. 16, 1827, Lincoln Collection, Brown University Library; JB to James A. Pearce, July 12, 1856, James A. Pearce Papers, box 2, Maryland Historical Society; and for the reconciliation, see JB to Thomas Elder, Dec. 10, 1827, Gratz Collection, case 2, box 24, folder 10, HSP.

23. On the factionalism among Pennsylvania Democrats, see Klein, *Pennsylvania Politics*; and Belohlavek, *George Mifflin Dallas*, esp. 23-35.

24. For the earlier comment about Barnard, see JB to Thomas Elder, Jan. 11, 1828, Gratz Collection, case 2, box 24, folder 10, HSP. For his later views, see JB to George B. Porter, Jan. 14, 1829 [misdated as 1828], George Bryan Porter Papers, Bentley Historical Library (quoted); and see also JB to Unknown, Feb. 7, 1829, and JB to Isaac D. Barnard, Mar. 11, and Aug. 20, 1829, JB Papers, box 1, folder 9, DCL. About Isaac D. Barnard, see Futhey and Cope, *History of Chester County,* 475–77. On Buchanan's messes of these years, see also JB to William Norris, Dec. 11, 1825, and Dec. 24, 1829, JB Papers, box 52, folders 27 and 28, HSP; and Goldman and Young, eds., *Congressional Directories*, 170, 184, 195, 206, and 281.

25. JB to John Reynolds, Jan. 27, 1830, Reynolds Family Papers, box 1, folder 6, F&M. See also Klein, *President James Buchanan*, 60–77.

26. For the anecdote of Buchanan's conversation with Jackson, see Duff, *Notes from a Diary*, 2:4; diary entry of John Quincy Adams, Jan. 31, 1831, in *Memoirs of John Quincy Adams*, ed. Adams, 8:307.

27. On this period, see Thornton, *Politics and Power in a Slave Society*, 117–62. On McKinley, see Brown, *John McKinley and the Antebellum Supreme Court*. On the visit of the Marquis de Lafayette to Alabama, see "Lafayette's Visit to Alabama," eds. McCall; and Bridges, "'The Nation's Guest.'"

28. On King's affair with Kenan, see Martin, "William Rufus King," 99–103; and Moore, *History of Alabama*, 168–72. For a different interpretation of the affair, see Brooks, "The Faces of William R. King," 18. On John C. Perry, see Owen, *History of Alabama Dictionary and Biography,* 4:1343.

29. For the letters of challenge, see Michael J. Kenan to WRK, May 22 and May 26, 1831, *Alabama State Intelligencer*, Oct. 29, 1831. On dueling among members of the Kenan family, see the newspaper clippings in WRK Papers, box 5, folder 7, ADAH. For the King family recollection of the affair, see the account of Bessie Hogan Williams, "King Family," in Johnston, *William R. King and His Kin*, 300.

30. WRK to John Coffee, July 13, 1831, John Coffee Papers, reel 2, ADAH. For the conversation between King and Perry, see Bessie Hogan Williams, "King Family," in Johnston, *William R. King and His Kin*, 300. For Perry's account of his initial encounter with King, see John C. Perry's letter "To the Public," Nov. 10, 1831, in *Alabama State Intelligencer*, Dec. 3, 1831; and for Perry's correspondence with King, see John C. Perry to WRK, June 25, 1831, and WRK to Perry, June 28, 1831, Huntsville *Democrat*, Nov. 11, 1831.

31. For John DeVane King's will, see Johnston, *William R. King and His Kin*, 107–108. On the affair, see Thomas DeVane King to William Taylor, July 12, 23, 30, and Nov. 17, 1831; Taylor to Thomas DeVane King, July 23, 1831; and John Coffee to William Taylor, Aug. 31, 1831, all in Huntsville *Democrat*, Nov. 17, 1831.

32. WRK to John Coffee, Dec. 10, 1831, John Coffee Papers, reel 2, ADAH; and WRK to Thomas S. Kenan, Nov. 28, 1839, WRK Papers, SHC. On the Kenans of North Carolina, see also Claude H. Moore, "James Kenan, Member of Provincial Congress," in *Heritage of Sampson County*, ed. Bizzell, 206–207.

33. For Anne Royall's observations on King's appearance, see *Black Book*, 3:122; and for the first Chesterfield comment, *Paul Pry*, Aug. 9, 1834. For the "Alabama Chesterfield" comment, see Will T. Sheehan, "Observations of the Only Vice President Alabama Furnished the United States, While Traveling in Europe," *Montgomery Advertiser*, Mar. 31, 1907. On Chesterfield more generally, see also Craig T. Friend, "Sex, Self, and the Performance of Patriarchal Manhood in the Old South," in *Old South's Modern Worlds*, eds. Barnes, Schoen, and Towers, 246–68, here 251. On King's many portraits, see esp. Brooks, "The Faces of William R. King."

34. On King's perceived grouping with Calhoun, see "Congressional Opposition," Washington *Union*, Oct. 13, 1831. See also Martin, "William R. King."

35. For King's remarks, see "General Convention," Baltimore *Republican*, May 22, 1832, reprinted in the *Washington Daily Globe*, May 24, 1832; and *Proceedings* (1832), 6. See also "History of the Two-Thirds Rule," April 28, 1860, *Camden Register*, in Jackson, "Alabama's First United States Vice-President," 12; Becker, "Unit Rule in National Nominating Conventions"; Gammon, *Presidential Campaign of 1832*, 100–101; McCormick, *Presidential Game*, 138–41; and Chase, *Emergence of the Presidential Nominating Convention*, 263–65.

36. For King's views on nullification, see WRK to John Coffee, Dec. 10, 1831, Coffee Papers, ADAH, reel 2; WRK to Martin Van Buren, Jan. 9, 1833, in *Papers of Martin Van Buren at the Library of Congress*, reel 12; and WRK to John Gayle, Feb. 26, 1833, copy in WRK Papers, box 1, folder 4, ADAH.

37. WRK to John Gayle, Feb. 26, 1833, WRK Papers, box 1, folder 4, ADAH; and Andrew Jackson to Hardy M. Cryer, Feb. 20, 1833, in *Correspondence of Andrew Jackson*, ed. Bassett, 5:19. On Dale's visit to Washington, see Claiborne, ed., *Life and Times of Gen. Sam Dale*, 177–213. On the feud between Louis McLane and Martin Van Buren, see Louis McLane to WRK, Dec. 25, 1836, and ca. spring 1836, McLane letters, NYPL

38. For the originating source for Jackson's quote about Buchanan's appointment to Russia, see Buell, *History of Andrew Jackson*, 2:404; and see also Boller, *Presidential Anecdotes*, 118. For Jefferson's reaction to offering Jackson the Russian mission, see diary entry of April 8, 1818, John Quincy Adams, *Memoirs of John Quincy Adams*, ed. Adams, 4:76; and on Jackson declining the Mexican mission, see Andrew Jackson to Edward Livingston, Mar. 24, 1823, in *Papers of Andrew Jackson*, eds. Moser et al., 5:264–66. For John Eaton's letter, see John Eaton to JB, May 31, 1831, in Curtis, *Life of James Buchanan*, 1:130.

39. Elizabeth Spear Buchanan to JB, Oct. 21, [1831], JB Family Papers, part 5.1.2, folder 1, LCHS. On Buchanan's acceptance of the Russian mission, see article from the *Susquehanna Register*, reprinted in the *Washington Daily Globe*, Aug. 6, 1831.

40. JB to Jared Sparks, Sept. 21, 1831, and April 7, 1832, Jared Sparks Papers, box 5, HUL.

41. John Barry to Susan Taylor, Mar. 30, 1832, in "Kentuckian in 'King Andrew's' Court," ed. Conover, 178; JB to Edward Y. Buchanan, July 15–17, 1832, in *Works of JB*, ed. Moore, 218; JB to Harriet Buchanan Henry, Aug. 15, 1832, JB Papers, box 45, HSP; JB to William T. Barry, Taylor Family Papers, Kentucky Historical Society. On Buchanan's time as Minister to Russia, see Binder, *James Buchanan and the American Empire*, 11–38. On Buchanan's relationship with John Randolph Clay, see also Oeste, *John Randolph Clay*, 103–20; and with John W. Barry, see also Conover, ed., " 'To Please Papa.' " See also JB to William W. Seaton, April 7, 1833, in Seaton, *William Winston Seaton*, 315–16.

42. JB to Stephen Pleasonton, July 6, 1832, Autograph Coll. B, HUL. On his relationship to Princess Lieven, see JB to John Reynolds, Reynolds Family Papers, box 1, folder 8, F&M; and JB to Princess Lieven, Nov. 13, 1855, Lieven Papers (Add MS 47378, Vol. CLVIII), British Library.

43. For the diary entry in question, see Tuesday, June 18, 1833, in *Works of James Buchanan*, ed. Moore, 2:363; and for letters that express similar sentiments, see JB to George G. Leiper, July 3, 1833, ibid., 2:367; and JB to John Reynolds, July 3, 1833, box 1, folder 13, DCL.

44. For the date of Buchanan's arrival home, see article of the *Boston Commercial Gazette*, reprinted in the *Washington Daily Globe*, Aug. 1, 1832. On this period, see Klein, *President James Buchanan*, 79–88.

45. JB to Mahlon Dickerson, Oct. 24, 1834, Dickerson Papers, box 1, folder 2, NJHS; "Dinner to Mr. Buchanan," *Washington Daily Globe*, Nov. 28, 1833; and "Pennsylvania Senator," ibid., Dec. 9, 1834. See also Klein, *Pennsylvania Politics*.

46. JB to William Norris, Jan. 15, 1826, JB Papers, box 52, folder 27, HSP. For the record of the purchase of the property at the corner of East King Street and Duke Street, see Feb. 21, 1829, Deed Book M, vol. 5, p. 145, Lancaster County Office of the Recorder of Deeds; and for the purchase of the Coleman residence, see Mar. 26, 1833, Deed Book Y, vol. 5, p. 198. On Buchanan's co-ownership of the Lucinda Furnace, see Davis, ed., *History of Clarion County*, 116; and for Buchanan's retrospection on the venture, see JB to James L. Reynolds, July 14, 1854, Reynolds Papers, box 11, folder 1, F&M.

47. JB to Harriet Buchanan, April 11, 1831, Buchanan letters, GLC.

48. For the "solitary abode" comment, see JB to John Randolph Clay, April 5, 1837, JB Papers, box 52, folder 31, HSP. For the surviving record on Buchanan's courtship with an unmarried Kittera relative, see JB to Thomas Kittera, Oct. 9, 1834, Sept. 25, 1837, and Jan. 13, 1839, JB to Anne Kittera, Oct. 30, 1840, and JB to Ann Kittera, April 25, 1843, JB Family Papers, part 1.1.1, folders 244a–f, LCHS.

49. JB to Eliza Violet Gist Blair, June 3, 1837, JB Papers, box 46, folder 2, HSP; JB to Ann Kittera, April 25, 1843, JB Family Papers, part 1.1.1, folder 244f, LCHS; and JB to Eliza Violet Gist Blair, May 15, 1839, Blair and Lee Family Papers, box 42, folder 5, PUL. See also Klein, *President James Buchanan*, 101 and 119–20; and Russ, "Mary Kittera Snyder's Struggle for an Income," 6.

CHAPTER 3

1. For an overview of this period, see Watson, *Liberty and Power*. On the major political issues of the Jacksonian era, see Russo, "The Major Political Issues of the Jacksonian Period"; McCormick, *Second American Party System*; Hofstadter, *Idea of Party*; Howe, *Political Culture of the American Whigs*; Peterson, *Great Triumvirate*; Freehling, *Road to Disunion, Vol. 1*; Holt, *Political Parties and American Political Development*; Holt, *Rise and Fall of the American Whig Party*; and Varon, *Disunion!*.

2. For the common practice of congressmen living as bachelors, see Zagarri, "The Family Factor," here 296–97; and Riley, "The Lonely Congressman." On the prevalence of bachelors in boardinghouses, see Chudacoff, *Age of the Bachelor*, esp. 32.

3. JB to Peter Wager, Jan. 13, 1838, JB Letters and Documents, NYPL; Young, *Washington Community*, 100. On Buchanan and other doughfaces, see Cox, "The Origin and Exhaustion of the Doughfaces," esp. 85–123; Wood, "'A Sacrifice on the Altar of Slavery'"; and Lynn, "A Manly Doughface." On the related concept of the slave power, see also Richards, *Slave Power*, esp. 197; Cooper, *The South and the Politics of Slavery*, esp. 257; and James L. Huston, "James Buchanan, the Slavocracy, and the Disruption of the Democratic Party," in *Companion to the Antebellum Presidents*, ed. Silbey, 421–45.

4. For the part played by the wives of politicians, see Allgor, *Parlor Politics*; and on Sarah Childress Polk, see Greenberg, *Lady First*.

5. Out of 167 senators, between the years 1790 and 1860, at least 6, and perhaps as many as 11, were unmarried, whether as bachelors or widowers (between 4 to 7 percent); see Radomsky, "Social Life of Politics," 469–88. A comparison to the "age of the bachelor," the period between 1890 and 1920, is instructive: in New York City, the epicenter of American bachelorhood, 11 percent of men between the ages of 45 and 64 were unmarried; see Chudacoff, *Age of the Bachelor*, esp. 21–44, 50.

6. For an overview of the gendered aspects of politics in the Jacksonian era, see Nancy Morgan, "'She's as Chaste as a Virgin!': Gender, Political Platforms, and the Second

American Party System," in *Companion to the Era of Andrew Jackson*, ed. Adams, 298–327. On the politicization of the marriage of Andrew Jackson in the election of 1828, see Basch, "Marriage, Morals, and Politics in the Election of 1828." On the Peggy Eaton affair, see Marzalek, *Petticoat Affair*; Kirsten E. Wood, "'One Woman So Dangerous to Public Morals'"; and Meacham, *American Lion*, esp. 98–114.

7. Watson, *Liberty and Power*, 131–71; and Freehling, *Road to Disunion*, 1:289–307.

8. On King's boardinghouses during the early 1830s, see Goldman and Young, eds., *United States Congressional Directories*, 228, 230, 241, 253, 268. See also Klein, *President James Buchanan*, 105–15.

9. For the early history of Washington and the population figures, see esp. Green, *Washington*, here 21, 48, 150 (quoted); on the C Street neighborhood, see Zevely, "Old Houses on C Street and Those Who Lived There," 152 (quoted); and Brown, *Washington*, 234.

10. For the description of King that mentions his height, see Pickett, *History of Alabama*, 647; for the description of King as an "old bachelor," see "Letters from Washington—No. 19" for the *Puritan Recorder*, June 12, 1852, enclosed in David Hitchcock to Caleb Cushing, June 18, 1852, Caleb Cushing Papers, box 61, folder 10, LC; and Caleb Cushing, "Biographical Sketch of William R. King, ca. 1834," Cushing Papers, box 201, folder 9, LC. See also Royall, *Paul Pry*, Aug. 4, 1832. On Van Buren, see Van Buren, *Autobiography of Martin Van Buren*, ed. Fitzpatrick, 724.

11. Schenck, *Personal Sketches of Distinguished Delegates of the State Convention*, 19; and Martin Van Buren to Theodore Miller, June 11, 1860, in "Correspondence of Bedford Brown," ed. Boyd, 20. On Bedford Brown, see also Jones, *Bedford Brown*; Walton, "Elections to the United States Senate in North Carolina, 1835–1861," esp. 172–74; and "Bedford Brown," in *Dictionary of North Carolina Biography*, ed. Powell, 1:240–41.

12. On Edward Lucas, see the entry for "Edward Lucas[IV], 1790–1858," in Trapnell, "Some Lucases of Jefferson County," 27–28. On drinking at Dickinson College, see Klein, "James Buchanan at Dickinson," in *John and Mary's College*, here 164; and Sumner, *Collegiate Republic*, esp. 101–102.

13. John Fairfield to Anna P. Fairfield, Jan. 7, 1836, in *Letters of John Fairfield*, ed. Staples, 65–66; *Poulson's Advertiser* (Philadelphia), Dec. 31, 1830, as reprinted in the *Journal of the Lancaster County Historical Society* 35 (1931), 95; "From Washington—Congressional Sketches," New York *Weekly Herald*, April 30, 1842; and JB to William F. Coplan, Mar. 23, 1837, JB Letters, HA (lot #49261). See also Klein, *President James Buchanan*, 100–104.

14. On the formal receptions and balls, see Allgor, *Parlor Politics*, esp. 147–89.

15. See the various listings in *Congressional Directories*, eds. Goldman and Young, 290–94. For Buchanan's comparison of King and Garret D. Wall, see JB to James W. Wall, Jan. 16, 1863, JB Papers, box 52, folder 2, HSP; and for a similar comment, see also JB to James W. Wall, July 14, 1860, ibid., box 51, folder 17. For the correspondence between Buchanan and Wall, see Garret D. Wall to JB, July 27, 1835, and

Sept. 23, 1835, ibid., box 3, folder 18, and JB to Garret D. Wall, Aug. 26, Sept. 18, Oct. 11, 1834, ibid., box 45, folder 15.

16. JB to Garret D. Wall, Nov. 19, 1835, JB Papers, box 52, folder 30, HSP. See also *Congressional Directories*, eds. Goldman and Young, 290–94; and Klein, *President James Buchanan*, 100–104.

17. On the election of 1836, see Joel Silbey, "Election of 1836," in *History of American Presidential Elections*, eds. Schlesinger and Israel, 2:575–600; and on the Whig strategy in the election of 1836, see Holt, *Rise and Fall of the American Whig Party*, 60–88.

18. WRK to JB, Oct. 5, 1836, JB Papers, box 4, folder 9, HSP.

19. WRK to JB, Oct. 5, 1836, JB Papers, box 4, folder 9, HSP; and JB to Thomas Elder, Nov. 7, 1836, ibid., box 45, folder 6. For a typical description of Buchanan's visits to Bedford Springs, see JB to L. Harper, Aug. 6, 1851, GLC.

20. Robert C. Nicholas to James P. Preston, July 16 (quoted) and Aug. 13, 1817, Preston Family Papers, VHS (see also "Letters from Old Trunks"). On the life of Robert C. Nicholas, see Thomas L. Bayne, "Genealogica, Vol. 1," VHS; "Nicholas Family of Virginia and Louisiana"; and Golladay, "The Nicholas Family of Virginia, 1722–1820," esp. 427–29. The source record of Robert Carter Nicholas (referenced as Robert Carter Nicholas II by genealogists) presents conflicting evidence: while some sources cite Nicholas as born in 1793 and as the son of George Nicholas, he was most likely born in 1787 to father Wilson Carey Nicholas and, keeping with this chronology, graduated from the College of William & Mary in 1803; see the note on the Nicholas family bible in Bayne's "Genealogica" noted above, and the listing of the class of 1803 in the *Catalog of Graduates of William and Mary* (1859).

21. JB to William Norris, Jan. 11, 1837, JB and HLJ Papers, LC, reel 1; "Austrian Mission," *Washington Daily Globe*, Mar. 14, 1837; John Catron to James K. Polk, March 13, [1837], in *Correspondence of James K. Polk*, eds. Cutler et al., 4:77–79. For Van Buren's offer of the attorney generalship to Buchanan, see Martin Van Buren to JB, Dec. 27, 1839, in *Works of James Buchanan*, ed. Moore, 4:124. At times, the messmates included others not directly affiliated with the Congress; for example, another man named King and his wife, "boarded with [Buchanan and William Rufus King] for seven years"; see diary entry of Sept. 1, 1846, *Diary of James K. Polk*, ed. Quaife, 2:109.

22. John P. King to JB, April 2, 1837, JB Papers, box 5, folder 12, HSP. On John P. King, see Mellichamp, *Senators from Georgia*, 107–109.

23. WRK to JB, June 2, 1837, JB Papers, box 5, folder 12, HSP; and for the various mess locations, see *Congressional Directories*, eds. Goldman and Young, 304, 318, 330, 344, and 358. For other notable Washington residences during this time, see Smith, "Historic Washington Homes."

24. WRK to JB, June 2, 1837, JB Papers, box 5, folder 12, HSP.

25. "Senator King of Alabama," *Lancaster Intelligencer*, reprinted in the *Washington Daily Globe*, Dec. 1, 1837; "Buchanan's Influence," *Lancaster Examiner and Democratic Herald*, Mar. 11, 1840.

26. For references to drinking by Webster and Buchanan, see Daniel Webster to JB, Mar. 21, 1835, box 3, folder 15, and for the dinner invitation, see Webster to JB, May 29, 1838, box 6, folder 8, JB Papers, HSP.

27. On Buchanan's trip to Virginia, see JB to Thomas J. Randolph, Feb. 20, 1838, JB Papers, box 1, folder 20, DCL; "Charlottesville, June 8," *Virginia Free Press*, June 6, 1838; and "White Sulphur Springs," *Lewisburg Enquirer*, Aug. 17, 1838, reprinted in the *Virginia Free Press*, Aug. 30, 1838. For King's trip to Virginia, see WRK to JB, June 20, 1839, JB Papers, box 7, folder 5, HSP. On elite society taking the waters, see Lewis, *Ladies and Gentlemen on Display*.

28. On the Panic of 1837, see Lepler, *The Many Panics of 1837*.

29. WRK to JB, June 2, 1837, JB Papers, box 5, folder 12, HSP; WRK to Asbury Dickens, June 1, 1837, Misc. Manuscripts Coll., box 1, LC; JB to Eliza Violet Gist Blair, June 3/7, 1837, box 46, folder 2, HSP.

30. "Speech, September 29, 1837, on Making Public Officers Depositories," in *Works of James Buchanan*, ed. Moore, 3:266, 270; "The Government and the Country," ed. J. T. Buckingham, *Boston Courier*, April 6, 1840. See also *Congressional Globe*, 25th Congress, 1st session, 85.

31. *Register of Debates*, 24th Congress, 2nd session, 618–19; "Remarks, March 1, 1839, on the Resolutions Concerning the Maine Boundary," in *Works of James Buchanan*, ed. Moore, 5:108. On the conservativism of the period, see Smith, *Stormy Present*, esp. 11–13.

32. For the initial debate precipitated by the Morris resolutions, see the proceedings for January 7 and 11, 1836, in the *Congressional Globe*, Appendix, 24th Congress, 1st session, 75–81, 83–84, here 77; and for the subsequent debate, see the proceedings for December 18, 1837, in *Congressional Globe*, Appendix, 25th Congress, 2nd session, 34–39. On the gag rule debates, see Wirls, " 'The Only Mode of Avoiding Everlasting Debate,' " esp. 125–29; and for Buchanan's involvement in the disenfranchisement of free African Americans in Pennsylvania, see Wood, " 'A Sacrifice on the Altar of Slavery,' " 75–106.

33. *Register of Debates*, 24th Congress, 1st session, 715; WRK, "Slavery in the District of Columbia," *Congressional Globe*, 24th Congress, 1st session, appendix, 142; and diary entry, Mar. 7, 1836, Mahlon Dickerson Diary, 1832–1845, Dickerson Papers, box 4, folder 1, NJHS.

34. "Remarks, March 2, 1836, on Petitions for the Abolition of Slavery in the District of Columbia," and "Remarks, February 6, 1837, on Memorial Praying for the Abolition of Slavery in the District of Columbia," *Works*, ed. Moore, here 3:9 and 3:205; JB "Intermeddling with Slavery," Jan. 10 and 11, 1838, *Works*, ed. Moore, 3:356.

35. "Remarks of William R. King," Dec. 18, 1837, *Niles' National Register*, vol. 3, no. 18 (Dec. 30, 1837), 275; and Thomas Elder to JB, Dec. 23, 1837, JB Papers, box 2, folder 20, HSP.

36. On the purchase of John Bell, see the account of Bessie Hogan Williams, ca. 1917, in Johnston, *William R. King and His Kin*, 295. On the African American

community in antebellum Washington, DC, see Mary Beth Corrigan, "The Ties That Bind: The Pursuit of Community and Freedom Among Slaves and Free Blacks in the District of Columbia, 1800–1860," in *Southern City, National Ambition*, ed. Gillette, 69–90. On Buchanan's role in the sale of enslaved people in the 1830s, see Klein, *President James Buchanan*, 100–101.

37. On the growth of partisanship, see Watson, *Liberty and Power*, 6; and Silbey, *Shrine of Party*.

38. For the record of the various votes, see *Register of Debates*: Wabash River improvement vote on Jan. 2, 1835, 23rd Congress, 2nd session, 90; Expunging Resolution vote on Jan. 16, 1837, 24th Congress, 2nd session, 504; surplus revenue vote on Feb. 19, 1836, 24th Congress, 1st session, 577–78; abolition of slavery votes on Mar. 11, 1836, and February 9, 1837, 24th Congress, 1st session, 804, and 24th Congress, 2nd session, 740; and on the subtreasury measures, see the various votes in 25th Congress, 1st session, passim.

39. For a study that utilizes roll-call analysis of congressional boardinghouses, see Bogue and Marlaire, "Of Mess and Men"; and for a comparison to congressional voting behavior in the 1840s, see Silbey, *Shrine of Party*. See also Bogue, *Clio & the Bitch Goddess*; and Poole, *Congress*, esp. 85–96.

40. On congressional activity during this period, see Watson, *Liberty and Power*, 198–230; Holt, *Rise and Fall of the Whig Party*, 89–121; and on Buchanan's personal life, see Klein, *President James Buchanan*, 116–50.

41. On William S. Ramsey, see the unattributed *History of Cumberland and Adams Counties*, 1:105, 160. On Buchanan's interest in Ramsey, see JB to John Reynolds, Jan. 2, 1833, JB Papers, box 1, folder 8, DCL; JB to Joel R. Poinsett, July 6, 1838, box 1, folder 21, DCL; and for more on their relationship, see William S. Ramsey to JB, May 29, 1838, and Aug. 25, 1839, JB Papers, box 6, folder 8, and box 7, folder 11, HSP. See also *Congressional Directories*, eds. Goldman and Young, 344.

42. On the currency debate, see JB, "Speech of Mr. Buchanan," Jan. 22, 1840, and "Small Bank Notes," Feb. 26, 1840, and John Davis, "Speech of Mr. Davis," Jan. 23, 1840, "Reply of Mr. Davis to Mr. Buchanan," Feb. 25, 1840, *Congressional Globe* (Appendix), 26th Congress, 1st session, 129–37 (quoted 136), 157–59 (quoted 159), 218–21. See also "Speech of Mr. John Davis of Massachusetts on the Sub-Treasury Bill," Jan. 23, 1840 (Washington, DC: Gale and Seaton, 1840).

43. JB, "Remarks of Mr. Buchanan," Mar. 3, 1840, "Remarks of Mr. Buchanan," Mar. 17, 1840; and Davis, "Remarks of Mr. Davis," Mar. 6, 1840, *Congressional Globe* (Appendix), 26th Congress, 1st session, 230–32, 244–47, 295–96. See also "Remarks of Messrs. Buchanan, King and Brown, in reply to Messrs. Davis, Preston and Clay, of Kentucky, on the subject of the currency," March 6, 1840 (Washington, DC: Globe, 1840), quoted 10, 12; "Reply of Mr. Davis, of Massachusetts to the Charge of Misrepresenting Mr. Buchanan's Argument in Favor of the Hard-Money System and the Consequent Reduction of Wages," Mar. 6, 1840 (Washington,

DC: Gales and Seaton, 1840). See also John Davis to Eliza B. Davis, Mar. 18, 1840, John Davis Papers, box 1, folder 7, AAS.

44. "Speech of Mr. Ramsey," June 6, 1840, *Congressional Globe* (Appendix), 26th Congress, 1st session, 560–64; William S. Ramsey to JB, Aug. 31, 1840, JB Papers, box 9, folder 1, HSP.

45. Jonathan M. Foltz to JB, Aug. 9, 1855, JB Family Papers, part 7.1.1, folder 39, LCHS; and JB to Jonathan M. Foltz, Sept. 21, 1855, Foltz Papers, LC. See also JB to William P. Schell, Aug. 17, 1848, JB Letters, HA (lot #34304). On Foltz, see Foltz, *Surgeon of the Seas*, esp. 130–40, 175–85; and Roddis, "Jonathan M. Foltz." See also Vincent J. Bertolini, "Fireside Chastity: The Erotics of Sentimental Bachelorhood in the 1850s," in *Sentimental Men*, eds. Chapman and Hendler, 19–42, here 19.

46. For local accounts of Ramsey's death, see *Baltimore Patriot*, Oct. 19, 1840, reprinted in the *Daily National Intelligencer*, Oct. 21, 1840; for Buchanan's obituary of Ramsey, see "William S. Ramsey," *American Volunteer*, Nov. 19, 1840, reprinted from the *Lancaster Intelligencer*; for the memoriam on Ramsey's life given before the House of Representatives, see *Congressional Globe*, 26th Congress, 2nd session, 17–18; *History of Cumberland and Adams Counties*, 160; and for the letter of condolence, see John M. Read to JB, Oct. 22, 1840, JB Papers, box 9, folder 5, HSP.

47. William H. Roane to Sarah Roane Harrison, Dec. 14, 1840, Dec. 23, 1840, Feb. 8, 1841, and Feb. 17, 1841, Harrison Family Papers, VHS; and *Congressional Directories*, eds. Goldman and Young, 372.

48. "Mess Parties of the Members of Congress," *New York Herald*, Jan. 6, 1841. On the marriage of Nicholas and Vinson, see also Plater, *Butlers of Iberville Parish*; and on Nicholas's defeat for re-election, see Sacher, *A Perfect War of Politics*, 101.

49. Robert C. Nicholas to JB, June 19, 1841, JB Papers, box 9, folder 8, HSP. For Nicholas's most recent visit to the springs, see *New York Morning Herald*, July 31, 1840.

50. William H. Roane to JB, April 14, 1842, JB Papers, box 10, folder 2, HSP. For the description of Sevier, see Walton, "Ambrose Hundley Sevier," here 39. On Ritchie, see Osthaus, *Partisans of the Southern Press*, 12–46.

51. JB to Bedford Brown, July 30, 1841, Bedford Brown Papers, box 1, DUL. For their later correspondence, see Brown to JB, Sept. 21, 1856, JB Papers, HSP, reel 29; and JB to Brown, Sept. 30, 1856, Bedford Brown Papers, box 1, DUL.

52. For more on the Buchanan siblings and their children, see "Descendants of James Buchanan, Father of President Buchanan," JB Family Papers, LCHS. For Miss Hetty's role in raising the two children, see the recollection of James Buchanan Henry to "Dear Madam," 1896, Henry Family Papers, box 1, HSP.

53. For the poem, see the draft copied in Buchanan's handwriting, dated Mar. 18, 1842, in the JB Family Papers, part 1.4.2, folder 2, LCHS. On the intended recipient of the poem, see also Klein, *President James Buchanan*, 156, who posits Anna Todd Payne; and Klein, "Senator 1834–'44" research notes, Klein Papers, box 10, folder 1,

PSU, who also suggests Mary Kittera Snyder. See also Russ, "Mary Kittera Snyder's Struggle for an Income."

CHAPTER 4

1. On the later Jacksonian era, see Watson, *Liberty and Power*, 232–54; and on its long-term effects on the administrative functions of the federal government, see White, *Jacksonians*. For the earliest and still most succinct argument for the "Age of Jackson," see Schlesinger, *Age of Jackson*; and for counterarguments, see variously Sellers, *Market Revolution*; and Howe, *What Hath God Wrought*.

2. On the democratization of the electorate, see Wilentz, *Rise of American Democracy*; on the election of 1828, see Parsons, *Birth of Modern Politics*; and on 1840, see Gunderson, *Log Cabin Campaign*. On the solidification of the Second Party System, see Holt, *Political Parties and American Political Development*; and McCormick, *Second American Party System*.

3. About Van Buren's selection as vice president in 1832, see Niven, *Van Buren*, 295–315.

4. On the election of 1836, see Shade, " 'The Most Delicate and Exciting Topics' "; and on the issue of Johnson's African American mistress in the election of 1836, see Brown, "Miscegenation of Richard Mentor Johnson"; and Snyder, *Great Crossings*, esp. 197–205.

5. On the vice presidential contest of 1840, see Klein, *President James Buchanan*, 129–41; and Sellers, *James K. Polk, Jacksonian*, 401–13. See also McCormick, *Presidential Game*, 164–206.

6. JB to John Randolph Clay, April 18, 1839, box 53, folder 2, JB Papers, HSP; JB to Eliza Violet Gist Blair, May 15, 1839, Blair and Lee Family Papers, box 42, folder 5, PUL; and JB to Charles M. Yates, [ca. Aug. 1839], Thomas H. Benton to JB, Aug. 17, 1839, and George S. Wharton to JB, Sept. 20, 1839, JB Papers, box 66, folder 2, and box 7, folders 11 and 13, HSP. See also Chambers, *Old Bullion Benton*, here 238.

7. WRK to JB, June 20, 1839, JB Papers, box 7, folder 5, HSP.

8. On Brown, see Jonathan M. Atkins, "Aaron Venable Brown," *American National Biography Online*.

9. WRK to CME, March 6, 1840, WRK Papers, box 1, folder 3, ADAH.

10. Aaron V. Brown to James K. Polk, April 3, 1840 [misdated May 3, 1840], in *Correspondence of James K. Polk*, eds. Cutler et al., 5:436. For earlier examples of King as "Miss Nancy," see the articles "From Washington," Mar. 17 and April 21, 1834, respectively, in the *Philadelphia Inquirer*, Mar. 19, 1834, and April 24, 1834; the untitled article from the *Alabama Beacon* reprinted in the Natchez *Daily Courier*, June 1, 1836; and the New Bedford *Emancipator and Weekly Chronicle*, May 1, 1844. See also the article "Washington, March 9th, 1837," *New York Herald*, Mar. 15, 1837, for the three nicknames, "Washington, April 10, 1844," printed in ibid., April 12, 1844; the diary entry of John Quincy Adams, May 10, 1844, in *Memoirs of John Quincy Adams*, ed. Adams, 12:25; and Poore, *Perley's Reminiscences*, 1:216. For a useful etymology of the term "Miss Nancy," see Saum, " 'Who Steals My

Purse,'" 189:fn38; Kimmel and Mosmiller, eds., *Against the Tide*, 6, 19; and for later usages, see Neaman and Silver, *Wordsworth Book of Euphemism*, 264–65.

11. Harvey M. Watterson to James K. Polk, May 2, 1842, in *Correspondence of James K. Polk*, eds. Cutler et al., 6:57.

12. "Buchanan's Influence," *Lancaster Examiner and Democratic Herald*, Mar. 11, 1840; Samuel H. Laughlin, May 4, 1840, in "Diaries of S.H. Laughlin of Tennessee, 1840–1843," ed. Sioussat, 54.

13. On the nominating convention of 1840, see Niven, *Martin Van Buren*, 463.

14. For the Harrison quote, see WRK to JB, Oct. 5, 1836, JB Papers, box 4, folder 9, HSP.

15. On violence in the Congress during this period, see Freeman, *Field of Blood*, 100-141.

16. For the affair of honor between King and Seaton, see Seaton, *William Winston Seaton*, 292–93.

17. On King's comment about Blair, see variously Alfred O.P. Nicholson to James K. Polk, Mar. 9 and 10, 1841, *Correspondence of James K. Polk*, eds. Cutler et al., 5:654–55. On Linn, see Hartley, "The Political Career of Lewis Fields Linn"; and on Sevier, see Walton, "Ambrose Hundley Sevier in the United States Senate." See also the Senate proceedings for Mar. 9, 1841, in the *Congressional Globe*, 27th Congress, 1st session, 243–46; John C. Calhoun to Thomas G. Clemson, Mar. 10, 1841, in *Calhoun Correspondence*, ed. Jameson, 2:477; Remini, *Henry Clay*, 574–75; and the notes in Hopkins et al., eds., *Papers of Henry Clay*, 9:511–12. For the characterization of Clay as a bully, see Freeman, *Field of Blood*, 346fn98.

18. Martin Van Buren to Andrew Jackson, Mar. 12, 1841, in *Correspondence of Andrew Jackson*, ed. Bassett, 6:93; and William L. Marcy to P. Montgomery Wetmore, Mar. 9, 1841, Marcy Papers, vol. 6, LC. See also "The Senate," *Daily National Intelligencer*, Mar. 16, 1841; and the account for Mar. 4 to Mar. 15, 1841, *Niles' National Register* 50 (Mar. 1841–Sept. 1841): 46–47. For the pinch of snuff exchange, see the report in the *Washington Globe*, reprinted in the *Jacksonville Republican*, April 7, 1841; and Poore, *Perley's Reminiscences*, 1:259–60. For the politicization of the bond to keep the peace, see "Henry Clay---'Law and Order,'" *Ohio Statesman*, April 24, 1844. For a later account of the affair, see Gobright, *Recollections of Men and Things*, 44-49.

19. Forney, *Recollections of Public Men*, 2:300-301; *New World* (New York), Mar. 9, 1841, p. 173; diary entry of John Quincy Adams, May 10, 1844, in *Memoirs of John Quincy Adams*, ed. Adams, 12:25; Henry W. Hilliard, "The Old Senate Chamber," *Appleton's Journal*, May 30, 1876. On the distinction between "fighting men" and "non-combatants" and for a succinct account of the affair, see Freeman, *Field of Blood*, 71–74 and 336–37fn117.

20. For a recent biography of Tyler, see May, *John Tyler*.

21. WRK to Arthur Bagby, Feb. 14, 1841, WRK Papers, box 1, folder 4, ADAH. On C.C. Clay's mess with Buchanan and King, see Nuermberger, *Clays of Alabama*, 63.

22. For memorable exchanges between Buchanan and Henry Clay, see the proceedings for July 17, 1841, in the *Congressional Globe*, 27th Congress, 1st session, 222–23. See also Sargent, *Public Men and Events*, 1:287–88; and for their later repartee, Remini, *Henry Clay*, 477, 586, and 604.

23. JB to A.J. Rockafeller, July 2, 1841, Andre De Coppett Collection, box 6, folder 4, PUL. For Buchanan's private views of Tyler, see JB to Samuel C. Humes, June 13, 1843 (quoted), and JB to Reah Frazer, Feb. 21, 1844, JB Papers, box 2, folders 5–6, DCL.

24. WRK to CME, Mar. 6, 1840, WRK Papers, box 1, folder 3, ADAH. For the recollection of Forney, see "XC," Dec. 8, 1872, in Forney, *Anecdotes of Public Men*, 1:395. For Julia Gardiner's comment on Buchanan, see Julia Gardiner to David L. Gardiner, Dec. 19–21, 1842, quoted in Seager, *And Tyler, Too*, 180.

25. "Speech, August 19, 1842, on the Webster-Ashburton Treaty," *Works of James Buchanan*, ed. Moore, 5:351. See the debate for March 7, 1842, *Congressional Globe*, 27th Congress, 2nd session, 287–88; and "Remarks, August 1, 1842, on the Tariff," *Works of James Buchanan*, ed. Moore, 5:332.

26. On the various messes of Buchanan and King, see the *Congressional Directories* for 1841–1844. On the Catrons as messmates, see JB to David R. Porter, Feb. 13, 1842, Porter Papers, box 6, folder 15, HSP. On King's dog, see William H. Roane to JB, Jan. 7, 1842, JB Papers, HSP, reel 7.

27. On the F Street neighborhood, see Brown, *Washington*, 334; and on the B Street neighborhood, see Wharton, *Social Life in the Early Republic*, 303–304.

28. For Calhoun's letter on the nominations in 1844, see John C. Calhoun to Robert M.T. Hunter, May 1, 1844, in *Papers of John C. Calhoun*, 18:384. See also Klein, *President James Buchanan*, 151–62.

29. JB to David R. Porter, Porter Papers, box 6, folder 17, HSP; and JB to John Reynolds, Feb. 22, 1842, JB Papers, box 2, folder 1, DCL.

30. JB to the Democrats of Pennsylvania, Dec. 14, 1843, in *Works of James Buchanan*, ed. Moore, 5:437–39; WRK to David Hubbard, May 14, 1844, George W. Campbell Papers, LC; and WRK to CME, Dec. 12, 1843, WRK Papers, box 1, folder 3, ADAH. On this period see, Klein, *President James Buchanan*, 151–59.

31. For the correspondence related to the King campaign sketch, see JB to Barnabas Bates, July 21, 1843, JB Papers, box 2, folder 5, DCL; and Bates to Jesse Miller, July 27, 1843 (acc. no I-SpahrB-1954-1), DCL. On the Pennsylvania nominating conventions of 1839 and 1843, see Snyder, *Jacksonian Heritage*, 144–50 and 171–86. For Jackson's correspondence, see Jackson to Martin Van Buren, November 29, 1843, in *Correspondence of Andrew Jackson*, ed. Bassett, 6:246.

32. For the first "Amicus" letter, see Washington *Daily Globe*, Jan. 8, 1844. On the role of William W. Payne as Amicus, see "Beauties of the Party Press," *New York Herald*, July 27, 1844.

33. For the related correspondence, see Cave Johnson to James K. Polk, Jan. 13, 21, and Feb. 6, 1844, in *Correspondence of James K. Polk*, eds. Cutler et al., 7:25–29, 51–56;

Polk to Johnson, January 21, 1844, in ibid., 7:38–44; and Aaron V. Brown to Polk, Jan. 22 and Feb. 2, 1844; in ibid., 7:44–46. For the various letters of "Amicus" and "A Tennessee Democrat," see Washington *Daily Globe*, Jan. 8, 15, 22, and Feb. 14, 1844.

34. For the "confidential" letter, see Aaron V. Brown to Sarah Childress Polk, Jan. 14, 1844, in *James K. Polk Papers*, reel 25. See also Sellers, *James K. Polk, Jacksonian*, 464–69; and the footnote in Cutler et al., eds., *Correspondence of James K. Polk*, 7:45-46fn3. On Mrs. Polk's social rebuff of Buchanan and King, see Nelson and Nelson, *Memorials of Sarah Childress Polk*, 51.

35. On the importance of women as political operators in their husband's campaigns, see Allgor, *Parlor Politics*, 102–46; Greenberg, *Lady First*, 56-137; DeFiore, "COME, and Bring the Ladies"; and Janet Coryell, "Superseding Gender," in *Women and the Unstable State in Nineteenth-Century America*, eds. Parker and Gordon, 84–112. See also Nelson and Nelson, *Memorials of Sarah Childress Polk*, 52; Greenberg, *A Wicked War*, 27–33; and Merry, *A Country of Vast Designs*, 32–33.

36. For the descriptions noted, see WRK to JB, July 1, 1844, JB and HLJ Papers, LC, reel 1 (on Polk); WRK to JB, Jan. 28, 1845, JB Papers, box 11, folder 23 (on Adams, Brown, and Toucey), HSP; WRK to Francis P. Blair, Dec. 27, 1844, Blair-Lee Family Papers, box 15, folder 3, PUL (on Adams); JB to Hugh Hamilton, Mar. 22, 1822, De Coppett Collection, box 6, folder 3, PUL (on Adams); and JB to Cornelia Roosevelt, May 13, 1844, box 46, folder 9, and WRK to JB, June 28, 1848, box 18, folder 18, HSP (on Van Buren).

37. For Tyler's view of King, see John Tyler to John S. Cunningham, Dec. 15, 1852, in *Letters and Times of the Tylers*, ed. Tyler, 2:205; and for the article approving King's appointment, see Baltimore *Patriot*, April 9, 1844, reprinted in the Washington *Daily Atlas*, April 13, 1844. See also Peterson, *Presidencies of William Henry Harrison & John Tyler*, 211; and Merk, *Slavery and the Annexation of Texas*, 3–32.

38. John C. Calhoun to WRK, April 12, 1844, and WRK to Calhoun, April 14, 1844, in *Papers of John C. Calhoun*, eds. Meriwether et al., 18:211, 237; WRK to Willie P. Mangum, April 15, 1844, printed in the *Daily National Intelligencer*, April 16, 1844; WRK to Benjamin Fitzpatrick, April 11, 1844, WRK Papers, box 1, folder, 4, ADAH; WRK to Joseph White, April 12, 1844, William Pinkney Papers, box 1, folder 20, PUL.

39. Article by the Washington correspondent, "By the Southern Mail," April 9, 1844, printed in the *New York Herald*, April 11, 1844; and John Catron to James K. Polk, June 8, 1844, *Correspondence of James K. Polk*, eds. Cutler et al., 7:214.

40. JB to Cornelia Roosevelt, May 13, 1844, and WRK to JB, May 14, 1844, JB Papers, box 46, folder 9, and box 11, folder 6, HSP.

41. Il Secretario, "Washington Correspondence," April 10, 1844, in *North American and Daily Advertiser*, April 12, 1844; article by the Washington correspondent, "By the Southern Mail," April 9, 1844, printed in the *New York Herald*, April 11, 1844; Royall, *The Huntress*, April 20, 1844.

42. WRK to JB, May 10, 1844, JB Papers, box 11, folder 6, HSP.

43. JB to Cornelia Roosevelt, May 13, 1844, JB Papers, box 46, folder 9, HSP.

44. Jonathan M. Foltz to JB, Nov. 22, 1855, JB Family Papers, part 7.1.1, folder 40, LCHS; Robert C. Nicholas to James P. Preston, July 16, 1817, Preston Family Papers, VHS; Bedford Brown to JB, Sept. 21, 1856, Bedford Brown Papers, DUL; WRK to Francis S. Claxton, May 2, 1844, JB Papers, box 56, folder 2, HSP; and WRK to John C. Calhoun, [ca. May 3, 1844], in *Papers of John C. Calhoun*, eds. Meriwether et al., 18:412.

45. For Benton's speech to expunge Andrew Jackson, see Thomas H. Benton, "Expunging Resolution," Jan. 12, 1837, *Register of Debates*, 13, part 1 (1836–1837): 380–91, here 391. For more on Benton's usage of the phrase "solitary and alone," see Tschachler, *Monetary Imagination of Edgar Allan Poe*, 85–87; and Chambers, *Old Bullion Benton*, 219. For other examples of Buchanan's use of "solitary and alone" in different contexts, see JB to David R. Porter, Feb. 17, 1841, Porter Papers, box 6, folder 17, HSP; JB to Eliza Watterston, Nov. 17, 1851, in *Works of James Buchanan*, ed. Moore, 8:424; and JB to C.L. Ward, Dec. 6, 1853, Buchanan Papers, N-YHS. Buchanan used the phrase in public remarks as much in private correspondence; see "Remarks on the Election of a Public Printer," Feb. 18, 1841, in *Works of James Buchanan*, ed. Moore, 4:384; and "Speech on the Veto Power, Feb. 2, 1842, in *Works of James Buchanan*, ed. Moore, 5:133. The phrase may have originated in the writings of Laurence Sterne; see *A Sentimental Journey*, 1:153.

46. On Buchanan's courtship of Cornelia Van Ness Roosevelt, see JB to Cornelia Van Ness Roosevelt, Feb. 14, 1863, JB Papers, box 52, folder 2, HSP; and John Crampton to Lord Clarendon, Sept. 10, 1854, *American Material in the Clarendon Papers*, reel 3. See also Moore, "James Buchanan and the Earl of Clarendon," 330; and Barnes and Barnes, eds., *Private and Confidential*, 182. On Buchanan's proposed visit to see Roosevelt in New York, see JB to Cornelia Van Ness Roosevelt, Nov. 8, 1842, JB Papers, box 2, folder 3, DCL; and for the Roosevelts' interest in renting the Madison's old Washington house, see Cornelia Van Ness Roosevelt to Dolley Madison, Nov. 12, 1842, *Dolley Madison Digital Edition*. On Cornelia Van Ness Roosevelt, see also James Buchanan Henry to John B. Moore, ca. 1908, Moore Papers, box 221, folder 1908, LC; Ellet, *Queens of American Society*, 281–94; and the obituary in *New York Times*, Feb. 20, 1876.

47. WRK to JB, May 10, 1844, and JB to Cornelia Roosevelt, May 13, 1844, JB Papers, box 11, folder 6, and box 46, folder 9, HSP. See also Buchanan's concern about a missing letter to Roosevelt in JB to HL, Mar 13, 1859, in *Works*, ed. Moore, 10:318–19.

48. WRK to JB, May 14, 1844, JB Papers, box 11, folder 6, HSP.

49. For the letters noted above, see Matilda Catron to JB, July 4, 1844, and JB to Catron, [n.d., ca. July 12, 1844], in *Works*, ed. Moore, 6:60–61; and John Catron to JB, July 25, 1844, JB and HLJ Papers, LC, reel 1. For King's inquiry about "Wiffie," see WRK to JB, n.d. [ca. May 1845], JB Papers, box 13, folder 14, HSP.

50. Article in the *Baltimore Clipper*, reprinted in the *National Intelligencer*, April 12, 1844.

51. "Col. King and Mr. Buchanan," Charleston *Mercury*, reprinted in the Alabama *Beacon*, April 20, 1844; Independent, "Washington Correspondence," Philadelphia *North American*, Dec. 9, 1846. On the Whig tendencies of the *Mercury*, see Osthaus, *Partisans of the Southern Press*, 69–94; and on those of the *North American*, see Robinson, "The *North American*."

CHAPTER 5

1. On Texas independence and the efforts of Jackson and Van Buren toward annexation, see Smith, *Annexation of Texas*, 1:58–81; and Pletcher, *Diplomacy of Annexation*, 72–74.

2. On the expansionist mood of this period, see Sellers, *James K. Polk, Continentalist*; Hietala, *Manifest Design*; Greenberg, *Manifest Manhood*; and Greenberg, *A Wicked War*. On manifest destiny and its relation to national politics, see Morrison, *Slavery and the American West*; Etcheson, *Bleeding Kansas*; and Childers, *Failure of Popular Sovereignty*.

3. For the "Treaty of Annexation," see Miller, ed., *Treaties and Other International Acts*, 4:1836–46. For Tyler's message accompanying the "Treaty of Annexation" of April 1844, see the Senate *Executive Journal*, 6:257–61 and 311–12. On Tyler's diplomacy with Mexico, see Reeves, *American Diplomacy under Tyler and Polk*; Seager, *And Tyler, Too*; and Merry, *A Country of Vast Designs*.

4. For Calhoun's early communications with King and legation secretary Jacob Martin, see Calhoun to Martin, April 18, 1844, and Calhoun to WRK, April 23, 1844, in *Papers of John C. Calhoun*, eds. Meriwether et al., 18:211, 237, 254, 273, 312–14, and 332. On King's instructions from Calhoun, see also St. George L. Sioussat, "John Caldwell Calhoun," in *American Secretaries of State*, ed. Bemis, 5:164–65.

5. WRK to John C. Calhoun, May 10, 1844, in *Papers of John C. Calhoun*, eds. Meriwether et al., 18:478. See also "Passengers Sailed," New York *Daily Herald*, May 17, 1844. For the "classic fame" comment, see Richard Rush to JB, Sept. 30, 1848, JB Papers, box 18, folder 24, HSP.

6. WRK to CME, Dec. 10, 1842, Dec. 12, 1843, and Mar. 15, 1844, WRK Papers, box 1, folder 3, ADAH.

7. WRK to CME, May 20, 1842, WRK Papers, box 1, folder 3, ADAH; JB to Cornelia Van Ness Roosevelt, May 13, 1844, JB Papers, box 46, folder 9, HSP.

8. William T. King to Thomas DeVane King, June 15, 1846, WRK Papers, box 1, folder 5, ADAH. On Alfred J. Beck and William T. King, see Johnston, *William R. King and His Kin*, 61 and 77.

9. Francis W. Pickens to JB, July 5, 1846, JB Papers, box 14, folder 8, HSP. On the romantic imagination of Lord Byron, see Thompson, *Suffering Traveller*, esp. 231–72; and Janes, *Oscar Wild Prefigured*, 129–57.

10. WRK to John C. Calhoun, July 13, and July 31, 1844, in *Papers of John C. Calhoun*, eds. Meriwether et al., 19:334–38 (quoted 336), and 482–86 (quoted 483). See also Johnson, *Guizot*, 295–96.

11. WRK to JB, July 1, 1844, JB and HLJ Papers, LC, reel 1. For letters that mention King, see Ashbel Smith to Anson Jones, Dec. 24, 1844, G.W. Terrell to Jones, Feb. 18, 1845, in *Memoranda and Official Correspondence*, ed. Jones, 411–12, 422–30. On King's mission, see also Merk, *Monroe Doctrine and American Expansionism*, 40–64; and Smith, *Annexation of Texas*, 385–40. On Smith, see Silverthorne, *Ashbel Smith of Texas*, esp. 19–36.

12. For the "Official Proceedings of the Democratic National Convention, Baltimore, May 27–30, 1844," see *History of American Presidential Elections*, eds. Schlesinger and Israel, 2:829–52. On the Democratic convention of 1844, see variously Lambert, "Democratic Nominating Convention of 1844"; Sellers, *James Knox Polk, Continentalist*, 67–107; Belohlavek, "The Democracy in a Dilemma"; Niven, *Martin Van Buren*, 530–41; and Wilentz, *Rise of American Democracy*, 547–76.

13. JB to Francis P. Blair, Nov. 27, 1849, Blair-Lee Family Papers, box 8, folder 1, PUL. On the convention, see also Charles Sellers, "Election of 1844," in *History of American Presidential Elections*, eds. Schlesinger and Israel, 2:764–73.

14. JB to William N. Irvine, June 29, 1844, JB Papers, box 2, folder 7, DCL; JB to John B. Sterigere, July 17, 1844, in *Works of James Buchanan*, ed. Moore, 6:62; WRK to JB, Nov. 14, 1844, JB Papers, box 11, folder 13, HSP. For Buchanan's letters of counsel to Polk, see JB to Unknown, Sept. 6, 1844, and JB to James K. Polk, Sept. 23, 1844, in *Works of James Buchanan*, ed. Moore, 70–71. For a summation of the votes in the election of 1844, see Charles Sellers, "Election of 1844," in *History of American Presidential Elections*, eds. Schlesinger and Israel, 2:849–52.

15. George M. Dallas to Robert J. Walker, [Dec. 6, 1844] (misdated Nov. 6, 1844), Walker Papers, vol. 3, LC. On the Polk cabinet selection, see Sellers, *James K. Polk, Continentalist*, 162–208; Belohlavek, *George Mifflin Dallas*, 99-108; and Ambacher, "George M. Dallas," esp. 328-35.

16. George M. Dallas to Sophia Dallas, Feb. 22, 1845, in "The Library," ed. Nichols, 363. On Dallas's relationship with Polk, see Belohlavek, *George Mifflin Dallas*, esp. 79–98; and Sellers, *James K. Polk, Continentalist*, 193–95; and on his relationship with Buchanan, see also Ambacher, "George M. Dallas"; and Ambacher, "George M. Dallas, Cuba, and the Election of 1856."

17. Aaron V. Brown to Alfred O.P. Nicholson, Feb. 18, 1845, in "Letters from Aaron V. Brown to Alfred O. P. Nicholson," ed. Parks, 173; and Andrew Jackson to William B. Lewis, Feb. 28, 1845, in "Andrew Jackson Comments on Polk's Cabinet," ed. Bonner, 288.

18. WRK to JB, Jan. 28, 1845, JB Papers, box 11, folder 23, HSP.

19. JB to Unknown [probably Matilda Catron], n.d. [ca. Sept. 1844], JB Papers, box 46, folder 10, HSP; JB to James K. Polk, Sept. 23, 1844, in *Works of James Buchanan*, ed. Moore, 6:70–71.

20. Joanna Lucinda Rucker to Elizabeth C. Price, n.d. (ca. Oct. 1845), Joanna Lucinda Rucker Papers, TSLA; and JB to Rucker, Aug. 20, 1848, Polk Memorial Association Collection of James Knox Polk Papers, TSLA, reel 1. Rucker eventually married Robert B. Jetton of Rutherford County, Tennessee. For another flirtation with one "Miss Jane," see also JB to Mrs. Jesse Miller, April 10, 1846, JB Letters, Shapell Manuscript Collection.

21. Anna Payne to JB, n.d., JB Papers, HSP, reel 45; JB to Payne, Nov. 8, 1847, in Sotheby's, *Fine Printed and Manuscript Americana from the Collection of Mrs. Philip D. Sang*, 148–49; JB to Payne, Mar. 3, 1850, JB Papers, box 2, folder 24, DCL. For the description of Payne, see Upton, *Our Early Presidents*, esp. 229–36 (quoted 236); and JB to Rucker, Aug. 20, 1848, Polk Memorial Association Collection of James Knox Polk Papers, TSLA, reel 1. For the silhouette, see JB Papers, box 5, folder 13, DCL; and on the album, JB to Payne, n.d., JB Letters, HA (#61124). On Payne's marriage, see Miller, "Dr. Thomas Miller and His Times," 312–13; and on Dr. James H. Causten Jr., see "Rambler Records Tale of Album Which Was a Real Benefactor," Washington *Evening Star*, Mar. 20, 1927. See also Anna Payne to JB, Aug. 30, 1849, Jan. 1, Feb. 25, and Mar. 16, 1850, JB Papers, HSP, reels 15–16.

22. *New York Herald*, Oct. 29, 1845. For the observation of Buchanan socializing with Dolley Madison, see George M. Dallas to Sophia Dallas, Dec. 16, 1845, in "Library," ed. Nichols, 371.

23. Poore, *Perley's Reminiscence*, 1:332. For more on the photograph, see Bergeron, "All in the Family"; Clifford Krainik, "The Earliest Photographs of the White House, 1840s," in *White House*, ed. Seale, esp. 39–43; and Krainik, "A 'Dark Horse' in Sunlight and Shadow." See also JB to HL, July 17 and 27, 1845, July 3, 1846 (quoted), July 19, 1847, July 8, Aug. 2 and 22, 1848, and Jan. 9, 1849, in JB and HLJ Papers, LC, reel 1.

24. WRK to JB, Nov. 14, 1844, Jan. 28, 1845, and April 30, 1845, JB Papers, box 11, folders 13 and 23, and box 12, folder 12, HSP.

25. WRK to JB, April 30, 1845, JB Papers, box 12, folder 12, HSP. For Buchanan's official correspondence to King, see JB to WRK, Mar. 25, May 6, Nov. 10, 1845, in *Works of James Buchanan*, ed. Moore, 127–28, 154, 292–93. See also the various messages from JB to WRK in Diplomatic Instructions to U.S. Ministers, France, NA, reel 55.

26. JB to Richard Pakenham, July 12, 1845, in *Works of James Buchanan*, ed. Moore, 6:194–203. On this period, see also Klein, *President James Buchanan*, 175–93; and Hietala, *Manifest Design*, 71–83.

27. For King's letters during these months, see WRK to JB, Nov. 28, 1845, Jan. 1, 1846, and April 30, 1846, JB Papers, box 13, folders 10, 15, and 24, HSP.

28. WRK to JB, April 16, 1845, Thomas Sidney Jesup Papers, vol. 9, LC.

29. Diary entries of Aug. 26 and 30, 1845, *Diary of James K. Polk*, ed. Quaife, 1:4, 11.

30. Diary entry of Oct. 29, 1845, *Diary of James K. Polk*, ed. Quaife, 1:80–81.

31. Diary entry of June 8, 1846, *Diary of James K. Polk*, ed. Quaife, 1:460. See also Pletcher, *Diplomacy of Annexation*, 246–49; and Merk, "Presidential Fevers," 28–29.

32. JB to James K. Polk, n.d. [ca. 1845], JB Papers, HSP, reel 47; WRK to JB, Nov. 28, 1845, JB Papers, box 13, folder 10, HSP; and diary entry of Nov. 18 and Dec. 25, 1845, and Jan. 24, 1846, in *Diary of James K. Polk*, ed. Quaife, 1:97, 143–46, and 190. For more on the Woodward nomination, see Curran, "Polk, Politics, and Patronage"; and Kahan, *Amiable Scoundrel*, 64–68.

33. JB to Louis McLane, Dec. 13, 1845, JB Papers, HSP, reel 47. On his defense of Judge Franklin and rejection of Tyler's offer to a Supreme Court position, see Klein, *President James Buchanan*, 23–26, 154. For more on Supreme Court nominations during this period, see Abraham, *Justices and Presidents*, 105–109.

34. Diary entry of June 10, 1846, *Diary of James K. Polk*, ed. Quaife, 1:464–65; JB to Edward Y. Buchanan, July 13, 1846, Cadwalader Papers, box 262, folder 4, HSP. See also Klein, *President James Buchanan*, 172–74.

35. WRK to JB, Feb. 28, 1846, JB Papers, box 13, folder 20, HSP. For rumors of King's nomination, see also New York *Evening Post*, June 19, 1846; and McLane to James K. Polk, Aug. 2, 1846, *Correspondence of James K. Polk*, eds. Cutler et al., 11:260

36. On McLane's view of King, see letters of Louis McLane to Robert McLane, July 18 and 19, 1846, McLane Papers, box 3, folder 1, LC ("imperious fellow" quote); on King's subsequent visit, see Louis McLane to Robert McLane, Aug. 2, 1846, ibid.; and for McLane's conversation with Polk, see diary entry of Sept. 11, 1846, *Diary of James K. Polk*, ed. Quaife, 2:133–36. On McLane's general disposition during this period, see Munroe, *Louis McLane*, 509–45.

37. Letters of WRK to JB, Jan. 27, 1846, box 13, folder 20; Mar. 28, box 14, folder 8; April 30, box 14, folder 9; July 3, box 14, folder 22; and July 15, 1846, box 14, folder 24, all in JB Papers, HSP. For others who opposed Buchanan's accepting a Supreme Court nomination, see John Slidell to JB, April 9, 1846, JB Papers, HSP, reel 10.

38. WRK to JB, July 3, 1846, JB Papers, box 14, folder 22, HSP.

39. Diary entry of Aug. 1, 1846, *Diary of James K. Polk*, ed. Quaife, 2:61.

40. On this period, see DeVoto, *The Year of Decision*; Graebner, *Empire on the Pacific*; Bauer, *Mexican War*; and Greenberg, *A Wicked War*.

41. Diary entries of May 9 and 11, 1846, *Diary of James K. Polk*, ed. Quaife, 385, 397–98. On the cabinet photograph, see Seale, *The President's House*, 1:254; Seale, "Editorial"; Krainik, "A 'Dark Horse' in Sunlight and Shadow"; and Krainik, "Discovered."

42. WRK to JB, April 30 and June 1, 1846, box 13, folder 24, and extract of letter from JB to WRK, June 23, 1846, JB Papers, box 14, folder 4, HSP. On the Buchanan-Rush relationship, see the letters from JB to Richard Rush, Jan. 5, Aug. 22, 1846, box 30, folder 24; Mar. 6, 1847, box 31, folder 3; and Aug. 8, 1848, box 32, folder 1, in Rush Family Papers, PUL.

43. WRK to JB, Oct. 1, 1846, JB Papers, box 14, folder 15, HSP. For an account of King's arrival in Washington, see *Daily National Intelligencer*, Nov. 11, 1846; and for his call to the White House, see diary entry of Nov. 12, 1846, *Diary of James K. Polk*, ed. Quaife, 2:232.

44. On this period, see the accounts in Greenberg, *A Wicked War*; and Bauer, *Mexican War*; WRK to JB, Feb. 10, JB Papers, box 15, folder 7, HSP; and for Buchanan's comment to King, see WRK to JB, June 11, 1847, JB Papers, box 15, folder 27, HSP.

45. Diary entry of April 10, 1847, *Diary of James K. Polk*, ed. Quaife, 2:467. For Trist's account of his final conversation with Buchanan, see Nicholas P. Trist to Winfield Scott, Jan. 12, 1861, quoted in Drexler, *Guilty of Making Peace*, 13. See also Greenberg, *A Wicked War*, 175–76; Ohrt, *Defiant Peacemaker*, 99–105; Mahin, *Olive Branch and Sword*, 41; and Smith, *War with Mexico*, 2:128.

46. WRK to JB, June 11, 1847, JB Papers, box 15, folder 27, HSP.

47. WRK to JB, June 11, 1847, JB Papers, box 15, folder 27, HSP.

48. For Buchanan's letters of recall, see JB to Nicholas Trist, Oct. 6 and 25, and Dec. 21, 1847, in *Diplomatic Correspondence*, ed. Manning, 8:214–19; WRK to JB, Oct. 5, 1847, JB Papers, box 16, folder 8, HSP; Nicholas Trist to Virginia Trist, Nov. 28, 1847, Trist Papers, LC, reel 2; and Nicholas Trist to JB, Dec. 6, 1847, in *Diplomatic Correspondence*, ed. Manning, 8:984–1020. On Trist's mission, see also Mahin, *Olive Branch and Sword*.

49. Diary entries of Feb. 21 and 25, 1848, *Diary of James K. Polk*, ed. Quaife, 347–51 and 362, here 350. For the movement to acquire more Mexican territory, see Fuller, *Movement for the Acquisition of All Mexico*, 94–97.

50. For the Galviensis attacks on Polk and Cass, see "Affairs in Washington," Feb. 9 and 12, 1848, *New York Herald*; and diary entries of Feb. 23 and Mar. 24, 1848, *Diary of James K. Polk*, ed. Quaife, 3:352–56 and 401. For Buchanan's denial, see JB to Simon Cameron, Mar. 27, 1848, in *Works of James Buchanan*, ed. Moore, 8:29. On this incident, see also Marbut, *News from the Capital*, 85–93; and Klein, *President James Buchanan*, 190–91. For the later defense, see Galviensis, "Galviensis and the Senate," April 14, 1848, *New York Herald*; and for Polk's comment, see diary entry of Mar. 27, 1848, *Diary of James K. Polk*, ed. Quaife, 3:410.

51. On John Nugent, see O'Meara, "Early Editors of California," 495 (quoted); Bancroft, "The Perils of Journalism," in *Works of Hubert Howe Bancroft*, 37:205–25; and Reid, "John Nugent."

CHAPTER 6

1. On the revolutions of 1848 in Europe, see Rapport, *1848*; and for its effects in America, Roberts, *Distant Revolutions*, esp. 1–41.

2. On this period, see Earle, *Jacksonian Antislavery*, 123–43; Potter, *Impending Crisis*, 63–89; Nevins, *Ordeal of the Union, Vol. 1: Fruits of Manifest Destiny*, 34–252; and Johannsen, *Stephen A. Douglas*, 235–82.

3. For the political backdrop to the election of 1848, see Silbey, *Party Over Section*, 45–85; and Holman Hamilton, "Election of 1848," in *History of American Presidential Elections*, eds. Schlesinger and Israel, 3:863–96.

4. For calls for a bachelor ticket, see Jackson *Southron*, Sept. 1, 1842; and Fayetteville *Weekly Observer*, Nov. 16, 1847.

5. WRK to CME, June 6, 1847, WRK Papers, box 1, folder 3, ADAH; and WRK to JB, Oct. 5, 1847, and June 11, 1847, JB Papers, box 16, folder 8, and box 15, folder 27, HSP. On the Senate election in Alabama, see also Thomas B. Cooper to Nancy Cooper, Dec. 13, 1847, Cooper Papers, ADAH; and articles in the *Huntsville Democrat*, Jan. 6 and Sept. 1, 1847. On this period, see also Thornton, *Politics and Power in a Slave Society*, 169–71; Dorman, *Party Politics in Alabama*, 27–42; and Williams, "Dixon H. Lewis."

6. On King's nomination to the vice presidency in 1848, see "Journal of the Democratic Convention," 15; and George Washington Gayle to JB, Mar. 9, 1848, JB Papers, box 17, folder 27, HSP.

7. James K. Polk to JB, Feb. 17, 1845, and JB to Polk, Feb. 18, 1845, in *Works of James Buchanan*, ed. Moore, 6:110–12. On Buchanan's dinners, see the uncatalogued book, Applications for Office (B 96.150.1), JB Family Papers, LCHS. On Buchanan's presidential aspirations in 1848, see Klein, *President James Buchanan*, 194–205; and Coleman, *Disruption of the Pennsylvania Democracy*, 19–31.

8. WRK to JB, Oct. 5, 1847, JB Papers, box 16, folder 18, HSP. For Polk's preference for Cass, see Merry, *A Country of Vast Designs*, 431; and on the Whig selection of Taylor, see Holt, *Rise and Fall of the American Whig Party*, 284–330.

9. For the full record of voting, see *Proceedings of the Democratic National Convention* (1848).

10. On this point, see Silbey, *Party Over Section*, 117–20; and Klunder, *Lewis Cass*, 175–94.

11. For Yancey's statements on King, see Yancey, "Address to the People of Alabama," 15, 19–22, 40, 58–61. For King's correspondence, see WRK to JB, June 28, 1848, JB Papers, box 18, folder 18, HSP; and WRK to William Garrett, Aug. 16, 1848, in Garrett, *Reminiscences*, 679–80. On King's return to Washington, see *Washington Daily Union*, July 18, 1848.

12. Francis P. Blair to Martin Van Buren, June 16, 1848, *Papers of Martin Van Buren*, reel 31; news items from Detroit *Free Press*, reprinted in the Gloucester *Telegraph*, May 19, 1849.

13. Robert C. Winthrop to John Clifford, June 4, 1848 (copy), *Winthrop Papers*, reel 39. Achilles and Patroclus were a pair of intimate male friends and lovers from Homer's *Iliad*, while Nisus and Euryalus were a similarly intimate dyad from Virgil's *Aeneid*.

14. For Buchanan's invitation to Rush, see JB to Richard Rush, April 6, 1847, Rush Papers, box 31, folder 3, PUL; and for mention of Shields's visit, see James Shields to JB, Oct. 20, 1848, JB Papers, box 19, folder 2, HSP. See also Sears, "Slidell and Buchanan."

15. On Buchanan's dinners, see the uncatalogued book, Applications for Office (B 96.150.1), JB Family Papers, LCHS; and on his visit to Saratoga Springs, see JB to Richard Rush, Aug. 8, 1848, Rush Papers, box 32, PUL.

16. *Congressional Directory*, 30th Congress, 2nd session (1849); Davis, *Jefferson Davis*, 1:281. For King's role on the joint committee, see diary entry of Dec. 4, 1848, and on his meeting with Polk, Jan. 17, 1849, *Diary of James K. Polk*, ed. Quaife, 4:222, 291. On King's talent for nonpartisanship, see "Anecdote of William R. King," *Mobile Register*, Nov. 12, 1870.

17. On Buchanan and King's dinner at the White House, see diary entry of Dec. 14, 1848, *Diary of James K. Polk*, ed. Quaife, 4:236; and on Buchanan's own dinners, see uncatalogued book, Applications for Office (B 96.150.1), JB Family Papers, LCHS.

18. For Polk's views of Buchanan's personality, see diary entries of Sept. 1, 1846, and Feb. 27, 1849, in *Diary of James K. Polk*, ed. Quaife, 2:110 and 4:355; and for Forney, see *Anecdotes of Public Men*, 1:64–65. The character "Miss Fribble" originated in the play by David Garrick, "Miss in Her Teens; or, the Medley of Lovers" (1746).

19. On the issues at stake in 1849–1850, see esp. Stegmaier, *Texas, New Mexico, and the Compromise of 1850*, 5–84; Freehling, *Road to Disunion*, 1:487–510; Peterson, *Great Triumvirate*, 415–48; and Hamilton, *Prologue to Conflict*, 1–42.

20. For the criticism of King, see George S. Houston to Howell Cobb, June 26, 1849, *Correspondence of Toombs, Stephens, and Cobb*, ed. Phillips, 2:166. On the party in Montgomery, see Thomas B. Cooper to Nancy Cooper, Dec. 11, 1849, Cooper Papers, ADAH; WRK to Alton Saltmarsh, Dec. 12, 1849, WRK Papers, box 1, folder 4, ADAH. On the burning of the state capitol, see Sulzby, *Historic Alabama Hotels & Resorts*, 124–27.

21. On the timing of Buchanan's possession of Wheatland, see the uncatalogued notebook, James Buchanan (B03.3.1), JB Family Papers, LCHS. For the observation about Buchanan at Wheatland, see "James Buchanan" (1859), Biog. Vol. 9, no. 24, HSP. For glimpses of Buchanan's lifelong drinking habits, see variously JB to John Reynolds, Jan. 9, 1827, JB Papers, box 1, folder 7, DCL; JB to John McSparren, Feb. 12, 1851, JB and HLJ Papers, box 5, folder 1, LC; and Nathaniel Hawthorne to William D. Ticknor, April 30, 1854, in *Works of Nathaniel Hawthorne*, ed. Woodson, 17:210–11. On Buchanan's first retirement to Wheatland, see Klein, *President James Buchanan*, 206–21; and on the sale of Wheatland, see also Klein, "Story of Wheatland," 10–18.

22. WRK to JB, Jan. 6 and 13, 1850, JB Papers, box 20, folders 7 and 9, HSP; and JB to WRK, Jan. 18, 1850, ibid., box 48, folder 3. On King's role during the Compromise of 1850, see Martin, "William R. King and the Compromise of 1850." On the congressional debates more generally, see Holt, *Rise and Fall of the Whig Party*, 459–563; and Freehling, *Road to Disunion*, 1:453–510.

23. JB to C.L. Ward, Jan. 22, 1850, JB Papers, N-YHS (the "strictly private letter" from King is dated Jan. 13, 1850 and available in the JB Papers, box 20, folder 9, HSP); and JB to Nathan Clifford, Jan. 8, 1850, in Clifford, *Nathan Clifford*, 250–51.

24. WRK to JB, Jan. 6, 1850, JB Papers, box 20, folder 7, HSP. For the timing of Buchanan's trip to Washington, see also JB to Jonathan M. Foltz, Dec. 18, 1849, and Feb. 2, 1850, Foltz Papers, LC; and Raleigh *Weekly Standard*, April 24, 1850. For the mention of Ellis, see also WRK to Alton Saltmarsh, Feb. 27, 1850, WRK Papers, box 1, folder 4, ADAH.

25. On Buchanan's flirtation with Margaret William King and King's meeting Harriet Lane, see WRK to JB, Jan. 13 and June 8, 1850, JB Papers, box 20, folders 9 and 20, HSP; and JB to WRK, Mar. 6 and 20, 1850, ibid., box 48, folder 4.

26. On Buchanan's bachelor complaints, see JB to William M. Gwin, May 22, 1850, Gwin Papers, Bancroft Library, University of California, Berkeley ("bachelor's home" quote); JB to Jacob S. Yost, March 6, 1851, JB Papers, N-YHS ("bachelor's abode" quote); JB to C.L. Ward, Dec. 6, 1853, ibid.; JB to WRK, May 13, 1850 (quoted), in *Works*, ed. Moore, 8:383–85; and WRK to JB, June 8 and 19, 1850, JB Papers, box 20, folders 20–21, HSP. On his flirtations with Eliza Watterston, see JB to Eliza Watterston, Nov. 17, 1851 and Nov. 18, 1852, JB and HLJ Papers, box 5, folder 3, LC; and JB to Eliza Watterston, May 5, 1853, Seth Kaller. On Buchanan's potential interest in marrying a Mrs. Reigart of Lancaster, see JB to HL, Aug. 4, 1850, JB and HLJ Papers, LC, reel 1.

27. On Buchanan's boardinghouse meetings, see two successive letters from David Outlaw to Emily B. Outlaw, both dated Feb. 2, 1850, Outlaw Papers, box 1, folder 7, SHC. See also JB to Robert Tyler, Feb. 25, 1850, GLC (quoted); JB to J. Glancy Jones, Mar. 8, 1850, JB and HLJ Papers, box 5, folder 5, LC; JB to WRK, Mar. 6, 1850, box 48, folder 4; WRK to JB, Mar. 11, 1850, box 20, folder 16; and WRK to JB, June 19, 1850, box 20, folder 21, in JB Papers, HSP.

28. WRK to JB, May 8, 1850, JB Papers, box 20, folder 19, HSP; and JB to WRK, May 13, 1850, ibid., box 48, folder 5 [see also transcript in *Works*, ed. Moore, 8:383].

29. For the attack made by Seward, see JB to WRK, Mar. 15, 1850, box 48, folder 4; WRK to JB, Mar. 20, 1850, box 20, folders 17; and JB to WRK, May 13, 1850, box 48, folder 5, in JB Papers, HSP. For King's letters that address the sectional crisis during this period, see WRK to Neil P. Blue, April 11, 1850, Blue Family Papers, box 6, folder 1, ADAH; WRK to Morgan Smith, April 23, 1850, published in Montgomery *Advertiser*, May 22, 1850; WRK to J.B. Clarke, April 29, 1850, published in Huntsville *Democrat*, May 23, 1850; WRK to Neal Smith, June 13, 1850, in "William R. King on Sectional Issues," ed. Owen, 45. On King's assumption of president pro tempore, see Raleigh *Weekly Standard*, May 15, 1850 (quoting reporter from the *Baltimore Sun*). See also Martin, "William R. King and the Compromise of 1850."

30. For relevant correspondence, see WRK to Bolling Hall, Nov. 19, 1850, Bolling Hall Papers, box 5, folder 2, ADAH; WRK to Dr. Alanson Saltmarsh, Aug. 25, 1850, WRK Papers, box 1, folder 18, ADAH; and WRK to JB, Aug. 4 and 26, 1850, JB Papers, box 20, folders 22 and 23, HSP.

31. For the immediate aftereffects of the compromise, see Holt, *Rise and Fall of the Whig Party*, 563–83; and Peterson, *Great Triumvirate*, 476–93. On the history of the "Union" print, see Holzer, Boritt, and Neely, *Lincoln Image*, 68-69.

32. Huntsville *Democrat*, Nov. 28, 1850; WRK to Thomas D. King, Nov. 21, 1850, WRK Papers, box 1, folder 3, ADAH. See also WRK to Tuscaloosa Committee, Oct. 23, 1850, in *National Intelligencer*, Nov. 7, 1850.

33. WRK to JB, Jan. 12, 1851, JB Papers, box 21, folder 1, HSP. On Buchanan's visit to Washington, see Jonathan M. Foltz to JB, Jan. 28, 1851, JB Family Papers, part 7.1.1, folder 22, LCHS; and JB to William Hopkins, Feb. 14, 1851, JB Papers, box 48, folder 12, HSP; and WRK to JB, Oct. 14, 1851, ibid., box 21, folder 21. See also King's frank on the letter of JB to Jonathan M. Foltz, Feb. 5, 1851, Foltz Papers, LC.

34. WRK to JB, Dec. 21, 1851, box 21, folder 28; Jan. 16, 1851, box 22, folder 3; and Mar. 6 and 24, 1852, box 22, folder 6, in JB Papers, HSP. On Buchanan's visit in February 1852, see "The Compromise Measures," *New York Tribune*, Feb. 17, 1852, in *First Blows of the Civil War*, ed. Pike, 115

35. JB to Cave Johnson, Mar. 30, 1852, in *Works*, ed. Moore, 8:447–49; Le Diable Boiteux, "Washington Correspondence," Feb. 20, 1852, in New Orleans *Times*, Mar. 2, 1852. On the growing political conservativism of the 1840s and 1850s, see Connolly, " 'Tearing Down the Burning House' "; and on the effect of age in presidential elections, see Eyal, *Young America Movement and the Transformation of the Democratic Party*.

36. For the banner in the Pittsburgh *Daily Post*, see issues from July 1851 to June 7, 1852; article of the Alabama *Advertiser and Gazette* quoted in "James Buchanan," Jackson *Mississippian and State Gazette*, Feb. 27, 1852; and Le Diable Boiteux, "Washington Correspondence," Feb. 20, 1852, in New Orleans *Times*, Mar. 2, 1852.

37. JB to David Lynch, May 11, 1852, Lynch Papers, LC [see also transcript in JB and HLJ Papers, box 5, folder 3, LC]. On Lynch, see Klein, *President James Buchanan*, esp. 101, 156–57, 195–96, and 219–20. On opposition to Buchanan within Pennsylvania, see Kahan, *Amiable Scoundrel*, 97–102.

38. Letters of WRK to JB, May 13, 17, 20, and 26, 1852, JB Papers, box 22, folders 15, 16, 17, and 19, HSP.

39. For the record of balloting, see *Proceedings of the Democratic National Convention* (1852).

40. Edmund Burke to Franklin Pierce, June 6, 1852, in "Some Papers of Franklin Pierce, 1852–1862," ed. Ray, 114.

41. For Buchanan's various correspondence following King's nomination, see JB to Robert Tyler, June 8, 1852, in *Letters and Times of the Tylers*, ed. Tyler, 2:498–99; JB to [unknown], June 11, 1852, JB Papers, box 53, folder 6, HSP; JB to Cave Johnson, June 24, 1852, in *Works*, ed. Moore, 8:450; "Letter of Hon. James Buchanan," June 8, 1852, printed in the New York *Weekly Herald*, June 26, 1852; JB to the Democratic

Citizens of Springfield, Pennsylvania, June 14, 1852, in *Tioga Eagle*, July 15, 1852; and JB to the editor, Washington *Daily Union*, June 18, 1852.

42. WRK to Robert Tyler, June 28, 1852, WRK Papers, box 1, folder 3, ADAH; and WRK to JB, June 12, 1852, JB Papers, box 22, folder 24, HSP. On Buchanan's trip to Saratoga Springs, see JB to HL, Aug. 8, 1852, JB and HLJ Papers, LC, reel 1.

43. JB to Rose O'Neal Greenhow, Aug. 28, 1852, Barbee Papers, box 9, LC; and WRK to Thomas Ruffin, John Everett, et al., Aug. 30, 1852, in Goldsboro *Republican and Patriot*, Sept. 7, 1852. On King's return to Alabama, see the coverage in the Alabama *Advertiser and State Gazette*, Oct. 6, 1852.

44. On the election of 1852, see Roy and Jeannette Nichols, "Election of 1852," in *History of American Presidential Elections*, eds. Schlesinger and Israel, 3:920–50.

45. Brooklyn *Daily Eagle*, June 7, 1852; and speech of Smith as reported in Wilmington *Daily Journal*, Sept. 5, 1852.

46. For the anonymous small foot comment, see Will T. Sheehan, "Observations of the Only Vice President Alabama Furnished the United States, While Traveling in Europe," *Montgomery Daily Advertiser*, Mar. 31, 1907; for the "flimsy" comment, see Charleston *Mercury*, June 11, 1852; and for Randolph story about King's boots, see "Presidential Qualifications," *New York Times*, June 15, 1852. For King's dismissal of the attacks, see WRK to Philip Phillips, June 26, 1852, Phillips Papers, box 1, LC.

47. For the Buchanan-Pierce correspondence, see Franklin Pierce to JB, Dec. 7 and 14, 1852, and JB to Pierce, Dec. 11, 1852, in *Works*, ed. Moore, 8:492–500. See also JB to Christopher L. Ward, Nov. 16, 1852, JB Papers, N-YHS.

48. JB to J. Glancy Jones, Dec. 13, 1852, JB and HLJ Papers, box 5, folder 7, LC; and WRK to JB, Dec. 13, 1852, JB Papers, box 23, folder 2, HSP.

49. For King's letter of resignation, see WRK to U.S. Senate, Dec. 20, 1852, *Congressional Globe*, 32nd Congress, 2nd session, 89; WRK to David R. Atchison, Feb. 20, 1853, Atchison Papers, folder 3, State Historical Society of Missouri; CME to JB, Jan. 1, 1853, JB Papers, box 23, folder 4, HSP; and on King's resignation of his Senate seat, see "Wayside Gatherings," *Gleason's Pictorial Drawing-Room Companion*, Jan. 29, 1853.

50. William Sharkey to William L. Marcy, Mar. 26, 1853, Despatches from U.S. Consuls in Havana, NA, reel 26. For accounts of King's trip to Cuba, see "Hon. William R. King," *Huntress*, Jan. 8, 1853; and Washington *Evening Star*, Jan. 17, 1853. For other accounts of King's inauguration, see Washington *Evening Star*, Mar. 2, 1853; Reese D. Gayle to unknown, ca. Mar. 1853, ADAH; and *National Intelligencer*, April 8, 1853. See also copy of affidavit of Vice Presidential Oath of William Rufus King, signed by W.L. Sharkey, Mar. 26, 1853, WRK Papers, box 1, folder 4, ADAH.

51. CME to JB, Mar. 9, 1853, JB Papers, box 23, folder 11, HSP. Margaret William King married the planter and doctor William Augustine Jones, a man much closer to her age, on October 16, 1854; see Johnston, *William R. King and His Kin*, 56. On King's health, see also the report from nephew G.H. Jones in the Raleigh *Register*, Mar. 5, 1853.

52. On the last days of William Rufus King, see "Interesting Intelligence from Cuba,"
    April 10, 1853, *New York Weekly Herald*, April 23, 1853; "Landing of the Vice
    President," Mobile *Daily Register*, April 12, 1853, reprinted in the Montgomery
    Advertiser and State Gazette, April 20, 1853; and "Death of Col. King," Montgomery
    Advertiser and State Gazette, April 27, 1853. For King's last words, see Johnston,
    William R. King and His Kin, 71. For memorials and obituaries, see "Death of Vice
    President King," *Mobile Daily Register*, April 20, 1853; obituary in the *New York
    Weekly Herald*, April 23, 1853; the public letter from Gov. Henry W. Collier, May 4,
    1852, printed as "Respect to the Memory of Mr. King," Montgomery *Advertiser and
    State Gazette*, May 11, 1852; Strange, "Eulogy on the Life and Character of William
    Rufus King"; the various addresses in the "Obituary Address on the Occasion of
    the Death of Hon. William R. King"; and Bagby, "Eulogy Pronounced on the
    Life and Character of William R. King." See also Brooks, "Faces of William Rufus
    King"; and Brooks, "Opulence and Intrigue."
53. JB to Francis W. Pickens, July 14, 1853, JB and HLJ Papers, box 5, folder 18, LC.
54. For the relevant correspondence, see Franklin Pierce to JB, Mar. 30, 1852, JB to
    Pierce, April 2 and 27, and June 7, 1853, in *Works*, ed. Moore, 8:504, 506, 510–12;
    JB to Pierce, June 11, 14, 23, 29, and July 7, 1853, Pierce to JB, June 26 and July 2,
    1853, and "Memorandum by Mr. Buchanan on His Appointment as Minister to
    England," July 12, 1853, in *Works*, ed. Moore, 9:1–22. See also Klein, *President James
    Buchanan*, esp. 221–33; and Binder, *James Buchanan and the American Empire*,
    esp. 161–73.

CHAPTER 7

1. On the events of the early Pierce administration, see variously Landis, *Northern
   Men with Southern Loyalties*, 76–142; Potter, *Impending Crisis*, 145–265; Nevins,
   Ordeal of the Union, Vol. 1: House Dividing, 3–77; Milton, *Eve of Conflict*, 79–96;
   and Nichols, *Democratic Machine*, 187–226. For biographical studies of Pierce, see
   Wallner, *Franklin Pierce*, vol. 2; and Nichols, *Franklin Pierce*, esp. 232–506.
2. On the introduction of the Kansas-Nebraska bill, see Shelden, *Washington
   Brotherhood*, 96–119; Nichols, *Franklin Pierce*, 302–24; and Balcerski, " 'A General
   Concurrence in the Propriety of the Repeal.' "
3. On this transformation, see esp. Gienapp, *Origins of the Republican Party*, 273–
   303; Anbinder, *Nativism and Slavery*, 20–52; and Kleppner, *Third Electoral
   System*, 16–47.
4. For a revealing letter, see James L. Bowlin to JB, JB Papers, April 21, 1854, box 25,
   folder 1, HSP; and for Buchanan's comment on Nebraska, see JB to James Reynolds,
   May 2, 1854, JB Papers, box 3, folder 15, DCL.
5. About Buchanan's transatlantic crossing, see the diary entry for Aug. 1, 1853, in the
   "Scrapbook of notes and memoranda relating to Clayton Bulwer Treaty," Vol. 17,

JB Papers, HSP. On Sickles, see Brandt, *Congressman Who Got Away with Murder*, 29–36; and Swanberg, *Sickles the Incredible*, 88–100. On Peabody's intimate friendship with Buchanan, see letters of George Peabody to William W. Corcoran, May 3 and 16, 1853, and Jan. 13, 1854 (quoted), in Corcoran, *A Grandfather's Legacy*, 111–12, 120–21; and for the fallout between the pair over Sickles, see Parker, *George Peabody*, 71–74. For details of Lane's activities in England, see esp. the letters to and from Lane and Buchanan, in Curtis, *Life of James Buchanan*, 2:142–68 (as well as those same letters in *Works*, ed. Moore, 8:32–258, 392–488, and 9:3–77); JB to Robert Tyler, Jan. 19, 1855, JB Letters, HA (lot #34235); and "Harriet Lane's Load of Wood," *Washington Post*, Feb. 7, 1892. See also Kilian, "Celebrated Harriet Lane," 7–8; Cahalan, "Harriet Lane," 26–37; Klein, "Harriet Lane," 3; and Klein, *President James Buchanan*, 246–47.

6. On this period in Anglo-American relations, see Barnes and Barnes, eds., *Private and Confidential*, 38–92; May, *Southern Dream of a Caribbean Empire*, 22–45; Donovan, "President Pierce's Ministers at the Court of St. James"; and Klein, *President James Buchanan*, 227–46. On Buchanan's efforts to acquire Cuba in 1848, see JB to Romulus Saunders, June 17, 1848, and JB to John M. Clayton, April 7, 1849, in *Works*, ed. Moore, 8:90–102, 360–61. See also Sioussat, "James Buchanan," in *American Secretaries of State*, ed. Bemis, 5:296–300; and Rauch, *American Interest in Cuba*, 48–100.

7. For Buchanan's suggestion to acquire Cuba, see JB to Franklin Pierce, Dec. 11, 1852, in *Works*, ed. Moore, 8:493–99; and for his views on the Ostend conference, see JB to Pierce, Sept. 1, 1854, and JB to William L. Marcy, Oct. 6 and 23, 1854, 9:251–52, 259–72. On Lane's time at Ostend, see Holloway, *Ladies of the White House*, 546–47. On Buchanan's involvement in shaping the Ostend Manifesto, see also Landis, *Northern Men with Southern Loyalties*, 91–95; May, *Southern Dream of a Caribbean Empire*, 46–75; Ettinger, *Mission to Spain of Pierre Soule*, 339–412; Rauch, *American Interest in Cuba*, 262–94; and Reineke, "Diplomatic Career of Pierre Soule," 313–28.

8. On the end of his mission, see variously JB to HL, Nov. 9, 1855, JB and HLJ Papers, LC, reel 2; JB to William L. Marcy, Nov. 16, 1855, in *Works*, ed. Moore, 9:460–61; JB to Eskridge Lane, Feb. 29, 1856, JB Family Papers, part 1.1.1, folder 74, LCHS; and JB to HL, April 3, 1856, JB and HLJ Papers, LC, reel 2. For Thurlow Weed's comment, see Ward, *Life and Times of Cardinal Wiseman*, 2:47. For political sentiments following the passage of the Kansas-Nebraska Act, see Landis, *Northern Men with Southern Loyalty*, 120–47; and Potter, *Impending Crisis*, 199–265.

9. For Buchanan's speech to crowds in New York, see "Speech, April 24, 1856," in *Works*, ed. Moore, 77–78; and on his trip to Lancaster, see Van Horn, "Old Buck Cannon." For other views of Buchanan at Wheatland, see the articles in *Frank Leslie's Illustrated Newspaper*, Mar. 14, 1857.

10. For a perceptive account of the various political conventions of 1856, see the articles by Murat Halstead in *Trimmers, Trucklers & Temporizers*, eds. Hesseltine and Fisher. On the rise of the American Party, see Anbinder, *Nativism and Slavery*,

esp. 220–45; and for the Republicans, see Gienapp, *Origins of the Republican Party*, esp. 305–46. See also Nevins, *Ordeal of the Union, Vol. 1: House Dividing*, 487–514.

11. For the balloting, see *Official Proceedings of the Democratic Party* (1856). For contemporary views of the candidates, see the various critical articles in *First Blows of the Civil War*, ed. Pike, 332–37.

12. On Buchanan's cultivation of political support in Virginia, see Auchampaugh, "John W. Forney, Robert Tyler and James Buchanan"; and Landis, *Northern Men with Southern Loyalties*, 148–52.

13. On Buchanan's manhood as a factor in his candidacy, see Lynn, "A Manly Doughface"; and on Buchanan's political rhetoric, see Robert E. Terrill, "James Buchanan: Romancing the Union," in *Before the Rhetorical Presidency*, ed. Medhurst, 166–93. On conservativism in the election of 1856, see Smith, *Stormy Present*, esp. 88–99.

14. For Black's speech at the convention, see *Official Proceedings of the Democratic Party* (1856), 59. For the account of the visit to Wheatland, see "For True Democrats," *Afro-Americana* (#3735), Library Company of Philadelphia. See also McCurdy, *Citizen Bachelors*, 198–200; and Lynn, "A Manly Doughface."

15. Horton, *Life and Public Services of James Buchanan*, 424; "Short Answers to Reckless Fabrications, Against the Democratic Candidate for President, James Buchanan" (Philadelphia, 1856).

16. For the results of the election, see Roy and Jeannette Nichols, "Election of 1856," in *History of American Presidential Elections*, eds. Schlesinger and Israel, 3:1094. See also Nichols, *Disruption of American Democracy*, 17–32 and 54–64; and on its gendered aspects, Pierson, *Free Hearts & Free Homes*.

17. On the mood of the nation to start 1857, see Stampp, *America in 1857*, here 9.

18. On the view of Buchanan's preparation for office, see Klein, *President James Buchanan*, 317; and Baker, *James Buchanan*, 4–5. On the selection of his cabinet, see Nevins, *Ordeal of the Union, Vol. 2: Emergence of Lincoln*, 67–79; and Klein, *President James Buchanan*, 261–69.

19. Greenhow, *My Imprisonment and the First Year of Abolition Rule at Washington*, 73. On the Buchanan inaugural, see Poore, *Perley's Reminiscences*, 1:511–16; Singleton, *Story of the White House*, 2:42 (quoted); Rosenberger, "Inauguration of President Buchanan a Century Ago"; Stampp, *America in 1857*, 63–66. Nephew Eskridge Lane eventually succumbed to the effects of the disease on March 26, 1857.

20. For a recent review of Buchanan's relationship to the *Dred Scott* case, see Paul Finkelman, "James Buchanan, Dred Scott, and the Whisper of Conspiracy," in *James Buchanan and the Coming of the Civil War*, eds. Quist and Birkner, 20–45. See also Stampp, *America in 1857*, 89–93; Fehrenbacher, *Dred Scott Case*, 197–98, 307–14; Swisher, *Taney Period*, 614–22; and for the letters of Buchanan with Grier and Catron, see Auchampaugh, "James Buchanan, the Court, and the Dred Scott Case," 231–40. See also Carrafiello, "Diplomatic Failure."

21. On Buchanan's struggles with patronage appointments, see Meerse, "Buchanan's Patronage Policy." For Buchanan's first annual message, see "First Annual Message," Dec. 8, 1857, in *Works*, ed. Moore, 10:129–63, here 135. On the Utah expedition, see "Proclamation on the Rebellion in Utah," April 6, 1858, in *Works*, ed. Moore, 10:203–206. See also MacKinnon, *At Sword's Point*; and Huston, *Panic of 1857 and the Coming of the Civil War*, 14–65.

22. For Buchanan's message on Kansas, see "Message on the Constitution of Kansas," Feb. 2, 1858, in *Works*, ed. Moore, 10:179–92. On the Lecompton Constitution controversy, see Landis, *Northern Men with Southern Loyalties*, 176–204; Etcheson, *Bleeding Kansas*, 139–67; Johannsen, *Stephen A. Douglas*, 576–613; Shenton, *Robert J. Walker*, 150–74; and Nevins, *Ordeal of the Union, Vol. 2: Emergence of Lincoln*, 264–70. On the split between Buchanan and Douglas, see also Meerse, "Origins of the Buchanan-Douglas Feud Reconsidered." On the connection between Buchanan and Walker, see Freehling, *Road to Disunion*, 1:418–20.

23. Pryor, *Reminiscences of Peace and War*, 48–49; and DeLeon, *Belles, Beaux and Brains*, 33. On Buchanan's connection to Greenhow, see Rose Greenhow to John C. Calhoun, April 3, 1849, Greenhow, *My Imprisonment and the First Year of Abolition Rule at Washington*, 163; the commentary in the *Calhoun Papers*, eds. Meriwether et al., 26:366–67; and Blackman, *Wild Rose*, 133–40. For other recollections of the Buchanan White House, see Davis, *Jefferson Davis*, 1:223; Forney, *Anecdotes of Public Men*, 2:312; and Clay-Clopton, *A Belle of the Fifties*, 58–137. On the Buchanan White House, see also Allman, "White House Collection from James Buchanan's Time"; Kilian, "James Buchanan's White House Hostess"; and Rosenberger, "Harriet Lane, First Lady."

24. On the triangulated relationship of Buchanan, Lane, and Roosevelt, which often included sister Marcia Van Ness Ouseley (wife of former British minister to the United States, William Gore Ouseley), see JB to HL, May 18, 1859, in *Works*, ed. Moore, 10:320–21. For Buchanan's line about Lane, see Kate Thompson to Mary Ann Lamar Cobb, June 8, 1859, Cobb Papers, box 46, folder 16, UGA. On Lane's courtships, see *Mary Chesnut's Civil War*, ed. Woodward, 115; and on Miles, see also HL to Lily Macalester, Nov. 29, 1859, Harriet Lane Letters, Mount Vernon Ladies' Association. On Buchanan's time at the Soldiers' Home, see Pinsker, *Lincoln's Sanctuary*, 3. On this period, see Klein, *President James Buchanan*, 273–75; and Auchampaugh, "James Buchanan, Bachelor of the White House." Nephew James Buchanan Henry served as the president's private secretary from March 1857 to March 1859.

25. For Thompson's comment about the relationship between Buchanan and Howell Cobb, see Kate Thompson to Mary Ann Lamar Cobb, May 18, 1859, box 46, folder 15, Cobb Papers, UGA. Thompson may also have called Buchanan by the nickname "Old Gurley," after Presbyterian minister Phineas Gurley. See also Klein, *President James Buchanan*, 276–78, 333–34; Updike, *Buchanan Dying*, 204–209; and Reid, *Howell Cobb*, 905–11. On Mary Ann Lamar Cobb, see also Mays, " 'The Celebrated Mrs. Cobb.' "

26. On Buchanan's rumored courtship of Sarah Childress Polk, see George Plitt to JB, Sept. 17, 1855, enclosing a newspaper clipping, JB and HLJ Papers, LC, reel 2. On Craig's interest in Buchanan, see Elizabeth C. Craig to Mary Ann Lamar Cobb, June 23, 1857, Cobb Papers, box 45, folder 18, UGA. For Craig's reactions to Buchanan and Lane, see her correspondence with her professed, though not confirmed, fiancé, James Robb from Oct. 25, 1858, to April 17, 1859, Robb Papers, folders 320–29, Historic New Orleans Collection. Elizabeth Craig later married James Robb of New York and relocated to Chicago. See also her surprise at Buchanan's snub of her husband in Elizabeth Robb to James Robb, June 24 and Aug. 5, 1860, ibid., folders 371 and 377; and for a continued recollection of kindness for Buchanan, see Robb to Mary Ann Lamar Cobb, Aug. 20, 1860, Cobb Papers, box 50, folder 11, UGA. For Craig's correspondence with Buchanan, see letters to JB, June 1, 1858, June 27, 1859, Jan. 1, 1860, and June 14 and 26, 1866, JB Papers, HSP, reels 35, 37, 38, and 44. For other comments on Craig's departure from the White House, see Kate Thompson to Mary Ann Lamar Cobb, May 18, 1859, Cobb Papers, box 46, folder 15, UGA. On Elizabeth Whipple Hunt Church Craig Robb more generally, see also "Mrs. Elizabeth Church Robb." On Buchanan's flirtation with Eugénie Patience Bate Bass, see Kate Thompson to Mary Ann Lamar Cobb, July 10, 1859 (on his change of clothes), box 64, folder 14, and Lenora Clayton to Mary Ann Lamar Cobb, Aug. 4 and 19, 1859 (on his trip to Bedford Springs), box 64, folder 16, in Cobb Papers, UGA; and the letter of Howell Cobb to Mary Ann Lamar Cobb, July 20, 1859, Cobb / Erwin / Lamar Papers, box 3, folder 1, UGA. On Bass, see also "The Napier Ball," *New York Times*, Feb. 19, 1859; Gouverneur, *As I Remember*, 231; and Durham, "Tennessee Countess." Mrs. Bass eventually remarried the Italian minister to the United States, Chevalier Giuseppe Bertinatti, in 1865.

27. JB to HLJ, Oct. 15, 1858, JB and HLJ Papers, LC, reel 2. On the dinner party, see Nevins, *Ordeal of the Union, Vol. 2: Emergence of Lincoln*, 400; and on the midterm elections, see also Nichols, *Disruption of American Democracy*, 208–21; Huston, *Panic of 1857 and the Coming of the Civil War*, 139–72; and Landis, "Old Buck's Lieutenant," 209. For Buchanan's second annual message, see "Second Annual Message," Dec. 6, 1858, in *Works*, ed. Moore, 10:235–77. On the executive and legislative efforts to purchase Cuba, see May, *Southern Dream of a Caribbean Empire*, 168–89.

28. For the newspaper coverage, see Philadelphia *Press*, June 10, 1859. For the comment about kissing hands, see Kate Thompson to Mary Ann Lamar Cobb, June 8, 1859, Cobb Papers, box 49, folder 16, UGA; and for Buchanan's eagerness to greet waiting women, see the article in the *New York Herald*, June 6, 1859. For the comment about King, see Buchanan's speech at Wilmington, June 3, 1859, quoted in "President Buchanan in North Carolina," Richmond *Enquirer*, June 7, 1859 [and compare to a similar remark recorded in a Raleigh newspaper, quoted in Auchampaugh, "Journey of a Forgotten President," 7]. On Buchanan's interest

in visiting North Carolina, see also JB to Thomas Ruffin, et al., Aug. 28, 1852, in Goldsboro *Republican and Patriot*, Sept. 7, 1852; and on the trip, see the articles in the *New York Herald*, June 1–8, 1857; and Howell Cobb to Mary Ann Lamar Cobb, June 7, 1859, Cobb Papers, box 41, folder 6, UGA.

29. On the raid of John Brown, see Freehling, *Road to Disunion*, 2:205–21; Potter, *Impending Crisis*, 356–84. On the start of the Thirty-Sixth Congress, see Freehling, *Road to Disunion*, 2:246–70. For Buchanan's third annual message, see "Third Annual Message," Dec. 10, 1859, in *Works*, ed. Moore, 10:339–70, here 339.

30. For Buchanan's messages on the Covode Committee investigation, see "Message," Mar. 28, 1860, and "Message," June 22, 1860, in *Works*, ed. Moore, 10:399–405 and 435–43, here 403. See also JB to James G. Bennett, June 18, 1860, in *Works*, ed. Moore, 10:434. On corruption in the Buchanan administration, see also Summers, *Plundering Generation*, 239–60.

31. On the various Democratic national conventions of 1860, see Holt, *Election of 1860*.

32. For Buchanan's speech, see "Speech, July 9, 1860," in *Works*, ed. Moore, 10:457–64, here 458 and 463.

33. While in Europe, Ellis carried a letter of introduction from Buchanan; see JB to Lady Clarendon, May 3, 1857, Van Sinderen Collection, box 1, folder 28, Yale University Library. For Ellis's interest in visiting Washington, see Sophie Plitt to HL, Sept. 5/7, 1860, JB and HLJ Papers, LC, reel 3; and for the mention of the gold belt, see HL to Sophie Plitt, Oct. 9, 1860, ibid., box 3, LC [note: the letter was excluded in the microfilm edition of the JB and HLJ Papers, LC]. For the suitors of Lane and Ellis, respectively, see the diary entries for Mar. 11 and May 9, 1861, in *Mary Chesnut's Civil War*, ed. Woodward, 22, 59.

34. Prince Albert Edward to Queen Victoria, Oct. 7, 1860, quoted in Ridley, *The Heir Apparent*, 59. On Ellis's part in the prince's visit, see HL to Sophie Plitt, Oct. 9, 1860, JB and HLJ Papers, box 3, LC; and Mary Ann Cobb to Lamar Cobb, Oct. 13/14, 1860, Cobb / Erwin / Lamar Papers, box 3, folder 5, UGA. Prince Albert Edward so enjoyed his visit that decades later, during his own coronation, he invited Harriet Lane Johnston to attend as his honored guest (her health prevented the trip). On the visit of the Japanese delegation, see also Finn, "Guests of a Nation"; and on the visit of Prince Albert Edward, see Faulkner, "President Buchanan Greets a Guest of State."

35. On the election of Lincoln and the secession that followed, see Egerton, *Year of Meteors*, 215–47; Burlingame, *Abraham Lincoln*, 1:684–718; Potter, *Impending Crisis*, 442–47; and Stampp, *And the War Came*, 63–82. See also McClintock, *Lincoln and the Decision for War*, 30–202.

36. For Buchanan's fourth annual message, see "Fourth Annual Message," Dec. 3, 1860, in *Works*, ed. Moore, 11:7–43, here 20. On the Crittenden Compromise, see Potter, *Impending Crisis*, 545–55; and Potter, *Lincoln and His Party in the Secession Crisis*, 101–11. For Buchanan's emotional response to the peace delegates, see Crittenden, *Recollections of President Lincoln and His Administration*, 33. For newspaper reactions to secession, see Dumond, ed., *Southern Editorials*.

37. For the "Siamese Twins" quote, see "Our Washington Correspondence," *New York Herald*, May 23, 1860; and on Buchanan's interview style, see Schouler, *History of the United States*, 5:481fn (quoted). On the intimate relationship of Toombs and Stephens, see Davis, *The Union That Shaped the Confederacy*. For various helpful interpretations of Buchanan's actions during the secession winter of 1860 to 1861, see Curtis, *James Buchanan*, 2:376–79; Klein, *President James Buchanan*, 353–67; and Michael A. Morrison, "President James Buchanan: Executive Leadership and the Crisis of the Democracy," in *James Buchanan and the Coming of the Civil War*, eds. Quist and Birkner, 134–64.

38. On the change in personnel in Buchanan's cabinet, see Auchampaugh, *James Buchanan and His Cabinet on the Eve of Secession*; and Daniel W. Crofts, "Joseph Holt, James Buchanan, and the Secession Crisis," in *James Buchanan and the Coming of the Civil War*, eds. Quist and Birkner, 208–36. For Black's role during the secession crisis, see Brigance, *Jeremiah Sullivan Black*, 92–112; and for Stanton's role, see Marvel, *Lincoln's Autocrat*, 120–37; and Thomas and Hyman, *Stanton*, 93–118.

39. On the final dinner with his cabinet officers, see Kate Thompson to Mary Ann Lamar Cobb, Feb. 3, 1861, Cobb Papers, box 65, folder 16, UGA (see also "Letters of Kate Thompson to Mary Ann Cobb," ed. Windham, 197–98). On the election of Jefferson Davis, see Cooper, *Jefferson Davis*, 325–32. On Ellis's departure, see Sophie Plitt to HL, Feb. 17, 1861, JB and HLJ Papers, LC, reel 3. Cornelia Van Ness Roosevelt also stayed at the White House for a time; see Sophie Plitt to HL, Jan. 15, 1861, ibid.

40. On the Lincoln inauguration, see Fiske, "When Lincoln Was First Elected"; Leech, *Reveille in Washington*, 43–45; Hurd, *Washington Cavalcade*, 104–105; Miller, *President Lincoln*, 7–13; Burlingame, *Abraham Lincoln*, 2:45–51; and John Hay's recollection of the conversation between Buchanan and Lincoln in *At Lincoln's Side*, ed. Burlingame, 118–19. For Buchanan's line about leaving the White House, see the speech addressed to "Mr. Mayor, my old Neighbors, Friends, and Fellow-Citizens," Mar. 4, 1861, in Curtis, *Life of James Buchanan*, 2:509–10. For appearances of the line in his correspondence, see, for example, JB to William Carpenter, Sept. 13, 1860, JB Papers, box 1, folder 13, LCHS. For other renderings, see also Sandburg, *Abraham Lincoln*, 1:139; and Klein, *President James Buchanan*, 402.

41. JB to William W. Seaton, June 26, 1862, in Seaton, *William Winston Seaton*, 313–14; on the medical bill, see Jonathan M. Foltz to Simon Cameron, Mar. 9, 1861, Simon Cameron Papers, LC, reel 6. For his financial net worth, see Buchanan's account book with the Chemical Bank of New York in the JB Family Papers, part 2.1, folder 14, LCHS; and Buchanan's Commonplace Book in the still unprocessed Papers of Hiram Swarr in the JB Family Papers, part 6.1, folder 19a, LCHS. The final inventory of his personal property and assets totaled $280,582.72. On Buchanan's communion in the Presbyterian Church, see Appel, *Life and Work of John Williamson Nevin*, esp. 601–604. On Buchanan's retirement years, see Auchampaugh, "James

Buchanan During the Administrations of Lincoln and Johnston"; Martin, *After the White House*, 235–50; Klein, *President James Buchanan*, 403–29; and Michael J. Birkner, "Epilogue: Buchanan's Civil War Years," in *James Buchanan and the Coming of the Civil War*, eds. Quist and Birkner, 266–80.

42. For Buchanan's various assignment of blame, see Buchanan, *Mr. Buchanan's Administration on the Eve of Rebellion*, 111, 134, 169–75; and for his belief in being vindicated, see the account of his final days in the Lancaster *Intelligencer*, June 3, 1868; and Cole, "Asserting His Authority."

43. On the wedding of Harriet Lane, see Hostetter, "Harriet Lane," 109; and on the honeymoon, see JB to James Buchanan Henry, Feb. 17, 1866, Gratz Collection, case 2, box 24, folder 7, HSP.

44. CME to HLJ, April 13, 1866, JB and HLJ Papers, LC, reel 4; and JB to CME, June 30, 1866, JB Papers, box 4, folder 11, DCL. See also JB to HLJ, June 30 and July 7 and 21, 1866, JB Family Papers, part 1.1.1, folders 190–92, LCHS.

45. CME to HLJ, Oct. 14, 1866, JB and HLJ Papers, LC, reel 4. For Ellis' slave ownership, see "Schedule 2—Slave Inhabitants in Eastern Division in the County of Wilcox, State of Alabama," Federal Census Records, 1860, p. 466. On the sororal model of female friendships, see Lasser, " 'Let Us Be Sisters Forever.' "

46. JB to CME, June 30, 1866, JB Papers, box 4, folder 11, DCL; and JB to HLJ, July 18, 1866, and CME to HLJ, Oct. 14, 1866, JB and HLJ Papers, LC, reels 2 and 4.

47. For the descriptions of Ellis, see JB to HLJ, Oct. 2 (quoted), 27, and 29, and Nov. 10, 1866, JB Family Papers, part 1.1.1, folders 195 and 197–99, LCHS; and JB to James Buchanan Henry, Nov. 10, 1866, ibid., folder 7.

48. For the response to the autograph request, see JB to Harrison Wright, Nov. 16, 1866, JB Letters, HA (lot #36055). On Wright, see his obituary notice in the *Wilkes-Barre Record*, Feb. 27, 1885.

49. For the note, see the docket of JB to WRK, May 11, 1844, JB Papers, box 11, folder 6, HSP.

50. On the preservation of the Buchanan-King correspondence, see the epilogue.

51. JB to CME, Dec. 14, 1867, JB and HLJ Papers, LC, reel 2 [note: pages 2 and 3 are missing from the microfilm edition of the JB and HLJ Papers, LC].

52. On Buchanan's final days, see the Lancaster *Intelligencer*, June 3, 1868; and Cahalan, *James Buchanan and His Family at Wheatland*, 14–15.

53. On the funeral of James Buchanan, see Cahalan, *James Buchanan and His Family at Wheatland*, 79–82; and Van Beck, "James Buchanan."

EPILOGUE

1. On northern and southern reunification during the immediate postbellum years, see esp. Blight, *Race and Reunion*; and Janney, *Remembering the Civil War*, 103-132.

2. CME to HLJ, Sept. 16, 1868, JB and HLJ Papers, LC, reel 4.

3. For the various letters, see WRK to JB, April 30, 1845, box 12, folder 12; Feb. 28, 1846, box 13, folder 20; and Dec. 13, 1852, box 23, folder 2, in JB Papers, HSP.

4. JB to WRK, Mar. 20, 1850, JB Papers, box 48, folder 4, HSP [transcript in *Works*, ed. Moore, 8:370]; William W. King to JB, Mar. 19, 1853, JB Papers, box 23, folder 13, HSP. The signature on the letter excludes King's nephew, William Thomas King, from being the correspondent. Buchanan had once loaned money to the William W. King in question, and he seems to have acted as Buchanan's Washington agent on occasion.

5. On the New York warehouse fire, see Moore, ed., *Works of James Buchanan*, 1:vii. For William Reed's incomplete manuscript of his Buchanan biography, see JB Papers, box 60, folders 3–4 and 8, HSP; and for Cadwalader's biographical notes, see Cadwalader Family Papers, box 262, HSP.

6. On the Battle of Selma, see McIlwain, *1865 Alabama*, 77–79; and Fitts, *Selma*, 74–85.

7. For newspaper coverage of the floods of the Alabama River, see "Falling in Sheets," St. Louis *Globe-Democrat*, Mar. 31, 1886; "Rain and Flood," New Orleans *Picayune*, Mar. 28, 1888; and the various articles in the Feb. to Mar. 1961 editions of the Selma *Times-Journal*. See also Barnes and Somers, "Floods of February–March 1961 in the Southeastern States," 6.

8. For the account of Buchanan's death and subsequent dispute over his estate, see Irelan, *The Republic*, 15:644–58; and on the preservation of the James Buchanan papers, see Rosenberger, "Protecting the Buchanan Papers."

9. Cornelia Van Ness Roosevelt to HLJ, Jan. 22, 1867, JB and HLJ Papers, LC, reel 4. See also Ellet, *Queens of American Society*, frontispiece and 281–94.

10. For the two letters of Ellis to Johnston misdated to 1883, see Elizabeth Fries Lummis Ellet to HLJ, Jan. 23 and April 16, [1869], JB and HLJ Papers, LC, reel 4. See also the copy of the Shunk memorandum (undated), JB Papers, box 60, folder 7, HSP.

11. For mention of Ellis's visit to Cape May, see HLJ to H.M. North, July 30, 1869, JB Papers, box 1, folder 15, LCHS. As compared to her later years, in 1868 alone, Ellis traveled to Richfield Springs, NY, Saratoga Springs, NY, and Newport, RI. On Ellis's final years and death, see Bessie Hogan Williams, "King Family," in Johnston, *William R. King and His Kin*, 302–303; and her will, dated Feb. 8, 1889, in the Wilcox County Loose Estate Case Files; and "Certificate of Probate of Will, Oct. 6, 1890," Wilcox County Will Books, 6:276–77. For the mention of the Ellis photograph, see HLJ to William U. Hensel, Feb. 27, 1899, Wheatland-Klein Collection, box 1, folder 4, LCHS. On Johnston's final years and death, see Rosenberger, "Passing of a Great Lady." For more on Johnston, see Thomas J. Balcerski, "Harriet Rebecca Lane Johnston," in *A Companion to First Ladies*, ed. Sibley, 197–213.

12. JB to CME, June 30, 1866, JB Papers, box 4, folder 11, DCL. For the marble bust in the US Senate, see *United States Senate Catalogue of Fine Art*, ed. McGoldrick, 238–39; and for the bronze bust at the Clinton County Courthouse, paid for by Congress and cast in 1930, see the mislabeled postcard "Bust of Rufus King Near Courthouse, Clinton, N.C.," Durwood Barbour Collection of North Carolina Postcards, SHC. On the relocation of the remains of William Rufus King, see the notice in the *Selma Times*, Jan. 12, 1883, reprinted in the *New York Times*, Jan. 15,

1883; the article on King's unmarked tomb in the *Wilmington Messenger*, Nov. 19, 1892; and the reminiscence in Bessie Hogan Williams, "King Family," in Johnston, *William R. King and His Kin*, 299. On the subsequent investigations of King's tomb and the Cuba memorial, see Jackson, "Alabama's First United States Vice President," 12; and Johnston, *William R. King and His Kin*, 72–76. See also "The William Rufus King Room," ed. Owen.

13. On the various memorials to King, see Rosenberger, "Two Monuments for the Fifteenth President of the United States."

14. William W. Dudley to Benjamin Harrison, Dec. 19, 1887, quoted in Calhoun, *Benjamin Harrison*, 57. On the relationship of Dudley and Harrison, see Jensen, *Winning of the Midwest*, 27–35. On the depiction of Hill and Peffer, see Fischer, "Rustic Rasputin." On Twain's conception of the Siamese twins, see Morris, *Gender Play in Mark Twain*, 61–62. On changing conceptions of manhood among politicians during this period, especially notions of effeminacy, see Murphy, *Political Manhood*, 1–10.

15. On congressional friendships in the twentieth century, see Baker, *Friend and Foe in the U.S. Senate*. On the specific congressional friendships noted, see the note of Richard Nixon to Jacqueline Kennedy, Nov. 23, 1963, quoted in Matthews, *Kennedy & Nixon*, 239–40; J.Y. Smith, "Ex-Senator George Aiken, 92," *Washington Post*, Nov. 20, 1984; and Lerner, "Unlikely Political Pals."

16. On the house on C Street, see Boyer, "Frat House for Jesus" (quoted); and Sharlet, *C Street*. Yet another group of congressional roommates—Senator Chuck Schumer, Senator Dick Durbin, and Representative George Miller (three Democrats from New York, Illinois, and California, respectively)—inspired the premise for the show *Alpha House*, released by Amazon Studios in 2013.

17. On the bromance of Obama and Biden, see Nguyen, "Barack Obama and Joe Biden"; and Tod Perry, "Barack Obama and Joe Biden's 'Bromance' Continues After the White House," *Good Magazine*, May 18, 2017. For studies that historicize these iterations of modern manhood, see Syrett, *The Company He Keeps*; and Bederman, *Manliness & Civilization*. On the future of male friendship, see William Deresiewicz, "Faux Friendship," *The Chronicle of Higher Education*, Dec. 6, 2009; and on the problematic deployment of the term "bromance," see Smith, "The 'Bromance' Problem."

18. On bromosexual relationships, see Jim Farber, "The Rise of the 'Bromosexual' Friendship," *New York Times*, Oct. 4, 2016.

Bibliography

MANUSCRIPT COLLECTIONS

Alabama
    Alabama Department of Archives and History
        Alabama Governor Administrative Files (Israel Pickens, John Gayle)*
        Alabama Secretary of State Correspondence (Thomas A. Rodgers)
        Arthur Pendleton Bagby Papers
        Matthew P. Blue Family Papers
        John Coffee Papers
        Thomas B. Cooper Correspondence
        Government Records Collections
        Bolling Hall Family Papers
        William Rufus King Family Papers
        Israel Pickens Family Papers
        Selma Land Company account book
        Tait Family Papers
    Wilcox County Courthouse
        Loose Estate Case Files*
        Will Books*
California
    Shapell Manuscript Foundation
        James Buchanan letters
    University of California, Berkeley, Bancroft Library
        William McKendree Gwin Papers
Connecticut
    Yale University, Manuscript and Archives Library
        Ethel Fogg and William Brooks Clift Memorial Collection
        S. Griswold Flagg Collection
        Gardiner-Tyler Family Papers

Southard Hay Autograph Collection
Harold Lamport Collection
Charlton Thomas Lewis Papers
Miscellaneous Manuscripts
Park Family Papers
Ulrich B. Phillips Papers
Alfred White Van Sinderen Collection
James Watson Webb Papers

Georgia
University of Georgia, Hargrett Rare Book & Manuscript Library
Cobb / Erwin / Lamar Family Papers
Howell Cobb Family Papers

Illinois
Abraham Lincoln Presidential Library
James Buchanan letters
Chicago Historical Society
James Buchanan letters and documents
John Russell Jones Papers

Kentucky
Kentucky Historical Society
Taylor Family Papers

Louisiana
Historic New Orleans Collection
James Robb Collection
Louisiana State University, Special Collections Library
William R. King Letter
Tulane University, Howard-Tilton Memorial Library
Louisiana Historical Association Collection
Jefferson Davis Papers (Series 55-D), vol. 18

Maine
Maine Historical Society
Nathan Clifford Papers

Maryland
Johns Hopkins University, Alan M. Chesney Medical Archives
Harriet Lane Home for Invalid Children Papers
Maryland Historical Society
Benjamin Howell Griswold Papers
Carolyn N. Horowitz Autograph Collection
John Eager Howard Papers
James A. Pearce Papers
National Archives, College Park
General Records of the Department of State

Despatches from US Consuls in Havana, Cuba, 1783–1906*
Despatches from US Ministers to France, 1789–1906*
Despatches from US Ministers to Russia, 1808–1906*
Diplomatic Instructions of the Department of State, France, 1829–1906*
Massachusetts
American Antiquarian Society
John Davis Papers
Boston Public Library
James Buchanan Letters
William Rufus King Letter
Harvard University, Houghton Special Collections Library
Autograph Collection (various)
Jared Sparks Letterbooks
John Updike Papers
Massachusetts Historical Society
Adams Family Papers*
Edward Everett Papers*
Winthrop Family Papers*
Michigan
Bentley Historical Library, Ann Arbor
George Bryan Porter Papers
University of Michigan, William L. Clements Library
US President Papers, 1776–1945
James Buchanan letters
Missouri
State Historical Society of Missouri
David Rice Atchison Letters
Nevada
Gallery of History, Las Vegas
James Buchanan autograph letters
University of Nevada, Reno
James Buchanan Letter
New Jersey
New Jersey Historical Society
Mahlon Dickerson and Philemon Dickerson Papers
Statesmen Autograph Collection
Princeton University, Rare Books and Special Collections Department
Andre De Coppett Collection
Blair and Lee Family Papers
Butler Family Papers
Cameron Family Papers
Lewis Cass Collection

            Delafield Family Papers
            Edward Livingston Papers
            General Miscellaneous Manuscripts
            William Pinkney Papers
            Rush Family Papers*
            Samuel L. Southard Papers
            Strauss Autograph Collection
            Wainwright Family Collection
New York
        Brooklyn Historical Society
            James Buchanan letters
        Columbia University, Rare Book and Manuscript Library
            Belmont Family Papers
            Hamilton Fish Letters
        Cornell University, Rare and Manuscript Collection
            James Buchanan Receipt and Letter
        New-York Historical Society
            Gilder Lehrman Collection
                James Buchanan Letters
            James Buchanan Papers (AHMC–Buchanan, James)
        New York Public Library, Manuscript and Archives Division
            James Buchanan Letters and Documents
            Clymer-Meredith-Read Family Papers
            George William Gordon Papers
            Horace Greely Papers
            James A. Hamilton Papers
            Edward S. and Mary Stillman Harkness Manuscript Collection
            Washington Irving Papers
            Louis McLane Letters
            T. H. Morrell Collection of Original Autograph Letters of the Presidents of
                the United States
            Theodorus Bailey Myers Collection
            Fernando Wood Letters and Documents
        New York Society Library
            James Buchanan Letters
        Pierpont Morgan Library
            American Literary and Historical Manuscripts, various
            Henry Wheaton Family Collection
        Seth Kaller, Inc., White Plains, NY
            James Buchanan letter
North Carolina
        Duke University, David M. Rubenstein Rare Book & Manuscript Library

George Booker Papers
Bedford Brown Papers
James Buchanan letters and documents (various)
Campbell Family Papers
Clement Claiborne Clay Papers
William Rufus King Papers
Charles Colcock Jones Jr. Papers
Joseph Long Papers
Edward Lucas Papers
Willie Person Mangum Papers
Henry Alexander Wise Papers
North Carolina Department of Archives
Katherine Clark Pendleton Conway Collection
Walter Clark Papers
Miscellaneous Papers
David L. Swain Papers
Southern Historical Collection, University of North Carolina
Durwood Barbour Collection of North Carolina Postcards*
Kenan Family Papers
William Rufus King Letters
David Outlaw Papers*
Nicholas Trist Papers
Pennsylvania
Crawford County Historical Society
James Buchanan letters
Dickinson College, Archives and Special Collections Library
James Buchanan Papers
Fendrick Library, Mercersburg
James Buchanan Vertical File
Early Tax Records of Mercersburg
Family Records: Buchanan
Harriet Rebecca Lane Johnston Vertical File
Franklin and Marshall College, Archives and Special Collections
Board of Trustees Minutes
Jonathan M. Foltz Papers
Reynolds Family Papers
Historical Society of Pennsylvania
James Buchanan Family Papers
James Buchanan Fund records
James Buchanan Papers*
Cadwalader Family Papers
Hampton L. Carson Collection

Conarroe Autograph Collection
Lewis Coryell Papers
George Mifflin Dallas Papers
Dreer Collection
Frank M. Etting Collection
S. L. Fallon Autograph Collection
Fayette County Collection
Genealogical Data: Surnames DA-DEK
Gilpin Family Papers
Simon Gratz Autograph Collection
John Harris Collection
Henry Family Papers
James Buchanan Henry Private Account Book
Charles Jared Ingersoll Collection
Irvine-Newbold Family Papers
Frank Willing Leach Papers
Ellis Lewis Papers
William David Lewis Papers
Frank B. Nead Documents
Joel Roberts Poinsett Papers
William W. Porter Collection
John M. Read Papers
John Sergeant Papers
Townsend Family Collection
Samuel Welsh Collection
Lancaster County Historical Society
James Buchanan Collection
James Buchanan Family Papers
David Lynch Collection
Samuel R. Slaymaker II, White Chimneys Collection
Swarr Scrapbooks
Wheatland-Klein Collection
Library Company of Philadelphia
John A. McAllister Collection of Civil War Era Printed Ephemera, Graphics
and Manuscripts
Luzerne County Historical Society, Wilkes-Barre
Hendrick B. Wright Papers
Pennsylvania Historical and Museum Commission, State Archives
James Buchanan Collection
Pennsylvania Masonic Library & Museum, Philadelphia
James Buchanan biographical file
Pennsylvania State University, Eberly Family Special Collections Library

James Buchanan Correspondence
James Buchanan Papers
Jacob Hibshman Papers
Philip S. Klein Collection
Rosenbach Museum & Library, Philadelphia
James Buchanan Papers
Upper West Conococheague Presbyterian Church, Mercersburg
James Buchanan letter
Church Records (various)
Villanova University, Falvey Memorial Library
John B. and Carroll R. Powell Collection*
David Lynch Collection*
Rhode Island
Brown University, John Hay Library
Lincoln Collection
Replies to Dinner Invitations from President Buchanan
Tennessee
Tennessee State Library and Archives
Aaron Venable Brown Papers
John Coffee Papers*
David Hubbard Papers
Sir Emil Hurja Collection*
Andrew Jackson Papers*
Polk Memorial Association Collection of James Knox Polk Papers
Joanna Lucinda Rucker Letter Folio
Texas
Heritage Auctions
James Buchanan Letters
William R. King Letter
Virginia
Mount Vernon Ladies' Association, Fred W. Smith National Library
Harriet Lane Letters
University of Virginia
George Ticknor Curtis Papers
Virginia Historical Society
Harrison Family Papers
Martha Waller Johnson Papers
Wise Family Papers
Washington, DC
Library of Congress, Manuscript Division
James Dodson Barbee and David Rankin Barbee Papers
George Plitt Papers

John Bell Papers
Breckinridge Family Papers
James Buchanan and Harriet Lane Johnston Papers*
Edmund Burke Collection
Simon Cameron Papers*
George Washington Campbell Papers
Caleb Cushing Papers
John Fairfield Correspondence
Hamilton Fish Papers
Jonathan Messersmith Foltz Papers
Elbridge Gerry Papers
James Henry Hammond Papers
Andrew Jackson Papers*
Thomas Sidney Jesup Papers
David Lynch Papers
Dolley Madison Papers*
William L. Marcy Papers
Gates W. McGarrah Collection of Presidential Autographs
Louis McLane Papers
Miscellaneous Manuscripts Collections
	John Pendleton King correspondence
	William Rufus King correspondence
John Bassett Moore Papers
Philip Phillips Family Papers
James Knox Polk Papers*
William Cabell Rives Papers
Nicholas Trist Papers*
John Tyler Papers*
US Executive Mansion Papers
Martin Van Buren Papers*
Robert J. Walker Papers
George Watterston Papers
United Kingdom
	British Library, London
		Aberdeen Papers
		Archive of the Royal Literary Fund
		Autograph Letters of Presidents of the United States of North America
		James Robert George Graham Papers
		Charles Griffin Letters
		Lieven Papers
		Miscellaneous Letters and Papers
		Palmerston Papers
		Robert Peel Papers

Oxford University, Bodleian Library
  American Material in the Clarendon Papers, 1853–1870*
  American Material in the Clarendon Papers, 1844–1856*

*collection consulted on microfilm or in digital format

GOVERNMENT DOCUMENTS, DIRECTORIES,
AND OFFICIAL REPORTS

Acts of Alabama.

Alabama State Census (1855, 1865).

Annals of Congress of the United States. 42 vols. Washington, DC: Gales and Seaton, 1834–1856.

Barnes, Harry H. Jr., and William P. Somers. "Floods of February–March 1961 in the Southeastern States." Geological Survey Circular 452. Washington, DC: US Department of the Interior, 1961.

Boyd's Washington and Georgetown Directory (1858, 1860).

Congressional Directories (32nd–36th Congresses). Washington, DC: J & G. S. Gideon, 1852–1861.

Congressional Globe. 46 vols. Washington, DC: Globe Office, 1833–1873.

Dictionary of the United States Congress: Compiled as a Manual of Reference for the Legislator and Statesman. Washington, DC, 1864.

Federal Census, Alabama. 1840–1890.

Goldman, Perry M., and James S. Young, eds. *The United States Congressional Directories, 1789–1840.* New York: Columbia University Press, 1973.

"Journal of the Democratic Convention Held in the City of Montgomery on the 14th and 15th February, 1848." Montgomery, AL: McCormick & Walshe, 1848.

Journal of the Executive Proceedings of the U.S. Senate. Washington, DC: US Senate, 1828–.

Proceedings of the Democratic National Convention (1840, 1848, 1852, 1856).

Register of Debates. 14 vols. Washington, DC: Gales & Seaton, 1825–1837.

Ten Eyck's Washington and Georgetown Directory, with a Complete Congressional and Department Directory (1855).

The Washington and Georgetown Directory, Strangers' Guide-Book for Washington, and Congressional and Clerk's Register (1853).

The Washington City Directory, and Congressional, and Executive Register (1850).

The Washington Directory and National Register (1843, 1846).

NEWSPAPERS AND CONTEMPORARY PERIODICALS

Alabama Advertiser and State Gazette (Montgomery)

Alabama Beacon (Greensborough)

Alabama State Intelligencer (Tuscaloosa)

American Volunteer (Carlisle, PA)

Arkansas Gazette (Little Rock)
Baltimore Clipper
Baltimore Patriot
Boston Courier
Boston Herald
Boston Post
Charleston Mercury
Daily Advertiser (Montgomery)
Daily American (Nashville)
Daily Atlas (Boston)
Daily Courier (Natchez)
Daily Post (Pittsburgh)
Detroit Free Press
Emancipator and Weekly Chronicle (New Bedford)
Fayetteville Weekly Observer
Frank Leslie's Illustrated Newspaper
Gleason's Pictorial Drawing-Room Companion
Gloucester Telegraph (MA)
Grand Gulf Advertiser (Claiborne, MS)
Harper's Weekly
Huntress (Washington, DC)
Huntsville Democrat
Jacksonville Republican (AL)
Lancaster Era
Lancaster Examiner and Democratic Herald
Lancaster Daily Intelligencer
Lancaster Journal
Mercersburg Journal
Mississippian and State Gazette (Jackson)
Mobile Daily Advertiser
Mobile Daily Register
National Intelligencer (Washington, DC)
National Quarterly Review
New Orleans Times-Picayune
New World (New York)
New-York Daily Times
New York Evening Post
New York Herald
New York Times
Niles' National Register (Washington, DC)
North American and Daily Advertiser (Philadelphia)
North-Carolinian (Fayetteville)

Ohio State Journal (Columbus)
Ohio Statesman (Columbus)
Paul Pry (Washington, DC)
Philadelphia Inquirer
Philadelphia Press
Portage Sentinel (Ravenna, OH)
Poulson's Advertiser (Philadelphia)
Public Opinion (Chambersburg, PA)
Punch
Raleigh Weekly Standard
Republican and Patriot (Goldsboro, NC)
Republican Banner (Nashville)
Selma Times-Journal
Southron (Jackson, MS)
St. Paul Daily Globe
Vanity Fair
Virginia Free Press (Charlestown)
Washington Constitution
Washington Globe
Washington Star
Wheeling Daily Intelligencer
Wilkes-Barre Record
Wilmington Daily Journal
Wilmington Messenger

PUBLISHED CORRESPONDENCE, CATALOGUES, DIARIES, MEMOIRS,
GENEALOGICAL WORKS, BIOGRAPHICAL REFERENCE, PAMPHLETS,
SPEECHES, AND PUBLIC PAPERS

Adams, John Quincy. *Memoirs of John Quincy Adams, Comprising Portions of His Diary from 1795 to 1848.* 12 vols. Ed. Charles Francis Adams. Philadelphia: J. B. Lippincott & Co., 1874–1877.

Appel, Theodore. *Recollections of College Life, at Marshall College, Mercersburg, Pa., from 1839 to 1845; A Narrative with Reflections.* Reading, PA: Daniel Miller, 1886.

Appel, Theodore. *The Life and Work of John Williamson Nevin.* Philadelphia: Reformed Church Publication House, 1880.

Bagby, Arthur. "Eulogy Pronounced on the Life and Character of William R. King, at the Request of the Citizens of Selma, on the 22d February, 1854." Camden, AL: Printed at the "Republic" Office, 1854.

Bancroft, Hubert H. *The Works of Hubert Howe Bancroft.* 39 vols. San Francisco: History Co. Publishers, 1887.

Barefield, Marilyn, ed. *Old Cahaba Land Office Records & Military Records, 1817–1853*. Easley, SC: Southern Historical Press, 1981.

Barnes, James J., and Patience P. Barnes, eds. *Private and Confidential: Letters from British Ministers in Washington to The Foreign Secretaries in London, 1844–67*. Selinsgrove, PA: Susquehanna University Press, 1993.

Bassett, John S., ed. *Correspondence of Andrew Jackson*. 7 vols. Washington, DC: Carnegie Institution, 1926–1935.

Battle, Kemp P., ed. *Letters of Nathaniel Macon, John Steele and William Barry Grove, with Sketches and Notes*. Chapel Hill, NC: University Press, 1902.

Bemis, Samuel F., ed. *The American Secretaries of State and Their Diplomacy*. 18 vols. New York: Pageant Book Co., 1963.

Bizzell, Oscar M., ed. *The Heritage of Sampson County, North Carolina*. Clinton, NC: Sampson County Historical Society, 1983.

Bizzell, Oscar M., and Virginia L. Bizzell, eds. *A Portrait of Nineteenth Century Sampson County as Revealed by Sampson County Court Minutes*. 4 vols. Clinton, NC: Sampson County Historical Society, 1987–1995.

Blaine, James G. *Twenty Years in Congress: From Lincoln to Garfield*. 2 vols. Norwich, CT: Henry Bill, 1884–1886.

Bonner, James C., ed. "Andrew Jackson Comments on Polk's Cabinet." *Tennessee Historical Quarterly*. Vol. 27, no. 3 (Fall 1968): 287–88.

Boyd, William K., ed. "Correspondence of Bedford Brown." *An Annual Publication of Historical Papers Published by the Historical Society of Trinity College*. Vols. 6–7 (1906–1907): 66–92, 16–31.

Brewer, Willis. *Alabama: Her History, Resources, War Record, and Public Men, from 1540 to 1872*. Montgomery, AL: Barrett & Brown: 1872.

Brown, George R. *Washington: A Not Too Serious History*. Baltimore: Norman Publishers, 1930.

Buchanan, A.W. Patrick. *The Buchanan Book*. Montreal: privately printed, 1911.

Buchanan, James. *Mr. Buchanan's Administration on the Eve of the Rebellion*. New York: D. Appleton & Co., 1866.

Burlingame, Michael, ed. *At Lincoln's Side: John Hay's Civil War Correspondence and Selected Writings*. Carbondale: Southern Illinois University Press, 2000.

Catalog of Graduates of William and Mary. Williamsburg, VA: College of William & Mary, 1859.

Claiborne, John F. H., ed. *Life and Times of Gen. Sam Dale, the Mississippi Partisan*. New York: Harper & Brothers, 1860.

Clay-Clopton, Virginia. *A Belle of the Fifties*. Ed. Ada Stirling. New York: Doubleday, Page, & Co., 1905.

Clemens, William M. *Buchanan Family Record*. New York: William M. Clemens, 1914.

Clifford, Philip G. *Nathan Clifford, Democrat (1803–1881)*. New York: G. P. Putnam's Sons, 1922.

Conover, Cheryl, ed. "Kentuckian in 'King Andrew's' Court: The Letters of John Waller Barry, Washington, D.C., 1831–1835." *Register of the Kentucky Historical Society*. Vol. 81, no. 2 (Spring 1983): 168–98.

Conover, Cheryl, ed. "'To Please Papa': The Letters of John Waller Barry, West Point Cadet, 1826–1830." *Register of the Kentucky Historical Society*. Vol. 80, no. 2 (Spring 1982): 183–212.

Corcoran, William W. *A Grandfather's Legacy; Containing a Sketch of His Life and Obituary Notices of Some Members of His Family, Together with Letters from His Friends*. Washington, DC: Henry Polkinhorn, 1879.

Creigh, Thomas. *History of the Presbyterian Church in Mercersburg, Penna*. Mercersburg, PA: Andrew M. Spangler, 1846.

Crittenden, Lucius E. *Recollections of President Lincoln and His Administration*. New York: Harper & Brothers, 1904.

Curtis, George T. *Life of James Buchanan: Fifteenth President of the United States*. 2 vols. New York: Harper & Brothers, 1883.

Cutler, Wayne, et al., eds. *Correspondence of James K Polk*. 13 vols. Nashville, TN: Vanderbilt University Press, 1969–.

Davis, A.J., ed. *History of Clarion County Pennsylvania*. Syracuse, NY: D. Mason & Co., 1887.

Davis, Varina. *Jefferson Davis: Ex-President of the Confederate States of America*. 2 vols. New York: Belford Co., 1890.

Day, Sherman. *Historical Collections of the State of Pennsylvania*. Philadelphia: George W. Gorton, 1843.

DeLeon, Thomas C. *Belles, Beaux and Brains of the 60's*. New York: G. W. Dillingham, 1907.

Duff, Mountstaurt E. Grant. *Notes from a Diary, 1892–1895*. 2 vols. London: John Murray, 1904.

Dumond, Dwight L., ed. *Southern Editorials on Secession*. Washington, DC: American Historical Association, 1931; reprint: Gloucester, MA: Peter Smith, 1964.

Ellet, Elizabeth Fries Lummis. *The Court Circles of the Republic, or the Beauties and Celebrities of the Nation*. Hartford, CT: Hartford Publishing Co., 1869.

Ellet, Elizabeth Fries Lummis. *The Queens of American Society*. New York: Charles Scribner & Co., 1867.

Ellis, Franklin, and Samuel Evans. *History of Lancaster County, with Biographical Sketches of Many of its Pioneers and Prominent Men*. Philadelphia: Everts & Peck, 1883.

Fiske, Stephen. "When Lincoln Was First Inaugurated." *Ladies' Home Journal*. Vol. 14, no 4 (Mar. 1897): 7.

Foote, Henry S. *Casket of Reminiscences*. Washington, DC: Chronicle Publishing Co., 1874.

Forney, John W. *Anecdotes of Public Men*. 2 vols. New York: Harper & Brothers, 1873–1881.

Futhey, J. Smith, and Gilbert Cope. *History of Chester County, Pennsylvania, with Genealogical and Biographical Sketches*. Philadelphia: Louis H. Everts, 1881.

Garrett, William. *Reminiscences of Public Men in Alabama*. Atlanta: Plantation Publishing, 1872.

Gobright, Lawrence A. *Recollection of Men and Things at Washington, During the Third of a Century*. Philadelphia: Claxton, Remsen & Haffelfinger, 1869.

Gouverneur, Marian. *As I Remember: Recollection of American Society during the Nineteenth Century*. New York: D. Appleton & Co., 1911.

Greenhow, Rose O'Neal. *My Imprisonment and the First Year of Abolition Rule at Washington*. London: Richard Bentley, 1863.

Grubbs, Lillie M., ed. *Martin and Allied Families*. Columbus, GA: n.p. 1946.

Hagood, Johnson. *Memoirs of the War of Secession*. 2 vols. Ed. Ulysses R. Brooks. Columbia, SC: State Co., 1910.

Hardy, John. *Selma: Her Institutions and Her Men*. Selma, AL: Times and Book Job Office, 1879; reprint: Spartanburg, SC: Reprint Co., 1978.

Hawthorne, Nathaniel. *The Centenary Edition of the Works of Nathaniel Hawthorne*. 23 vols. Eds. Thomas Woodson et al. Columbus: Ohio State University Press, 1962–1994.

Hesseltine, William B., and Rex G. Fisher, eds. *Trimmers, Trucklers & Temporizers: Notes of Murat Halstead from the Political Conventions of 1856*. Madison: State Historical Society of Wisconsin, 1961.

Historical Register: Notes and Queries, Historical and Genealogical, Relating to Interior Pennsylvania, for the Year 1883. 2 vols. Harrisburg, PA: Lane S. Hart, 1883.

Holler, Rose G. "Some Rare Items Regarding James Buchanan and Thaddeus Stevens." *Kittochtinny Historical Society Papers*. Vol. 14 (1957–1963): 229–36.

Holloway, Laura Carter. *Ladies of the White House*. New York: US Publishing Co., 1870.

Hopkins, James F., et al., eds. *The Papers of Henry Clay*. 10 vols. Lexington: University Press of Kentucky, 1959–1991.

Horton, Rushmore G. *The Life and Public Services of James Buchanan*. New York: Derby and Jackson, 1856.

Johnston, Henry P. Sr. *William R. King and His Kin*. Birmingham, AL: Featon Press, 1975.

Jones, Anson, ed. *Memoranda and Official Correspondence Relating to the Republic of Texas, its History and Annexation*. New York: D. Appleton & Co., 1859.

Journal of the Convention of the Alabama Territory, begun July 5, 1819. Huntsville, AL: John Boardman, 1819; reprint: n.p.: Statute Law Book Co., 1909.

"King Family of Virginia." *William and Mary Quarterly*. Vol. 16, no. 2 (Oct. 1907): 105–10.

King, Oscar Benjamin. *Our King Family: Their Ancestors, In-Laws, and Descendants*. Fort Worth, TX: Manney Co., 1970.

Klein, Philip S., ed. "Memoirs of a Senator from Pennsylvania: Jonathan Roberts, 1771–1854." *Pennsylvania Magazine of History and Biography*. Vol. 62, no. 2 (April 1938): 213–48.

Landis, Mrs. James D. "Who Was Who in Lancaster One Hundred Years Ago." *Papers Read Before the Lancaster County Historical Society.* Vol. 9, no. 10 (Dec. 1907): 363–421.

"Letter of Condolence and Other Subjects from Senator William Rufus King to Governor Israel Pickens." *Alabama Historical Quarterly.* Vol. 3, no. 2 (Summer 1941): 231–34.

"Letters from Old Trunks: From Coles Collection of Preston Papers." *Virginia Magazine of History and Biography.* Vol. 47, no. 3 (July 1939): 239–43.

Lucas, Silas E., ed. *Marriages from Early Tennessee Newspapers, 1794–1851.* Easley, SC: Southern Historical Press, 1978.

Manning, William R., ed. *Diplomatic Correspondence of the United States, 1831–1860.* 12 vols. Washington, DC: Carnegie Endowment for International Peace, 1932–1939.

Marraro, Howard, ed. *Diplomatic Relations Between the United States and the Kingdom of the Two Sicilies.* 2 vols. New York: Vanni, 1951.

McCall, D.L., ed. "Lafayette's Visit to Alabama, April 1825." *Alabama Historical Quarterly.* Vol. 17, no. 1 and 2 (Spring and Summer 1955): 33–77.

McGoldrick, Jane R., ed. *United States Senate Catalogue of Fine Art.* Washington, DC: US Government Printing Office, 2002.

Meriwether, Robert L., et al. eds. *The Papers of John C. Calhoun.* 28 vols. Columbia: University of South Carolina Press, 1959–2003.

Miller, David H., ed. *Treaties and Other International Acts of the United States of America.* 8 vols. Washington, D.C.: US Government Printing Office, 1931–1948.

Miller, Virginia. "Dr. Thomas Miller and His Times." *Records of the Columbia Historical Society.* Vol. 3 (1900): 303–23.

Mombert, J.I. *An Authentic History of Lancaster County in the State of Pennsylvania.* Lancaster, PA: J. E. Barr & Co., 1869.

Moore, John B., ed. *The Works of James Buchanan, Comprising his Speeches, State Papers, and Private Correspondence.* 12 vols. Philadelphia: J. B. Lippincott Co., 1908–1911.

Moser, Harold D., et al., eds. *The Papers of Andrew Jackson.* 10 vols. Knoxville: University Press of Tennessee, 1980–.

Neaman, Judith S., and Caroline G. Silver. *The Wordsworth Book of Euphemism.* Reprint; Hertofdshire, England: Wordsworth Editions, Ldt., 1995.

Nelson, Anson and Fanny Nelson. *Memorials of Sarah Childress Polk.* New York: Anson D. F. Randolph & Co., 1892; reprint: Newtown, CT: American Political Biography Press, 1994.

Newsome, A. R. "Twelve North Carolina Counties in 1810–1811." *North Carolina Historical Review.* Vol. 5, no. 4 (Oct. 1928): 413–46.

"Nicholas Family of Virginia and Louisiana." *Virginia Magazine of History and Biography.* Vol. 57, no. 1 (Jan. 1949): 83–85.

Nichols, John B., ed. *History of the Medical Society of the District of Columbia, 1817–1909.* Washington, DC: Medical Society, 1909.

Nichols, Roy F., ed. "The Library: The Mystery of the Dallas Papers (Part 1)." *Pennsylvania Magazine of History and Biography*. Vol. 73, no. 3 (July 1949): 349-92.

"Obituary Address on the Occasion of the Death of Hon. William R. King." Washington: R. Armstrong, 1854.

O'Neall, John B. *Biographical Sketches of the Bench and Bar of South Carolina*. 2 vols. Charleston, SC: S. G. Courtenay, 1859.

Owen, Thomas M., ed. *History of Alabama and Dictionary of Alabama Biography*. 4 vols. Chicago: S. J. Clarke Co., 1921.

Owen, Thomas M., ed. "William R. King on Sectional Issues." *Gulf State Historical Magazine*. Vol. 1, no. 1 (July 1902): 45.

Quaife, Milo M., ed. *The Diary of James Knox Polk*. 4 vols. Chicago: A. C. McClurg & Co., 1910.

Parks, Joseph H., ed. "Letters from Aaron V. Brown to Alfred O. P. Nicholson, 1844– 1850." *Tennessee Historical Quarterly*. Vol. 3, no. 2 (June 1944): 170–79.

Patterson, Alta K. *Kennard, King, Knight, Hardin, Goodin, Their Ancestors & Descendants*. Chelsea, MI: n.p., 1988.

Phillips, Ulrich B., ed. *Annual Report of the American Historical Association for the Year 1911, Vol. 2: The Correspondence of Robert Toombs, Alexander H. Stephens, and Howell Cobb*. Washington, DC, 1913.

Pickett, Albert J. *History of Alabama and Incidentally of Georgia and Mississippi, from the Earliest Period*. 2 vols. Charleston, SC: Walker and James, 1851; re- print: Birmingham, AL: Webb Book Co. 1900.

Pike, James S., ed. *First Blows of the Civil War: The Ten Years of Preliminary Conflict in the United States, from 1850 to 1860*. New York: American News Co., 1879.

Plischke, Elmer. *U.S. Department of State: A Reference History*. Westport, CT: Greenwood Press, 1999.

Poore, Benjamin P. *Perley's Reminiscences of Sixty Years in the National Metropolis*. 2 vols. Philadelphia: Hubbard Bros., 1886.

Powell, William S., ed. *Dictionary of North Carolina Biography*. 6 vols. Chapel Hill: University of North Carolina Press, 1988.

Pryor, Sara Agnes Rice. *Reminiscences of Peace and War*. New York: Macmillan Co., 1905.

Ray, P. Orman. "Some Papers of Franklin Pierce, 1852–1862." *American Historical Review*. Vol. 10, nos. 1–2 (Oct. 1904–Jan. 1905): 110–27, 350–70.

Reilly, Bernard F. Jr. *American Political Prints, 1766–1876: A Catalog of the Collections in the Library of Congress*. Boston: G. K. Hall, 1991.

Riddle, William. *The Story of Lancaster: Old and New*. Lancaster, PA: n.p., 1917.

Riley, B. F. *Makers and Romance of Alabama History*. Birmingham, AL: n.p., 1915.

Royall, Anne. *The Black Book, or a Continuation of Travels in the United States*. 3 vols. Washington, DC: n.p., 1828–1829.

Sanderson, Alfred. *Historical Sketch of the Union Fire Company, No. 1, of the City of Lancaster, Penna., from 1760 to 1879*. Lancaster, PA: Union Fire Co., 1879.

Sargent, Nathan. *Public Men and Events.* 2 vols. Philadelphia: J. B. Lippincott & Co., 1875.

Scarborough, William K., ed. *The Diary of Edmund Ruffin.* 2 vols. Baton Rouge: Louisiana State University Press, 1972–1989.

Schenck, David. *Personal Sketches of Distinguished Delegates of the State Convention 1861-2.* Greensboro, NC: Thomas, Reece, & Co., Printers, 1885.

Schlesinger, Arthur Jr., and Fred L. Israel, eds. *History of American Presidential Elections, 1789-2001.* 11 vols. Philadelphia: Chelsea House Publishers, 2002.

Seaton, William W. *William Winston Seaton of the "National Intelligencer": A Biographical Study with Passing Notes of His Associates and Friends.* Boston: James R. Osgood & Co., 1871.

Shanks, Henry T., ed. *Papers of Willie Person Mangum.* 5 vols. Raleigh, NC: State Dept. of Archives and History, 1950–1956.

Singleton, Esther. *The Story of the White House.* 2 vols. New York: McClure Co., 1907.

Sioussat, St. George L., ed. "Diaries of S.H. Laughlin of Tennessee, 1840–1843." *Tennessee Historical Magazine.* Vol. 2 (Mar. 1916): 43–85.

Smith, Hal H. "Historic Washington Homes." *Records of the Columbia Historical Society, Washington, D.C.* Vol. 11 (1908): 243–67.

Sotheby's. *Fine Printed and Manuscript Americana from the Collection of Mrs. Philip D. Sang.* New York: Sotheby's, 1985.

Staples, Arthur G., ed. *Letters of John Fairfield.* Lewiston, ME: Lewiston Journal Co., 1922.

Sterne, Laurence. *A Sentimental Journey Through France and Italy.* 2 vols. London: T. Becket, 1768.

Strange, Robert. "Eulogy on the Life and Character of William R. King, Delivered in Clinton, on the 1st Day of June, 1853." Raleigh, NC: William W. Hollden, 1853.

Tyler, Lyon G., ed. *The Letters and Times of the Tylers.* 3 vols. Richmond: Whittett and Shepperson, 1884–1896; reprint: New York: Da Capo Press, 1970.

Van Buren, Martin. *Autobiography of Martin Van Buren.* Ed. John C. Fitzpatrick. Washington, DC: Government Printing Office, 1920.

Ward, Wilfrid. *The Life and Times of Cardinal Wiseman.* 2 vols. New York: Longmans, Green, & Co., 1897.

Welchans, George R. *History of Lodge No. 43, F.&A.M.* Lancaster, PA: Inquirer Printing Co., 1885.

Wharton, Anne Hollingsworth. *Social Life in the Early Republic.* Philadelphia: J. B. Lippincott Co., 1903.

Wheaton, Henry, ed. *Some Account of the Life, Writings, and Speeches of William Pinkney.* New York: J. W. Palmer & Co., 1826.

Wilson, Reba S., and Betty S. Glover. *The Lees and Kings of Virginia and North Carolina, 1636-1976.* Ridgely, TN: Wilson and Glover Pub. Co., 1975.

Windham, Frank, ed. "The Letters of Kate Thompson to Mary Ann Cobb (1858–1861)." *Journal of Mississippi History.* Vol. 50, no. 3 (1988): 173–98.

Woodward, C. Vann, ed. *Mary Chesnut's Civil War*. New Haven, CT: Yale University Press, 1981.

Wright, John K., ed. *Atlas of the Historical Geography of the United States*. New York: Carnegie Institution of Washington, 1932.

Yancey, William L. "An Address to the People of Alabama." Montgomery, AL: Flag & Advertiser, 1848.

Zevely, Douglass. "Old Houses on C Street and Those Who Lived There." *Records of the Columbia Historical Society, Washington D.C.* Vol. 5 (1902): 151–75.

BOOKS

Abernethy, Thomas P. *The Formative Period in Alabama, 1815–1828*. Montgomery, AL: Brown Printing Co., 1922.

Abraham, Henry J. *Justices and Presidents: A Political History of Appointments to the Supreme Court (Second Edition)*. New York: Oxford University Press, 1985.

Adams, Sean P., ed. *A Companion to the Era of Andrew Jackson*. Malden, MA: Wiley-Blackwell, 2013.

Allgor, Catherine. *Parlor Politics: In Which the Ladies of Washington Help Build a City and a Government*. Charlottesville: University of Virginia Press, 2000.

Anbinder, Tyler. *Nativism and Slavery: The Northern Know Nothings and the Politics of the 1850s*. New York: Oxford University Press, 1992.

Anthony, Carl S. *First Ladies: The Saga of the Presidents' Wives and Their Power*. New York: William Morrow & Co., 1990.

Appleby, Joyce. *Inheriting the Revolution: The First Generation of Americans*. Cambridge, MA: Harvard University Press, 2000.

Argersinger, Jana L., and Leland S. Person, eds. *Hawthorne and Melville: Writing a Relationship*. Athens: University of Georgia Press, 2008.

Auchampaugh, Philip G. *James Buchanan and His Cabinet on the Eve of Secession*. Privately printed, 1926.

Bailey, Hugh C. *John Williams Walker: A Study in the Political, Social, and Cultural Life of the Old Southwest*. Tuscaloosa: University of Alabama Press, 1964.

Baker, Jean H. *Affairs of Party: The Political Culture of Northern Democrats in the Mid-Nineteenth Century*. Ithaca, NY: Cornell University Press, 1983.

Baker, Jean H. *James Buchanan*. New York: Henry Holt and Company, 2004.

Baker, Ross K. *Friend and Foe in the U.S. Senate*. New York: Free Press, 1980.

Barnes, Diane L., Brian Schoen, and Frank Towers, eds. *The Old South's Modern Worlds: Slavery, Region, and Nation in the Age of Progress*. New York: Oxford University Press, 2011.

Barzman, Sol. *Madmen and Geniuses: The Vice-Presidents of the United States*. Chicago: Follett Publishing Co., 1974.

Bauer, K. Jack. *The Mexican War, 1846–1848*. Lincoln: University of Nebraska Press, 1974.

Bederman, Gail. *Manliness & Civilization: A Cultural History of Gender and Race in the United States, 1880–1917*. Chicago: University of Chicago Press, 1995.

Belohlavek, John M. *George Mifflin Dallas: Jacksonian Patrician*. University Park: Pennsylvania State University Press, 1977.

Benemann, William. *Male–Male Intimacy in Early America: Beyond Romantic Friendships*. New York: Routledge, 2006.

Billias, George A. *Elbridge Gerry: Founding Father and Republican Statesman*. New York: McGraw-Hill, 1976.

Billingsley, Carolyn E. *Communities of Kinship: Antebellum Families and the Settlement of the Cotton Frontier*. Athens: University of Georgia Press, 2004.

Binder, Frederick M. *James Buchanan and the American Empire*. Selinsgrove, PA: Susquehanna University Press, 1994.

Birkner, Michael J., ed. *James Buchanan and the Political Crisis of the 1850s*. Selinsgrove, PA: Susquehanna University Press, 1996.

Blackman, Ann. *Wild Rose: The True Story of a Civil War Spy*. New York: Random House, 2006.

Blight, David. *Race and Reunion: The Civil War in American Memory*. Cambridge, MA: Harvard University Press, 2001.

Bogue, Alan G. *Clio & the Bitch Goddess: Quantification in American Political History*. Beverly Hills, Calif.: Sage Publications, 1983.

Boller, Paul F. Jr. *Presidential Anecdotes*. New York: Oxford University Press, 1996.

Bomberger, Christian M. *Twelfth Colony Plus: The Formative Years of Pennsylvania and a Biography of James Buchanan*. Jeannette, PA: Jeannette Publishing Co., 1934.

Bowling, Kenneth R., and Donald R. Kennon eds. *Establishing Congress: The Removal to Washington, D.C., and the Election of 1800*. Athens: Ohio University Press, 2005.

Brandt, Nat. *The Congressman Who Got Away with Murder*. Syracuse, NY: Syracuse University Press, 1991.

Brigance, William N. *Jeremiah Sullivan Black: A Defender of the Constitution and the Ten Commandments*. Philadelphia: University of Pennsylvania Press, 1934.

Brown, Steven B. *John McKinley and the Antebellum Supreme Court: Circuit Riding in the Old Southwest*. Tuscaloosa: University of Alabama Press, 2012.

Brown, William B. *The People's Choice: The Presidential Image in the Campaign Biography*. Baton Rouge: Louisiana State University Press, 1960.

Buell, Augustus C. *History of Andrew Jackson: Pioneer, Patriot, Soldier Politician, President*. 2 vols. New York: Charles Scribner's & Sons, 1904.

Burlingame, Michael. *Abraham Lincoln: A Life*. 2 vols. Baltimore: Johns Hopkins University Press, 2008–2013.

Bushman, Richard. *The Refinement of America: Persons, Houses, Cities*. New York: Knopf, 1992.

Cahalan, Sally S. *James Buchanan and His Family at Wheatland*. Lancaster, PA: privately printed, 1988.

Calhoun, Charles W. *Benjamin Harrison*. New York: Times Books, 2005.

Carnes, Mark C., and Clyde Griffen, eds. *Meaning for Manhood: Constructions of Masculinity in Victorian America*. Chicago: University of Chicago Press, 1990.

Cassell, Frank A. *Merchant Congressman in the Young Republic: Samuel Smith of Maryland, 1752–1839*. Madison: University of Wisconsin Press, 1971.

Catton, Bruce, ed. *John and Mary's College*. Westwood, NJ: Fleming H. Revell Co., 1956.

Cawthorne, Nigel. *Sex Lives of the Presidents: An Irreverent Expose of the Chief Executive form George Washington to the President Day*. New York: St. Martin's, 1996.

Chambers, William N. *Old Bullion Benton, Senator from the New West: Thomas Hart Benton, 1782–1858*. New York: Little, Brown, 1956.

Chapman, Mary, and Glenn Hendler, eds. *Sentimental Men: Masculinity and the Politics of Affect in American Culture*. Berkeley: University of California Press, 1999.

Chase, James S. *Emergence of the Presidential Nominating Convention, 1789–1832*. Urbana: University of Illinois Press, 1973.

Childers, Christopher. *The Failure of Popular Sovereignty: Slavery, Manifest Destiny, and the Radicalization of Southern Politics*. Lawrence: University Press of Kansas, 2012.

Chudacoff, Howard P. *The Age of the Bachelor: Creating an American Subculture*. Princeton, NJ: Princeton University Press, 1999.

Cleves, Rachel H. *Charity and Sylvia: A Same-Sex Marriage in Early America*. New York: Oxford University Press, 2014.

Cohen, Jeffrey J., ed. *Monster Theory: Reading Culture*. Minneapolis: University of Minnesota Press, 1996.

Coleman, John F. *The Disruption of the Pennsylvania Democracy, 1848–1860*. Harrisburg: Pennsylvania Historical and Museum Commission, 1975.

Cooper, William J. Jr. *Jefferson Davis, American*. New York: Knopf, 2000.

Cooper, William J. Jr. *The South and the Politics of Slavery, 1828–1856*. Baton Rouge: Louisiana State University Press, 1978.

Crain, Caleb. *American Sympathy: Men, Friendship, and Literature in the New Nation*. New Haven, CT: Yale University Press, 2001.

D'Emilio, John, and Estelle B. Freedman. *Intimate Matters: A History of Sexuality in America*. Chicago: University of Chicago Press, 1988.

Dangerfield, George. *The Era of Good Feelings*. New York: Harcourt, Brace, Co., 1952.

Davis, William C. *Breckinridge: Statesman, Soldier, Symbol*. Baton Rouge: Louisiana State University Press, 1974.

Davis, William C. *The Union That Shaped the Confederacy: Robert Toombs & Alexander H. Stephens*. Lawrence: University Press of Kansas, 2001.

DeVoto, Bernard. *The Year of Decision: 1846*. New York: Little, Brown, & Co., 1942.

Donehoo, George P., ed. *A History of the Cumberland Valley in Pennsylvania*. 2 vols. Harrisburg, PA: Susquehanna History Association, 1930.

Dorman, Levy. *Party Politics in Alabama from 1850 Through 1960*. Tuscaloosa: University of Alabama Press, 1995.

Drexler, Robert W. *Guilty of Making Peace: A Biography of Nicholas P. Trist*. Lanham, MD: University Press of America, 1991.

Duberman, Martin B. *About Time: Exploring the Gay Past; Revised and Expanded Edition*. New York: Plume, 1991.

Earle, Jonathan H. *Jacksonian Antislavery and the Politics of Free Soil, 1824–1854*. Chapel Hill: University of North Carolina Press, 2004.

Edmonds, Bobby F. *George McDuffie: Southern Orator*. McCormick, SC: Cedar Hill, 2007.

Egerton, Douglas R. *Year of Meteors: Stephen Douglas, Abraham Lincoln, and the Election that Brought on the Civil War*. New York: Bloomsbury Press, 2010.

Etcheson, Nicole. *Bleeding Kansas: Contested Liberty in the Civil War Era*. Lawrence: University of Kansas Press, 2004.

Ettinger, Amos A. *The Mission to Spain of Pierre Soule, 1853-1855: A Study in the Cuban Diplomacy of the United States*. New Haven: Yale University Press, 1932.

Eyal, Yonatan. *The Young America Movement and the Transformation of the Democratic Party, 1828–1861*. Cambridge: Cambridge University Press, 2007.

Faderman, Lillian. *Surpassing the Love of Men: Romantic Friendship and Love between Women from the Renaissance to the Present*. New York: Morrow, 1981.

Faflik, David. *Boarding Out: Inhabiting the American Urban Literary Imagination, 1840–1860*. Evanston, IL: Northwestern University Press, 2012.

Fehrenbacher, Don E. *The Dred Scott Case: Its Significance in American Law and Politics*. New York: Oxford University Press, 1978.

Finkelman, Paul, and Donald R. Kennon, eds. *In the Shadow of Freedom: The Politics of Slavery in the National Capital*. Athens: Ohio University Press, 2011.

Fitts, Alston, III. *Selma: Queen City of the Blackbelt*. Selma, AL: Clairmont Press, 1989.

Foltz, Charles S. *Surgeon of the Seas: The Adventurous Life of Surgeon General Jonathan M. Foltz in the Days of Wooden Ships*. New York: Bobbs-Merrill, 1931.

Foster, Thomas A., ed. *Long Before Stonewall: Histories of Same-Sex Sexuality in Early America*. New York: New York University Press, 2007.

Freehling, William W. *The Road to Disunion*. 2 vols. New York: Oxford University Press, 1990–2007.

Freeman, Joanne B. *Affairs of Honor: National Politics in the New Republic*. New Haven, CT: Yale University Press, 2002.

Freeman, Joanne B. *The Field of Blood: Violence in Congress and the Road to Civil War*. New York: FSG, 2018.

Friend, Craig T., ed. *Southern Masculinity: Perspectives on Manhood in the South Since Reconstruction*. Athens: University of Georgia Press, 2009.

Friend, Craig T., and Lorri Glover, eds. *Southern Manhood: Perspectives on Masculinity in the Old South*. Athens: University of Georgia Press, 2004.

Fuller, John D. P. *The Movement for the Acquisition of All Mexico, 1846–1848*. Baltimore: Johns Hopkins University Press, 1936.

Gamber, Wendy. *The Boardinghouse in Nineteenth-Century America*. Baltimore: Johns Hopkins University Press, 2007.

Gammon, Samuel R., Jr. *The Presidential Campaign of 1832*. Baltimore: Johns Hopkins University Press, 1922.

Gienapp, William E. *The Origins of the Republican Party, 1852–1856*. New York: Oxford University Press, 1987.

Gillette, Howard Jr., ed. *Southern City, National Ambition: The Growth of Early Washington, D.C., 1800–1860*. Washington, DC: American Architectural Foundation, 1995.

Godbeer, Richard. *The Overflowing of Friendship: Love between Men and the Creation of the American Republic*. Chapel Hill: University of North Carolina Press, 2009.

Good, Cassandra A. *Founding Friendships: Friendships between Men and Women in the Early American Republic*. New York: Oxford University Press, 2015.

Graebner, Norman A. *Empire on the Pacific: A Study in American Continental Expansion*. New York: Ronald Press, 1955.

Green, Constance M. *Washington: Village and Capital, 1800–1878*. Princeton, NJ: Princeton University Press, 1962.

Green, Edwin L. *George McDuffie*. Columbia, SC: State Company, 1936.

Greenberg, Amy S. *A Wicked War: Polk, Clay, Lincoln, and the 1846 U.S. Invasion of Mexico*. New York: Knopf, 2012.

Greenberg, Amy S. *Cause for Alarm: The Volunteer Fire Department in the Nineteenth-Century City*. Princeton, NJ: Princeton University Press, 1998.

Greenberg, Amy S. *Lady First: The World of First Lady Sarah Polk*. New York: Knopf, 2019.

Greenberg, Amy S. *Manifest Manhood and the Antebellum American Empire*. New York: Cambridge University Press, 2005.

Greven, David. *Gender Protest and Same-Sex Desire in Antebellum American Literature*. Routledge: New York, 2016.

Gunderson, Robert G. *The Log-Cabin Campaign*. Lexington: University of Kentucky Press, 1957.

Hall, Claude H. *Abel Parker Upshur: Conservative Virginian, 1790–1844*. Madison: State Historical Society of Wisconsin, 1963.

Halperin, David M. *How to Do the History of Homosexuality*. Chicago: University of Chicago Press, 2004.

Hamilton, Holman. *Prologue to Conflict: The Crisis and Compromise of 1850*. Lexington: University Press of Kentucky, 1964.

Hardwick, Elizabeth. *Herman Melville*. New York: Penguin, 2000.

Hartog, Hendrick. *Man and Wife in America: A History*. Cambridge, MA: Harvard University Press, 2000.

Hietala, Thomas R. *Manifest Design: American Exceptionalism and Empire (Revised Edition)*. Ithaca, NY: Cornell University Press, 2003.

Hildt, John C. *Early Diplomatic Negotiations of the United States with Russia*. Baltimore: Johns Hopkins University Press, 1906.

Hoffman, Ronald, and Peter J. Albert, eds. *Women in the Age of the American Revolution*. Charlottesville: University of Virginia, 1989.

Hofstadter, Richard. *The Idea of Party: The Rise of Legitimate Opposition in the United States, 1780–1840*. Berkeley: University of California Press, 1969.

Holt, Michael F. *Political Parties and American Political Development from the Age of Jackson to the Age of Lincoln*. Baton Rouge: Louisiana State University Press, 1992.

Holt, Michael F. *The Election of 1860: "A Campaign Fraught with Consequences."* Lawrence: University Press of Kansas, 2017.

Holt, Michael F. *The Political Crisis of the 1850s*. New York: Wiley, 1978.

Holt, Michael F. *The Rise and Fall of the American Whig Party: Jacksonian Politics and the Onset of the Civil War*. New York: Oxford University Press, 1999.

Holzer, Harold, Gabor S. Boritt, and Marc E. Neely, Jr. *The Lincoln Image: Abraham Lincoln and the Popular Print*. New York: Scribner Press, 1984; reprint: Urbana: University of Illinois Press, 2001.

Horrocks, Thomas A. *President James Buchanan and the Crisis of National Leadership*. Hauppauge, NY: Nova Science Publisher's, Inc., 2011.

Howe, Daniel W. *The Political Culture of the American Whigs*. Chicago: University of Chicago Press, 1979.

Howe, Daniel W. *What Hath God Wrought: The Transformation of America, 1815–1848*. New York: Oxford University Press, 2007.

Hurd, Charles. *Washington Cavalcade*. New York: E. P. Dutton & Co., 1948.

Huston, James L. *The Panic of 1857 and the Coming of the Civil War*. Baton Rouge: Louisiana State University Press, 1987.

Irelan, John R. *The Republic; or, a History of the United States of America in the Administrations, From the Monarchic Colonial Days to the Present Times*. 18 vols. Chicago: Fairbanks and Palmer, 1888.

Jabour, Anya. *Marriage in the Early Republic: Elizabeth and William Wirt and the Companionate Ideal*. Baltimore: Johns Hopkins University Press, 1998.

Jackson, Walter M. *Alabama's First United States Vice-President: William Rufus King*. Decatur, AL: Decatur Printing Co., 1952.

Janes, Dominic. *Oscar Wilde Prefigured: Queer Fashioning and British Caricature, 1750–1900*. Chicago: University of Chicago Press, 2016.

Janney, Caroline E. *Remembering the Civil War: Reunion and the Limits of Reconciliation*. Chapel Hill: University of North Carolina Press, 2013.

Jensen, Richard J. *The Winning of the Midwest: Social and Political Conflict, 1888–1896*. Chicago: University of Chicago Press, 1971.

Johannsen, Robert W. *Stephen A. Douglas*. Urbana: University of Illinois Press, 1973.

Johnson, Douglas. *Guizot: Aspects of French History, 1787–1874*. Toronto: University of Toronto Press, 1963.

Jones, Houston G. *Bedford Brown: State Rights Unionist*. Carrollton: West Georgia College, 1955.

Kahan, Paul. *Amiable Scoundrel: Simon Cameron, Lincoln's Scandalous Secretary of War*. Lincoln, NE: Potomac Books, 2016.

Kann, Mark E. *A Republic of Men: The American Founders, Gendered Language, and Patriarchal Politics*. New York: New York University Press, 1998.

Kaplan, Catherine. *Men of Letters in the Early Republic: Cultivating Forums of Citizenship*. Chapel Hill: University of North Carolina, 2008.

Karp, Matthew. *This Vast Southern Empire: Slaveholders at the Helm of American Foreign Policy*. Cambridge, MA: Harvard University Press, 2016.

Katz, Jonathan N. *Love Stories: Sex between Men before Homosexuality*. Chicago: University of Chicago Press, 2001.

Katz, Jonathan N. *The Invention of Heterosexuality*. New York: Plume, 1995.

Kelly, Catherine E. *Republic of Taste: Art, Politics, and Everyday Life in Early America*. Philadelphia: University of Pennsylvania Press, 2016.

Kimmel, Michael S., and Thomas E. Mosmiller, eds. *Against the Tide: Pro-Feminist Men in the United States, 1776-1990, a Documentary History*. Boston: Beacon Press, 1992.

Klein, Harry M. J. *A Century of Education at Mercersburg, 1836–1936*. Lancaster, PA: Lancaster Press, Inc., 1936.

Klein, Harry M. J. *Lancaster's Golden Century, 1821–1921: A Chronicle of Men and Women Who Planned and Toiled to Build a City Strong and Beautiful*. Lancaster, PA: Hagar and Bro., 1921.

Klein, Harry M. J., and William F. Diller. *The History of St. James' Church (Protestant Episcopal), 1744–1944*. Lancaster, PA: St. James' Church, 1944.

Klein, Herbert. *A Population History of the United States (Second Edition)*. New York: Cambridge University Press, 2012.

Klein, Philip S. *Pennsylvania Politics, 1817–1832: A Game Without Rules*. Philadelphia: Historical Society of Pennsylvania, 1940; reprint: Philadelphia: Porcupine Press, 1974.

Klein, Philip S. *President James Buchanan: A Biography*. Newtown, CT: Pennsylvania State University Press, 1962.

Klepp, Susan E. *Revolutionary Conceptions: Women, Fertility, and Family Limitation in America, 1760-1820*. Chapel Hill: University of North Carolina Press, 2009.

Kleppner, Paul. *The Third Electoral System, 1853–1892: Parties, Voters, and Political Cultures*. Chapel Hill: University of North Carolina Press, 1979.

Klunder Willard C. *Lewis Cass and the Politics of Moderation*. Kent, OH: Kent State University Press, 1996.

Kramer, Larry J. *The American People: Volume 1: Search for My Heart: A Novel*. New York: Picador, 2015.

Landis, Michael J. *Northern Men with Southern Loyalties: The Democratic Party and the Sectional Crisis*. Ithaca, NY: Cornell University Press, 2014.

Leech, Margaret. *Reveille in Washington, 1860–1865*. New York: Harper & Brothers, 1941.

Lepler, Jessica M. *The Many Panics of 1837: People, Politics, and the Creation of a Transatlantic Financial Crisis*. Cambridge: Cambridge University Press, 2013.

Lewis, Charlene M. Boyer. *Ladies and Gentlemen on Display: Planter Society at the Virginia Springs, 1790–1860*. Charlottesville: University of Virginia Press, 2001.

Lewis, Herbert J. *Clearing the Thickets: A History of Antebellum Alabama*. New Orleans: Quid Pro Books, 2013.

Lincoln, W. Bruce. *Nicholas I: Emperor and Autocrat of All the Russias*. Bloomington: Indiana University Press, 1980.

Loewen, James W. *Lies Across America: What Our Historic Sites Get Wrong*. New York: New Press, 1999.

MacKinnon, William P., ed. *At Sword's Point: A Documentary History of the Utah War*. 2 vols. Norman, OK: Arthur H. Clark Co., 2008–2016.

Mahin, Dean B. *Olive Branch and Sword: The United States and Mexico, 1845–1848*. Jefferson, NC: McFarland & Co., 1997.

Marbut, F. B. *News from the Capital: The Story of Washington Reporting*. Carbondale: Southern Illinois University Press, 1971.

Marcus, Sharon. *Between Women: Friendship, Desire, and Marriage in Victorian England*. Princeton, NJ: Princeton University Press, 2007,

Martin, Asa E. *After the White House*. State College, PA: Penns Valley Publisher, 1951.

Martin, Robert K. *Hero, Captain, Stranger: Male Friendship, Social Critique, and Literary Form in the Sea Novels of Herman Melville*. Chapel Hill: University of North Carolina Press, 1986.

Marvel, William. *Lincoln's Autocrat: The Life of Edwin Stanton*. Chapel Hill: University of North Carolina Press, 2015.

Marzalek, John F. *The Petticoat Affair: Manners, Mutiny, and Sex in Andrew Jackson's White House*. Baton Rouge: Louisiana State University Press, 1997.

Matthews, Christopher. *Kennedy & Nixon: The Rivalry that Shaped Postwar America*. New York: Simon & Schuster, 1996.

May, Gary. *John Tyler*. New York: Times Books, 2008.

May, Robert E. *The Southern Dream of a Caribbean Empire, 1854–1861*. Baton Rouge: Louisiana State University Press, 1973; reprint: Gainesville: University Press of Florida, 2002.

McCall, Laura, and Donald Yacovone, eds. *A Shared Experience: Men, Women, and the History of Gender*. New York: New York University Press, 1998.

McClintock, Russell. *Lincoln and the Decision for War: The Northern Response to Secession*. Chapel Hill: University of North Carolina Press, 2008.

McCormick, Richard. *The Presidential Game: The Origins of American Presidential Politics*. New York: Oxford University Press, 1982.

McCormick, Richard. *The Second American Party System: Party Formation in the Jacksonian Era*. Chapel Hill: University of North Carolina Press, 1966.

McCurdy, John G. *Citizen Bachelors: Manhood and the Creation of the United States*. Ithaca, NY: Cornell University Press, 2009.

McIlwain, Christopher L. Jr. *1865 Alabama, from Civil War to Uncivil Peace*. Tuscaloosa: University of Alabama Press, 2017.

McMillan, Malcolm C. *Constitutional Development in Alabama, 1798–1901: A Study in Politics, the Negro, and Sectionalism*. Chapel Hill: University of North Carolina Press, 1955.

Meacham, Jon. *American Lion: Andrew Jackson in the White House*. New York: Random House, 2009.

Medhurst, Martin J., ed. *Before the Rhetorical Presidency*. College Station: Texas A&M University Press, 2008.

Mellichamp, Josephine. *Senators from Georgia*. Huntsville, AL: Strode Publishers, 1976.

Merk, Frederick. *Slavery and the Annexation of Texas*. New York: Knopf, 1972.

Merk, Frederick. *The Monroe Doctrine and American Expansionism, 1843–1849*. New York: Knopf, 1966.

Merry, Robert W. *A Country of Vast Designs: James K. Polk, the Mexican War, and the Conquest of the American Continent*. New York: Simon & Schuster, 2009.

Merry, Robert W. *Where They Stand: The American Presidents in the Eyes of Voters and Historians*. New York: Simon & Schuster, 2012.

Miller, William L. *President Lincoln: The Duty of a Statesman*. New York: Vintage, 2008.

Milton, George F. *The Eve of Conflict: Stephen A. Douglas and the Needless War*. Boston: Houghton Mifflin Company, 1934.

Moore, Albert B. *History of Alabama*. Tuscaloosa: Alabama Book Store, 1934.

Morgan, James H. *Dickinson College: The History of One Hundred and Fifty Years, 1783–1933*. Carlisle, PA: Dickinson College, 1933.

Morris, Linda A. *Gender Play in Mark Twain: Cross-dressing and Transgression*. Columbia: University of Missouri Press, 2007.

Morrison, Michael A. *Slavery and the American West: The Eclipse of Manifest Destiny*. Chapel Hill: University of North Carolina Press, 1997.

Munroe, John A. *Louis McLane: Federalist and Jacksonian*. New Brunswick, NJ: Rutgers University Press, 1973.

Murphy, Kevin P. *Political Manhood: Red Bloods, Mollycoddles, & the Politics of Progressive Era Reform*. New York: Columbia University Press, 2008.

Murphy, Teresa A. *Citizenship and the Origins of Women's History in the United States*. Philadelphia: University of Pennsylvania Press, 2013.

Neely, Marc E. Jr. *The Boundaries of American Political Culture in the Civil War Era*. Chapel Hill: University of North Carolina Press, 2005.

Nelson, Dana D. *National Manhood: Capitalist Citizenship and the Imagined Fraternity of White Men*. Durham, NC: Duke University Press, 1998.

Nevins, Allan. *Ordeal of the Union, Vol. 1: Fruits of Manifest Destiny, 1847–1852; A House Dividing, 1852–1857*. New York: Collier Books, 1992.

Nevins, Allan. *Ordeal of the Union, Vol. 2: The Emergence of Lincoln: Douglas, Buchanan, and Party Crisis, 1857–1859; Prologue to Civil War, 1857–1861*. New York: Collier Books, 1992.

Nichols, Roy F. *Franklin Pierce: Young Hickory of the Granite Hills (Second Edition)*. Philadelphia: University of Pennsylvania Press, 1958.

Nichols, Roy F. *The Democratic Machine, 1850–1854*. New York: Columbia University Press, 1928.

Nichols, Roy F. *The Disruption of American Democracy*. New York: Macmillan Co., 1948.

Niven, John. *Martin Van Buren: The Romantic Age of American Politics*. New York: Oxford University Press, 1983.

Nuermberger, Ruth K. *The Clays of Alabama: A Planter-Lawyer-Politician Family*. Lexington: University of Kentucky Press, 1958.

Oates, John A. *The History of Fayetteville and the Upper Cape Fear*. Fayetteville, NC: privately printed, 1950.

Oeste, George I. *John Randolph Clay: America's First Career Diplomat*. Philadelphia: University of Pennsylvania Press, 1966.

Ohrt, Wallace. *Defiant Peacemaker: Nicholas Trist in the Mexican War*. College Station: Texas A&M University Press, 1997.

Orser, Joseph A. *The Lives of Chang & Eng: Siam's Twins in Nineteenth-Century America*. Chapel Hill: University of North Carolina Press, 2014.

Osthaus, Carl R. *Partisans of the Southern Press: Editorial Spokesmen of the Nineteenth Century*. Lexington: University Press of Kentucky, 1994.

Pace, Robert F. *Halls of Honor: College Men in the Old South*. Baton Rouge: Louisiana State University Press, 2004.

Parker, Alison M., and Sarah B. Gordon. *Women and the Unstable State in Nineteenth-Century America*. College Station: Texas A&M University Press, 2000.

Parker, Franklin. *George Peabody, a Biography (Revised Edition)*. Nashville, TN: Vanderbilt University Press, 1995.

Parsons, Elaine F. *Manhood Lost: Fallen Drunkards and Redeeming Women in the Nineteenth-Century United States*. Baltimore: Johns Hopkins University Press, 2003.

Parsons, Lynn H. *The Birth of Modern Politics: Andrew Jackson, John Quincy Adams, and the Election of 1828*. New York: Oxford University Press, 2009.

Peterson, Merrill D. *The Great Triumvirate: Webster, Clay, Calhoun*. New York: Oxford University Press, 1987.

Peterson, Norma L. *The Presidencies of William Henry Harrison & John Tyler*. Lawrence: University Press of Kansas, 1989.

Pierson, Michael D. *Free Hearts & Free Homes: Gender and American Antislavery Politics*. Chapel Hill: University of North Carolina Press, 2003.

Pinsker, Matthew. *Lincoln's Sanctuary: Abraham Lincoln and the Soldiers' Home*. New York: Oxford University Press, 2003.

Plater, David D. *The Butlers of Iberville Parish, Louisiana: Dunboyne Plantation in the 1800s*. Baton Rouge: Louisiana State University Press, 2015.

Pletcher, David M. *The Diplomacy of Annexation: Texas, Oregon, and the Mexican War*. Columbia: University of Missouri Press, 1973.

Poole, Keith T., and Howard Rosenthal. *Congress: A Political-Economic History of Roll Call Voting*. New York: Oxford University Press, 1997.

Potter, David M. *Lincoln and His Party in the Secession Crisis*. New Haven, CT: Yale University Press, 1942.

Potter, David M. *The Impending Crisis, 1848–1861*. New York: Harper & Row, 1976.

Quist, John W., and Michael J. Birkner, eds. *James Buchanan and the Coming of the Civil War*. Gainesville: University Press of Florida, 2013.

Rapport, Michael. *1848: Year of Revolution*. New York: Basic Books, 2009.

Ratcliffe, Donald J. *The One-Party Presidential Contest: Adams, Jackson, and 1824's Five-horse Race*. Lawrence: University Press of Kansas, 2015.

Rauch, Basil. *American Interest in Cuba: 1848–1855*. New York: Columbia University Press, 1948.

Reeves, Jesse S. *American Diplomacy under Tyler and Polk*. Baltimore: Johns Hopkins Press, 1907.

Reid, Robert L. *Howell Cobb: A Biography*. Baton Rouge: Louisiana State University Press, 1995.

Remini, Robert V. *Andrew Jackson*. 3 vols. New York: Harper & Row, 1977–1984.

Remini, Robert V. *Henry Clay: Statesmen for the Union*. New York: Norton, 1991.

Rhodes, James F. *History of the United States from the Compromise of 1850*. New York: Macmillan, 1892.

Richards, Leonard L. *The Slave Power: The Free North and Southern Domination, 1780–1860*. Baton Rouge: Louisiana State University Press, 2000.

Ridley, Jane. *The Heir Apparent: A Life of Edward VII, the Playboy Prince*. New York: Random House, 2013.

Robb, Graham. *Strangers: Homosexual Love in the Nineteenth Century*. New York: Norton, 2003.

Roberts, Timothy M. *Distant Revolutions: 1848 and the Challenge to American Exceptionalism*. Charlottesville: University of Virginia Press, 2009.

Ross, Shelley. *Fall from Grace: Sex, Scandal, and Corruption in American Politics from 1702 to the Present*. New York: Ballantine Books, 1988.

Rotundo, E. Anthony. *American Manhood: Transformations in Masculinity from the Revolution to the Modern Era*. New York: Basic Books, 1993.

Sacher, John M. *A Perfect War of Politics: Parties, Politicians, and Democracy in Louisiana, 1824–1861*. Baton Rouge: Louisiana State University Press, 2003.

Sandburg, Carl. *Abraham Lincoln: The War Years*. 4 vols. New York: Harcourt, Brace, & Co., 1939.

Saul, Norman E. *Distant Friends: The United States and Russia, 1763–1867*. Lawrence: University Press of Kansas, 1991.

Schlesinger, Arthur, M. Jr. *The Age of Jackson*. New York: Little, Brown, 1945.

Schouler, Justin. *History of the United States under the Constitution*. 7 vols. New York: Dodd, Mead, & Co, 1880–1913.

Schweitzer, Ivy. *Perfecting Friendship: Politics and Affiliation in Early American Literature*. Chapel Hill: University of North Carolina Press, 2006.

Seager, Robert II. *And Tyler, Too: A Biography of John & Julia Gardiner Tyler*. New York: McGraw-Hill, 1963.

Seale, William. *The President's House: A History.* 2 vols. Washington, DC: White House Historical Association, 1986.

Seale, William, ed. *The White House: Actors and Observers.* Boston: Northeastern University Press, 2002.

Sellers, Charles G. *James K. Polk, Continentalist, 1843–1846.* Princeton, NJ: Princeton University Press, 1966.

Sellers, Charles G. *James K. Polk, Jacksonian, 1795–1843.* Princeton, NJ: Princeton University Press, 1957.

Sellers, Charles G. *The Market Revolution: Jacksonian America, 1815-1846.* New York, Oxford University Press, 1991.

Sharlet, Jeff. *C Street: The Fundamental Thread to American Democracy.* New York: Little, Brown & Co., 2010.

Shelden, Rachel A. *Washington Brotherhood: Politics, Social Life, and the Coming of the Civil War.* Chapel Hill: University of North Carolina Press, 2013.

Shenton, James P. *Robert John Walker: A Politician from Jackson to Lincoln.* New York: Columbia University Press, 1961.

Sibley, Katherine A.S., ed. *A Companion to First Ladies.* Malden, MA: Wiley-Blackwell Publishing, 2016.

Silbey, Joel H., ed. *A Companion to the Antebellum Presidents, 1837–1861.* Malden, MA: Wiley Blackwell, 2014.

Silbey, Joel H. *Party Over Section: The Rough and Ready Presidential Election of 1848.* Lawrence: University of Kansas Press, 2009.

Silbey, Joel H. *The Shrine of Party: Congressional Voting Behavior, 1841–1852.* Pittsburgh: University of Pittsburgh Press, 1967.

Silverthorne, Elizabeth. *Ashbel Smith of Texas: Pioneer, Patriot, Statesman, 1805–1886.* College Station: Texas A&M University Press, 1982.

Slaymaker, Samuel R., II. *Captives' Mansion.* New York: Harper & Row, 1973.

Smith, Adam I. P. *The Stormy Present: Conservatism and the Problem of Slavery in Northern Politics, 1846–1865.* Chapel Hill: University of North Carolina Press, 2017.

Smith, Elbert B. *The Presidency of James Buchanan.* Lawrence: University Press of Kansas, 1975.

Smith, Justin H. *The Annexation of Texas.* New York: Macmillan Co., 1911.

Smith, Justin H. *The War with Mexico.* 2 vols. New York: Macmillan Co., 1919.

Snyder, Charles M. *The Jacksonian Heritage: Pennsylvania Politics, 1833–1848.* Harrisburg: Pennsylvania Historical and Museum Commission, 1958.

Snyder, Christina. *Great Crossings: Indians, Settlers, and Slaves in the Age of Jackson.* New York: Oxford University Press, 2017.

Sparks, Patricia M. *Gossip.* New York: Knopf, 1985.

Stampp, Kenneth M. *America in 1857: A Nation on the Brink.* New York: Oxford University Press, 1990.

Stampp, Kenneth M. *And the War Came: The North and the Secession Crisis, 1860–1861.* Baton Rouge: Louisiana State University Press, 1950.

Stegmaier, Mark J. *Texas, New Mexico, and the Compromise of 1850: Boundary Dispute and Sectional Crisis.* Kent, OH: Kent State University Press, 1996.

Stowe, Steven M. *Intimacy and Power in the Old South: Ritual in the Lives of the Planters.* Baltimore: Johns Hopkins University Press, 1987.

Strauss, Robert. *Worst. President. Ever.: James Buchanan, the POTUS Rating Game, and the Legacy of the Least of the Lesser Presidents.* Guilford, CT: Lyons Press, 2016.

Strozier, Charles B. *Your Friend Forever, A. Lincoln: The Enduring Friendship of Abraham Lincoln and Joshua Speed.* New York: Columbia University Press, 2016.

Sulzby, James Jr. *Historic Alabama Hotels & Resorts.* Tuscaloosa: University of Alabama Press, 1960.

Summers, Charles, ed. *Homosexuality in Renaissance and Enlightenment England: Literary Representations in Historical Context.* Binghamton, NY: Haworth Press, 1992; reprint: New York: Routledge, 2013.

Summers, Mark W. *The Plundering Generation: Corruption and the Crisis of the Union, 1849–1861.* New York: Oxford University Press, 1987.

Sumner, Margaret. *Collegiate Republic: Cultivating an Ideal Society in Early America.* Charlottesville: University of Virginia Press, 2014.

Swanberg, William A. *Sickles the Incredible.* New York: Scribner, 1956.

Swisher, Carl B. *The Taney Period, 1836–64.* New York: Macmillan Publishing Co., 1974.

Syrett, Nicholas. *The Company He Keeps: A History of White College Fraternities.* Chapel Hill: University of North Carolina Press, 2009.

Thomas, Benjamin P., and Harold M. Hyman. *Stanton: The Life and Times of Lincoln's Secretary of War.* New York: Knopf, 1962; reprint: Westport, CT: Greenwood Press, 1980.

Thompson, Carl. *The Suffering Traveller and the Romantic Imagination.* New York: Oxford University Press, 2007.

Thornton, John M., III. *Politics and Power in a Slave Society: Alabama, 1800–1860.* Baton Rouge: Louisiana State University Press, 1978.

Travers, Len. *Celebrating the Fourth: Independence Day and the Rites of Nationalism in the Early Republic.* Amherst: University of Massachusetts Press, 1997.

Tripp, C. A. *The Intimate World of Abraham Lincoln.* New York: Thunder's Mouth Press, 2005.

Tschachler, Heinz. *The Monetary Imagination of Edgar Allan Poe: Banking, Currency and Politics in the Writings.* Jefferson, NC: McFarland, 2013.

Updike, John. *Buchanan Dying: A Play.* New York: Knopf, 1974.

Updike, John. *Memories of the Ford Administration.* New York: Knopf, 1992.

Upton, Harriet Taylor. *Our Early Presidents, Their Wives and Children.* Boston: D. Lathrop Co., 1891.

Varon, Elizabeth R. *Disunion!: The Coming of the American Civil War, 1789–1859.* Chapel Hill: University of North Carolina Press, 2008.

Vicinus, Martha. *Intimate Friends: Women Who Loved Women, 1778–1928.* Chicago: University of Chicago Press, 2004.

Vipperman, Carl J. *William Lowndes and the Transition of Southern Politics*. Chapel Hill: University of North Carolina Press, 1989.

Wallace, Irving, and Amy Wallace. *The Two: The Story of the Original Siamese Twins*. New York: Simon & Schuster, 1978.

Wallner, Peter A. *Franklin Pierce*. 2 vols. Concord, NH: Plaidswede Publishing, 2004–2007.

Walther, Eric H. *The Fire-Eaters*. Baton Rouge: Louisiana State University Press, 1992.

Watson, Elbert L. *Alabama United States Senators*. Huntsville, AL: Strode Publishers, 1982.

Watson, Harry L. *Liberty and Power: The Politics of Jacksonian America (Second Edition)*. New York: Hill & Wang 2006.

Watson, Robert P. *Affairs of State: The Untold History of Presidential Love, Sex, and Scandal, 1789–1900*. Lanham, MD: Rowman & Littlefield, 2012.

White, Leonard D. *The Jacksonians: A Study in Administrative History, 1829–1861*. New York: MacMillan, 1954.

Wilentz, Sean. *The Rise of American Democracy, Jefferson to Lincoln*. New York: Norton, 2006.

Williams, Timothy J. *Intellectual Manhood: University, Self, and Society in the Antebellum South*. Chapel Hill: University of North Carolina Press, 2015.

Wood, Gordon S. *Empire of Liberty: A History of the Early Republic, 1789–1815*. New York: Oxford University Press, 2011.

Young, James S. *The Washington Community, 1820–1828*. New York: Columbia University Press, 1963.

Zagarri, Rosemary. *Revolutionary Backlash: Women and Politics in the Early American Republic*. Philadelphia: University of Pennsylvania Press, 2007.

Zakim, Michael. *Ready-Made Democracy: A History of Men's Dress in the American Republic, 1760–1860*. Chicago: University of Chicago Press, 2006.

ARTICLES AND CHAPTERS

Allman, William G. "The White House Collection from James Buchanan's Time." *White House History*. Vol. 12 (Winter 2003): 62–65.

Ambacher, Bruce. "George M. Dallas, Cuba, and the Election of 1856." *Pennsylvania Magazine of History and Biography*. Vol. 97, no. 3 (July 1973): 318–32.

Atkins, Jonathan M. "'The Purest Democrat': The Career of Congressman George W. Jones." *Tennessee Historical Quarterly*. Vol. 65, no. 1 (Spring 2006): 2–21.

Auchampaugh, Philip G. "A Forgotten Journey of An Antebellum President: The Trip and Addresses of James Buchanan Delivered During His Journey to the Commencement of the University of North Carolina at Chapel Hill in 1859." Richmond, VA: privately printed, 1935.

Auchampaugh, Philip G. "James Buchanan During the Administrations of Lincoln and Johnston." *Historical Papers and Addresses of the Lancaster County Historical Society*. Vol. 43, no. 3 (1939): 67–111.

Auchampaugh, Philip G. "James Buchanan, the Bachelor of the White House: An Inquiry on the Subject of Feminine Influence in the Life of Our Fifteenth President." *Tyler's Quarterly Historical and Genealogical Magazine*. Vol. 20, no. 3 and 4 (Jan. and April 1939): 154–66, 218–34.

Auchampaugh, Philip G. "James Buchanan, the Court, and the Dred Scott Case." *Tennessee Historical Magazine*. Vol. 9, no. 4 (Jan. 1926): 231–40.

Auchampaugh, Philip G. "James Buchanan, the Squire from Lancaster: The Squire's Home Town." *Pennsylvania Magazine of History and Biography*. Vol. 55 and 56, no. 4 and 1 (1931–1932): 289–300, 15–32.

Auchampaugh, Philip G. "John W. Forney, Robert Tyler and James Buchanan." *Tyler's Quarterly Genealogical Magazine*. Vol. 15, no. 2 (Oct. 1934):

Bailey, Hugh C. "Israel Pickens, People's Politician." *Alabama Review*. Vol. 17 (April 1964): 83–101.

Balcerski, Thomas J. "'A General Concurrence in the Propriety of the Repeal': Male Friendship, Party, and Section in the Kansas-Nebraska Bill." *Civil War History*. Vol. 65, no. 2 (June 2019): 157-183.

Balcerski, Thomas J. "'A Work of Friendship': Nathaniel Hawthorne, Franklin Pierce, and the Politics of Enmity in the Civil War Era." *Journal of Social History*. Vol. 50, no. 4 (Summer 2017): 655–79.

Basch, Norma. "Marriage, Morals, and Politics in the Election of 1828." *Journal of American History*. Vol. 80, no. 3 (Dec. 1993): 890–918.

Becker, Carl. "The Unit Rule in National Nominating Conventions." *American Historical Review*. Vol. 5, no. 1 (Oct. 1899): 64–82.

Belohlavek, John M. "The Democracy in a Dilemma: George M. Dallas, Pennsylvania, and the Election of 1844." *Pennsylvania History*. Vol. 41, no. 4 (Oct. 1974): 390–411.

Bergeron, Paul H. "All in the Family: President Polk in the White House." *Tennessee Historical Quarterly*. Vol. 46, no. 1 (Spring 1987): 10–20.

Binder, Frederick M. "James Buchanan and the Earl of Clarendon: An Uncertain Relationship." *Diplomacy and Statecraft*. Vol. 6, no. 2 (July 1995): 323–41.

Birkner, Michael. "A Conversation with Philip S. Klein." *Pennsylvania History*. Vol. 56, no. 4 (Oct. 1989): 243–75.

Bogue, Allan, and Mark P. Marlaire. "Of Mess and Men: The Boardinghouse and Congressional Voting, 1821–1842." *American Journal of Political Science*. Vol. 19, no. 2 (May 1975): 207–30.

Boyer, Paul. "Notes of a Disillusioned Lover: John Updike's 'Memories of the Ford Administration.'" *American Literary History*. Vol. 13, no. 1 (Spring 2001): 67–78.

Boyer, Peter J. "Frat House for Jesus: The Entity Behind C Street." *The New Yorker*. Sept. 13, 2010.

Bridges, Edwin C. "'The Nation's Guest': The Marquis de Lafayette's Tour of Alabama." *Alabama Heritage*. Vol. 102 (Fall 2011): 8–17.

Brooks, Daniel F. "The Faces of William R. King." *Alabama Heritage*. Vol. 69 (Summer 2003): 14–23.

Brown, Thomas. "The Miscegenation of Richard Mentor Johnson as an Issue in the National Election Campaign of 1835–1836." *Civil War History*. Vol. 39 (March 1993): 5–30.

Carrafiello, Michael L. "Diplomatic Failure: James Buchanan' Inaugural Address." *Pennsylvania History*. Vol. 77, no. 2 (Spring 2010): 145–65.

Casper, Scott E. "An Uneasy Marriage of Sentiment and Scholarship: Elizabeth F. Ellet and the Domestic Origins of American Women's History." *Journal of Women's History*. Vol. 4, no. 2 (Fall 1992): 10–35.

Churcher, Sharon. "First Gay President?" *Penthouse Magazine*. Vol. 19, no. 3 (Nov. 1987): 16.

Clark, Martha B. "Who Was Jacob Hibshman, the Congressman from Lancaster County?" *Historical Papers and Addresses of the Lancaster County Historical Society*. Vol. 15, no. 7 (1911): 219–21.

Cleves, Rachel H. "'What, Another Female Husband?': The Prehistory of Same-Sex Marriage in America." *Journal of American History*. Vol. 101, no. 4 (Mar. 2015): 1055–81.

Cole, Allen F. "Asserting His Authority: James Buchanan's Failed Vindication." *Pennsylvania History*. Vol. 70, no. 1 (Winter 2003): 81–97.

"Colonel John McKee." *Alabama Historical Quarterly*. Vol. 3, no. 1 (Spring 1941): 15–22.

Connolly, Michael J. "'Tearing Down the Burning House': James Buchanan's Use of Edmund Burke." *American Nineteenth Century History*. Vol. 10, no. 2 (June 2009): 211–21.

Cullen, Elizabeth O. "The Coming of the Railroads to Washington, D.C." *Records of the Columbia Historical Society, Washington, D.C.* Vol. 57/59 (1957/1959): 26–32.

Curran, Daniel J. "Polk, Politics, and Patronage: The Rejection of George W. Woodward's Nomination to the Supreme Court." *Pennsylvania Magazine of History and Biography*. Vol. 121, no. 3 (July 1997): 163–99.

DeFiore, Jayne C. "COME, and Bring the Ladies: Tennessee Women and the Politics of Opportunity during the Presidential Campaign of 1840 and 1844." *Tennessee Historical Quarterly*. Vol. 51 (Winter 1992): 197–212.

Ditz, Toby L. "The New Men's History and the Peculiar Absence of Gendered Power: Some Remedies from Early American Gender History." *Gender and History*. Vol. 16, no. 1 (April 2004): 1–35.

Donovan, Theresa A. "President Pierce's Ministers at the Court of St. James." *Pennsylvania Magazine of History and Biography*. Vol. 91, no. 4 (Oct. 1967): 457–70.

Durham, Walter T. "Tennessee Countess." *Tennessee Historical Quarterly*. Vol. 39, no. 3 (Fall 1980): 323–40.

Earman, Cynthia D. "A Census of Early Boardinghouses." *Washington History*. Vol. 12, no. 1 (Spring/Summer 2000): 118–21.

Faulkner, Claire. "President Buchanan Greets a Guest of State: The Prince of Wales." *White House History*. Vol. 12 (2003): 410–19.

Finn, Dallas. "Guests of the Nation: The Japanese Delegation to the Buchanan White House." *White House History*. Vol. 12 (2003): 372–96.

Fischer, Roger A. "Rustic Rasputin: William A. Peffer in Color Cartoon Art, 1891–1899." *Kansas History*. Vol. 11 (Winter 1988–1989): 222–39.

Gendzel, Glen. "Political Culture: Genealogy of a Concept," *Journal of Interdisciplinary History*. Vol. 28, no. 2 (Autumn 1997): 225–50.

Hatfield, Mark O. "Vice Presidents of the United States, 1789–1993: William Rufus King." Washington, DC: US Government Printing Office, 1997.

Hensel, William U. "James Buchanan as a Lawyer." *University of Pennsylvania Law Review and American Law Register*. Vol. 60, no. 8 (May 1912): 546–81.

Hensel, William U. "The Attitude of James Buchanan, a Citizen of Lancaster County, Towards the Institution of Slavery in the United States." Lancaster, PA: New Era, 1911.

Herrmann, Steven B. "Melville's Portrait of Same-Sex Marriage in *Moby-Dick*." *Jung Journal: Culture & Psyche*. Vol. 4, no. 3 (Summer 2010): 65–82.

Hostetter, Ida L. K. "Harriet Lane (Later Harriet Lane Johnston)." *Historical Papers and Addresses of the Lancaster County Historical Society*. Vol. 32, no. 6 (1929): 97–112.

Jabour, Anya. "Male Friendship and Masculinity in the Early National South: William Wirt and His Friends." *Journal of the Early Republic*. Vol. 20, no. 1 (Spring 2000): 83–111.

Kilian, Pamela. "James Buchanan's White House Hostess: The Celebrated Harriet Lane." *White House History*. Vol. 12 (2003): 362–71.

Klein, Frederic S. "Robert Coleman, Millionaire Ironmaster." *Journal of the Lancaster Historical Society*. Vol. 54 (Winter 1960): 17–33.

Klein, Philip S. "Bachelor Father and Family Man." *Western Pennsylvania Historical Magazine*. Vol. 50, no. 3 (July 1967): 199–214.

Klein, Philip S. "Harriet Lane: 'Our Republican Queen.'" *Valleys of History*. Vol. 2 (Autumn 1966): 1–5.

Klein, Philip S. "James Buchanan and Ann Coleman." *Journal of the Lancaster County Historical Society*. Vol. 59, no. 1 (1955): 1–20.

Klein, Philip S. "The Inauguration of President James Buchanan." *Journal of the Lancaster County Historical Society*. Vol. 61, no. 4 (Oct. 1957): 145–68.

Klepp, Susan E. "Revolutionary Bodies: Women and the Fertility Transition in the Mid-Atlantic Region, 1760-1820." *Journal of American History*. Vol. 85, no. 3 (Dec. 1998): 910–45.

Krainik, Clifford. "A 'Dark Horse' in Sunlight and Shadow: Daguerreotypes of President James K. Polk." *White House History*. Vol. 2, no. 1 (June 1997): 38-49.

Krainik, Clifford. "Discovered: An Unknown Brady Portrait of James K. Polk and Members of His Cabinet." *White House History*. Vol. 21 (Fall 2007): 78-81.

Lambert, Robert S. "The Democratic Nominating Convention of 1844." *Tennessee Historical Quarterly*. Vol. 14, no. 1 (Mar. 1955): 3–23.

Landis, Michael T. "Old Buck's Lieutenant: Glancy Jones, James Buchanan, and the Antebellum Democracy." *Pennsylvania Magazine of History and Biography*. Vol. 140, no. 2 (April 2016): 183-210.

Lasser, Carol. "'Let Us Be Sisters Forever': The Sororal Model of Nineteenth-Century Female Friendship." *Signs*. Vol. 14, no. 1 (Autumn 1985): 158–81.

Leff, Mark H. "Revisioning U.S. Political History." *American Historical Review*. Vol. 100, no. 3 (June 1995): 829–53.

Lerner, Adam B. "Unlikely Political Pals: Some of the Most Memorable Bipartisan Friendships." *Politico Magazine*. Oct. 27, 2014.

Lindman, Janet M. "Histories of Friendship in Early America: An Introduction." *Journal of Social History*. Vol. 50, no. 4 (2017): 603–608.

Lynn, Joshua A. "A Manly Doughface: James Buchanan and the Sectional Politics of Gender." *Journal of the Civil War Era*. Vol. 8, no. 4 (Dec. 2018): 591–620.

Marraro, Howard R. "William Pinkney's Mission to the Kingdom of the Two Sicilies, 1816." *Maryland Historical Magazine*. Vol. 43, no. 4 (Dec. 1948): 235–65.

Martin, John M. "William R. King and the Compromise of 1850." *North Carolina Historical Review*. Vol. 39, no. 4 (Oct. 1962): 500–18.

Martin, John M. "William R. King and the Vice Presidency." *Alabama Review*. Vol. 16 (Jan. 1963): 35–40.

Martin, John M. "William R. King: Jacksonian Senator." *Alabama Review*. Vol. 18 (Oct. 1965): 243–45.

Mattingly, Carol. "Elizabeth Fries Lummis Ellet (1818–1877)." *Legacy* 18, no. 2 (2001): 101–107.

Mayfield, John. "'The Soul of a Man!': William Gilmore Simms and the Myths of Southern Manhood. *Journal of the Early Republic*. Vol. 15, no. 3 (Autumn 1995): 477–500.

Mays, Elizabeth. "'The Celebrated Mrs. Cobb': Mrs. Howell Cobb." *Georgia Historical Quarterly*. Vol. 24, no. 2 (June 1940): 101–23.

McMillan, Malcolm C. "The Alabama Constitution of 1819: A Study of Constitution-Making on the Frontier." *Alabama Lawyer*. Vol. 12 (Jan. 1951): 74–91.

McMurtry, R. Gerald. "James Buchanan in Kentucky, 1813." *Filson Club History Quarterly*. Vol. 8, no 2 (April 1934): 73–87.

Meerse, David E. "Buchanan's Patronage Policy: An Attempt to Achieve Political Strength." *Pennsylvania History*. Vol. 40, no. 1 (Jan. 1973): 36–57.

Meerse, David E. "Origins of the Buchanan-Douglas Feud Reconsidered." *Journal of the Illinois State Historical Society*. Vo. 67, no. 2 (April 1974): 154–74.

Merk, Frederick. "Presidential Fevers." *Mississippi Valley Historical Review*. Vol. 47, no. 1 (June 1960): 3–33.

Moffat, Charles H. "Charles Tait, Planter, Politician, and Scientist of the Old South." *Journal of Southern History*. Vol. 14, no. 2 (May 1948): 206–33.

Morris, Francis G., and Phyllis M. Morris. "Economic Conditions in North Carolina about 1780." *North Carolina Historical Review*. Vol. 16, nos. 2–3 (April–July 1939): 107–33, 296–327.

Nguyen, Tina. "Barack Obama and Joe Biden: The Ultimate Friendship." *Vanity Fair*. Dec. 2016.

O'Meara, James. "Early Editors of California." *Overland Monthly (Second Series)*. Vol. 14, no. 83 (Nov. 1889): 489–99.

Owen, Marie B. "The William Rufus King Room." *Alabama Historical Quarterly*. Vol. 3, no. 1 (Spring 1941): 4–7.

Reid, Robie L. "John Nugent: The Impertinent Envoy." *British Columbia Historical Quarterly*. Vol. 8 (Jan. 1944): 53–76.

Reineke, J. A. Jr. "The Diplomatic Career of Pierre Soule." *Louisiana Historical Quarterly*. Vol. 15 (1932): 283–329.

Riley, Padraig. "The Lonely Congressmen: Gender and Politics in Early Washington, D.C." *Journal of the Early Republic*. Vol. 34, no. 2 (Summer 2014): 243–73.

Rindfleisch, Bryan C. "'What It Means to Be a Man': Contested Masculinity in the Early Republic and Antebellum America." *History Compass*. Vol. 10/11 (2012): 852–65.

Robinson, Elwyn B. "The *North American*: Advocate of Protection." *Pennsylvania Magazine of History and Biography*. Vol. 64, no. 3 (July 1940): 345–55.

Roddis, Jonathan. "Jonathan M. Foltz, Surgeon General of the Navy (1871–72)." *Military Surgeon*. Vol. 90, no. 4 (April 1942): 445–49.

Rosenberger, Homer T. "Harriet Lane, First Lady: Hostess Extraordinary in Difficult Times." *Records of the Columbia Historical Society, Washington, D.C.* Vol. 66/68 (1966/1968): 102–53.

Rosenberger, Homer T. "Inauguration of President Buchanan a Century Ago." *Records of the Columbia Historical Society, Washington, D.C.* Vol. 57/59 (1957/1959): 96–122.

Rosenberger, Homer T. "Protecting the Buchanan Papers." *Journal of the Lancaster County Historical Society*. Vol. 72, no. 3 (1970): 137–69.

Rosenberger, Homer T. "The Passing of a Great Lady: Mrs. Harriet Lane Johnston." *Journal of the Lancaster County Historical Society*. Vol. 75, no. 1 (1971): 1–18.

Rosenberger, Homer T. "Two Monuments for the Fifteenth President of the United States." *Journal of the Lancaster County Historical Society*. Vol. 78, no. 1 (1974): 29–48.

Russ, William A., Jr. "Mary Kittera Snyder's Struggle for an Income." *Snyder County Historical Society Bulletin*. Vol 4, no 1 (Jan. 1960): 1–27.

Russo, David J. "The Major Political Issues of the Jacksonian Period and the Development of Party Loyalty in Congress, 1830–1840." *Transactions of the American Philosophical Society* Vol. 62 (n.s.), no. 5 (1972): 3–51.

Saum, Lewis O. "'Who Steals My Purse': The Denigration of William R. King, the Man for Whom King County Was Named." *Pacific Northwest Quarterly*. Vol. 92, no. 4 (Fall 2001): 181–89.

Seale, William. "Editorial." *Nineteenth Century*. Vol. 2 (Spring 1976): 4–5.

Sears, Louis M. "Slidell and Buchanan." *American Historical Review*. Vol. 27, no. 4 (July 1922): 709–30.

Sener, Samuel M. "Mayor John Passmore." *Journal of the Lancaster County Historical Society*. Vol. 5, no. 5 (1900/1901): 113–15.

Shade, William G. "'The Most Delicate and Exciting Topics': Martin Van Buren, Slavery, and the Election of 1836." *Journal of the Early Republic*. Vol. 18, no. 3 (Autumn 1998): 459–84.

Skeen, C. Edward. "'Vox Populi, Vox Dei': The Compensation Act of 1816 and the Rise of Popular Politics." *Journal of the Early Republic*. Vol. 6, no. 3 (Autumn 1986): 253–74.

Smith, Dainty. "The 'Bromance' Problem." *Gender, Popular Culture and Media Freedom*. Vol. 10 (2012): 16–18.

Stenberg, Richard. "Jackson, Buchanan, and the 'Corrupt Bargain' Calumny." *Pennsylvania Magazine of History and Biography*. Vol. 58, no. 1 (1934): 61–85.

Struble, Robert Jr. "House Turnover and the Principle of Rotation." *Political Science Quarterly*. Vol. 94, no. 4 (Winter 1979–1980): 649–67.

Thornton, Julia F. "North Carolina's Own Huguenot Families. *The Huguenot*. Vol. 12 (1943): 113–16.

Trapnell, Frederica H. "Some Lucases of Jefferson County." *Magazine of Jefferson County Historical Society*. Vol. 60 (Dec. 1994): 17–34.

Van Beck, Todd W. "James Buchanan." *American Cemetery*. Vol. 63 (Mar. 1990): 19–24, 39.

Walton, Brian. "Ambrose Hundley Sevier in the United States Senate, 1836–1848." *Arkansas Historical Quarterly*. Vol. 32 (Spring 1973): 25–60.

Walton, Brian. "Elections to the United States Senate in North Carolina, 1835–1861." *North Carolina Historical Review*. Vol. 53, no. 2 (April 1976).

Walton, Brian. "The Elections for the Thirtieth Congress and the Presidential Candidacy of Zachary Taylor." *Journal of Southern History*. Vol. 35, no. 2 (May 1969): 186–202.

Weatherman, Donald V. "James Buchanan on Slavery and Secession." *Presidential Studies Quarterly*. Vol. 15 (Fall 1985): 796–805.

Williams, Thomas M. "Dixon H. Lewis." *Alabama Polytechnic Institute Historical Studies (Fourth Series)*. Ed. George Petrie. Auburn, AL: n.p., 1910.

Wirls, Daniel. "'The Only Mode of Avoiding Everlasting Debate': The Overlooked Senate Gag Rule for Antislavery Petitions." *Journal of the Early Republic*. Vol. 27, no. 1 (Spring 2007): 115–38.

Wood, Kirsten E. "'One Woman So Dangerous to Public Morals': Gender and Power in the Eaton Affair." *Journal of the Early Republic*. Vol. 17, no. 2 (Summer 1997): 237–75.

Wood, Nicholas. "'A Sacrifice on the Altar of Slavery': Doughface Politics and Black Disenfranchisement in Pennsylvania, 1837–1838." *Journal of the Early Republic*. Vol. 31, no. 1 (Spring 2011): 75–106.

Worner, William F. "Military Activities in Lancaster during the War of 1812." *Journal of the Lancaster County Historical Society*. Vol. 35 (1931): 205–27.

Worner, William F. "The Washington Association of Lancaster." *Journal of the Lancaster County Historical Society*. Vol. 35 (1931): 146–49.

Zagarri, Rosemarie. "The Family Factor: Congressmen, Turnover, and the Burden of Public Service in the Early American Republic." *Journal of the Early Republic*. Vol. 33, no. 2 (Summer 2013): 283–316.

UNPUBLISHED SOURCES

Ambacher, Bruce I. "George M. Dallas: Leader of the 'Family' Party." PhD diss. Temple University. 1970.

Brooks, Daniel F. "Opulence and Intrigue: Odiot, Rihouët, and the Diplomatic Service of Alabama's William Rufus King." Paper presented at the Antiques Forum, New Orleans, 2011.

Cahalan, Sally S. "Harriet Lane: The Public Years with James Buchanan, 1854–1861: A Study of Proper Victorian Womanhood." MA thesis. Pennsylvania State University at Harrisburg, 1991.

Campbell, John A. Jr. "James Buchanan: Advocate in Congress, Cabinet, and Presidency." PhD diss. University of Florida, 1968.

Cox, Nicholas P. "Origins and Exhaustion of the Doughfaces." MA thesis. University of Houston, 2007.

Earman, Cynthia D. "Boardinghouses, Parties and the Creation of a Political Society: Washington City, 1800–1830." MA thesis. Louisiana State University, 1992.

Golladay, Victor D. "The Nicholas Family of Virginia, 1722–1820." PhD diss. University of Virginia, 1973.

Hartley, James R. "The Political Career of Lewis Fields Linn." MA thesis. University of Missouri, Columbia, 1951.

Kramer, Eugene F. "The Public Career of Elbridge Gerry." PhD diss. Ohio State University, 1955.

Martin, John M. "William Rufus King: Southern Moderate." PhD diss. University of North Carolina, 1955.

Radomsky, Susan. "The Social Life of Politics: Washington's Official Society and the Emergence of a National Political Elite, 1800–1876." PhD diss. University of Chicago, 2005.

Thompson, Joseph C. "Willie Person Mangum: Politics and Pragmatism in the Age of Jackson." PhD diss. University of Florida, 1995.

Index

For the benefit of digital users, indexed terms that span two pages (e.g., 52–53) may, on occasion, appear on only one of those pages.

Page references followed by *f*, and *t* refer to figures, and tables respectively.